Advertising worldwide

Advertising worldwide

Concepts, theories and practice of international, multinational and global advertising

Marieke K. de Mooij
Managing Director, BBDO College and
World Secretary, IAA Education Programme

with

Warren J. Keegan
Pace University, New York

Prentice Hall

New York London Toronto Sydney Tokyo Singapore

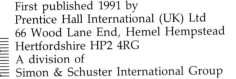

First published 1991 by
Prentice Hall International (UK) Ltd
66 Wood Lane End, Hemel Hempstead
Hertfordshire HP2 4RG
A division of
Simon & Schuster International Group

Typeset in 11 pt Palacio
by MCS Ltd, Salisbury, England

Printed and bound in Great Britain at the
University Press, Cambridge

Library of Congress Cataloging-in-Publication Data

Mooij, Marieke K. de, 1943–
    Advertising worldwide : concepts, theories, and practice of
international, multinational, and global advertising / Marieke K. de
Mooij, with Warren J. Keegan.
      p.   cm.
    Includes bibliographical references and index.
    ISBN 0-13-471897-6
    1. Advertising. 2. Advertising media planning. 3. Advertising,
Comparison. I. Keegan, Warren J. II. Title.
HF 5823.M48 1991
659.1—dc20
                                          91-12208
                                             CIP

British Library Cataloguing in Publication Data

Mooij, Marieke K. de 1943–
  Advertising worldwide.
  1. Advertising
  I. Title II. Keegan, Warren J. (Warren Joseph) 1936–
  659.1

ISBN 0-13-471897-6

---

1 2 3 4 5 95 94 93 92 91

To: Rein Rijkens

Contents

Foreword

The publication of a thorough and contemporary treatment on international advertising, which will be of value to students (of all ages), is quite a major event.

In spite of the 'globalization' of the advertising market, there has been a rather slow response to this dominant trend on the part of educators, writers and publishers.

So I very much welcome this book. I expect it to make a very real contribution to our understanding of an important, complex and rapidly changing subject.

Roger Neill
Chief Executive, Bozell Europe
World President, International Advertising Association

Preface

'Fools rush in where angels fear to tread.'

Alexander Pope

This book is about the impact of the globalization of markets on marketing communication, and particularly on advertising. Much has been written about global corporations, strategy, management and marketing, but to date there is almost nothing available on global or worldwide advertising. Why is this?

Advertising is not a science. Anyone who wants to write about global communications must draw on the experience of practitioners of the art and the craft of advertising. We have not only drawn on our knowledge of global marketing and communications but have taken advantage of the vast body of accumulated experience of busy practitioners of global advertising, who themselves do not have the time to sit down and write a book.

We have broken new ground with this first book on worldwide advertising, and we confess that we feel an appreciation of Alexander Pope's wise observation that 'fools rush in where angels fear to tread'. We assembled our knowledge from interviews, published marketing literature, private communications, seminars and conferences where practitioners and academicians share their experience and ideas.

A word about change. The task of keeping up to date a book with the word 'worldwide' in the title is an impossible one, because the world we describe is changing so fast. Sections written in October 1989 had to be deleted in December of the same year because of the changes in Eastern Europe. No doubt between the time the manuscript goes to the printer and the publication date there will be further changes.

These changes do not, however, alter the principles, concepts or tools which we present. Anyone who wishes to master the basic concepts, techniques and practices that enable a company to move from domestic to international, multinational, global or transnational advertising will find guidance and direction in this book.

We hope that our readers will enjoy and profit from reading *Advertising Worldwide*. We do plan to revise the book, and would appreciate comments and suggestions from readers which we will be able to incorporate into the next edition. Please write to us at the following addresses or care of our publisher, Prentice Hall International (UK) Ltd.

Marieke K. de Mooij
Dellaertlaan 37
1171 HE Badhoevedorp
Netherlands

Warren J. Keegan
210 Stuyvesant Avenue
Rye, NY 10580
USA

Acknowledgements

This book could not have been written without the help of many people. We would especially like to thank Leo van Os of Lintas Worldwide for screening the material from the start. Joop Roomer and Les Kellen encouraged us to write the book. We would like to thank Hetje Honig of SA, who did the first translations from Dutch into English, Hall and the late Evelyn Duncan, advertising consultants and educators, for evaluating and correcting the first chapters, and Gordon Miracle, Professor of International Advertising and his students for screening and evaluating the text of the first five chapters. The same counts for Kaarina Iltanen of Markkinointi Instituutti in Finland. Geert Hofstede, Professor of International Management in the Netherlands, was kind enough to let us use his ideas on intercultural management and marketing. ESOMAR kindly gave permission to use its material.

We would like to thank all those members of BBDO around the world who screened several chapters: Karen Olshan (USA) and Elzo Boerema (Netherlands) for research, Eymert van Manen (Netherlands) for sales promotion, Goos Geursen (Netherlands) for planning, Les Margulis and Arnie Semsky (USA), Tim Cox (UK) and Peter Teillers, Anja Aarsse and Paul Turken (Netherlands) for media, and Henk Koenders (Netherlands) for sponsorship. Thanks are also due to Ki-Hung Lee (Korea Broadcast Advertising Corporation) for data on the Seoul Olympics, Leo van Deutekom (DE/Sara Lee, Netherlands) for research, Erik van Vooren (Direct Marketing Know How Institute, Belgium) for direct marketing, Barbara Taylor (Hill & Knowlton International, USA) for PR, Victor Kiu (Ogilvy & Mather, Singapore) for life-style research in Asia, Ton Otker (Philips, Netherlands) for sponsorship, Hans du Chatinier (Lintas) for media, Steve Winram (Zenith Media Worldwide, UK) for data on media, Hein Becht (Scan, European agency selection consultancy, Netherlands) for the organizational aspects, Miriam P. Wallk (Nielsen) and all those people from the research institutes quoted who were willing to check parts of the text.

We must also thank Cathy Peck and Jos de Jong of Prentice Hall for their valuable advice and support, and Linda Clare, the copy-editor, who did the splendid job of making Marieke's English real English.

Finally, we want to thank our readers, practitioners, students and teachers of advertising. We are anxious to hear from you. Let us know what you like and what you don't like, and let us know your suggestions for change in the next edition.

We reserve our last acknowledgements for those who made this book possible.

In particular Marieke would like to thank Angeline Noordstar of BBDO College and her neighbour, friend and secretary for IAA, Hannie van Driel for their support, her fax machine (Canon) for never failing to swallow and spit out endless information and corrections sent from many places in the world, IAA for their help, and particularly everyone at BBDO College and FHV/BBDO in the Netherlands for providing appropriate spiritual and creative surroundings, moral backing and support. Most of all she would like to thank her husband, Anne van 't Haaff for his patience, support and love, and most of all for not giving unwanted advice at the wrong moments.

Warren would like to thank his secretary Marf Knowles and his research assistants Jessie Huang and Mark Keegan for their many contributions and creative assistance.

The authors and publishers would like to thank the following for their kind permission to reproduce copyright material:

ESOMAR for Table 3.2 and Figures 3.1, 3.2, 5.8, 5.9, 10.1 and 10.2.

Geert Hofstede for the Working Paper 'Marketing and Culture', WP 90-006, University of Limburg at Maastricht.

Lexington Books for extracts from *International Advertising Handbook* by Barbara Sundberg Baudot (Lexington, Mass.: Lexington Books, D. C. Heath and Company, copyright 1989, Lexington Books).

Penguin Books USA Inc. for an extract from Saul Bellow, *Mr Sammler's Planet*, copyright 1970 by Saul Bellow.

Saatchi and Saatchi Communications Limited for an extract from 'Television in Europe to the Year 2000'.

Part One

The environment of worldwide advertising

Chapter 1
The global advertising environment

◾ Introduction

Worldwide expenditure on advertising has been growing faster than the world gross product, the value of all goods and services produced in the world, which exceeds 18 trillion dollars. According to figures provided by Starch Inra Hooper, in cooperation with the International Advertising Association, total advertising expenditure grew from 180 billion US $ based on 66 countries in 1986, to 228 billion US $ based on 58 countries in 1988.

The relative importance of particular regions is changing. The United States is the largest single market in the world but its gross national product has declined as a proportion of gross world product from almost 50 per cent at the end of the Second World War to approximately 27 per cent in 1991.

Theodore Levitt generated a storm of controversy in 1983 when he wrote in the *Harvard Business Review*[1] that companies must learn to operate as if the world were one large market, ignoring superficial regional and national differences and selling the same products in the same way throughout the world. This global approach makes sense, according to Levitt, because consumers around the world are motivated by the same desires for modernity, quality and value. At the same time, new technology and standardized methods of production have made global marketing programmes feasible. Japan's success, he says, is based on standardization, high quality and low costs.

In support of his view that regional differences are disappearing Levitt points to McDonald's on the Champs Elysees in Paris and the Ginza in Tokyo, Coca-Cola in Bahrain, Pepsi-Cola in Moscow, and

Revlon cosmetics, Sony televisions and Levi jeans everywhere. Levitt's thesis is not new. It was expressed repeatedly in the early 1960s by Eric Elinder, head of a Swedish advertising agency, who argued that consumer differences were diminishing.[2]

On the other hand, many have argued that Levitt's thesis is unfounded.

> Not even the mass-marketing Japanese demand complete subjugation to a single, world master plan.[3]

However, globalization of markets is a fact, and company structures, marketing and communication strategies are either driving the process of change or following in its wake.

In July 1990, over a billion people around the world watched the closest thing there is to a world game, the World Cup football (soccer) match between Argentina and Germany. Matches like this have become global marketing events.

The 1990s will clearly launch the new era of global business. Economic integration, the extent to which economic activity crosses national boundaries, continues to increase. A hundred and fifty years ago, almost everything that was produced was consumed by people who lived no further than 75 kilometres from the site of production. At the turn of the century, economic integration was growing: today, in the high-income countries of the world, integration is approaching 50 per cent.

Take a look around you: you get up in the morning, put on your Italian shoes, get in your Japanese car, go to your office where you use an American computer, and in the evening you watch your Japanese television set, eating a piece of Dutch cheese and drinking a glass of French wine or Scotch whisky. This is the environment of worldwide advertising: the integration of domestic, international, multinational and global or transnational business.

The objective of this chapter is to describe the environment of worldwide advertising, providing concepts and definitions, and outline the process of company internationalization. In addition it will give an overview of the history of world trade, the growth of international trade after the Second World War and the origins and growth of multinational companies. This is necessary in order to understand the concepts of marketing and communication worldwide.

◼ Language, concepts and definitions

Language can be an efficient communication vehicle, but it can also be an obstacle. This is why it is important to be aware of how language is used. The English language has developed as a lingua franca for the advertising world. This does not mean that the English or the Americans are necessarily well understood by the rest of the (advertising) world. Neither 'English English' nor 'American English' are by definition the best means of communication. To take one example, the meaning of 'advertising overseas' or 'offshore advertising' may appear clear to advertising people from the United Kingdom or the United States, but it is not a clear concept for most Europeans, since for them crossing borders does not necessarily imply crossing a sea. These words sound very insular to many people who use English as a second language.

Colloquialisms can also cause gross misunderstandings. An example of British colloquialism which caused serious misunderstanding was provided by Mrs Thatcher: when the then UK Prime Minister, launching Super Channel in 1988, wished the European audience 'the best of British', few understood that she just meant to say 'good luck' and was not implying a desire to impose British culture on continental Europe. In fact, the British at that time had been members of the EC for years, but they still talked about the inhabitants of the European continent as 'Europeans' as if to contradict themselves.

On the other hand, not all the advertising specialists whose native language is not English have yet understood that they need to become fluent in the English language. It is the only way to become a true advertising 'international', since most international, multinational or global companies, as well as international advertising agencies, use English for their inter-office communications. They will not hire people who have not mastered the English language.

Readers for whom English is a second language should note that the words 'international', 'multinational' and 'foreign', and the concept 'across borders', are often used interchangeably. 'Global' or 'world-wide' expresses 'all over the world'. However, in many languages 'global' means 'general', as with the French *globale* or Dutch *globaal*; while in these languages *mondiale* is then the right translation of 'worldwide'. One has to be careful to select exactly the right word to express the desired meaning. Common business words are: 'subnational', 'domestic', 'national', 'international', 'multinational', 'multidomestic', 'regional', 'global', 'worldwide', and 'transnational'.

The pattern of growth for a company or strategy starts at the subnational level and progresses through the following levels: national/domestic, multinational/multidomestic, regional/global/worldwide, transnational. The same terms are used for corporate business strategies as for the related marketing and advertising strategies. Definitions of business and marketing strategies will be given in the next section.

Some words or concepts are obsolete, while in order to be truly international, others need to be redefined. Obsolete terms include for example 'The Far East', a concept with overtones of colonial times. The Far East refers to Asia as seen from Europe. In this book terms such as Asia or Pacific Rim will be used. For marketing purposes the word 'foreign' is also obsolete. For the worldwide marketer there is no such thing as a 'foreign' market, only an unfamiliar market. Export marketing is another example of an obsolete term, although many books have been written under this title. Exporting, like importing, is simply the sourcing of a product from outside the purchaser's country. Therefore the term export marketing combines a sourcing arrangement with marketing. This linking of sourcing outside the country of purchase with marketing is a contradiction in terms. Companies that practise global marketing make sourcing decisions based on an assessment of all relevant facts concerning price, quality and market access. Marketing in these companies is the drive and sourcing is a tool which may or may not involve sourcing outside the country of purchase or exporting.

Concepts and definitions

Concepts such as 'international', 'multinational', 'global' and 'transnational' marketing and advertising have several definitions. Whatever definition one gives, there are basic similarities in terms of activities, marketing philosophies and processes. The differences lie in the location and types of markets and the organization of the enterprise which operates both in the homeland and, simultaneously, in other national markets.

'International', 'multinational' and 'global' marketing and advertising are not well-defined concepts in general usage, even among marketing practitioners. They are used as synonyms, but may be used in a specific differentiated sense as well. The following definitions are based on different marketing strategies, which are related to organizational typology.

Definitions of international, multinational, global and transnational marketing

International marketing is the extension of the home country marketing strategy and plan to the world.

Multinational marketing is the development of a strategy for each country that responds to the unique differences and conditions in each country.

Global marketing is the integration of the international and multinational approach where the objective is to create the greatest value for customers and the greatest competitive advantage for the company.

Transnational marketing consists of centralizing some resources at home and others abroad, while distributing others among local operations in different countries. The transnational company extends, adapts and creates a marketing mix.[4]

Supranational is another frequently encountered word. This term is mainly used in the framework of cross-border media advertising, where differences in culture, religion and legislation affect the transmission and reception of the advertising message.

■ Stages of development in the internationalization of companies

There are five stages in the international evolution of companies.[5] These are outlined below.

Domestic or national companies

A domestic or national company is focused upon serving customers in its home country. It is 'ethnocentric' or home-country oriented. Its strategy is domestic: it targets domestic markets, and uses domestic resources to create customer value. Almost all companies begin by serving customers in their home countries, often in a single region of the home country if that market provides a significant share relative to marketing worldwide. For instance, Coca-Cola and Deere typify domestic American companies that later grew into global marketing powers.

International companies

International companies are simply companies that do some business in another country, whether sourcing goods or financial capital, or marketing goods to customers. When a company decides to go international, it makes sense to start by extending the existing, standard business and marketing mix it uses in its home market so that it can focus on learning how to do business in new, unknown markets. Given limited resources and experience, these companies must concentrate on what they do best.

In time, the international company discovers that it must adapt its marketing mix to differences in markets around the world in order to succeed. Toyota, for example, discovered this when it entered the US market in 1957 with its Toyopet. The Toyopet was not a big hit: critics said the cars were 'overpriced, underpowered and built like tanks'.[6] The car was so unsuited for the US market that unsold models were shipped back to Japan. Toyota regarded its rejection as a learning experience and a source of invaluable intelligence about marketing preferences. Note that Toyota did not define the experience as a failure. For companies which are in a process of transition there is no such thing as a failure: only learning experiences and successes in the constantly evolving strategy and experience of the company.

Multinational companies

When a company decides to respond to market differences, it evolves into a multinational company pursuing a multidomestic or multinational strategy. This company formulates a unique strategy for each country in which it conducts business and has a polycentric or host-country orientation. The great strength of the multinational is that it sees the differences in each country and market. Its great weakness is that it does not see the similarities.

Competitors tracking these companies find their behaviour relatively predictable. Each subsidiary based in a different country is managed as if it were an independent city-state. Organized into an area structure, subsidiaries are grouped into regional organizations reporting to world headquarters.

Philips of the Netherlands in the 1960s provides a classic example of a multinational company pursuing a multidomestic strategy. Philips at the time relied upon relatively autonomous organizations (called NOs) in each country. Each country developed its own strategy. Until the company faced competition from Matsushita and other globally oriented Japanese companies, this approach worked well. But once faced with competition from other countries, Philips operated at a distinct disadvantage. Matsushita, for example, adopted a global strategy that focused its resources on serving a world market for home entertainment products.

Global companies

Global companies focus upon building cost advantages through centralized global-scale operations. In the global company strategic assets, resources, responsibilities, and decisions are centralized. The mentality of the global company is to treat operations in other countries or regions as a delivery pipeline to a unified global market. The strength of the global company is that it sees the differences *and* the similarities in world markets. This is the first level at which there is a focus upon global customers in determining basic marketing strategy. The international company designs for the home-country customer and extends home-country products to the world. The multinational designs products for each of the countries in which it does business.

Matsushita demonstrated the superiority of a global strategy approach by correctly assessing that European customers would accept limited choice in television receivers in exchange for lower price. Meanwhile, Philips offered European customers seven different models based on four different chassis, because its factories worldwide produced seven models. If European customers had demanded this variety, it would have made Philips a stronger competitor. Philips' offering of greater variety in the technical design was based not upon what customers were asking for, but rather on Philips' structure and strategy.

An excellent example of a global consumer products company is the Coca-Cola company. It gained true global recognition during the Second World War as Coke bottling plants followed the march of US troops around the world. Management in Atlanta, USA, made all the strategic decisions then as now. In general the brand name, concentrated formulas, positioning and advertising are virtually standard worldwide.[7] 'Coca-Cola provides a simple moment of refreshment, a simple moment of pleasure to consumers in 160 countries, 559 million times every single day, with a consistent, high product quality.'[8]

Transnational companies

A transnational company is an integrated business system which uses global resources to serve global customers. The transnational company seeks efficiency as a means of achieving global competitiveness. It acknowledges the need for local responsiveness as a tool for flexibility. Innovations are regarded as an outcome of a wider process of organizational learning that encompasses every member of the company.

Philips realized that it would continue to lose market share until it adopted either a global or a transnational strategy. It changed its organization and created Industry Main Groups in the Netherlands, responsible for developing a global strategy for R&D, marketing and manufacturing. Since Philips already had key resources such as research and engineering groups located in many countries, by deciding to adopt a strategy of targeting global markets it successfully made the transition from multinational to transnational. This illustrates the important point that the company does not have to go through each stage in turn in the course of its development.

Overview

Table 1.1 gives a summary of the characteristics of each company type.

Advertising strategies should be consistent with business and marketing strategies. Therefore, the definitions for domestic, international, multinational and global advertising are similar to those for marketing. However, companies which are in transition may vary their advertising strategies for some brands and not for others.

Like marketing definitions, advertising definitions are often not used very precisely. In many parts of the world, 'international advertising' and 'global advertising' are used as umbrella words for everything relating to advertising across borders. Further chapters will go into more depth regarding international and global advertising. For

Table 1.1 Stages in the development of the transnational corporation

Stage	Company type	Orientation	Scanning horizons	Marketing strategy
1	Domestic corporation	Ethnocentric/ home country	Domestic	Domestic
2	International corporation	Ethnocentric/ home country	Operating countries	Extension
3	Multinational corporation	Polycentric/ host country	Operating countries	Adaptation
4	Global corporation	Ethnocentric/ geocentric	Global markets	Extension, adaptation and creation
5	Transnational corporation	Geocentric/ world	Global business environment	Extension, adaptation and creation

Source: Warren J. Keegan, Working Paper No. 2, May 1990, The Center For International Business Studies, Pace University, New York, NY 10038.

the purpose of this book the following definition of advertising worldwide will be used:

> The formulation of communications vision, intent, strategy and the implementation of a communications plan, including media advertising, sales promotion, direct marketing communication and public relations activities that simultaneously support the sales of goods and services in more than one country in several parts of the world.

■ History of world trade

The world economy

Wallerstein[9] describes the history of our capitalist world economy from the Middle Ages to the present day. He explains that in a specifically capitalist world economy the economic decisions in the first instance were directed towards the arena of the world economy, while political decisions in the first instance were directed towards smaller structures with legal systems, such as nations, city states and kingdoms. One of the most important themes in the history of the world economy is the balance between nationalism and internationalism – not in an ideological sense, but in terms of organization.

During some periods a country's important political and economic institutions are directed towards operating in the international arena, and local interests are directly related to developments in other parts of the world. At other times the emphasis is on local activity, the country's priority is the strengthening of its own borders, and there is a lack of interest in external events. The changes in orientation that occur over time mainly involve geographical situation and political structure.

Wallerstein differentiates three zones in the world economy:

1. The core states or core areas (high-income areas).
2. The peripheral areas (low-income).
3. The semi-periphery (middle-/low-income).

As far as trade is concerned the core controls the periphery. In the core states there is often a strong state machinery combined with a national culture. Wallerstein specifies peripheral areas instead of states, because a characteristic of a peripheral area is that the indigenous state is weak, ranging from non-existence (a colonial situation) to a low degree of autonomy (a neo-colonial situation).[10] There are also semi-peripheral areas which fall between the core and the periphery on a series of dimensions, such as complexity of economic activities and strength of state machinery. Some of these areas had been core areas in earlier versions of the world economy. Some had been peripheral areas that were later promoted, so to speak, as a result of the changing geopolitics of an expanding world economy. A world economy shows a hierarchy of occupational tasks, in which tasks requiring higher levels of skill and greater capitalization are reserved for higher-ranking areas. The development of a world economy also shows a widening of the social and economic gaps among the various areas. Some regions of the world may change their role in the world economy to their advantage.

The external arena of one country often becomes the periphery of the next, or its semi-periphery. Core states can also become semi-peripheral and semi-peripheral ones peripheral. The ability of a particular state to remain in the core sector is not beyond challenge. Core states tend to be replaced over time by other countries. During the sixteenth century, Antwerp co-ordinated the international commerce of the Habsburg empire and was the link which connected England as well as Portugal to the European world economy. Antwerp was functioning as a market place for England and in this way Antwerp also became the financial centre of Europe. However, this core function was later taken over by Amsterdam, because the Republic of the Netherlands allowed greater economic integration than any other European monarchy. The bourgeoisie of Holland had carried through just that degree of reform which was necessary to promote economic expansion with enough retention of freedom to prevent overcentralization. The Dutch became, after the revolution, not only the centre of the Baltic trade, but a centre of world trade.

Such changes in the status of areas need to be closely watched by those who practise international trade and production. Currently Japan, Singapore, Taiwan and South Korea can be termed core areas. A number of other countries in the Pacific Basin are still in a phase of the semi-peripheral area. Nepal, China and similar countries are still peripheral areas. Thailand is an example of a semi-peripheral area which may change into a core area in the near future. The same could be said for some Eastern European countries such as Hungary, now that the political situation may allow it. Lebanon was a core state a few decades ago; its role as a commercial centre is now being taken over by the United Arab Emirates (Dubai).

Technological advances play the most important role in altering the economic importance of certain areas. In this way certain areas in the world can change their structural role in the world economy to their advantage.

Examples from the Middle Ages

During the Middle Ages a reasonable trade balance existed between Christian Europe and the Arabian world. Gold and silver flowed eastward and spices and precious stones went westwards. However, a shortage of gold caused problems for Florence and Genoa who needed to produce coins. Gold had to be obtained elsewhere. The Portuguese were the only nation interested in travelling further afield than the usual kind of discovery voyages. Due to its geographical position Portugal could only expand via the sea. Furthermore, Portugal enjoyed internal stability, with no internal wars as was the case in the rest of Europe. Consequently, financed by Genoa, the Portuguese set out on their voyages of discovery.

Looking at China during that same period, it seems that Europe and China had similar population levels between the thirteenth and sixteenth centuries. From the second century to the fifteenth century China had a technological advantage. It was only in around 1450 that Europe began to increase its technological development. One reason was political: Europe could not afford to lag behind in the development of its arms industry, because of many wars between the different states. In China, on the other hand, the government decided to restrict the development of the arms industry, in order to improve internal peace.

The Portuguese and the Chinese went on their discovery voyages in the same period. However, eighteen years later the Chinese stopped abruptly with the death of eunuch-admiral Cheng Ho in 1434. The main reason lay in an important cultural difference: the Chinese did not travel to *obtain* something but to *take* something. By bringing gifts of high quality to far-away countries, they wanted to assure those countries of their superiority. They were not interested in colonizing because they believed that they were already the whole world. When their treasuries were depleted due to the escapades of Cheng Ho, the discovery voyages were stopped and China cut itself off. China changed from a core area to a peripheral area.[11]

A good description of the interdependence of political stability and industrial development can be found in the history of the Royal Dutch Oil Company (later Shell) written by Dr C. Gerritson.[12] In the introduction of the first chapter he writes:

> Due to its experience of exploiting oil in the Dutch Indies, the Royal Dutch Company is closely linked to the country of its origin. The rise of the Royal Dutch Oil Company has only been possible as a result of the victory, in the colonial framework, of liberal principles, which have best served the interests of the colonial power in Asia by free competition of western

capital and western labour with the exploitation of the natural resources of these tropical regions.

The international trade houses are examples of the origin of global trade. As far as trade with Asia is concerned, one good example is the Dutch Verenigde Oost-Indische Compagnie (VOC) or Dutch East India Company. After Antwerp fell into Spanish hands in 1585, the centre of the spice trade moved to Amsterdam. Lisbon, the most important port for the spice trade, was in Spanish hands, so it was necessary to set up an organization to circumvent the Spaniards. In order to build a strong fleet and to reduce the negative influence of competition among the Hollanders, the VOC was founded. It managed a fleet which created an economical and political weapon against the Spaniards. The VOC was a capitalist trading corporation, with three main functions: speculative investment, long-term investment and colonization.

■ The growth of international trade after the Second World War

International trade and investments have been the two fastest growing sectors since the Second World War.[13] Between 1913 and 1948 the volume of world production grew at an average yearly rate of 2 per cent; population growth and the increase in productivity accounted for half this growth. The volume of world trade grew by 5 per cent yearly. Between 1948 and 1973 total world production grew at an average of 5 per cent yearly, and population growth accounted for 40 per cent of this. Trade grew at a yearly average of 7 per cent. This changed with the oil crisis of 1973: from 1973 to 1978 world trade grew by only 4 per cent and world production by 3.5 per cent. In 1981 the volume of world trade dropped for the first time since 1945.

The growth of international trade and international marketing after the Second World War is based on six basic factors which did not previously exist.

Six factors affecting growth of international trade

The international monetary system

In 1944 economists and diplomats from the United Nations came together in order to set up an international monetary system. This was the origin of the International Monetary Fund (IMF). The main objective was to set up a system of international liquidity based on money, gold or other means of payment to facilitate the interchange of goods and services between countries. Until 1969 this was based on the gold standard; subsequently other standards were used, and the system of International Drawing Rights was created. The system had to function in such a way that it would be possible for enterprises to finance trade and investments across borders. However, the system is not foolproof. The growing debts of countries such as Argentina, Brazil, Mexico and some African states, and the imbalance, particularly between the United States and Japan, can become serious handicaps for international trade.

The world trade system

The trading system of the post-war years was based on a mutual wish to avoid the return of the limited and discriminatory trade practices of the 1920s and 1930s. The aim was to create a free world in which a free stream of goods and services could transfer freely between countries. From this commitment developed the General Agreement on Tariffs and Trade (GATT) which provided for freedom of trade through its rules and parameters.

One of the complications of a world trade system is that governments tend to subsidize or otherwise assist national exporting enterprises. This leads to a situation whereby the target countries feel the need to protect themselves. Protectionism occurs either where the exporter is unusually successful, like Japan in the areas of electronics and cars, or where exporting countries have a relative advantage such as inexpensive labour, as is the case where textiles are produced in low-wage countries. It also occurs when a country's trade balance is unfavourable and debts are too high.

The greatest challenge for the trading system in the late 1980s and early 1990s is not the decline of tariff levels, but the so-called 'non-tariff barriers' (NTBs). Examples are import quotas and exclusive distribution practices used in order to protect an industry, and there are also very subtle methods such as administrative regulations and procedures with which it is difficult to comply or which have a delaying effect. Such measures are used by Japan. One example is the use of strict quality requirements; a product must, before being allowed into a country, comply with that country's specified requirements. Another method is to impose requirements with which some products simply cannot comply, such as the *Reinheitsgebot* for beer in Germany, or requirements which for various reasons result in prohibitively high prices. The variety of different requirements in each country hinders the production of specific products. Products increase in price and imports are restricted.

World peace

Although since 1945 there has always been at least one war in progress somewhere in the world, and one cannot really speak of world peace, there has not been a world war. This has led to fast growth in the international economy.

National economic growth

Factors such as technological development and improved management skills have led many countries to open their borders and admit international enterprises. A growing economy makes it possible for countries to allow in international enterprises without directly damaging existing local enterprises. Economic growth creates market opportunities without creating resistance against newcomers.

Communication

The improved speed and capacity and reduced cost of communication have also increased the pace of growth in international trade. The jet aeroplane, telecommunications and electronic data transmission have really made the world into what Marshall McLuhan[14] called the 'global village'.

Global enterprise

Enterprises aiming at world trade make links between the available sources and market opportunities in two or more countries simultaneously. Such companies have made use of the first five opportunities listed above. Within the international monetary system, and under the umbrella of world peace, global enterprise has made use of new communications technology and has taken advantage of worldwide economic growth. It has identified markets, mobilized personnel, exploited financial resources, developed and carried out research and made use of the results, produced and executed market planning and exported products. At the same time advertising and sales promotion efforts have developed markets for world products and brands. All this has contributed to growth on an international and global scale.

The last decade

The greatest and most profound change lies in the emergence of global markets and global competitors, who have steadily displaced their local competitors. The integration of the world economy has increased from less than 10 per cent at the turn of this century to approximately 50 per cent in 1989.

The changes continue. Within the past decade, there have been four major changes:

1. Capital movements rather than trade have become the driving force of the world economy.
2. Production has become 'uncoupled' from employment.
3. Primary products have become 'uncoupled' from the industrial economy.
4. The world economy is in control. The macro-economics of the nation-state are no longer in control.

Of these, the last is the most important – the emergence of the world economy as the dominant economic unit. Companies and countries that recognize this fact have the greatest chance of success. The real secret of the success of Germany and Japan is their focus on the world economy and world markets. The first priority of their governments and businesses has been to secure their competitive position in the world. In contrast, the United Kingdom and to a lesser extent the United States have focused on domestic objectives and priorities to the exclusion of a global competitive position.

■ Origins and growth of the multinational

Christopher Tugendhat, vice-president of the Commission of the European Communities from 1981 to 1985, describes in his book *The Multinationals*[15] the development, characteristics, activities and organizational structures of a large number of multinationals. What follows is a summary of the history of the development of multinationals.

The forerunners of the present multinationals were founded in the 1860s. Bayer took a share in the aniline factory in Albany, New York, in 1865. In 1866 the Swedish inventor of dynamite, Alfred Nobel, started a factory in Hamburg. The US firm Singer built its first factory on the other side of the ocean, in Glasgow, in 1867 – a mass-production operation with sufficient capacity to serve all of Europe and export sewing machines to Asia, Africa and even back to the United States. Singer was the first enterprise to produce and market a product worldwide under one name. Singer may be called the first multinational.[16] The largest advertisers in China in the early 1900s included the British American Tobacco Company and Singer.[17]

Each enterprise which went to other countries in search of higher profits had its own reasons for doing so, but there were several factors which influenced them all:

1. As industrial enterprises grew, mass markets developed.
2. The improvement of transport and communication possibilities through the development of the steamship, the railway and the telegraph prompted the entrepreneurs to look for opportunities further afield and made it possible to control business activities from a distance.
3. Sometimes it was cheaper to produce in a foreign country, near the ultimate consumer, than producing at home and adding transport costs. For this reason Bayer settled in the United States and Singer in Scotland.
4. Nationalism also played a role. Enterprises began to realize that it would be more effective to supply local needs through a local management team which could understand the local clients better than could an export manager at head office. Edison built a factory in Germany because in a nationalistic political climate national suppliers were given priority
5. The most important reason for the growth of multinational enterprises was a growth in protectionism. Except for Great Britain, practically all governments introduced import duties in order to limit imports and to support their own national industries. William Lever, the founder of Lever Brothers, stated in 1902, that the decision about whether to develop a separate, self-managed production unit was a matter of profits and costs. If import duties in the target country surpass the costs of having one's own operation there, the choice is easy. High import duties are the reason why Bayer built dye factories in Russia in 1876 and in France in 1882.[18]

In the United States between 1880 and 1890 there was an enormous concentration of industrial activity. More than 5,000 enterprises were linked to form about 300 trusts. The resulting giants dominated the industrial stage. Most of them had no need to expand their activities beyond North America, except in order to get rid of their surpluses. If they did open a settlement somewhere else, they could afford to do so at a loss because of their high profits at home.

The emphasis on research and innovation, combined with high labour costs in the United States, meant that research activity moved to Europe. Many inventions were made in Europe and then mass-produced in the United States. However, there was definitely a two-way traffic: the British firm Courtaulds dominated the fast-growing rayon industry, the Royal Dutch Shell group was a formidable competitor in the American oil market and Lever Brothers was a leading enterprise in the soap industry. The latter was later to merge with the Dutch company Van den Bergh & Jurgens to form the Anglo-Dutch company Unilever.

Between the two world wars several enterprises continued to expand their international interests. These were primarily the technologically progressive industries or producers of mass consumer goods. General Motors, Ford, and Procter & Gamble are examples. In 1939 more than half of Philips' employees worked outside the Netherlands.

During the period encompassed by the two world wars the most characteristic form of international industrial enterprise was the cartel. Cartels were agreements about exchanging information on prices and investments, and even included joint marketing efforts. The most important aim was to consolidate prices and profits and eliminate any conflict of interest. In some cases the internal agreements were so extensive and the degree of cooperation went so far that, on paper, the cartels looked like international enterprises. In fact, though, cartels are much looser structures, and they weakened under pressure.

After the Second World War American investments in Europe grew faster than the other way round. Until 1956 European interests in the United States exceeded those of the United States in Europe, but later Europe fell far behind. The so-called American invasion took place in Europe. The Americans, however, were less experienced and less interested in international operations than the established European multinationals. The companies were mostly American-directed enterprises, with an American management philosophy, and were mainly directed towards the US market. However, they were the forerunners of the present large international enterprises. Europe woke up, prompted among other things by the book *Le Défi Américain* by Servan-Schreiber.[19]

Europe began to build her own multinationals, and to do more research, development and innovation. The creation of the European Economic Community (EEC) in 1957 strongly influenced the attitude of American enterprises towards establishing operations in Europe. The Americans expected greater stability in Europe to result from a market more like their own. As a result a number of large American enterprises went through the following phases: first, exporting products from the United States, and secondly setting up subsidiaries in the countries where these goods were sold.

Earlier in this chapter several reasons were mentioned for establishing factories and sales organizations. One further reason was to gain the trust of the consumer, by demonstrating the ability to offer long-term service. For the enterprise it was also easier to keep track of changes in demand in terms of product quantity or product type. The decision to open a factory was taken when the alternatives were a slower pace of growth than competitors who had set up in the same country, or sometimes a complete loss of market. Setting up a local organization is the only way to enter some countries as governments sometimes demand that employment opportunities are created before products are allowed onto the market.

When an enterprise has started in a particular country in a region such as Europe, it often soon opens factories in other countries in the same region because of the advantages those surrounding countries can offer. For instance, the port facilities in the Netherlands and the available labour force in Scotland have provided firms with valid reasons for settling in Europe. One other good reason for further dispersal was that companies often did not want to appear too large in a particular country in order to avoid political pressure and nationalist resentment.

■ The 1990s: global economic integration

There are a number of driving forces which have led to a growing competition and an expansion in world industry. There are also restraining forces. Some elements can be both a driving force and a restraining force. The rapidly increasing integration of the global economy is a consequence of the interplay between driving and restraining forces.

Driving forces

Driving forces leading to expansion include the following:

1. The exponential increase in innovation and the shorter economic life of new technology, together with further differentiation in products and distribution methods.
2. Faster transport and communication, such as air freight, telefax and satellite television.
3. The impact of rising income on country infrastructure – countries become more similar in terms of infrastructure, distribution channels and market needs.
4. The growing similarity in marketing approaches and the tendency towards standardization for economies of scale.
5. Globalization – manufacturers either drop specific local products and introduce the same products in different markets, or develop products intended for a global buying public. New products in the sector of consumer durables, which are often based on new technology and new concepts, are often viewed as an international concept from the outset. Surf boards, VCRs, solaria, digital wrist-watches, hi-fi equipment, etc., have barely known specific local markets; within a few years the same designs were obtainable worldwide. The fight between Betamax, V2000 and VHS to become the established video recording system was perhaps the last big struggle in which producers and countries competed to raise their system to the status of world standard. With the advent of the compact disc, manufacturers immediately adopted a uniform system.
6. The high cost of development and the enormous investments needed to produce innovative products and introduce them into the world make it necessary nowadays to think in terms of a global approach with the resulting economies of scale.
7. Economic integration: companies join forces. Life-cycles of products become shorter, and so does the period of technological advantage over the competition. Massive investments in R&D and in advertising are needed in order to prolong the brand life-cycle and to create long-term brand images. These huge investments are impossible to manage alone, so enterprises join forces to maximize the technical and commercial possibilities.
8. Falling tariff barriers and regional economic pacts such as those of the European Community facilitate trade between countries. Import duties are removed for political reasons.
9. A changing industry structure leads increasingly to, for example, the production of world goods composed of parts from several countries.

All these factors have triggered shifts in the international competitive position. New players are taking part in the game, from Asia, from developing countries, and also from previously non-capitalist countries. There are, however, also restraining forces.

Restraining forces

Restraining forces include the following:

1. National controls: new types of protectionism include anti-dumping procedures, a blockade on all mergers and acquisitions over a certain size which have trans-frontier trade implications, and controls on ways of evading anti-dumping procedures such as the so-called 'screwdriver' plants where imported components are assembled.[20]
2. Management myopia: the company history may be a restraining force. Changes in top management may be necessary if change is to occur. Both smaller local companies and large multinationals will have to adapt their views and organizations to the changing global environment. Changes in attitudes, organizational procedures, education and training are necessary.
3. Cultural values: insensitivity to cultural differences, both in management and in marketing strategy, can be a serious constraint on developing a successful global strategy.

Table 1.2 gives an overview of the forces at work in global industry.

Table 1.2   Global industry forces

Driving Forces		Restraining forces
Technology ⟶		
Cost ⟶		
Market needs ⟶	⟵	Market needs
Free markets ⟶	⟵	National controls
Economic integration ⟶	⟵	Globalism
Peace ⟶	⟵	War
Cultural values ⟶	⟵	Cultural values
Management vision ⟶	⟵	Management myopia
Industry structure ⟶	⟵	Industry structure
Strategic intent ⟶	⟵	Organization history
0		100
	Percentage integration	

Source: Warren J. Keegan, 'Strategies for successful market entry', Institute for Global Business Strategy, Pace University, New York, NY 10038.

■ Summary

This chapter provided an introduction to worldwide advertising. It described the global environment, the history of world trade and more recent developments in global trade. It provided concepts and definitions of marketing worldwide which form the basis for worldwide advertising.

Chapter 2 will consider in more detail the world's most important regions.

■ Notes and references

1. Theodore Levitt, 1983: 'The globalization of markets', *Harvard Business Review*, May–June, pp. 92–102.
2. Eric Elinder, 1961: 'How international can advertising be?', *International Advertiser*, December, pp. 12–16.
3. Warren J. Keegan: *Principles of Global Marketing*, not yet published.
4. Christopher Bartlett and Sumantra Ghoshal, 1989: *Managing Across Borders*, Hutchinson Business Books.
5. This draws heavily on Warren J. Keegan, 1990: 'Competing in global industries: the transnational advantage', Working Paper No. 2, The Center For International Business Studies, Pace University, NY 10038, USA.
6. Ibid.
7. John A. Quelch and Edward J. Hoff, 1986: 'Customizing global marketing', *Harvard Business Review*, May–June.
8. George Gourlay, Assistant Vice President, The Coca-Cola Company, Second Annual Quality Conference, Conference Board, 16–17 May 1989, New York.
9. This section is an adaptation of sections from part one of Immanuel Wallerstein, 1974: *The Modern World System*, Academic Press.
10. Ibid.
11. Ibid.
12. Dr C. Gerritson, 1939: *Geschiedenis der 'Koninklijke'*, N.V. A. Oosthoek's Uitg. Mij.
13. This section is adapted from Warren J. Keegan, 1989: *Global Marketing Management*, Prentice Hall.
14. Marshall McLuhan, 1964: *Understanding Media: the Extensions of Man*, McGraw Hill Book Company.
15. This section is an adaptation of sections from Christopher Tugendhat, 1971: *The Multinationals*, Pelican Books.
16. Ibid.
17. Barbara Sundberg Baudot, 1989: *International Advertising Handbook, A User's Guide to Rules and Regulations*, Lexington Books.

18. Tugendhat, 1971: op. cit.
19. Jean-Jacques Servan-Schreiber, 1967: *Le Défi Américain*, Denoël. Translated as *The American Challenge*, 1967: Avon, New York.
20. Jos Willenborg, 1989: 'Confronting Europe', *KOREA Business World*, September.

Chapter 2
Developments in world regions

■ Introduction

Chapter 1 described the development of a world economy: how core areas developed, and the role of the periphery and the semi-periphery. The world economy of the 1980s and 1990s is a logical result of these developments. Relationships between countries – core areas, semi-peripheral areas and the periphery – are in continuous movement. In order to develop strategies for the future, it will be necessary to understand what is happening now.

The recent developments in the major world regions and their interrelationships will therefore be described, focusing on the three continents which are most relevant for global advertising: North America, Europe and Asia. Further chapters will provide data on many more regions. However, for global marketing and advertising these three continents are the most interesting and the fastest developing. The population of these areas wields extensive buying power. Figure 2.1 shows what the world looks like when mapped in terms of Gross Domestic Product.

Table 2.1 shows the three largest advertising spending markets, Europe, the United States and Japan. Total world advertising expenditures are approximately US $228 billion, of which these three markets comprise the majority.

The EC currently has a population of 325 million and this is growing fast. With the addition of 16.5 million East Germans, the EC will have a population which is 38 per cent larger than that of the United States and three times that of Japan. The European Free Trade Association (EFTA), consisting of Austria, Switzerland, Sweden, Norway, Finland

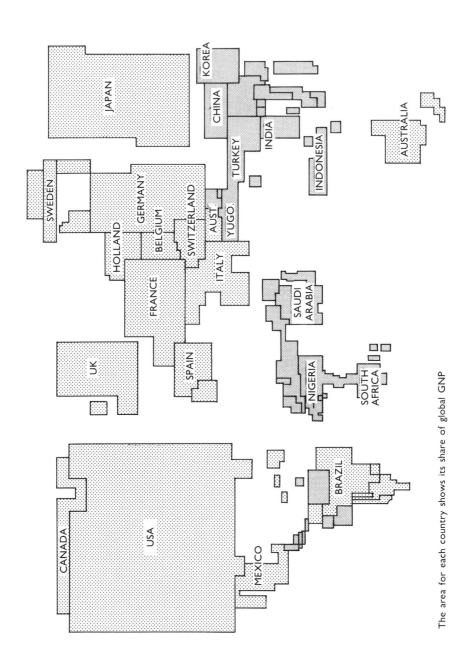

The area for each country shows its share of global GNP

Figure 2.1 *GDP map of the world (source: Nielsen)*

Table 2.1 The three largest markets for advertising expenditure

1988	Population millions	Advertising expenditure US $ millions	Advertising expenditure per capita US $	Advertising expenditure % of GDP
Europe*	355	53,753	153.3	1.0
USA	246	118,050	480.2	2.4
Japan	123	34,471	281.6	1.3
	724	206,274	305.0	1.6

* 16 countries in Europe, including most EFTA countries, such as Switzerland, Austria, the non-EC Scandinavian countries and Finland.

Source: World Advertising Expenditures, 23rd edition, Starch Inra Hooper, in cooperation with the International Advertising Association.

and Iceland, has a population of 32 million. EFTA is losing its individual importance, but for some uniform, high quality products EFTA and the EC can be seen as one market, so this region will clearly be very important for global corporations.

There will be major shifts in investment: Japan is stepping up its efforts to enter Europe, and a new wave of American investment in Europe is to be expected if the single market proves effective.

In all three regions the communications industry is developing very fast: 90 per cent of telephones and 96 per cent of computers are owned by less than twenty developed countries. Although some developing countries have been successful in improving technology in areas such as transport and computerization, many will find it difficult to participate or progress in this area.

Trade relationships between Western Europe and Asia are changing, while the USSR and the Eastern European countries are in an economic transition to a market-oriented economy for which their government institutions and business structure are not yet ready.

■ Europe, the 'single market' and international trade

The European Community was founded on 25 March 1957. Initially it consisted of the European Coal and Steel Community (ECSC), Euratom and the European Economic Community. These three organizations merged in July 1967 as a first step towards a true European Community, governed by communal treaty. The EC now consists of twelve member states: Belgium, Denmark, France, Germany, Greece, Ireland, Italy, Luxembourg, the Netherlands, Portugal, Spain and the United Kingdom. Since 1988 the European Community has been the largest trading bloc in the world.

In 1987 the Gross National Product (GNP) of the EC was estimated at US \$4,263.7 billion, compared to US \$4,436.2 billion for the United States and US \$2,379.3 billion for Japan.

In 1990 the EC will consist of 325 million consumers, compared to 249 million in the United States and 123 million in Japan.[1] EC exports are three times those of the United States, four times those of Japan, and seven times those of the USSR. This development will cause a considerable upheaval in traditional international marketing. When Austria, Norway and Sweden are admitted to membership in 1995, the EC will consist of 348 million consumers, compared to 256 million in the United States and 126 million in Japan.

The process of creating the single European market consists of the following measures:

1. Removing all border controls and customs facilities.
2. Guaranteeing free movement of persons and the right of citizens in one member state to settle in any other.
3. Removal of technical barriers.
4. Removal of fiscal barriers.
5. Liberalization of governmental purchasing policies.
6. Liberalization of the transfer of services and money.

These measures are designed to ensure a free flow within the member nations of everything necessary to healthy marketing. The process involves removal of trade barriers like the German *Reinheitsgebot*, the 20,000 industrial standards which protect German products against competition from France and Italy, and the twenty-five types of electric plugs used in different European countries. A lot has already changed: the number of customs forms used for international transport has been reduced from thirty-five to one.

Originally the initiatives came from Brussels, but since 1988 the business world has emerged as the driving force behind Euromarketing. Major corporations have awakened to the cost-savings which standardized trans-European marketing can bring, and are acting accordingly. One of Europe's largest manufacturers of household cleansers, for example, has cut the number of lemon scents used in their products in Europe from twenty-two to just three. Further evidence is provided by the many corporate take-overs within Europe and the rush of foreign investment into the EC. The winners after 1992 will be the big companies with a pan-European presence.

The consumer will most likely have a greater array of goods and services at his or her disposal, in some cases at lower prices. However, this will not turn an individual into a uniform Euroconsumer. A single advertising campaign, run throughout Europe, would miss its target: 66 per cent of all EC citizens speak only one language; less than 25 per cent speak two, while only 8 per cent are trilingual. Europeans do not display homogeneous buying behaviour. National aspects of buying behaviour will not disappear immediately with the abolition of national borders. Figure 2.2 shows the use of mineral water in various European countries, which is a good example of national differences in consumption.

Geographically and economically there are large differences. In 1985 the population of West Germany, the largest EC country, was 165 times larger than the population of Luxembourg, the smallest country. In 1988 the GNP of the Danes, the richest inhabitants of the EC, was more than twice that of the Portuguese, while Portugal's population was twice that of Denmark. The Northern European countries are richer than their neighbours in the South. In 1990 27.8 per cent of the EC population lives in Denmark, Western Germany and the Benelux countries, with 35.2 per cent of the GNP.[2] Many expect that Euroconsumers will gradually come to show similarity in their desires for products and services, and tastes, life-styles and buying behaviour will draw closer together. This can be seen already in developments in the electronic media and information technology. 1992 will bring greater standardization and internationalism to advertising in Europe. At least, advertisers are organizing themselves for more standardization.

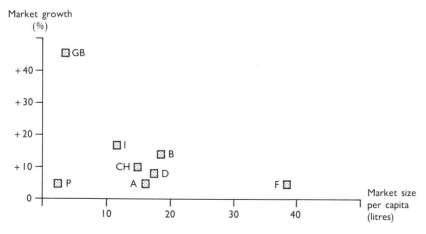

Figure 2.2 *Mineral water sales in Europe (source: Nielsen)*

However, non-Europeans, even if they place great emphasis on pan-European strategies, must still take into account the national characteristics of each EC country. The differences between the twelve individual nations – cultural, historic and linguistic – run deeper than one may imagine. Consumer values and behaviour may not change as quickly or as extensively as some would expect. There is a trend towards growing nationalism, and many individuals simply do not believe closer union is really going to happen.

The developments are, however, technologically driven, and ultimately no government will be able to stop them. National borders meant 'legal space'. Their abolition will change this 'legal space' into 'marketing space' and 'psychological space'.

The impact of changes in the media will be very important: the Europeanized media will have their impact on the consumer, leading towards convergence and integration. Restraints will be provided by language barriers, company cultures, differences in decision-making and operational style, and the 'Not Invented Here' syndrome.

Market growth, market segmentation, and the availability of an increased array of goods and services will necessitate increased advertising. Whether it concerns a new product introduction, or a re-launch of a product which has been standardized for the EC market, advertising will be essential to communicate details of the new or reworked product to the consumer in an increasingly active market.[3] The advertising and marketing world has been actively reorganizing itself to meet the challenge of the 1990s.

In 1988 Johnson & Johnson's $35 million rollout of Silhouettes feminine hygiene products was the result of their first effort in approaching Europe as a single market rather than a collection of distinct countries. Saatchi and Saatchi coordinated the advertising effort.[4] United Pictures International, the export marketing organization for the US studios Paramount, Universal and MGM/UA, fired their local agencies in each country and appointed Young & Rubicam to manage $30 million worth of film promotion, mostly in Europe. Johnson Wax has realigned most of its household and personal care brands, which have an advertising budget of about $60 million, with DDB Needham Worldwide, Belier, and Foote, Cone & Belding, to allow for the preparation of European brand strategies. Agencies are gearing up because multinational clients are increasingly assigning budgets for specific brands on a pan-European basis. Colgate toothpaste has been adapted into a single formula for sale across the region, replacing a situation where the same brand sold in different price categories in various parts of Europe. In 1988 Gillette's personal care division began selling a natural deodorant called Natrel Plus in the United Kingdom, the Netherlands, Spain and parts of Scandinavia. Saatchi & Saatchi in London handled the account.

These efforts by multinationals may pave the way for easier marketing by small companies, which have so far confined their sales to local markets. Greek yoghurt was typically a product only eaten by the Greeks, but it is now being introduced as a niche product in several countries, partly because regular yoghurt has been made more palatable to mass-market taste by General Mills with Yoplait and Gervais Danone with Dannon. Some brands, however, may disappear; for example, Nestlé may eventually drop yoghurt brand names such as Chambourcy and Elita.

When the barriers come down, smaller companies not previously organized for complex export trade will be able to move products across borders with the same ease as multinationals. This means that previously unknown brands will suddenly be competing with established market leaders. Small, local, good-idea, new-product companies will probably become more dangerous competitors to large companies than are other large companies.[5] They have a competitive advantage in terms of speed of implementation, speed of decision-making, and more personal and local trade and consumer relations.

Eastern Europe

After the events of late 1989, when most communist regimes in the Eastern European countries were abolished, and with so many changes still in progress, it would be presumptuous to sketch a commercial future for Eastern Europe. However, some events which occurred shortly before the major changes are still relevant.

In June 1988 the European Community and Comecon, the Eastern Bloc trading group, agreed to recognize each other. After that, one after the other, consortia from Germany, Italy, France and Britain offered upwards of $7 billion in trade finance to the Soviet Union.[6] Companies as diverse as Siemens, Rank Xerox, French aluminium producer Pechiney and construction giant Bouygues, the Italian state oil and chemicals group ENI as well as Fiat and engineering giant Asea Brown Boveri have rushed to set up joint ventures, taking advantage of the growing openness of the Soviet economy. Hungary has acted as the testing ground for many of the changes which Gorbachev has initiated in the Soviet Union, while Czechoslovakia, Bulgaria and Poland have lagged behind.

The development of a free market economy is impossible in countries where the political and bureaucratic system does not support it. In the Soviet Union and in the East European countries, Western investment is being sought to improve the domestic economy, but all these countries need Western help with quality improvement and management techniques to boost their ability to export manufactured goods into the world markets.

Among Western European countries, West Germany led the way in setting up joint ventures, while Finnish and Austrian companies profited from their traditional role as the middlemen between East and West. French enterprises have been closing deals rapidly, while British firms have only been making half the number of deals concluded by the French.

Flow of capital is the major problem, as private capital does not yet exist in the Eastern Bloc. Organizational aspects are also important. In the Soviet Union, for example, all Xerox machines and typewriters previously had to be registered by the police. It is very difficult to get modern equipment into the country in order to improve ways of doing business because of valuta problems.

Of the Eastern Bloc countries, Czechoslovakia has the most motivated workforce, and there is a first-rate economic team in government, but the greatest problem is nationalism. Poland has a high level of debt and a poor infrastructure, but its advantages include natural resources and several institutions which unite the country such as the Catholic Church and Solidarity. Ten years of opposition have been used to educate the people in what a free economy means. Early extensions of a brand name in the Eastern European countries and the initiation of advertising will be an interesting investment for the future.

Pepsi-Cola is selling in the Soviet Union, and its advertising agency BBDO has set up an office in Moscow. Western media owners are getting into the newly opened Eastern Bloc markets too: McGraw Hill is planning to launch a Hungarian edition of *Business Week*, there are plans to launch a commercial TV station in Czechoslovakia, and the Dutch publisher VNU has published a cultural and business magazine, *Moscow*, in association with the Moscow branch of the union of Soviet journalists and the Interbranch Commercial Bank, aimed at the development of wholesale trade in the USSR.

■ Developments in Asia, the Pacific and the Middle East

There are several bodies for economic and political cooperation in Asia and the Pacific Basin. These include the South Asian Association for

Regional Cooperation (SAARC), the Association of South-East Asian Nations (ASEAN) and Asia Pacific Economic Cooperation (APEC).

SAARC consists of Bhutan, Bangladesh, India, Maldives, Nepal, Pakistan and Sri Lanka. The total population of these countries is almost one-fifth of the world population. The objective of SAARC is cooperation in economic development. The member countries have divergent cultures, but they are similar in religious affiliation and levels of poverty. Half the population is between 15 and 40 years old. Future trends will see more women participating as consumers, and more people moving from rural areas to the cities.

Advertising expenditure is expected to grow, especially for television advertising. The growth of television will spread knowledge of new trends, changing buying behaviour accordingly. Yearly advertising expenditure per capita varies from $0.14 in Bangladesh to $1.00 in Sri Lanka.

ASEAN was established in 1967 in Bangkok to accelerate economic progress and to increase the stability of the South-East Asian region. The members are Brunei, Indonesia, Malaysia, the Philippines, Singapore and Thailand. Brunei has the world's highest per capita annual income – more than $20,000; GNP growth rates for ASEAN nations averaged nearly 5 per cent in 1987, as opposed to the US rate of 1.7 per cent. ASEAN exports grew by an average of 35.7 per cent from 1986 to 1987. Imports rose by an average of 33.8 per cent over the same period. Advertising expenditure has grown by an average of 25 per cent annually during the last years. Multinationals and joint ventures in the advertising industry have captured large market shares in the region, except in Indonesia, where the law prescribes local control.

APEC established in October 1989, is an Asia-Pacific economic bloc representing Australia, New Zealand, Japan, Korea, the ASEAN countries, and eventually Taiwan, Hong Kong and the People's Republic of China. The Pacific economy is growing strongly, with an average growth in GNP of 7 per cent.

The 'little dragons' of Asia, China and Japan

The 'little dragons' are Hong Kong, Taiwan, South Korea and Singapore. Asia's four little dragons have long followed Japan's brilliant economic example. They have learned to nurture their export-led economies and fight for the massive market shares required to sustain economic growth. Their advertising industry has grown – at the rate of 19 per cent in Hong Kong, to 30 per cent in South Korea and 50 per cent in Taiwan. In 1987–8 total advertising expenditure grew in Hong Kong by 68 per cent, in South Korea by 23 per cent, in Singapore by 21 per cent and in Taiwan by 26 per cent. The advertising industry in Japan represents 15 per cent of world advertising expenditure. China has been 'open' for ten years, and since 1978 advertising expenditure has been growing at a yearly rate of 50 per cent. This growth in Asia has continued in 1990. During the first half of the year, advertising expenditure increased by 13.5 per cent in Taiwan, 27.5 per cent in Korea, 23 per cent in Singapore, 29 per cent in Thailand, 57 per cent in Indonesia and 35 per cent in Malaysia.

Japan and the 'dragons': trade with the United States and Europe

The United States was the prime outlet for the dragons till the late 1980s. While the US market is gradually setting limits on their exports, Hong Kong, Singapore, South Korea and Taiwan – like Japan – are also beginning to encounter serious obstacles throughout Europe, as they arrive with their cheap exports of shoes, textiles, appliances and computers. Exploding trade surpluses have driven them towards Europe's 325 million relatively affluent consumers.

On 1 January 1989 the United States expelled the Newly Industrialized Countries (NICs) – also termed Newly Industrialized Economies (NIEs) – from its Generalized System of Preferences (GSP), reflecting the extent to which they have grown from developing nations into major economic powers. South Korea, Taiwan and Hong Kong show an average real economic growth rate of 12.4 per cent in 1987, while Singapore's real economic growth rate climbed from 1.8 per cent in 1986 to 8.8 per cent in 1987. This dynamic expansion depends heavily on massive export markets, which account for 40 per cent or more of their GDP. The push into Europe is accelerating.

Taiwan's exports to the European Community soared by 65.2 per cent to $7.8 billion in 1987, while imports climbed by 60.8 per cent to $5.2 billion. Europe's share of Taiwan's total trade is expected to grow to about 20 per cent by 1992; in contrast Europe accounted for only 12.6 per cent of Taiwan's foreign trade in 1986. South Korea has moved even faster and further into Europe. The US market absorbs 40 per cent of South Korea's exports, earning the country a trade surplus with the United States of $9.7 billion in 1987. Seoul's campaign to diversify export markets helped to expand the European share of South Korea's exports at an average rate of 23.3 percent between 1983 and 1987. The two smaller dragons – Hong Kong and Singapore – have more diverse trade accounts, but both saw trade with Europe grow by 50 per cent or more in 1987 alone. Because of Asia's low labour costs and favourable exchange rates, the dragons can set prices with which Europe can hardly compete. Their most important exports are electronics, textiles and shoes. For example, 1.7 million South Korean microwave ovens were shipped into EC countries in 1987, slightly more than the 1.6 million produced in the EC. The EC commission has started to impose provisional dumping duties on some products. Taiwan and Hong Kong pose the greatest threats for Europe. Apart from their electronic goods, they are also gearing up for high quality expansion into other, more traditional areas of European production. The Taiwanese in particular have invested heavily in sophisticated capital equipment for textiles, leatherware and shoes. This may enable them to produce the same range, quality and style as Italy's clothing industry. The NICs are also following Japan's example by setting up factories in Europe. The South Koreans have built over a dozen factories in Europe and more are planned. Trade figures indicate that the NICs, by retaining more control over their marketing and distribution in Europe than in the United States, are adapting successfully to business in the EC. The four dragons have adjusted their export strategy to suit the special requirements of Europe's diverse markets by setting up European-based marketing and production to enable them to quickly shift strategies to suit a variety of customer needs.

Compared to the mass merchandisers in the United States, Europe is very different as far as distribution is concerned. Buyers tend to be small, and to hold lower levels of stock; when they want merchandise, they want it urgently. Garment manufacturers have found the diversity of colour preferences, styles and even clothing sizes require exporters to move more cautiously than when approaching the relatively homogeneous US markets. The just-in-time production techniques of the NICs confer a competitive advantage.

While Europe is the leader in Asia's luxury goods markets, the NICs will clearly continue to export more to the EC than they import. Despite the popularity of French cognac and German BMWs among Asia's growing population of affluent urban professionals, the dragons are competitors, not merely an outlet for exports. Moreover, the purchasing power of the NICs' 70 million consumers is not really equal to the task. South Korea is a big market, but its per capita purchasing power is low – about $3,000 annually. The Taiwanese and Hong Kong Chinese, on the other hand, are rich, but they are not very numerous.

While Hong Kong and Singapore have historically operated as free ports, South Korea and Taiwan are gradually dismantling the tariffs that have protected their domestic markets from imports of foreign agricultural and consumer goods.[7]

In order to retain their competitiveness, the Japanese have been pushing much of their manufacturing into neighbouring countries. Japan has been investing throughout China and South-East Asia. Japanese companies have been quietly moving into Bangkok, Hong Kong, China and South Korea. Over 3,000 Japanese firms now have Asian operations and employ more than 700,000 local workers. The Japanese economic push into Asia is also accompanied by some important changes in management attitudes. There is evidence of a greater willingness among Japanese firms to hire and promote local managers, transfer less sophisticated technologies and involve local partners in equity participation.

South-East Asia, not America or Europe, is the most promising area for long-term investment as far as Japan is concerned. An implication of Japan's Asian investment moves is a pragmatic accommodation to a larger trend – the emergence of what may amount to three major trading blocs in Europe, North America and Asia. The traditional trading pattern of Asia's NICs – importing capital goods from Japan and exporting industrial products to the United States – began to change in 1988. Asian nations are now importing increasingly from the United States and exporting to Japan. Japanese imports of manufactured goods from Asia grew at a rate of nearly 50 per cent in 1988.

The strongest growth in Asia in 1988 occurred in Thailand, due to low labour costs, relatively high educational levels and a number of cultural similarities between two apparently dissimilar peoples. Both the Japanese and the Thai are Buddhist, which means they share a flexible outlook. Both want to do business. In 1988 Japan became the largest single investor in Thailand.

Elsewhere in South-East Asia, Malaysia, offering labour costs some 30–50 per cent lower than Singapore and Thailand, is beginning to attract additional investment, especially in the car industry.

A wide range of Japanese companies, from toothpaste makers to software houses, have moved into China. More than 500 new Japanese projects totalling close to $2 billion were announced in China in 1988. There are, however, a number of major barriers to investment in China, such as the lack of a foreign exchange market, which means that any venture is forced to export in order to earn foreign currency. Low production quality, poor factory organization and lack of trained technicians are also major problems. The most serious difficulty, however, is with infrastructure – long power failures, unreliable telecommunication facilities, unreliable supplies of pure water for production and even a lack of such basics as well-built highways and harbour facilities. China has an underdeveloped market system, bureaucratic control, no freedom of speech, no single language, many ethnic groups and a lack of adequate information and infrastructure. Also, the Chinese are not outward looking; the characters used to write 'China' translate as 'the centre of the world', and this indicates what is still the basic mentality.[8]

The success of Japan and the other booming countries in the region is based on a number of factors. Factors which have helped Japan and the other successful countries are related to Confucianism and include, among others, the view that success and happiness in life are more important than a possible after-life, the high value placed on education, the entrepreneurial spirit, good information systems, the development of capitalism and relatively authoritarian systems of government. The Chinese share some of these advantages, but in China because of the problems already mentioned they have not come to fruition.

The Middle East

This group consists of the Arab speaking countries: Saudi Arabia, Kuwait, Bahrain, Qatar, United Arab Emirates (UAE), Oman, Lebanon, Jordan, North Yemen, Iraq, Syria and South Yemen.

The last three countries have a controlled economy. In the others the advertising industry is developing fast. Advertising expenditure per capita varied in 1988 from $4.4 in Saudi Arabia to $29.4 in Kuwait.* The UAE, with its capital Dubai, is developing as a leading centre for international trade and communications.

The average population of the Middle East countries can be characterized in the following terms:

1. High illiteracy.
2. Limited exposure to culture and to the outside world.
3. Limited advertising.
4. Limited consumer sales promotion.
5. Plenty of money, so that prices are not a problem.

As a result there is a likelihood of high loyalty to the first brand in a category, and easy benefits for long-established brands.

Marketing is becoming easier in the Arab countries as the research and marketing infrastructure improves. For example, research in the Middle East has traditionally been difficult because of legal, social and religious constraints, but attitudes are changing rapidly, and research agencies have become more professional. Arab women are now

---

* After the invasion of Kuwait by Iraq, the situation is completely different. The position in the other Gulf states was unchanged at the time of going to press.

interviewing other Arab women, although the method of contact and the way the interviewer approaches her respondent must still take into account Islamic sensitivities.[9]

◼ North America and its attitude towards international marketing and advertising

North America is a major world region. Geographically North America includes the United States, Canada and Mexico. The two largest countries of this region, the United States and Canada, have recently signed a trade agreement which during the 1990s will totally eliminate barriers to the movement of goods and services between the two countries. This agreement will create a unified market in an area which, in 1988, accounted for 30 per cent of the Gross World Product.

North America is a distinctive regional market. In the United States there is a concentration of wealth and income within the framework of a single national economic and political environment that presents unique marketing characteristics. Per capita GNP in the United States in 1988 was $19,700. When this is converted to a standard of living, the United States comes out as one of the highest-income countries in the world.

The distinctive characteristic of the United States is the unique combination of high per capita income, large population, vast space, and plentiful natural resources. High product ownership levels are associated with a high income and relatively high receptivity to innovations and new ideas both in consumer and industrial products. The industrial product market is particularly receptive to innovations and products that reduce the labour hours necessary for production. The intensive application of computers and automated equipment in the United States reflects the high cost of labour, which creates an incentive to increase levels of mechanization in manufacturing and other processes. In general US industry is the most automated and efficient in the world, although there are notable exceptions.

Canada's income levels are roughly similar to those of the United States. The Canadian federation of provinces is politically distinctive with a growing emphasis on the individual character of each province. This is especially true for Quebec which is an island of French Canadian culture and language in the sea of the North American English-speaking culture. Ironically and paradoxically, the US-Canada trade pact has, by integrating Canada and the United States, made it more rather than less feasible for Quebec to consider separation from the Canadian federation.

The United States presents a unique foreign market opportunity for companies based outside the United States. It represents, in a single national market, an opportunity as large as that presented by all the countries of Western Europe, and is twice as large as the Japanese market. Indeed, its size is so great that most foreign countries wisely enter the US market with regional strategies, focusing their programmes initially on target regions before eventually going national. The United States was formerly a unique market also in terms of product saturation levels for consumer products, and receptiveness to innovation in both consumer and industrial products. Although these qualities are no longer unique to the US market, the United States remains a leader in accommodating innovative ideas, especially in the consumer products area.

The US market is probably the most communications-saturated market in the world. The degree of saturation is reflected in the high percentage of GNP expended on advertising in the United States – the highest in the world. The same is true for annual advertising expenditure per capita, currently (1990) $480.2. These figures reflect the wide access to the media and the crowded communications environment.

Technologically, the United States has slipped recently in relation to other countries. Akio Morita, co-founder of Sony, has recently and often described his views on this.[10] He says that America is by no means lacking in technology.

> But it does lack the creativity to apply new technologies commercially. US industry has itself to blame for much of the trade deficit. If they want to rectify the trade imbalance, they should devote their efforts to making products that really appeal to Japanese people and that they want to buy. Even Americans themselves prefer many Japanese-made products to American products.[11]

The biggest problem, Morita feels, is that America has opted out of manufacturing:

> Real business entails adding value to things by adding knowledge to them. That terrifies me. America no longer makes things, it only takes pleasure in making profits from moving money around.[12]

Another distinctive feature of the US market is that because of the size of the country, there is to an unusual degree an arm's-length – even an adversary – relationship between business and government. For the non-US-based marketer this arm's-length relationship provides greater opportunities for competing as a foreign firm than is true in most countries of the world, where closer partnership between government and business often excludes foreign suppliers from major product categories, especially industrial products. For example, the United States is one of the few industrial countries in the world where foreign manufacturers can bid on and obtain orders for power generation equipment.

■ Summary

This chapter has provided a description of the three major trading blocs – Europe, Asia and North America. Developments in South America, Africa, Australia and New Zealand were not covered because of lack of data or rapid change.

Although cultures and consequently buying behaviour differ within and between the regions described, buying behaviour and attitudes are tending to converge, especially for some products and services aimed at specific socio-economic groups. Standardized marketing operations will accelerate this process. This theme will be developed in the following chapters. Further details will also be given on the demographics of various countries, particularly when discussing media. When planning a global marketing campaign, it is vital to have a reasonable knowledge of this.

■ Notes and references

1. Sandra   Vandermerwe   and   Marc-Andre   l'Huillier,   1989: 'Euroconsumenten, hoe zien ze eruit', *PEM*, Autumn.
2. *Advertising Age*, 11 July 1988: '1992: Europe becomes one', p. 46.
3. *Stern* Marketing Series, 1989: *The New Marketing Challenge in Germany*.
4. *Advertising Age*, 11 July 1988: op. cit.
5. Keith Monk, 1989: *Go International*, McGraw-Hill, p. 175.
6. *International Management*, March 1989: 'Breaching the frontiers of Eastern Europe.'
7. *International Management*, October 1988: 'Dragons against the fortress'.
8. *International Management*, February 1989: 'Are the Japanese hollowing out their economy?'.
9. John Prawle, 1990: 'Efforts to bridge the Gulf', *Media & Marketing Europe*, July.
10. *Fortune*, 25 September, 1989.
11. Ibid.
12. Ibid. Data on growing advertising expenditure in Asia: Proceedings of Adasia Conference, Lahore, Pakistan, February 1989, and Adasia '90, Kuala Lumpar, November 1990.

Chapter 3
Global management and marketing strategy

■ Introduction

All worldwide advertising campaigns are set within the context of a worldwide marketing strategy and plan. Because strategy focuses a company's efforts, the quality of a company's strategy and planning is perhaps the single most important element determining its success or failure. No matter how hard you work, you will not be successful if your goal and focus are wrong.

Strategic planning has four distinguishing features: an external orientation that assesses the nature of environmental opportunities and threats; a process for formulating strategies; methods for analysis of strategic situations and alternatives; and a commitment to action.[1] Analysis of these factors is necessary to formulate a vision, intention and strategy for the organization so that it mobilizes the energy and creativity of each organization member. A business mission and a product vision are necessary in order to define the basics of the marketing communications strategy and plan.

Marketing strategy is that part of the business strategy which identifies target markets and addresses the needs and wants of customers to formulate an integrated marketing mix of product, price, place (channels of distribution) and promotion or communication. Advertising is a part of the broader promotion or communications strategy of the organization. Powerful advertising must be integrated into the broader framework of the marketing and business strategy.

This chapter reviews the development of worldwide marketing and the role played by advertising in this process. First the organization of export and international sales will be discussed, followed by the transition to international and global marketing, global strategy and the organization of global activities, global marketing strategies, global brands and megabrands and the changing role of the marketing manager.

◼ From international trade to marketing worldwide

This section will outline the progression from export to international trade and describe the accompanying changes in organizational structure. First two theoretical concepts, which should be familiar to students of international marketing, will be examined: the theory of comparative advantage and the product trade cycle model.

The theory of comparative advantage

The theory of comparative advantage is a demonstration, given certain assumptions, that a country can gain from trade even if it has an absolute disadvantage in the production of all goods, or that it can gain from trade even if it has an absolute advantage in the production of all goods. In other words, if the United States is better (more efficient) in the production of everything than Tanzania, the United States can still gain from specialization and trade. If Tanzania is inferior (less efficient) in the production of everything than the United States, Tanzania can still gain from specialization and trade.

This is a complicated economic theory, and it does not relate to the situation of an individual company. In addition, reality is far more complex than the limiting assumptions upon which the theory is based. Rather than going deeper into this theory with complicated business examples, we will take the simple example of the famous impresario Billy Rose, who was also the world's fastest typist. He faced a decision: 'Should I do my own typing, or should I pursue a career as a typist?'. The answer to both questions was no, because even though he had an absolute advantage as a typist over all typists in the world, his *comparative advantage* was as an impresario. If the objective is to maximize material well-being, both individuals and countries are better off specializing in their area of comparative advantage and then engaging in trade and exchange with others in the market-place.

The international product life-cycle model

This empirical model (developed by Professor Raymond Vernon of the Harvard Business School) is based on actual patterns of trade. It describes the relationship between the product life cycle, trade and investment. The international product life-cycle model suggests that many products go through a cycle during which high-income, mass-consumption countries are initially exporters, then lose their export markets, finally becoming importers of the product. At the same time other advanced countries shift from being importers to being exporters of the product, and later less developed countries shift from being importers to being exporters of a product. These shifts correspond to the three stages of the product life cycle: introduction, growth and maturity, and decline.

New products are initially introduced in high-income markets. This happens because high-income markets offer the greatest potential demand for new products, and it is useful to locate production facilities close to the product's market because of the need in the early stages of a product's life to respond quickly to consumer needs. Thus it is typical for products to be produced initially in the market where they will be sold. The first manufacturers of the new product have a virtual monopoly in world markets. Those in other countries who want the new product must order it from companies in the high-income country. Unsolicited orders begin to appear from other countries.

This develops into an export trade in the product. In the relatively high-income countries, entrepreneurs are quick to recognize and take advantage of lower labour and other costs in low-income markets. Production of the new product is then initiated abroad. As low-cost country producers gain experience and expand, competition from the lower-cost production country displaces the high-income country's export production as the main source for the product. At this point companies in high-income countries often decide to invest in low-income markets to retain their market share.

The final phase of this cycle occurs when the original high-income country manufacturer achieves mass production based on home and export markets and, due to lower costs, is able to produce more cheaply than the original high-income country. The low-income country manufacturer then begins to export to the high-income country market. The cycle is now complete and high-income country companies that once had a virtual monopoly in the product, find themselves facing competition from low-income countries in their home market. The personal computer industry is an industry which has just entered this last phase. Textile production has also been through the complete cycle.

The international product life cycle is basically a 'trickle down' model of world trade and investment. First products are introduced to the home market, then to other, advanced, countries, and finally to developing and less developed countries.

Another strategy is the 'waterfall' model: this consisting of developing a product and simultaneously introducing it to world markets. This approach recognizes that we live in a global village, and that markets develop simultaneously around the world. In the case of typical 'life-style' products or brands, for which there is a worldwide life-style target market, and the brand-concept is targeted at that specific market, the waterfall strategy may be very appropriate. For new, innovative or industrial products, however, this approach may not be appropriate.

Five international business tools

There are five business tools which can be used in the development of international trade: exporting, licensing, joint ventures, alliances and strategic partnerships. Each of these will be described in turn together with its organizational implications.

Exporting

Exporting is a basic tool for international growth and expansion. It is the sourcing of a product from another country. A small company which exports on a regular basis begins with an export manager who travels to the export markets, while sales and advertising are controlled from the home base. In larger companies there is usually a more distinct division of responsibilities, based on product type, geographical area or nature of the clients (for example, agent, wholesaler, direct sales etc.). The type of organization adopted is determined by the company itself, the product and the market.

The company

The greatest influence on the structure of the organization is the history of the company and the way in which it has grown. The bigger the company, the more structured it is likely to be, but managers often leave their own personal mark on an organization. American companies and multinationals attach a great deal of importance to reports and titles, but a 'whizz-kid' director leaves a distinctive mark on the company and on the team he works with. A man with special skills or contacts working outside the system will be tolerated. Factors like this play an important role in international trade.

The product

The type of product will determine whether it can be sold easily in other countries or unfamiliar markets. Technologically advanced products can be sold easily to technologically advanced buyers in any country, but culture-bound products that serve basic needs are less international. Each country or perhaps each region has its own specific sausage or speciality dish, but all countries use computers, aeroplanes and machine parts in the same way. A product like the bicycle, which is a luxury consumer durable in one country, forms a basic means of transport in another country. A convenience consumer product in Europe such as Pepsi-Cola is a luxury elsewhere, enjoyed only once a year. In Holland, milk is drunk everyday and bought in the supermarket. In Thailand it is sold in the streets from stalls, like ice-cream in Holland.

The more advanced the product, the more after-sales support it requires. Cars and machines break down and need both maintenance and regular servicing. It is essential to be able to respond to the questions and complaints of consumers and dealers in the country where the product is sold. High-volume goods need special means of transport, and raw materials and semi-manufactured goods determine the way in which they must be marketed. Labour-intensive products are most appropriately produced in low-wage countries, and capital-intensive products in a country in which capital finance is more readily available. Technically-advanced products demand technically-trained personnel.

When a multinational offers a large range of products, they are usually marketed by product type and adapted to the local markets. For some products, however, the national background is of great importance; examples include Scotch whisky and French cheese.

The market

The markets to which products are exported influence the way in which marketing organizations are structured. Are the orders big or small? What are the tax laws? Are there requirements for a special kind of packaging, either by law or because of the physical environment? How does the distribution work?

Too few enterprises structure their organizations formally in order to handle their exports efficiently. Many enterprises use exporting as a means of dumping their excess products. Enterprises which structure their organization for global operations and set up their organization so that it can react to the needs of the consumers who want to buy their products will be successful. However, in doing this the enterprise will have changed from an export/sales-oriented company into a customer/market-oriented company, multinational or global.

From export to other types of international operations

Production abroad

When export activities are successful, and particularly when sales abroad exceed sales in the home country, it is appropriate to set up production units in other countries in order to reduce transport costs and to make use of cheaper labour or raw materials.

Product development

At this point the similarities in consumer wants and needs in different countries must be taken into consideration in order to reach the highest possible level of standardization. Another approach is to find out how the same, standardized product can, in different stages of its life cycle, be marketed in different countries in the same or in different ways. In the home market a product may be in its ripening phase, earning maximum profits. However, in a country where it has been newly introduced, it will be in its pioneer phase and will therefore require a larger investment in communication and promotion.

The sales organization

The sales organization develops through four phases. Initially, export sales are handled from head office. The next step is to appoint an export-agent abroad. Thus may be a one-person business or a large organization. Agents usually specialize in a certain category of products or in a geographical area. Some control a wider range of products. Using an agent is a flexible way to start an export business. However, the producer must be sure that his agent has the right contacts and that he is honest. This kind of relationship is based on trust.

An agent can function as a distributor and thus as a wholesaler, receiving goods in bulk from the producer and distributing his client's orders in his own country. The agent may have his own sales, marketing, advertising and research organization. Sometimes he might even have his own outlets. He can stock spare parts, handle complaints and take the necessary action against the competition. This implies that he will also give the producer feedback with respect to product development or other activities. This system works well for consumer non-durables, but not so well for consumer durables and even less for high-value capital-intensive products which require lengthy sales negotiations. In the latter case salesmen from head office must be appointed. Even if there is an agent it may still be necessary to send someone from head office for the more important sales orders.

Another method is 'piggy-back' marketing. This means using the sales facilities of a producer who is already selling a complementary product in a certain country. A producer of paint brushes can collaborate with a producer of paint, sharing sales costs in proportion to turnover. This system only works when both parties gain by it. When the more important producer finds it a burden to carry the other with him, the arrangement will fail.

The fourth phase involves establishing one's own subsidiary abroad. This can be a 'sleeping' corporation for registration purposes, but it can also be a sales/service/marketing organization or a warehouse/wholesale business, or even a complete production or assembly plant, which operates in the same way as those in the home country. The latter becomes especially necessary when import duties are so high that it pays to start one's own production unit.

Other advantages of working without agents include savings in agents' commission, savings on transport of goods and personnel, and the chance to build up profits outside the home country, which can finance further expansion or act as reserves which cannot be taxed in the home country.

Licensing

Licensing basically involves selling know-how and trade and brand reputation to a buyer. The know-how may be technical or it may involve marketing. A licence is a right to use a valuable name or method or particular form of know-how.

Many enterprises use licensing as a method of establishing production abroad. This is easiest if the licence concerns a process which can be controlled, for example where it requires the use of an exclusive ingredient (as with Coca-Cola), or where the level of technology is such that the producer can guard the process by employing its own personnel. This happens only in countries which are willing to comply with the licence demands. Countries such as the USSR and developing countries in particular make use of this method because they lack technological knowledge and have an abundance of cheap labour. The production of Zastava and Lada cars (both varieties of the Fiat 124) in Eastern European countries was formerly an example of this.

Local production and local presence also has the advantage of establishing greater credibility in the eyes of the consumer. Moreover it can prevent 'pirating' (parallel import).

Joint ventures

A joint venture is an agreement between two companies to form an enterprise for the purpose of pursuing some business objective. Usually a joint venture has a limited and clearly defined scope in terms of markets, technology and business objectives. A typical joint venture is a company that is formed by two investors to pool assets and know-how in order to manufacture and market a product in a single country.

Alliances or strategic partnerships

In an alliance, each side seeks to learn the skills of the partner in addition to making and selling a product without carrying the sole investment responsibility. The real pay-off in creating competitive advantage is the process of learning and transferring know-how.

■ Corporate strategy and the organization of global corporate activities

Corporate strategy

In large multilevel organizations, strategy should provide guidance and direction to each reporting unit. The strategic planning process at the corporate level leads to the formulation of a corporate strategy, which defines the business in which a diversified company will compete. For example, IBM's United States operations include five independent units, each representing a different business for IBM: personal systems, enterprise systems, application business systems, technology products and communication systems. Although IBM is an integrated company, each unit enjoys considerable autonomy within the framework of corporate strategy which is pulled together at regional and worldwide headquarters. Thus, the corporate strategy will integrate all the strategies of IBM's individual businesses. Corporate strategy defines the businesses in which a diversified company will compete, and integrates the strategies of the businesses within an organization.

Mission statement

One key aspect of corporate planning has traditionally been the development of a mission statement, which answers the questions 'Who are we?' and 'What business(es) are we/will we be in?'. An organization's mission is 'the fundamental, unique purpose that sets it apart from other firms of its type and that identifies the scope of its operations in product and market terms. *The mission is a general, enduring statement of organizational intent.'*[2] The mission statement should define the purpose of the company and guide the organization's members in their decision-making and strategic planning. It should inspire creative effort and mobilize energy. A good mission statement is neither too broad nor too narrow. Consider, for example, the broad statement 'Our mission is to be a leader in the information industry'. The information industry is a one trillion dollar-plus industry. To be a leader in this industry begs the critical questions: in what part of the industry? for which customers? On the other hand, the statement 'Our mission is to sell 10,850 widgets in 1992' focuses only on the product and is too narrow. A good mission statement should provide focus for a company and it should be motivating and energizing. All good mission statements address the ultimate source of every company's existence: the customer. For example, IBM's mission, is stated in its Annual Report as follows:

> IBM is in the business of applying advanced information technology to help solve the problems of business, government, science, space exploration, defense, education, medicine, and other areas of human activity.

A comparison with the mission statement contained in Apple's Annual Report should, and does, provide a good view of how the two companies differ:

> What sets Apple apart from other companies is also what sets our computers apart from other computers: Our total focus on the human experience. What sets Apple computers apart is the performance of the people who use them. Only Apple gives users powerful technology that is easy to use, with thousands of consistent applications that work together, a broad product line to run them, and easy access to other computer environments.

As these examples illustrate, a mission statement that emphasizes how much money the company wants to make or how many units it wishes to sell is useless. It provides no focus and direction, and by suggesting that the purpose of the company is to obtain a reward without indicating *how* the reward will be earned, it mistakenly emphasizes ends and not means.

A mission statement is exceptionally difficult to formulate: defining a mission requires a deep understanding of customers and their needs. Without a clear mission statement it is impossible to develop a consistent communications strategy.

Strategic intent

While the word 'intent' has traditionally been used in strategic planning to describe a firm's mission, a new strategy model uses 'intent' somewhat differently. This model, described by Hamel and Pralahad, is based on the concept of strategic intent. For example, over the past two decades Japanese companies such as Honda, Komatsu and Canon which have achieved global leadership began with lofty ambitions, 'out of all proportion to their resources and capabilities' and then created and sustained an obsession for winning in the quest for global leadership. This obsession with winning is a strategic intent.[3] Strategic intent is a powerful concept for mobilizing corporate resources, energy and creativity to create competitive advantage and customer value.

The organization of global activities

A corporation that competes globally must decide how to spread its activities among various countries. The activities related to the buyer, are usually tied to where the buyer is located. A company selling in Japan must provide sales and service in Japan. The supporting activities can, in most industries, be detached from the place where sales take place.

There are two key aspects of global organization:[4]

1. The configuration of a company's activities worldwide, or the choice of where to perform each activity in the world, and in how many places.
2. The coordination of all activities in different countries.

The activities performed by a company include things like sales, service, product development and administration. Some are linked to specific countries, others can be dispersed. If the activities can be well integrated on a worldwide basis, the company is likely to have the best competitive advantage.

Industries globalize when the benefits of configuring and/or coordinating globally exceed the costs of doing so. The pattern of global organization can differ by segment or industry stage, and also by sub-system, e.g. groups of countries. Configuration and coordination possibilities may be high in specific competing countries, for example in countries which have similar climatic conditions and thus similar product needs. The sub-systems can be based on geographical regions, language, phase of development, amount of influence exercised on competition by the government, and historical and present political ties.[5]

A company can standardize (concentrate) some activities and adapt (disperse) others. Flexibility is important, the more so because traditional advantages are shifting more often and more quickly. A low-wage country may be quickly overtaken by another country, and a technological lead may also be overtaken very fast. In the shipping construction business, Japan overtook Europe, but was caught up soon afterwards by Korea. *A global strategy means more than only the choice between global standardization and adaptation to local needs.*

Marketing and global strategy

Many marketing activities are linked to the location of the buyer/consumer, but there are also many opportunities for global marketing coordination in most industries, especially as regards brand name, sales organization, service network and price.

The product development function in global industries is particularly complex, because it requires the collection and coordination of information from around the world. The already difficult matter of coordination between marketing and R&D becomes more difficult where global strategies are concerned.[6]

International and global marketing distinguishes itself from national marketing by an extra dimension: marketing must understand local consumer needs, marketing systems and media not only in one country, but in many countries simultaneously. Therefore marketing has the greatest need of global coordination as well as of response to local market conditions.

The future of international competition[7]

The configuration aspects

The need both to standardize products across countries and to segment markets will remain. Packaged consumer goods will increasingly become global products. Some services will also, due to progress in information technology, become suitable for global strategies. In many industries, though, the limits of the advantages which economies of scale can bring have already been reached. Although in one sense the limits of lower transport costs seem to have been reached, since containers and ships can barely become bigger, components are still becoming smaller and materials lighter, so there is still some possibility that transport costs can decrease, but for how long? The advantages of low-wage countries have decreased due to advances in information technology and as a result the influence of labour costs has diminished.

The coordination aspects

Here the picture looks different. Communication and coordination costs keep dropping strongly due to the breathtaking developments in information systems and telecommunications technology. Using computer-aided design technology, engineers in different countries work with each other via computer screens across the whole world. Marketing systems and business practice are increasingly standardized, making it easier to organize activities across various different countries. This emphasizes the importance of consistency in the way activities are organized throughout the world.

■ Global marketing strategies

When the pattern of international competition in an industry shifts from 'multidomestic' to global, this will have implications for the strategy of a company. There are three generic strategic approaches to outperforming other firms in an industry. These are overall cost leadership, differentiation and focus.[8]

Overall cost leadership

This strategy has become increasingly popular in recent years. Basically, a firm seeking to base its competitive strategy on overall cost leadership must aggressively pursue a position of cost leadership by constructing the most efficient scale facilities and obtaining the largest share of the market so that its cost per unit is the lowest in the industry. Cost leadership does not mean minimization of expenditure. For example, the cost leader in an industry will probably be the largest advertiser, but because of its greater volume, its advertising cost per unit will be the lowest. Similarly, this ratio will apply to all aspects of the competitor's programme, including selling costs, administrative costs, research and development, distribution and servicing. Cost leadership has been the cornerstone of highly successful strategies. In the United States, Ivory Soap and power tool manufacturer Black & Decker provide examples. In Japan, companies producing cameras, consumer electronics and entertainment equipment, motorcycles, and cars have achieved leadership on a world basis.

Differentiation

Differentiation involves the creation of a product or service that is *perceived* as being unique. This is an extremely effective strategy for defending market position and obtaining above-average returns. Examples of successful differentiation are Caterpillar in construction equipment, Mercedes in luxury cars and almost any successful branded consumer product.

Focus or 'niche' strategy

A focus or 'niche' strategy is based on serving a particular market segment more effectively and efficiently than any other competitor. Again, as with overall cost leadership and differentiation, successful focusing will yield above-average return. A focus strategy means finding a segment or a cluster of customers whose particular needs can best be met by a company focused on this market segment. The key to the market niche strategy is to identify the segment basis for defining the niche. When used as a marketing strategy this strategy is also called 'micro marketing'.

Competition and the product life-cycle

The requirements for an effective competitive strategy vary at different stages of the product life-cycle (PLC). The global enterprise must address each of the stages and decide whether to pursue them on a single- or a multi-country basis. Consider innovative entry, for example, the indicated strategy for the infancy stage of the PLC. Should a company concentrate on a single- or multi-country strategy? The answer depends on the company's resources.

In the global environment, the PLC concept is becoming less relevant for mass consumer brands, for which there need not be a declining phase since their life can be extended by adding value through intensive advertising (this is demonstrated by Listerine, Lux toilet soap and Coca-Cola, among other products).

■ Opposing concepts of global marketing: local adaptation versus global standardization

There are two opposing views about the role of marketing in global strategies. One view is that marketing is a local problem. The emphasis is on the differences between consumer needs and marketing systems, and this calls for a marketing strategy which is entirely directed towards the country involved. The opposing concept is based on the emerging similarities of consumers worldwide, which make it possible to use a common product, price, distribution and promotion programme on a worldwide basis.

There is no real choice between the two concepts. There can be degrees of standardization. A variety of external and internal factors influence the standardization decision, and the likelihood of standardization depends on a variety of factors – target market, market position, nature of the product and environment.

Global marketing will be discussed from first a local and then a standardized viewpoint. Next the configuration possibilities of global marketing and the necessary coordination of activities will be discussed. The section concludes with a summary of the main conditions for standardization.

The local viewpoint

The concept of directing all activities locally is based on the existence of essential differences which influence marketing in different countries. There are three categories of differences:

1. Cultural differences which influence consumer behaviour.
2. Differences in infrastructure.
3. Economic and technological differences.

Cultural differences

A global corporation must have a feeling for differences in culture. The marketing manager in particular must be aware of the similarities and differences in cultures in relation to his or her own country.

There are many cultural elements which influence marketing. These include attitudes towards consumption of goods; the use of colour, brand names, design and music; education and literacy; religion and beliefs; sex roles in society; and the political situation. In each culture attitudes towards work and ambition, management and the concept of profit vary. In economically developed countries the influence of the consumer is much stronger than in underdeveloped countries where some enterprises still dump products which do not meet the quality or safety standards of developed countries. Lack of education, illiteracy and defective communication channels mean that there is no active consumer movement in underdeveloped or developing countries.

In some countries, as in South and Central America, religion plays a very important role. Religious beliefs affect the amount of time spent in prayer and may involve fasting, as in the Muslim Ramadan, or abstinence from alcohol. Climatic differences also lead to different lifestyles and eating habits. In countries with a warm climate social life takes place out-of-doors and furniture is less important than in Northern Europe, where people entertain in the home. Barbecues are more common in countries with a hot climate.

Different nationalities eat at different times of the day, and the content of meals varies. The British are traditionally thought to eat a large, cooked breakfast. The Belgians eat soup with their supper. The French eat vegetables and potatoes as a separate course in the menu. In many cultures men and women eat separately, while in other nations mealtimes are seen as the highpoint of family life.

Other, related aspects of cultural differences will be discussed further in Chapters 4 and 5.

The need for product adaptation

Some products and communication programmes can be taken to other markets without major modifications; many consumer electronics fit into this category, although prices and distribution strategies still vary from country to country. On the other hand, many of the most notable international product failures have resulted from a lack of product adaptation. Philips, for instance, began to earn profits in Japan only after it had reduced the size of its coffee-makers to fit the smaller proportions of Japanese kitchens; Coca-Cola withdrew its two-litre bottle in Spain after discovering that few Spanish refrigerators had large enough compartments.[9]

Differences in infrastructure

Differences in transport systems, distribution, available media, legal conditions, the physical environment and communications systems can force multinationals to use an approach which differs from country to country.

The non-availability of commercial television in some countries affects advertising, as does the media buying system.

The concentration of distribution (as, for example, in the Scandinavian countries) calls for a completely different approach than a system with many small retail stores and a large number of wholesale trade organizations.

Legal and voluntary restrictions may include strict laws for handling promotions, patents and trademarks.

The physical environment is an important factor. A high degree of humidity in a country affects packaging and product design. Electrical equipment must meet different requirements in terms of plug type and voltage, etc. The sheer size of countries such as the Soviet Union or China has extensive consequences.

Transport and communications systems must be carefully considered. Differences in the telephone system, road networks and postal services affect how products can be sold. Mail order selling is clearly more difficult in Italy than in the United States due to the unreliability of the national postal services.

Economic and technological differences

Different economic situations bring about different consumer needs and attitudes. Advanced technological economies produce skills and working environments which are not found in agricultural societies. The latter are less aggressive and less competitive. The more prosperous people are, the more they desire luxury products and services. Only when basic needs are fulfilled is there a market for luxury articles. Often a market is seen as an enormous market, without taking into account the fact that there is not (yet) enough spending power to do more than satisfy basic needs. Many people consider the Chinese market to have a huge potential, but few realize that the basic needs are not yet met: in 1988 only one in every 27,000 people had access to a telephone.

The technological development of a country is important, because if there is no efficient energy system and no electricity, and there are no trained personnel available, it is very difficult to establish a production unit. However much modern equipment is installed, if the infrastructure is not available, it is difficult to operate. Telefaxes do not work when there is a power cut! A glossy, full-colour advertising campaign becomes a pale imitation in countries with mainly black and white newspapers.

The economic environment does not just differ from country to country, but also within each country. Southern Italy, for example, is poor in comparison to the North, while the South of England is the richest part of the country. The Northern Yugoslavian state of Slovenia is the most developed part of Yugoslavia, while the South lags behind. Import restrictions such as quotas, import duties and quality requirements also contribute to the economic environment.

Finally, competition is a key factor. When competition is particularly strong in one country, it will be necessary to adapt the strategy used in that country, for example in terms of price setting, sales activities and advertising.

The standardized viewpoint

The ultimate form of standardization means offering identical products worldwide at identical prices via identical distribution channels, supported by identical sales and promotion programmes. The advocates of this type of strategy point to successful examples in product categories which one would expect to be sensitive to local preferences and other local conditions: Coca-Cola, Esso, McDonald's.

The growing homogenization of needs across borders is the most frequently mentioned reason for standardization. Levitt[10] calls it 'the globalization of markets'. The successful examples he mentions are: McDonald's, Coca-Cola, Revlon Cosmetics, Sony Television and Levi jeans – products which can be bought to an identical design throughout the whole world.

Companies which make their profits by following this trend of globally homogenizing needs and preferences can, as a result, achieve economies of scale in procurement, logistics, production and marketing, and also in the transfer of management expertise which will all eventually add up to lower prices.

Still more important is the fact that standardization offers the possibility of building a uniform worldwide corporate image, world brand or global brand with a global image. It simplifies the development of a global marketing mix, especially with respect to brand names, advertising concepts, after-sales service, sales training and sales promotion.

The advantage of standardization for global advertising

Like product standardization, standardization of advertising helps create a consistent brand image, recognizable worldwide, which reduces the risk of confusion for the consumer. Standardized advertising also can reduce the costs of producing artwork, film and other advertising material.

However, Yoram Wind states

> that there are tremendous differences among countries. Ted Levitt correctly stresses that one should not focus only on differences, one should look for commonality and similarity; however, one cannot ignore the differences and the need to adapt to them. Most international blunders stem from instances of cultural insensitivity – lack of awareness of values, and attitudes – that cause a strategy which is extremely successful in one country to prove wrong in another.[11]

The best strategy is to 'think globally' and 'act locally', which implies that the 'overall' strategy is worldwide, but that the details of the marketing strategy follow the specific characteristics and cultural differences of each country.

Global coordination of marketing activities[12]

There are a number of ways in which marketing activities dispersed in different countries can be coordinated. These include the following:

1. Using similar methods across countries.
2. Transferring marketing know-how and skills from country to country.
3. Sequencing of marketing programmes across countries.
4. Integrating the efforts of various marketing groups in different countries.

Using similar methods across countries

Using similar methods across countries implies giving preference to standardizing the marketing activities in several countries instead of adapting to local needs. The advantage is the strengthening of the reputation of a brand which occurs when buyers and information are internationally mobile. Even if buyers are not mobile, information will cross borders due to the speed of information technology.

The decision about adopting a standardized marketing strategy must be taken separately for each marketing activity. The choice might be to go for the same brand name everywhere, and for the same sales strategy, even if this differs from local distribution patterns. An example is the way in which Coca-Cola in Japan deviated from the existing distribution system by refusing to use the traditional Japanese wholesale trade and instead starting its own bottling network. McDonald's got the Japanese to change centuries-old eating habits and now has over 500 outlets in Japan. German hair product manufacturers Wella used beauty salons and Schick distribute their razor blades through the Hattori Seiko distribution network. [13]

Companies which pursue decentralized strategies usually use different brand names in different countries. Most of the examples can be found in the packaged consumer goods industry. Examples are Nestlé and Unilever. However, in Europe the advent of the single market will increase the need for standardized strategies.

Some marketing activities are easier to standardize than others. It is easier to introduce and maintain a global brand name than it is to maintain a uniform qualitative sales force approach. Table 3.1 summarizes marketing activities according to ease or difficulty of standardization.

Table 3.1 Marketing activities according to ease or difficulty of standardization

Easy to standardize	Difficult to standardize
– brand name	– distribution
– product positioning	– personal selling
– service standards	– training sales personnel
– warranties	– pricing
– advertising theme	– media selection
– packaging	

Source: Michael E. Porter, 1986: *Competition in Global Industries*, Harvard Business School Press, Boston, Mass. Ch. 4.

Transfer of marketing know-how and skills from country to country

Of particular importance is the transfer of a market-entry approach that has worked in one country to other countries. Exchange of information about buying patterns, life-styles, attitudes, successful product introductions, new merchandising ideas, etc., are also of great importance. This exchange does not happen automatically. There is a need for communication and openness between headquarters and subsidiaries, but also among subsidiaries themselves. The corporate culture of a company plays an important role in this respect.

Sequencing of marketing programmes across countries

New products or services can also be introduced in a planned sequence in various countries. This sequence can be determined by the country's level of economic or technological development, by the acceptance of certain product appeals, or other factors. This strategy can prove economical since the costs can be shared across countries.

Integration of efforts of marketing groups across countries

The most frequent form of integration is the 'international account management system'. Such structures have existed for a long time, especially in service industries such as advertising agencies and banking. Advantages include a more efficient use of the sales force and the provision of a single contact for each international client. Sales to clients other than large international customers remain on a local basis. Disadvantages include increased travel time, language barriers and cultural differences in methods of conducting business.

Summary: standardization versus differentiation in marketing

A set of propositions developed by Subhash C. Jain,[14] sums up this section. He has compiled from the literature a definitive list of arguments for and against standardization. His definition of standardization is as follows:

> using a common product, price, distribution and promotion programme on a worldwide basis.

His propositions are as follows:

1. 'In general, standardization is more practical in markets which are economically alike.'
2. 'Standardization strategy is more effective if worldwide customers, not countries, are the basis for identifying the segments to serve.'
3. 'The greater the similarity in the markets in terms of customer behaviour and life-style, the higher the degree of standardization.'
4. 'The higher the cultural compatibility of the product across the host countries, the greater the degree of standardization.'
5. 'The greater the degree of similarity in a firm's competitive position in different markets, the higher the degree of standardization.'
6. 'Competing against the same adversaries, with similar share positions, in different countries leads to greater standardization than competing against purely local campaigns.'
7. 'Industrial and high technology products are more suitable for standardization than consumer products.'
8. 'The more similar the marketing infrastructure in the home and host countries, the higher the degree of standardization.'
9. 'Companies in which key managers share a common world view, as well as a common view of the critical tasks flowing from the strategy, are more effective in implementing a standardization strategy.'
10. 'The greater the strategic consensus among parent–subsidiary managers on key standardization issues, the more effective the implementation of standardization strategy.'
11. The greater the centralization of authority for setting policies and allocating resources, the more effective the implementation of standardization strategy.'

▪ World brands

A world brand, global brand or megabrand is one which shares the same strategic principles, positioning and marketing in every market throughout the world, although the marketing mix can vary.

A world brand is guided by the same strategic principles in every market in the world. Take for example Marlboro, which is positioned around the world as an urban brand appealing to the universal desire for freedom and physical space, something which urban dwellers typically lack. Freedom and space are symbolized by the 'Marlboro man'.

A world brand is positioned the same way in every market. If the brand is a premium-priced brand, it will be premium-priced around the

Table 3.2 Company/brand ranking by country

	Order	Association by Japanese	Association by Americans	Association by French
Global brands	1st	Sony 40%	Sony 67%	IBM 39%
	2nd	Chanel 40%	IBM 55%	Coca-Cola 27%
	3rd	Toyota 36%	Ford 38%	Sony 27%
	4th	IBM 36%	Toyota 30%	Christian Dior 23%
	5th	Louis Vuitton 34%	GM 27%	Renault 22%
	6th	Coca-Cola 16%	Coca-Cola 23%	Chanel 20%
	7th	Mercedes Benz 14%	GE 17%	Ford 19%
	8th	Honda 12%	Honda 15%	Honda 16%
	9th	GM 11%	McDonald's 13%	Ferrari 13%
	10th	McDonald's 11%	BMW 11%	Philips 13%
Japanese brands	1st	Sony	Sony	Sony
	2nd	Toyota	Toyota	Honda
	3rd	Honda	Honda	Mitsubishi
	4th	Matsushita	Mitsubishi	Akai
	5th	Seiko	Panasonic	Toyota
	...	Nissan, Hanae Mori, Mitsubishi	Toshiba, Nissan, Nikon	Yamaha, Toshiba, Canon, Hitachi
US brands	1st	IBM	IBM	Ford
	2nd	McDonald's	Ford	Coca-Cola
	3rd	Ford	GM	IBM
	4th	GM	GE	McDonald's
	5th	Coca-Cola	Coca-Cola	Levi Strauss
	...	Tiffany, Hunting World	McDonald's, Chrysler	Chrysler, GM, Apple
French brands	1st	Chanel	Peugeot	Renault
	2nd	Louis Vuitton	Chanel	Peugeot
	3rd	Hermes	Renault	Christian Dior
	4th	Christian Dior	Christian Dior	Chanel
	5th	Yves Saint Laurent	Yves Saint Laurent	Yves Saint Laurent
	...	Renault, Cartier, Renoma	Pierre Cardin, Hermes, Lancome	Philips, Citroen

Table 3.2 *(continued)*

	Order	Association by Japanese	Association by Americans	Association by French
West German brands	1st	Benz	BMW	Benz
	2nd	BMW	Benz	BMW
	3rd	Volkswagen	Volkswagen	Volkswagen
	4th	Solingen	Porsche	Schneider
	5th	Henkel	Adidas	Bosch
	...	Porsche, Beer, Braun	Audi, Krups, Braun	Krups, Porsche
UK brands	1st	Burberry's	Jaguar	Marks & Spencer
	2nd	Wedgwood	Rolls-Royce	Rolls-Royce
	3rd	Rolls-Royce	Burberry's	Jaguar
	4th	Aqua Scutum	Reebok	Austin
	5th	Jaguar	Wedgwood	Lipton
	...	Dunhill, Harrod's	Lloyds of London, London Fog	Rover, J&B, Weston
Italian brands	1st	Armani	Gucci	Fiat
	2nd	Ferrari	Ferrari	Benetton
	3rd	Gucci	Fiat	Ferrari
	4th	Valentino	Armani	Barilla
	5th	Fiat	Fendi	Panzani
	...	Benetton, Alfa Romeo	Benetton, Alfa Romeo	Minelli, Buitoni
Korean brands	1st	Hyundai	Hyundai	Daewoo
	2nd	Samsung	Samsung	Samsung
	3rd	Lotte	Gold Star	Gold Star
	4th	Kimchi	Daewoo	
	5th	Gold Star	Korean Airlines	
	...	Daewoo, Korean Airlines, Pony		

Note: The recognized brands shown above include non-specific brands and brands that are obviously from other countries.

Source: S. Hiromura, ESOMAR Conference, June 1990.

world. If it is positioned *vis-à-vis* an age segment of the market, the positioning will be the same in every market. For example, Benetton has positioned its main lines *vis-à-vis* the 16–24 youth market around the world.

A world brand is marketed in the same way in every market in the world, except that the marketing mix can vary to meet local consumer and competitive requirements. For example, both Coca-Cola and Pepsi-Cola increased the sweetness of their beverages in the Middle East where consumers prefer a sweeter drink. The issue is not exact uniformity, but rather whether it is essentially the same product which is being offered. Other elements of the marketing mix, such as price, promotion, appeal, media, distribution channels and tactics may also vary.

The perception of world brands

As a result of international mergers creating massive conglomerates, household goods, personal care goods and high class

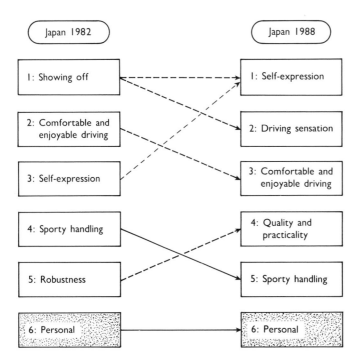

Figure 3.1 *Important factors in Japanese choice of car in 1982 and 1988 (source: T. Hisatomi, ESOMAR conference, June 1990)*

cosmetics are in the midst of intensive oligopolistic competition worldwide. Yet there are still very few brands which are seen as world brands. A brand may be sold worldwide, but that does not make it into a brand which is perceived as global. Many 'global brands' are seen as local brands in different nations. Table 3.2. shows how the same brands are perceived in different ways by the Japanese, Americans and French.[15]

Although there is a growing similarity in customers' awareness of megabrands, there is still a major choice to be made: the choice between global or micro marketing. An example of growing similarities can be found in the car industry. Both worldwide and within countries, values attached to cars have changed, and cars are looking more alike than ever before. It is no longer possible to distinguish from a car's appearance the country of manufacture. Also the factors which people consider important in choosing a car have changed and are increasingly similar across countries, as shown in Figures 3.1 and 3.2.[16]

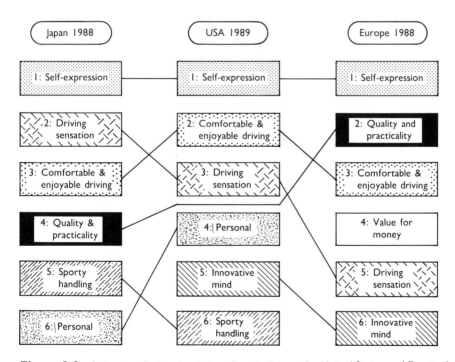

Figure 3.2 *Important factors in choice of car in Japan, the United States and Europe (source: T. Hisatomi, ESOMAR conference, June 1990)*

■ Global versus micro or 'niche' marketing

Globalization of marketing is rapidly advancing, but it is accompanied not just by the need to 'act local', implying adaptation of brand name, package and mass communications, but also by fragmentation of local markets, and a growing need for clearer focus on small niches or even individual consumers. This is coupled with an ever-increasing need for manufacturers to respond to the requirements of individual retailers and their particular customers. Markets are both getting bigger and getting smaller at the same time. This growth of micro marketing is stimulated by the fast-developing research techniques related to scanning in supermarkets. In the United States this phenomenon has grown rapidly in the last decade. In Europe as yet no grocery chain has more than a 5 per cent share of the European market, so global marketers still have to deal with local chains, but these local chains will tend to merge or turn into larger buying networks, and soon there will be large European chains of supermarkets. One of the causes for this is also the changing consumer behaviour: the daily shopping trips are declining everywhere.

Nielsen, the largest marketing research company worldwide, already offers scanning services in thirteen countries, including the United States and Japan. As a result, retail scanning and electronic panels will facilitate the micro marketing process.

A global company does not necessarily have to opt for megabrands; acting local in some ways may be more profitable, as may micro marketing. Selecting niches and targeting products and marketing support at specific groups of consumers – and understanding their behaviour in depth – may be a profitable strategy.

The two strategies are very different strategies and should be kept separate. If the aim is to develop a megabrand, it is no good launching a niche brand and later trying to make it into a megabrand.

A true world brand has the following characteristics:

1. It is present in all category segments and relevant product types.
2. There are opportunities for line extensions.
3. The brand is available and visible in all key retail sectors.
4. There is a comprehensive range of package and delivery types on offer.
5. There is no significant consumer demographic bias.
6. It is a market leader with good promotional support.[17]

Brand names for megabrands

There are three main strategies for brand names on a regional basis. Unilever, for example, uses the following strategies for Europe:

1. A one-brand-name European/worldwide strategy, e.g. Lux
2. A one-product European strategy with different brand names, e.g. Jif, Viss, Cif.
3. A niche or local positioning in certain countries, e.g. Knights Castille. [18]

When launching a new brand, with a new name, it is essential to take care in selecting the right name. Real global brand names, to be successful, must be easily identifiable, available and appropriate for use on a wide range of products, able to convey a desirable image to all audiences, and free from legal restrictions.

When changing a local brand name into a global name it is possible to use one of the existing names, perhaps that used in the largest market, add the company name to the local brand as an endorsement, and gradually make it stronger, as has been done by Nestlé. Alternatively it is possible to increase emphasis on the corporate name, as Gillette has shown. Mars changed their confectionery product named M&Ms in the United States and Treets in Europe into M&Ms worldwide. The chocolate bar it once called Marathon in the United Kingdom and Snickers in the United States is now called Snickers in both. Changing different local names into one global brand name, like Exxon did to replace Esso, Enco and Humble, is a costly exercise.

■ The changing role of the marketing manager

A strong management philosophy is needed for the management of a large multinational or global corporation and (marketing) managers who operate internationally have to adjust their role to meet the organization's changing needs.

Openness in communication

Open communication is essential for the exchange of experience and ideas. Efficient information systems are necessary for the coordination of both centralized and decentralized marketing efforts. A flow of information from marketing to R&D is also a condition for successful product development.

Central management must have an open mind regarding information from the subsidiaries in other countries. A local manager of Coca-Cola had a hard time convincing his head office in the United States of the opportunity for introducing iced coffee in Japan.[19]

Different management philosophies in different cultures

The North American emphasis on 'profit-performance' can be detrimental to the development of long-term strategies, especially with respect to pricing. An example is provided by General Foods, which had been producing instant coffee in Japan since 1954 with a market share of 85 per cent. When the competition entered the market, the market share held by General Foods decreased to 15 per cent in 1970. One of the most plausible explanations is that the expatriate US managers kept prices too high because they wanted to show high profits during their short transfer period in Japan.

This example shows the difference between the Japanese long-term approach and the American 'bottom line now' emphasis. US managers are often criticized for this short-term outlook, supposedly forced on them by Wall Street. Akio Morita, co-founder of Sony, recalls a chat with a money trader in New York: 'I enquired how far ahead he looks. One week? "No, no", came the reply. "Ten minutes"'.[20]

This orientation towards short-term profits also places obstacles in the way of making essential investments, for example investment in the research needed to build a long-term global strategy. The fast turnover of marketing managers and product managers also contributes to this. Building a global brand with a global image and keeping the brand personality alive requires a continuous screening of markets in order to find the trends on which a brand can be positioned.

New approach to in-company management

In order to solve the kind of problems mentioned above, new management processes will have to be developed. Bartlett and Ghoshal state that

> a large number of multinational corporations operating in today's environment are being forced to develop the organizational capabilities to respond to diverse national interests and demands, while *simultaneously*

co-ordinating and controlling these activities to allow the companies to act as efficient and effective global competitors. To manage this way, multinational corporations require a very different kind of internal management process than existed in the relatively simple multinational or global organizations they may have had previously. The result is the 'transnational organization', i.e. learning how to create and manage the transnational organization could be the major challenge for the MNC managers in the next decade.[21]

In a global corporation organizational renewal is the major task of management. Wisse Dekker of Philips, in his inaugural speech on the occasion of his appointment as Professor of International Management at the Rijksuniversiteit Leiden, stated:

In international management there are three important changes: globalizing, changing forms of cooperation and dynamizing (products and production processes are subject to ever faster changes). In a dynamic society the transfer of know-how and keeping that know-how up to date are a condition for survival for the multinational. It not only concerns technological innovation but also the organization of production and marketing will have to adapt. Renewal of the organization becomes the major task of management. Entrepreneurs must become 'change masters'. Renewal of the organization affects the total structure of the multinational corporation.

Globalization and new forms of cooperation will be the result. Innovation does not automatically mean growth. Innovation means selection, strengthening the strategic basis and, if necessary, rejecting some activities. Organizational renewal is closely related to strategy management. Dynamizing means that it becomes ever more difficult to learn from the past and to extrapolate the past into the future.

The future becomes more uncertain. This calls for new forms of consultation and policy making. Flexibility, willingness to change, anticipation and contingency-management; recognizing challenges and thinking in terms of transformation instead of continuity. These are the aspects which are going to belong to the culture of the multinational corporation. Cooperation and global structure will be assessed according to these aspects. In this connection corporate management must develop a global perspective, In this perspective, political, economical and technological developments have their place.

Reaching consensus between partners who have different ideas about 'what business are we in' is becoming an ever more important task for corporate management. In that respect the corporation plays a most important role.

Creating or changing a corporate culture is very difficult. By change-oriented training and management policies, management can increase cohesion within the corporation and influence the development of its corporate culture.[22]

A philosophy of wanting to win is developed through an improved management approach and investment in training. The president of the American Management Association, Thomas Horton (1986) writes in his 'Memo for Management':

> What can we do to improve our attitudes? We must act on the belief that the person who actually does a job knows more about that job than anyone else. But we can't stop there. We need, through training, to give our people the skills and tools which will enable them to suggest improvements in process and design. We also need to train our managers – to develop world-class managers. An improved managerial approach towards both our customers and our workforce is critical to our ability to win in global markets. We must bear in mind that without these two groups, we will have no business – and we must act accordingly. In summary, we must all make winning a top priority. We must implement carefully thought-through strategies.
>
> But we will have the greatest chance of winning – and really the only chance – by remembering that satisfying the customer is one ingredient necessary for success, and that drawing full on the talent of our human capital is another.[23]

■ Summary

This chapter has described the global strategies underlying global marketing and advertising decisions. Three basic global strategies were mentioned: global cost leadership, differentiation and focusing. Global marketing strategies follow the same strategies. There is, however, rarely one simple choice: both global marketing and niche or micro marketing can have their advantages. These, as well as the advantages for the organization, were described. The chapter concluded with a comment on the changes in management view needed for the implementation of global strategies. Global marketing and management means managing change, and therefore we will end with a Chinese proverb:

> Resisting change is something like holding one's breath. If you keep it up it will end badly.

■ Notes and references

1. Peter D. Bennett, 1988: *Dictionary of Marketing Terms*, American Marketing Association, Chicago.

2. Adapted from John A. Pearce II, 1981: 'An executive-level perspective on the strategic management process', *California Management Review*, Fall issue.
3. Gary Hamel and C. K. Prahalad, 1989: 'Strategic intent', Harvard Business Review, May/June.
4. Adapted from Michael Porter, 1986: *Competition in Global Industries*, Harvard Business School Press, 1986.
5. Ibid.
6. Ibid.
7. Ibid.
8. This draws on Warren J. Keegan, 1989: *Global Marketing Management*, Prentice Hall.
9. Philip Kotler, 1986: 'Global standardization – courting danger', *The Journal of Consumer Marketing*, Vol. 3, No. 2, Spring issue.
10. Theodore Levitt, 1983: 'The globalization of markets', *Harvard Business Review*, May–June, pp. 92–102.
11. Yoram Wind, 1986: 'The myth of globalization', *The Journal of Consumer Marketing*, Vol. 3, No. 2, Spring issue.
12. Porter, 1986: op. cit.
13. Fujio Hayashi, 1987: 'Opportunities in the Japanese market', *Management Review*, July.
14. Subhash C. Jain, 1989: 'Standardization of international marketing strategy: some research hypotheses', *Journal of Marketing*, January.
15. Shungo Hiromura, 'Global strategies for Japanese products in major Asian and Western countries – international comparative survey', ESOMAR Conference on 'America, Japan and EC '92: The Prospects for Marketing, Advertising and Research', Venice, Italy, June 1990.
16. Takashi Hisatomi, 'Global marketing by Nissan Motor Co. Ltd – simultaneous market study of users' opinions/attitudes in Europe, the USA and Japan', ESOMAR Conference, June 1990.
17. Colin Buckingham and Mike Penford, A.C. Nielsen, 'Thinking global and acting local – integrated information services for European companies in the 90s', ESOMAR conference on 'America, Japan and EC '92: The prospects for Marketing, Advertising and Research', Venice, Italy, June 1990.
18. Ibid.
19. Hayashi, 1987: op. cit.
20. Akio Morita, 1989: in *Fortune*, 25 September.
21. Christopher Bartlett and Sumantra A. Ghoshal, 1989: *Managing Across Borders*, Hutchinson Business Press.
22. Wisse Dekker, 1987: in *NRC/Handelsblad*, 11 February.
23. Thomas R. Horton, 1986: 'Winning in the global market', Memo for Management, *Management Review*, April.

Chapter 4
Communication and culture

■ Introduction

Everyone who introduces an international element to their work will have to confront the concept of the 'foreigner' in a very different way to that required when travelling as a tourist.

'Foreign' implies a potential threat to existing patterns of action and behaviour, and usually means a confrontation with different cultures. 'Culture' means learned behaviour, and this differs from society to society.

The international advertising executive will have to cooperate with people of different cultures. He or she will have to build strategies for communicating with consumers who have different values, attitudes and buying behaviour. Knowledge of the basic aspects of culture is essential in order to understand why people in different countries behave differently. This chapter will give definitions of culture and will describe several basic aspects of culture which are of importance for international advertising. The influence of global communication on the relationships which exist between people around the world is enormous. Therefore, alongside culture and cultural differences which influence communication, changes in world information and communication will also be described.

■ Culture and levels of culture

Hofstede[1] defines culture as follows

the collective mental programming of the people in an environment.

> Culture is not a characteristic of individuals; it encompasses a number of people who were conditioned by the same education and life experience.

Tylor[2] gives the following definition of culture:

> Culture is that complex whole which includes knowledge, beliefs, art, morals, law, customs and any other capabilities and habits acquired by man as a member of society.

Culture is learned behaviour, passed on from generation to generation and sometimes difficult for the outsider to understand. Assumptions about culture and behaviour are common, to the extent that people are often blind to the true nature of cultural differences. Any Westerner raised outside Asia who claims he or she fully understands and can communicate with the Japanese or Chinese is likely to be deluding himself or herself.[3] Even the people of the various European Community countries, although often seen by outsiders as one homogeneous market, are culturally very different. What makes it difficult to understand and accept the existence of cultural differences is the tendency to perceive other cultures in terms of one's own. Cultural projection of this kind makes it very difficult to understand other cultures. The businessman who does not change his approach when selling in a different culture, because he thinks his prospects will be influenced by the quality or the price of the product and not by his behaviour, will learn the hard way.

The important thing in getting to know another culture is to understand and accept the way peoples' minds work. Differences in thinking style are subtle and may not become obvious through superficial contact. The trouble begins when people have to start working together. Often, even after years of working together, both sides discover that neither can make the system work. American businessmen in Japan tend to ignore Japanese successes and American failures and persist in telling the Japanese how to do business the American way, forgetting that the Japanese favour a different approach.[4]

In the global village it is important to understand the culturally conditioned control systems. One of the important aspects is the identification process, of understanding one's own culture, in order to see how others differ. International business people, and especially those who call themselves communication specialists, cannot afford to be culturally illiterate.

Cultures differ in the way they experience and use aspects such as time, space, relationships, power, risk, masculinity, femininity and many others. These aspects vary within cultural groups too, depending on the level of culture being considered.

Levels of culture

The term 'culture' may apply to ethnic or national groups, or to groups within society at different levels[5]: a country, an age group, a profession or a social class, for example. The cultural programming of an individual depends on the groups or categories to which he or she belongs. The expressions of culture belonging to a certain level of cultural programming will differ: eating habits may differ by country, dress habits by profession, and gender roles by both country and social class. When discussing 'culture' it is important to be specific about the level, whether 'national culture', 'corporate culture' or 'age culture', in order not to create confusion. What is true at one level need not apply to another level.

Expressions of culture

Culture is expressed in several ways. Of the many terms used to describe expressions of culture Hofstede[6] states that the following four embody the total concept: symbols, heroes, rituals and values. In Figure 4.1, these have been depicted like the skins of an onion, indicating that symbols represent the most superficial and values the deepest manifestations of culture, with heroes and rituals falling somewhere in between.

Symbols are words, gestures, pictures or objects which carry a

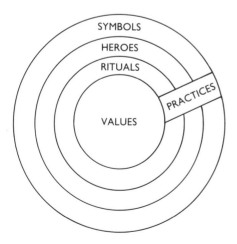

Figure 4.1 *Expressions of culture at different levels (source: Geert Hofstede, Working Paper 90-006, May 1990, University of Limburg, The Netherlands)*

particular meaning only recognized by those who share the culture. The words of a language or particular kind of jargon belong to this category, as do dress, hair-do, flags, status symbols and individual commodities such as Coca-Cola. New symbols are easily developed and old ones quickly disappear; symbols from one cultural group are regularly copied by others. This is why symbols are shown in the outer, most superficial layer in Figure 4.1.

Heroes are persons, alive or dead, real or imaginary, who possess characteristics that are highly prized in a culture, and thus serve as models for behaviour. Even fantasy or cartoon figures, like Batman or Charlie Brown in the United States and Asterix in France, can serve as cultural heroes. In the television age, outward appearances have become more important in choosing heroes than they were before.[7]

Rituals are collective activities considered socially essential within a culture: they are carried out for their own sake. Examples include ways of greeting and paying respect to others, and social and religious ceremonies. Business and political meetings organized for seemingly rational reasons often serve mainly ritual purposes, for example allowing the leaders to assert themselves. Sporting events are rituals both for the players and for the spectators.

In Figure 4.1, symbols, heroes and rituals have been included in the term '*practices*'. They are visible to an outside observer. However, their cultural meaning is invisible; it lies in the way these practices are interpreted by the insiders of the culture.

At the core of culture lie *values*. Values are broad tendencies to prefer certain states of affairs over others. Values embody contrasts:

evil	*v.*	good
dirty	*v.*	clean
ugly	*v.*	beautiful
unnatural	*v.*	natural
abnormal	*v.*	normal
paradoxical	*v.*	logical
irrational	*v.*	rational

Values are among the first things children learn, not consciously but implicitly. Developmental psychologists believe that by the age of ten most children have their basic value system firmly in place and that after this age changes are difficult to obtain. Many people are not consciously aware of the values they hold, so it is very difficult to discuss or observe them. Researchers have tried to describe values by asking people to state a preference among alternatives. The answers however should not be taken too literally: in practice people will not always act according to their answers on a questionnaire. Another difficulty in researching values is interpreting what people say. There is a distinction between the desirable and the desired: how people think the world ought to be versus what people want for themselves. This should be borne in mind when using the concept of values in advertising, and will be discussed further in Chapter 5.

In the context of international marketing and trade cultural differences can be approached in several ways. First, it is important to observe the cultural environment – the worldwide changes in communication and information which affect cultural change. In relation to any marketing communication strategy, the differences and similarities in consumer behaviour, must be considered before deciding on a strategy direction. Hofstede[8] describes this as the consumer side of the cultural approach; it operates at the level of national, social class, age group and gender cultures. For industrial products it may also take into account the professional cultures of the people influencing the buying decisions. In relation to selling or interpersonal communication, it is essential to be aware of those cultural differences which are important in interpersonal contacts – when negotiating, for example – and also of differences in decision-making in a seller-buyer relationship. Hofstede[9] calls this the producer side of the cultural approach; it operates at the level of organizational, business and professional cultures.

Corporate cultures may influence the image of an organization, and this in turn may influence a brand image. The phenomenon of international corporate or organizational cultures is beyond the scope of this book. However, some aspects of culture and interpersonal communication will be considered as differences in this area may influence the way advertising messages are stated. Differences in decision-making, for example, may be relevant not only to the negotiating process but also to the consumer decision process and the way it is depicted in advertising.

First, however, recent changes in world information and communication will be described.

■ Worldwide information and communication

The most important changes in information and communication are those which affect the flow of information and communication between people. Hamid Mowlana describes these in his book *Global Information and World Communication*.[10] In his opinion international relations are now determined not only by political and economic relations, but also – and to a greater extent – by culture and communication. In studying the communication aspect, it is not sufficient to take the traditional approach of analyzing mass media messages and communication. The human aspects must be considered alongside the technological aspects.

The international flow of information

The international flow of information is the movement of messages across national borders and between two or more national and cultural systems. There are many developments in this area, and this section will outline the changes in information flow and the possible effects in terms of contacts between peoples and cultures. Unfortunately, little research has yet been done to determine the precise nature of these effects, but it is none the less important to consider them.

Although *mass communication* in general can increase or even strengthen national feelings, communications technology has clearly affected national sovereignty. As a result, the responsibilities of international organizations which control communications across borders have increased. The location of decision-making has moved from the national to the international and transnational level. Differences of opinion have to be solved in an international environment.

With regard to *marketing communications* the world is clearly divided into areas as far as culture, trade development and the development of communication channels are concerned. These areas are Western Europe, the United States and Canada, Latin America, the Middle East, Asia, and the Pacific Basin. To some extent these areas overlap, and within them the various countries are grouped according to common features, such as similarity of language, culture, infrastructure, information channels, product consumption and the composition of the population.

Important factors which influence the international flow of information are: television worldwide and its national and international images, worldwide advertising, the movements of people, and education.

Television worldwide: national and international images

In 1950 only five countries had regular television broadcasts. At the end of the 1970s there were 400 million TV sets in 138 countries, and the number has grown considerably since then. Originally, existing films were shown; later many countries began importing material from the more developed countries. In each region some countries assumed a gate-keeping function. For example, there has been a steady flow of US films to the Latin American countries. Further distribution depends on whether the country importing the films is able to dub them. Originally this was done in Cuba for Latin America, but in the late 1950s this function was taken over by Mexico. Although both Peru and Brazil are now able to dub American films, Mexico has been able to maintain the gate-keeping function. A trend emerged whereby programmes were only shown in Latin America once they had been shown in Mexico. Egypt and Lebanon used to be gate-keepers for television in the Middle East, and in Asia the gate-keeping function was carried out by Singapore, Hong Kong and Japan.

It is often thought that the effects of mass communication by television broadcasting include loss of national identity and culture. As a result, at the end of 1989, both Asian and European countries were starting to reject the overdoses of American culture provided by US mass-produced films. In October 1989 the EC member nations discussed the idea of imposing quotas on the import of American shows in order to stimulate European production. Then US Trade Representative Ms Carla Hills called this 'blatantly discriminatory',[11] but nations or trading blocs are able to decide for themselves whether they want another nation's culture imposed on them.

There are other, often unexpected effects of this form of mass communication. The use of imported programmes gives a window on the outside world. However, in most countries all programmes are dubbed. The locals are still free to believe that the whole world speaks their language! The domestic servant of a multinational couple who lived in Spain several years ago, discovered through them that there was obviously, besides Spanish, yet another language: 'foreign'.

Studies of the effects of international television
Studies are in progress to assess the effects of international television. Research covers many aspects including the following:

1. The relationship between cultural identity, language and political conflicts.
2. The effect of too many US-produced TV programmes on local cultures.
3. The possible homogenizing of languages.
4. The possibility of using visual symbols in different cultures.
5. Whether it maintains obsolete stereotypes, for example those relating to the image of women or of ethnic minority groups.
6. The exploitation of cultural stereotypes of particular nations.
7. The effects of violence on television.

The influence of worldwide advertising

The emergence of global corporations and the development of international advertising agencies and mass media could change the 'cultural ecology' of a country; this might adapt itself to those who finance the system. It is doubtful, however, that this would occur; this is the kind of criticism often expressed by those who overrate the influence of the mass media on culture. The effect of advertising in its aim of 'global persuasion' may be relative, too. Although advertising of Nescafé and Maxwell coffee seems to have changed China's tea-culture for certain life-style groups, and although many young Chinese wear jeans and drink Coca-Cola, a Chinese person wearing jeans is a long way from being an American. The various China Towns around the world have spread more Chinese culture to the West than American TV advertising has spread American culture to China. Some western life-style groups interested in concepts like Zen, Yoga and I Ching have set up thriving businesses and coffee shops in Kathmandu, Nepal, where they sell Western books on Zen Buddhism, I Ching and Tarot and play Bach. These are a small minority. However, the phenomenon became real enough for the Suharto government to abolish TV advertising in Indonesia in 1979 – the fear was that the rural population would become Westernized too quickly, while lacking the financial means for Western consumption, which could result in discontent and rebellion.

The flow of professional information has not long been globalized. Until recently there was a lack of international professional and trade media, and indeed a lack of local specialized media in many countries. This is changing rapidly, though, because of segmented advertising. Now the professional and industrial market in several countries or regions is being covered by specialized media – for example Europe, Eastern Europe to a certain extent, Russia and China. Direct mail is growing fast, and in some countries, where the quality of the press is not very high, cinema advertising is growing in importance.

Movement of people

Both business people and entrepreneurs are adapting themselves to an international framework, and so are consumers. Furthermore information technology, television and radio allow an exchange of facts and experience. So does the movement of people.

The movement of people across borders implies communication of experiences, ideas, attitudes, religious beliefs, meanings, motivations and aims. The human factor must be taken into account in international communication research.

There are nine main kinds of 'across the border' movement; these can be classified as follows:

1. Migration and fugitive movements.
2. Movement of labourers and professionals.
3. Tourism.
4. Movement of military, diplomatic and intelligence service personnel.
5. Education, scientific and cultural exchange programmes and conferences.
6. Business trips and financial exchange.
7. Interchange of mass media, pop music, art and theatre.
8. Sporting events.
9. Movement arranged by voluntary and aid organizations.

Tourism is already one of the largest industries in many countries. This is due to the fast growth of the travel industry, the mass communications industry which brings interesting and attractive countries physically and psychologically closer, and economic growth, which allows individuals more money and more leisure time. However, tourism causes concern for two reasons.

First, the travel industry takes a stereotyped image of potential holiday destinations and exaggerates it. The French become great lovers; the Germans great beer-drinkers; Polynesian natives wear aprons made of grass; the Dutch wear wooden clogs; Africans are natives happy in their primitive cultures. Countries become branded articles with their main values amplified.

Secondly, tourists flow from 'core' areas towards peripheral or semiperipheral areas. Sociologists term this cultural imperialism. The developed country 'floods' the underdeveloped country and stimulates a kind of accelerated osmosis. Stereotypes of the developed country's culture observed in imported television programmes are confirmed by the tourists' physical presence.

Education

More and more people are participating in educational exchange programmes. Most students from developing countries are educated in the United States, but students from developing countries also tend to study in countries which are historically strongly linked to their own country, whether by language or culture.

Students from African countries such as Algeria, Morocco, Senegal, Tunisia, Cameroon and Madagascar tend to study in France. England receives most of its foreign students from Zambia, Zimbabwe, Sudan, Brunei, Cyprus, Iraq, India, Malaya, Singapore, Sri Lanka, Malta and Nigeria. The Soviet Union has naturally accommodated students from Bulgaria, Czechoslovakia, Hungary, Cuba, North Korea, Laos and Mongolia. However, for many Eastern European students, the events of late 1989 will give access to a wider choice of places in which to study.

▣ Cultural differences which influence marketing and communication

Intellectual man had become an explaining creature. Fathers to children, wives to husbands, lecturers to listeners, experts to laymen, colleagues to colleagues, doctors to patients, man to his own soul, explained.[12]

The extent to which advertisements contain explanations and use a lot of words, or are predominantly picture-based, varies. It is not only a matter of taste or professional view point; it often has to do with culture. Each culture reflects in its language and communication what is of value to the people. Culture is man's medium. Culture includes personality, how people express themselves and show emotion, the way they think, how they move, how problems are solved, how cities are built and how economies and governments function.[13]

There are many aspects of culture which influence consumer behaviour; usually several operate at the same time to influence behaviour. For example, people in more individualistic societies behave differently to those in collectivistic societies.[14]

The discussion here will be restricted to some important general cultural concepts. Practical implications, such as the measurement of cultural differences, will be considered in Chapter 5. The concepts of relevance here are as follows:

1. Context: high and low context cultures.
2. Conflicts.
3. Influence of culture on decision-making.
4. Uncertainty avoidance.
5. Thinking patterns.
6. Time.
7. Values.

Context: high- and low-context cultures

What one pays attention to or ignores is largely a matter of context. Context makes possible a kind of screening process giving protection from information overload.

In a high-context communication or message most of the information is either part of the physical context or internalized in the person; very little is made explicit as part of the message. The information of a low-context message is carried in the explicit code of the message. Twins who have grown up together are an example of high-context communication; they do not need to explain to each other why they behave in a certain way. Two lawyers in a courtroom are an example of low-context; they need the words and rhetorics of their coded, professional language. One reason most bureaucrats are so difficult to deal with is that they write for each other and are insensitive to the context required by the public. In general high-context communication is economical, fast and efficient. However, time must be devoted to programming. If this programming does not take place, the communication is incomplete. This is particularly important for those who do not know the culture. In general, high-context cultures are more predictable, but only if one is familiar with the system. To the observer, an unknown high-context culture can be completely mystifying, although he may not realize this if his own stereotypes are so strong that they distort what he sees.

In the communication field it is of great importance to be aware of the differences between high- and low-context. These intangible differences between cultures should help practitioners understand the behaviour patterns of other people with whom they come into contact. Such differences may also explain differences in message content and execution in the advertisements of different cultures and help understand why certain advertising messages work in some cultures and not in others.

Most European marketing people are saturated with decision theories based on the North American low-context culture. The underlying assumption is that in communication one needs arguments and persuasion by rhetoric: large numbers of words. In many other countries, especially Asian countries, the approach is completely different.

Within low-context cultures (LCCs), there are clear communication codes; these cultures attach value to individual orientation, have heterogeneous patterns of standards and low cultural requirements and limits. On the other hand high context cultures (HCCs) attach value to group identity, have implicit communication codes, and maintain a homogeneous standard pattern with high requirements and restrictions in respect of standards and values. Germany, Scandinavia, Switzerland and the United States are examples of LCC countries. China, Japan, Korea and Vietnam are examples of HCC countries.[15] HCCs are collective societies, while LCCs are more individualistic.[16] For the Japanese, the verbal mode is only one aspect of communication; the non-verbal is often seen as having greater importance than the verbal. This is in contrast to the emphasis on rhetoric and the domination of the word seen in the West. In the HCC system, that which is unsaid is often more important than what is said. On the other hand, in LCC systems words represent truth and power.

Conflicts

Knowledge of how cultures handle conflicts is important both for selling techniques and for mass communication. Conflicts can be placed in the context of LCC and HCC cultures, but they also have to do with other variables, such as collectivism v. individualism or the extent to which people want to avoid uncertainty.[17]

According to Western theories, there are two kinds of conflicts:[18] 'instrumental' and 'expressive'. An instrumental conflict is characterized by conflicting objectives. An expressive conflict is aimed at relaxation, the removal of hostile feelings. Take for example the refusal of a proposition during a sales meeting: the North American will enter a heated discussion, and will supply figures, diagrams and other material to support the argument. The Japanese, with their HCC system, will be highly surprised by the direct rejection and will analyze the situation as a personal assault or a sign of distrust. LCC individuals are more able to separate the dispute from the person involved; they can fight and scream over a conflict and yet become good friends afterwards. In the HCC system the instrumental point of difference is strongly linked to the person who causes the conflict. To disagree publicly or to confront somebody in public with a difference of opinion is an extreme insult which will make both parties lose face. Especially when communicating in a boss–subordinate relationship, individuals are expected to show mutual sensitivity appropriate to the rituals surrounding senior–junior relations. On the other hand, HCC individuals need to learn that a rejection from a LCC individual in business does not mean a personal insult.

The LCC individual may have a lower need for uncertainty avoidance. HCC individuals look at conflicts in a more sensitive and expressive way. The subject of the disagreement and the person with whom one disagrees are the same. This also goes for decision-making. The issue is who you are, and what values you hold. A person's position in society is crucial. In an HCC culture, bank loans are obtained on the basis of personal background, rather than analysis of the person's financial situation. LCC individuals, who tend to look at the world in analytical, linear-logical terms, are more inclined to view a conflict as instrumentally orientated. The concept of high- and low-context culture provides some useful explanations and guidance. However, most of the time there are additional variables involved, and a few of these are also described in this chapter. Germany for example, is a low-context culture country. However, Germans do not fight and scream over a conflict and remain good friends afterwards. A professional conflict may often become personal. Conflicts can originate from a faulty perception of the negotiating process.

The negotiating process differs strongly according to culture. In the United States, negotiating is seen as a competitive process of offers and counter-offers. In some cultures, negotiation is seen as a more wide-ranging discussion. For the French, negotiation is a grand debate. Brazilians expect to socialize before getting down to business. [19]

Influence of culture on decision-making

The fundamental assumption in Western decision-making theory is that a decision does not happen by itself, *somebody makes it*. This view derives from the North American culture. The Japanese, on the other hand, *let necessary action arise* as a result of events, instead of controlling them by making decisions. [20]

In the United States, decisions are *individual processes*, whereby the decision maker always makes his or her decisions in the context of a particular social role. In other cultures the individual has a special meaning (he represents a particular class or caste) in which the limitations of social class, family profession, etc., are implicit. In Japan the individual is defined as a member of a group. In India, the framework to refer to is the caste of which the individual serves as an example. Little attention is given to personal characteristics. Individualism and grand performance are valued by the Americans, French and Swedes. They are not so greatly prized by Asians. [21]

The notion that the 'locus of control' in the decision process lies in the individual also originates from the United States. This is the idea that one can implicitly control one's own fate, using factual information to adapt oneself to new developments. This is not a universal concept. The Russians put more weight on value-patterns and concepts than on facts. The Germans are more deductive and theoretical than the Americans.

In the United States class, profession and place of birth are seen as not restricting the possibilities open to each individual. In non-Western countries things are very different. Fundamental decisions about the personal life of the individual, such as choice of a marriage partner or profession, are taken by the parents or even grandparents. The decision-maker is not the person directly affected by the decision.

Likewise concepts of debt and responsibility differ from one culture to another. When dealing with damage compensation it is important to learn about those different concepts.

Group decisions are more often taken in the East than in the West, although they occur in both. The way in which the individual participates in a group differs considerably. The North American tries to influence the decision as much as possible and put his opinion forward clearly. To do this he uses procedures such as an agenda, voting procedures, etc. The assumption is that everybody must have a chance to give his opinion and everyone must have an equal vote when the decision is made. In other cultures which do not emphasize equality for all group members, and where honesty is seen differently, the introduction of such procedures might lead to the accusation of acting evasively. [22]

According to the old Confucian philosophy, which still applies in Japan, there must be unanimity; in order to respect the rights of the minority, the majority must come to an agreement in each dispute until consensus has been reached. This principle holds for government, for business life, and for the family. Nobody must be defeated entirely, this would result in losing face, and losing face is the worst that can happen to anyone.

The role of the chairman in a group is also different in different cultures. In the West the chairman's role is to give everybody a chance to speak and express an opinion. In the East the role involves 'guessing' the wish of the group and deciding the matter in hand on this basis. This is called 'haragei' (belly-art). The Japanese consider it impertinent for an individual to make a definite decision concerning himself or someone else. It is also insulting to insist on a decision. One must be evasive and reserved.

Uncertainty-avoidance[23]

The North Americans can easily live with uncertainty, and base many of their daily decisions on probabilities. Learning by trial and error and experimentation, searching for innovation, and acceptance of a high level of mobility, all express an easy attitude towards insecurity. The Japanese businessman, on the other hand, shuns insecurity. Comparative research in forty different countries show that Japanese businessmen have a stronger need to avoid uncertainty than businessmen of any other nationality. Instead of engaging in decision-making, Japanese businessmen rely on rules, precedents and patterns. They avoid making assessments or assumptions, and do not like to publish or discuss their plans before these are complete.

Thinking patterns

Although everybody applies dichotomies (yes–no), the country where this is most evident is the United States. Digital thinking and decision-making is a characteristic of the North American communication system. The Japanese are more inclined towards the analogical. The North Americans are structural and analytical; they lack the dynamics of the Chinese Yin-Yang, European dialectics (the process aimed at abolishing differences of opinion) or the Japanese holistic pattern-recognition approach, which involves recognizing the feeling of the overall situation before looking at details.[24] The North American approach works towards extremes in order to facilitate decision-making, posing 'problems' or mentioning 'conflicts' in order to instigate the search for a solution or justify taking action. In European culture the emphasis is on making an analysis in order to generate ideological and theoretical arguments. In Japan the controversy between two parties or interests will only be 'enlightened' if it provides a contribution to human relations. The tension which arises from this is accepted as being one of the conditions belonging to it.[25]

The way in which arguments are supported also varies across cultures. Some tend to rely on facts, others on ideology or dogma, and others on tradition or emotion. For the Japanese, the 'kimochi', or feeling, has to be right; logic is cold. The Saudis seem to be intuitive in approach and avoid persuasion based primarily on empirical reasoning, which is more characteristic of Western cultures. Mexicans rely on emotional appeals as a basis for persuasion.[26]

Time

Different cultures have different concepts of time. The Americans have a linear time concept, with clear structures, such as beginning, turning point, climax and end. Time is used as a measuring instrument and a means of controlling human behaviour by setting deadlines and objectives. Time is tangible; like an object, it can be saved, spent, found, lost and wasted.

Hall (1977, 1973)[27] describes this way of handling time as *monochronic* as opposed to *polychronic*. People from monochronic cultures tend to do one thing at a time; they are organized and methodical, and their workdays are structured to allow them to complete one task after another. Polychronic people, on the other hand, tend to do many things simultaneously. Their workday is not a chain of isolated, successive blocks; time is more like a vast, never-ending ocean extending in every direction. The Germans adhere to the more rigid and compartmentalized way of dealing with time, and are in fact one of the most well-organized peoples of all. To people who do many things at the same time, such as the French, Arabs, Pakistanis or South Americans, however, punctuality is nice but by no means an absolute necessity in the middle of a typically hectic day. So when a French person is delayed and arrives late for a meeting with a German, the latter might well be offended – although no offence was intended. The problem lies simply in the fact that the two speak different 'languages' of time, a fact which is usually overlooked by all the parties involved.[28] Meetings in Arab countries involve many people discussing their problems and ideas at the same time. People from a monochronic culture tend to become annoyed in meetings with polychronic people; due to the numerous interruptions, they cannot concentrate, and they feel that nothing is being accomplished. Northern Europeans are in general more monochronic and Southern Europeans more polychronic.

These differences in the concept of time give rise to one of the things which the Japanese find hardest to accept about American management culture. The Japanese prefer personal control of human relations rather than impersonal management via deadlines.

Time also relates to the concept of cause and effect used to explain the sequence of events. The cause-effect paradigm appears mainly in North American decision-making culture. Symbolic and mystical explanations of events are not accepted; preference is given to concrete and measurable causes, which precede the consequence or effect. Concepts in other cultures are very different. With the Chinese, for instance, causes and results do not have to follow each other; often they happen simultaneously. One event can be explained by another event which is happening at the same time.

Values

Attitudes are the most widely-studied aspect of consumer decision-making. An examination of values provides an analysis of the underlying motives which structure attitudes and behaviour. Values must be seen as predating and colouring our attitudes.[29] Thus, marketing researchers have used values as a means of understanding consumer motivation. Values are used to help describe market segments, together with or as a substitute for other socio-economic variables.

Earlier in this chapter, a value was defined as 'a preferred state of affairs over others'; in the marketing literature a value is also defined as 'a preferred state of being', which means an enduring belief about how good for one a particular broad class of activities and commodities are. For example, having an exciting life may be an important value for one person, while having a comfortable life is an important value for another.[30] A person's ranking of values represents his or her personal value system. Rankings of values differ from culture to culture.

The Rokeach Value Survey is a well-known questionnaire developed by psychologist Milton Rokeach for measuring values in American society.[31] The list of values resulting from this has been used in many other cultures with doubtful results. Value questionnaires designed for one country cannot easily be adapted to other countries. Furthermore, commercial researchers, are not always very precise in their definition of 'values'. Value questionnaires must be devised for each culture by indigenous researchers, in order to avoid any potential influence of the foreign researcher's own culture on the results.

Geert Hofstede[32] has investigated values in many countries and has identified four dimensions by which cultures may be ranked: power distance (large v. small), uncertainty avoidance (strong v. weak), individualism v. collectivism and masculinity v. femininity. (These will be described in more detail in Chapter 5.) However, questionnaires used by Hofstede were devised by Western researchers. Recently Michael Harris Bond[33] extended this research by Eastern made or compiled (Chinese) questionnaires, which were later translated to Western languages and used in both Western and Eastern countries. The objective was to try to explain the economic success of the East Asiatic countries – no Western value survey had been able to find an explanation for this. The Chinese survey identified a fifth dimension. The difference in outcome occurred because the tools were designed by different people, not because of the countries researched. This is a powerful illustration of how fundamental a phenomenon culture is.

Comparison of the surveys indicated that one of Hofstede's dimensions, uncertainty-avoidance, was only relevant to Western cultures. This dimension deals with a society's search for truth; uncertainty-avoiding cultures believe in an absolute truth, while uncertainty-accepting cultures take a more relativist position. The research in Eastern countries using the Chinese questionnaire suggested that there was another dimension, which was uniquely Eastern, called

Confucian Dynamism. This dimension deals with virtue. The research found that the other three Western dimensions were valid for both Western and Eastern cultures.

Culture grids

Grids are useful for marketing and communication decisions relating to different culture groups. Using grids is not an easy process, but simple grids can help the international marketing communication strategist. It is possible to draw up grids for global cultural differences or for the specific cultural differences which are relevant to a particular communication 'problem'.

As an example, Table 4.1 shows a grid giving a simple description of the cultural differences between Japanese and Westerners.[34] It is important to remember, though, that when comparing two societies, neither is static; Japanese society in particular is changing fast (see Table 4.1).

Table 4.1   Grid showing characteristics of Japanese behaviour

1. 'Culture of shame' in contrast to 'culture of sin'.
2. Standard of good behaviour: 'not to disturb others'.
3. Traditional ethical emphasis:
    − vertical relationship
    − standing on ceremony
    − politeness and deference
    − cleanliness
4. Emotion/feeling ranked very high, in contrast to logic.
    Greater emotional sensitivity:
    − to national environment
    − to opinions of others
    But outright expression of emotions discouraged.
5. Tendency to work together as members of groups rather than individuals.
6. Stronger sense of seclusionism, distinguishing *uchi* (inside) from *soto* (outside).
7. Sense of dependence (*amaeru*) and paternalism.
8. Tendency to avoid arguments and saying 'no'. An ambiguous response or even 'I'll consider it' means 'no'.

■ Summary

Cultural differences are among the most important variables involved when assessing the business environment in an unknown market. The information in this chapter should facilitate communication between parties involved in the communication industry, and help develop cultural sensitivity in producing effective cross-culture advertising. Culture and a variety of cultural concepts have been defined and the global flow of information described. This chapter has been based on the main literature on cultural differences, and this can be used as reference for marketing decisions. Reading about culture is only the beginning. The next step involves travelling and staying for longer than a two-week holiday in countries with different cultures. Guided tours are to be avoided – the only culture one really gets to know well is one's own.

◼ Notes and references

1. Edward B. Tylor quoted in Geert Hofstede, 1980: 'Motivation, leadership and organisation: do American theories apply abroad?', *Organisational Dynamics*, Summer issue, American Management Association.
2. Geert Hofstede, 1990: 'Marketing and culture' Working Paper 90-006, University of Limburg, Maastricht, The Netherlands. We are indebted to Professor Geert Hofstede, who wrote this Working Paper at the time this book was written, for us to use as background material.
3. This draws heavily on Edward T. Hall, 1977: *Beyond Culture*, Anchor Books.
4. Ibid.
5. Hofstede, 1990: op. cit.
6. Ibid.
7. Ibid.
8. Ibid.
9. Ibid.
10. Hamid Mowlana, 1989: *Global Information and World Communication*, Longman.
11. *USA Today*, 13 September 1989.
12. Saul Bellow, 1970: *Mr Sammler's Planet*, Penguin, New York.
13. Hall, 1977: op. cit.
14. Hofstede, 1980: op. cit.
15. Stella Ting-Toomey, 1985: in William B. Gudykunst, Lea P. Stewart and Stella Ting-Toomey (eds), *Communication, Culture and Organizational Processes*, Sage Publications, Chapter 4.
16. Geert Hofstede, 1981: *Culture's Consequences*, Sage Publications.
17. Ibid.
18. M. Olsen, 1978: *The Process of Social Organization*, 2nd ed., Holt, Rinehart & Winston, p. 308.
19. Robert T. Moran, 1987: 'Cross-cultural contact: for effective negotiating, know your cultural variables', *International Management*, January issue.

20. Ibid.
21. Ibid.
22. Edward C. Stewart, 'Culture and decision making', in: Gudykunst W. B., Stewart L. P. and Ting-Toomey S. (eds), 1985: op. cit.
23. Hofstede, 1981: op. cit.
24. Stewart, 1985: op. cit.
25. Ibid.
26. Moran, 1987: op. cit.
27. Hall, 1977: op. cit. and Hall, 1973: *The Silent Language*, Anchor.
28. Hall, 1973: op. cit.
29. Ernest Dichter, 1984: 'How values influence attitudes', in Robert Pitts Jr. and Arch G. Woodside (eds), *Personal Values and Consumer Psychology*, Lexington Books, pp. 139–40.
30. John A. Howard and Arch G. Woodside, 'Personal values affecting consumer psychology', in Pitts and Woodside, 1984: op. cit, p. 3.
31. Milton Rokeach, 1973: *The Nature of Human Values*, Free Press.
32. Hofstede, 1981: op. cit.
33. Geert Hofstede and Michael Harris Bond, 1988: 'The Confucius connection: from cultural roots to economic growth', *Organizational Dynamics*, American Management Association.
34. Peter Kersten, 1987: Canon Inc., unpublished.

Chapter 5
Consumer behaviour

■ Introduction

Among the important issues in marketing and advertising are whether to standardize a brand and/or its advertising, and how to find homogeneous market segments. With regard to standardizing brands, it is necessary to determine whether there are cultural similarities as far as values, needs and wants are concerned. With regard to finding homogeneous market segments, it is necessary to analyze differences in demographic and social characteristics as well as in values in order to find common characteristics and define clusters.

Different societies may share common cultural characteristics. These similarities may be the result of geographical proximity, but may also result from other causes. For each country, research is needed into environment and culture in order to establish similarities and differences in choice and buying behaviour.

A basic rule of international advertising is that people show more similarities than differences. If buying motives have more similarities than differences, this is also true of the advertising techniques which will influence them. The similarities justify advertising across borders. Furthermore, there are cultural sub-groups whose needs and wants transcend borders, for example certain professionals, or young people.

Once particular culture clusters have been identified the next step is to establish whether there is a connection between these and consumer behaviour.

While there has been a good deal of theorizing about cross-cultural behaviour, applications to consumer behaviour have not yet been very well researched. Therefore the advertiser has to rely on those general theories of behaviour which are most applicable to cross-cultural situations.

This chapter provides an overview of some general consumer behaviour theories and of developments in the field of cross-cultural research.

◼ Social and psychological aspects

Culture

In Chapter 4 several aspects of culture were discussed, including the practical problem of cultural projection – outsiders often fail to perceive cultural differences for this reason. Cultural projection is a form of selective perception, as people tend to project what they perceive in other cultures onto their own cultural background. Therefore it is only possible to understand other cultures by first becoming aware of one's own culture.

It is important to remember that most people do not understand either themselves or others very well. Generally our perception system is very limited, and selective perception plays an important role in everything we perceive. Most of our energy is spent in organizing what we perceive in a way which suits our own frame of reference. In dealing with people from a different culture, it is important to realize that there is usually a reason for behaviour which seems strange to the outsider, based on a cultural system of opinions, values and norms which are not obvious or explicit. In order to work effectively in a foreign culture one must make every effort to understand its concepts, motives and values. It is essential to be open-minded and adopt a mentality which reaches across borders.

When studying consumer behaviour, both openness to other cultures and research into values are needed. Research into values will be discussed later in this chapter. First several important social and psychological influences on consumer behaviour will be discussed:

1. The role of the family and of women in the buying process.
2. The educational system.
3. Social class.
4. Nationalistic views, national ideology and concepts of national pride.
5. The adoption process.
6. The hierarchy of needs.

The role of the family and of women in the buying process

The influence of the family on buying behaviour and on the consumer selection processes varies. In traditional societies with extended families, roles are different from those in industrial and post-industrial societies. Religion also influences behaviour and, more important, the cultural role of women. In societies which only accept women in traditional roles, buying decisions for some product categories are taken by men, while in other societies these decisions are taken by women.

The educational system

Countries with formal educational systems generally have the highest literacy levels. The consequence of this for marketing and advertising is that consumers are more critical, and want more sophisticated information. In such countries there is usually more extensive legislation protecting the consumer against unfair advertising practices, and there are often active consumer movements.

Social class

Definitions of class structures differ from country to country. The social class structure most often used for marketing in developed countries is that of the United States or adaptations of it. American society is usually described as a three-tier society, divided into upper, middle and lower classes. Consumption patterns are strongly related to social class, and the class structure has a distinctive shape: it can be portrayed as a pyramid with a narrowing bottom. Class structures of other societies vary in shape. Several examples are given in Figure 5.1.

Not only do class systems differ in various parts of the world; the relative sizes of the classes vary with the relative prosperity of countries.[1] Some class systems have a greater influence on buying behaviour than others. In some Western European countries 'lower' classes may exhibit upward mobility, showing buying behaviour similar to that of the 'upper' classes, but in other cultures, where the class system has a distinctive role, buying behaviour is more firmly linked to a particular social class.

Upper classes in almost all societies seem to be more similar to each other than they are to the rest of their own society.[2] Lower classes tend

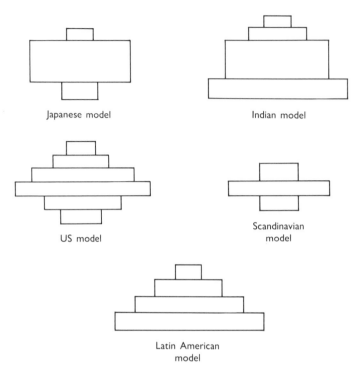

Japanese model

Indian model

US model

Scandinavian
model

Latin American
model

Figure 5.1 *Class structure in different societies (source: Adaptation from Edward W. Cundiff and Marye T. Hilger, 1988: Marketing in the International Environment, Prentice Hall)*

to be more culture-bound. Middle classes go in for cultural 'borrowing'. The upper and middle classes make choices which are less culture bound when selecting products and services, including food, clothing, household items and personal care products than the lower classes.

Nationalistic views

Nationalistic views can be considered in two ways. National ideology influences the way a company can operate in a foreign country, while concepts of national pride can be used for branding and advertising.

National ideology

Economic philosophy is an important element in national ideology. Governments have a strong influence on how freely a company can operate in particular countries. They may be involved to a greater or lesser extent in business and in establishing rules and regulations. In some cultures foreign products are perceived as inferior, in others as superior. In order to avoid being seen as foreign, many companies play down this aspect. In many countries where Philips manufactures and sells products, people do not know that it is a Dutch company.

Concepts of national pride

Some products and brands base their communication strategies on national pride or the specific expertise of a country. Many foreign products are marketed on the basis of a high quality image of the country of origin. For these products the 'made in' concept works very well.

Consumers are sensitive to the country of origin.[3] In 1965, by way of experiment, four identical cans of mixed fruit juice were labelled as the product of different Central American countries, and were then evaluated in Guatemala. It turned out that to consumers mixed fruit juice from Guatemala and Mexico tasted far better than mixed fruit juice from Costa Rica or El Salvador, although it was exactly the same drink.[4]

'Made in Germany' is immediately associated with reliability, precision and punctuality. 'Made in Japan' means: good quality. 'Made in France' means style and elegance. 'Made in Sweden' means strong and solid. A good example of the use of the 'made in' theme is the slogan 'Pizza, Bratwurst or nouvelle cuisine', used in 1986 when the Renault V6 Turbo was introduced to the English market. Another example is provided by the advertising campaign for Löwenbräu beer in Great Britain: a man is shown wearing Lederhosen along with the text 'Thankfully they sent us their lager, not their shorts'.[5]

Most 'made in' communications make use of stereotypes. Stereotypes are used because they provide instant communication. They trigger associations and can enrich a brand's perception. A 'made in' label enables manufacturers to position their brands simply, strongly, quickly and straightforwardly. The 'made in' issue has been analyzed repeatedly; the following are the main findings:[6]

1. Consumers hold stereotyped images both of foreign countries and of their own country.
2. These images are used as information cues in judging products originating from different countries.
3. Buyers are not always aware of a product's true origin, yet they are always able to express preferences for production locations.

4. Consumers in some countries tend to prefer domestic brands whereas consumers in other countries prefer foreign brands.
5. Like price or brand name, country of origin may serve as a proxy variable for product evaluation when other information is lacking.
6. Country of origin identifications may serve as a surrogate for branding.

The following are examples of things which tend to be seen as associated with particular countries:[7]

Italy:	Pizza, pasta, Parmesan cheese, espresso coffee, fashion, art, design, Ferrari, culture, music, wine, ice-cream, shoes.
Germany:	Beer, Bratwurst, Sauerkraut, cars.
Netherlands:	Wooden clogs, cheese, windmills, flower bulbs, diamonds, eggs, potatoes, coffee.
Great Britain:	Rain, tea, sandwiches, bowler hats, three-piece suits, whisky, bacon and eggs.
France:	Fashion, perfume, wine, haute couture, baguettes, Cognac, garlic, Champagne, cheese, cars.
Japan:	Raw fish, kimonos, rice, sake, cars, audio/video equipment, cameras, copiers.
United States:	Corn-on-the-cob, hamburgers, Coca-Cola, large cars, the dollar, peanuts, donuts, popcorn, hotdogs, chewing gum, ketchup, T-bone steaks.

The adoption process

Rogers' theory of 'diffusion of innovations' distinguishes adoption categories as follows: innovators, early adopters, early majority, late majority and laggards.[8] Adoption categories classify individuals within a market according to their willingness to accept new products. What is a new product in one market may not be new in another market. If an international marketer introduces a product which is new in one market but known in other markets, he will need to consider whether the target adoption groups are different and, if necessary, to create different strategies for those different markets. When the low-price Polaroid instant camera was introduced simultaneously in the United States and France, no consideration was given to the fact that the instant camera concept was well known in the United States but not in France. In France the target group was innovators, in the United States it was the majority.

Another aspect of the diffusion of innovations process is the extent to which cultures are open to change. It may well be that products or ideas which are compatible with cultural values and traditional ways of doing things will be adopted faster than those which are not.[9] The adoption process is a social phenomenon, characterized by the statistical normal distribution. One of the major reasons why the normal distribution is observed is the interaction effect. This is the process through which the innovators influence the early adopters, and so on. The acceptance of a new idea or product is the result of human interaction. It is particularly important to remember this when introducing new or existing products or services into other cultures.

The hierarchy of needs

In the search for universal cultural elements, Maslow's motivation theory has often been described as universal for all cultures.[10] Hofstede's research shows that it is based on the American culture, and is not universal.[11]

Maslow's theory states that human needs are fulfilled in phases. Only after the basic physical needs for food, water and housing have been fulfilled does the individual seek safety and security; beyond this lies the search for even higher levels of fulfilment – self-esteem and status, and ultimately the need for self-actualization. According to this theory the more developed a market is, the more it can offer goods and services which appeal to status. Any further development of the already

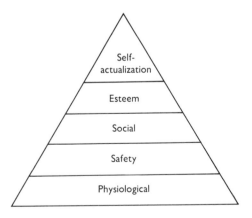

Figure 5.2 *Maslow's hierarchy of needs (source: Warren Keegan, 1989: Global Marketing Management, Prentice Hall)*

developed countries should involve self-actualization becoming even more important than status. Some experts argue that this is culturally defined. The highest level of the hierarchy, self-actualization, is a highly individualistic motive, which fits American society, but not many others.[12] In other countries, the highest level of the hierarchy of needs may be very different. For example, in Japan, German-speaking countries, some Latin countries and Greece, people are motivated by the need for personal, individual security. In France, Spain, Portugal, Yugoslavia, Chile and other Latin and Asian countries, people are motivated by the need for security and belonging, while in North European countries, success and belonging are the main motivators.[13] See Figure 5.2.

■ Marketing and the culture of the consumer[14]

Marketing and advertising people aim to compare cultures and find common qualities within cultures which are relevant to marketing. Research is often based on models which simplify reality in order to discuss, explain, classify and/or predict the impact of culture on the phenomena studied.

There are two types of models which try to order or quantify cultures: dimensional models and typologies. Dimensional models distinguish a number of dimensions, on which cultures can be compared. Another way of picturing differences among cultures is through typologies. A typology describes a number of ideal types, each of them more or less easy to imagine. Dividing countries into the First, Second and Third World is such a typology.

The 'life-style' typologies described later in this chapter were originally developed by US market research agencies and have been replicated more recently in Europe and Asia. These represent more sophisticated classifications, in which consumers are divided into groups such as 'believers', 'pleasurists' or 'Euro rockies'. Typologies are easier to grasp than dimensions, but they hold more problems for empirical research. Real cases seldom correspond exactly to one single, ideal type. However, outcomes of life-style research used by the advertising industry is mostly based on typologies, because these are easier to grasp, and appeal more to the imagination, than dimensional models.

Culture undoubtedly affects consumer behaviour. The question for marketing people is whether knowledge of certain aspects of the cultural background will make it possible to predict an individual's consumer behaviour. The prime factors are the consumer's disposable income and the availability of the commodity. Next in line come cultural factors; these affect the choice between alternative buying decisions. The practices described in Chapter 4 – rituals, heroes and symbols – are most likely to affect the buying decision. One commodity or service is preferred over another because of its symbolic value, because it is associated with a hero figure, or because it enables one to take part in a ritual. Values play a role in this process, but buying decisions are only rarely directly value-driven. Classifications of culture, on the other hand, tend to start from the level of values.

Research into classifications of culture

Geert Hofstede, professor of international management at the University of Limburg in the Netherlands, [15,16] has researched different dimensions of national cultures in sixty-four IBM subsidiaries. He identified four dimensions of national culture, based on values: these are power distance, uncertainty avoidance, individualism and masculinity.

Power distance is the degree of inequality among people which the population of a country considers normal, ranging from extreme inequality to relative equality.

Uncertainty avoidance is the degree to which people prefer structured to unstructured situations, the range is from extremely rigid to relatively flexible.

Individualism is the degree to which people in a country learn to act as individuals rather than as members of cohesive groups, with cultures ranging from individualistic to collectivist.

Masculinity is the degree to which 'masculine' values such as assertiveness, performance, success and competition prevail over 'feminine' values such as quality of life, warm personal relationships, service, care for the weak and solidarity: cultures range from tough to tender.

By applying these four dimensions to fifty countries, it appeared that definite culture clusters can be defined. Thus Southern European countries and the Latin American countries score high on both the power distance dimension and the uncertainty-avoidance dimension. With regard to uncertainty-avoidance versus masculinity, it seems that the masculine risk-takers appear to be the entire 'Anglo' cluster, plus a few Asian countries such as India, the Philippines and Hong Kong (interestingly, former English or American colonies). Figure 5.3 shows,

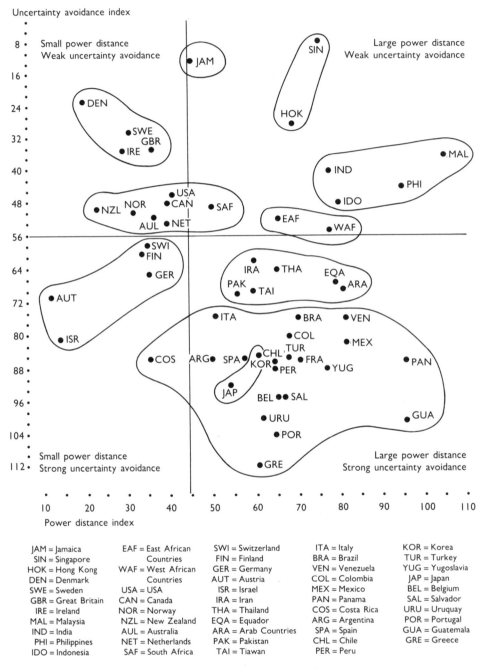

Figure 5.3 *Power distance versus uncertainty-avoidance plot for fifty countries and three regions (source: Geert Hofstede, 1990: Institute for Research on Intercultural Cooperation, Maastricht, The Netherlands)*

as an example, a power distance and uncertainty-avoidance plot for fifty countries and three regions.

The results of this research have mainly been used in international management theory. Researchers who want to test whether the scores on these four dimensions correlate with buying decisions in different countries should be aware that both individualism and small power distance are correlated with a country's wealth (per capita GNP). As wealth (disposable income) has a more direct effect on buying decisions than values, which influence buying behaviour indirectly, correlation studies involving the four dimensions should also include a correlation with per capita GNP. A cultural explanation for buying behaviour can only be upheld if any of the culture scores correlates more strongly with buying behaviour figures than with the per capita GNP.

Other cross-national studies of values are potentially relevant to an explanation of differences in buying behaviour. These will be discussed in the next section. However, the predictive value of these studies is limited as far as buying behaviour is concerned. The same values may produce different buying behaviours and different values may lead to similar buying behaviours. Some people think that the growing similarity in consumer behaviour resulting from the increasing number of global brands implies that national cultures will become more similar. On a superficial level this may be true, but fundamentally it is not. Practices become similar: people dress the same, buy the same products, use the same fashionable words (symbols), they see the same TV shows and advertising (heroes), they perform the same sports and leisure activities (rituals). These superficial manifestations of culture are sometimes mistaken for deeper underlying values, which determine the meaning various practices hold. Studies at the values level do not suggest a growing similarity between nations. The concept of life-style marketing developed for the marketing and advertising industry and the related studies described in the next section must be viewed in the light of the knowledge that if a life-style typology is developed by measuring values, its ability to predict consumer behaviour becomes doubtful. Also, if it is based on actual consumption of certain products and services, its interpretation in terms of values is highly speculative.

Nevertheless, attempts are made to relate people's values to brands in order to develop concepts for international life-style advertising. Knowing how consumers structure the world around them and how they perceive themselves can help in explaining their behaviour. There are now several research institutes which aim to assess and describe these constructs for different countries or markets, so that any similarities which emerge can be used as a basis for developing international brands and advertising strategies.

■ Value and life-style research

The strategy of focusing on the 'product plus' in advertising is still highly rated by some advertising people. However, few products or brands still carry a unique selling proposition. This is why most media advertising now concentrates on consumer benefits and life-styles, adding imagery and motivating values. Advertising presents the product as used in the context of a particular life-style, which allows projection and for identification and thus builds the brand personality. The values referred to here are not the core or central values described earlier, but are more instrumental or product-related.

Value marketing

We have progressed from product marketing to an era of what might be termed value marketing: the consistent linking of brands to product-related values. Mercedes-Benz fits in with self-respect, social recognition and a comfortable life; Volvo fits in with family security, a comfortable life and self-respect; BMW fit in with self-respect, pleasure and a world of beauty.[17] Advertisers connect values with life-styles: every life-style is characterized by a number of values which are shared to a greater or lesser extent by the members of a group. Clustering these value patterns may reveal life-style segments at which advertising can be targeted.

The applications of value and life-style research include the following:

1. New product development.
2. Positioning new brands.
3. Re-evaluation of existing brands in order:
   (a) to strengthen the current position;
   (b) to reposition brands;
   (c) to extend the brand life-cycle.
4. Redefining target groups and market segments.
5. Decision-making on brand advertising strategies, with regard to:
   (a) target groups;
   (b) proposition and/or brand personality;
   (c) concept development.

Life-style research linked to media usage can also help in media planning.

Although value and life-style research can be very useful, it is usually an addition to more basic research, for example socio-demographic data, or usage and attitude studies directly related to the product or market.

Cross-cultural life-style research may proceed by first defining life-style segments and then attempting to find similarities. Alternatively, one can begin by researching the social structure and value patterns of each different culture or market, and then proceed to look for similarities. This latter approach is preferable.

The next section will describe a few of the major studies of values and life-styles, which often claim to be able to predict trends. However, the doubts expressed earlier about the predictive value of such studies should be borne in mind.

Value research

The first value research to be used for marketing purposes was that of Rokeach.[18] Through lengthy analyses he devised a list of central values. Some people consider these to be universal and timeless. Others believe they are only applicable to the United States. In China, for example, values like perseverance and thriftiness are fundamental, but they do not appear on Rokeach's list.

Central values can be categorized as relating to human nature, to man's relationship with nature, to time and how man deals with it and to the concept of the ideal human being.

According to Rokeach's study the ten highest ranking central values of Americans are as follows:[19]

1. Honest.
2. Loving.
3. Responsible.
4. Broadminded.
5. Forgiving.
6. Ambitious.
7. Cheerful.
8. Helpful.
9. Independent.
10. Capable.

Rokeach divided central values into terminal values and instrumental values. *Terminal values* are values which relate to an ideal situation which does not currently exist or which has not yet been achieved. They relate to goals pursued by the whole of humanity. *Instrumental values* relate to the way in which people behave, or ought to behave, if they are pursuing the end-states referred to above. Instrumental values describe a form of ideal behaviour.[20]

Rokeach distinguished eighteen terminal values and eighteen instrumental values. These are as follows:

Terminal values	Instrumental values
a comfortable life	ambitious
an exciting life	broadminded
a sense of accomplishment	capable
a world at peace	cheerful
a world of beauty	clean
equality	courageous
family security	forgiving
freedom	helpful
happiness	honest
inner harmony	imaginative
mature love	independent
national security	intellectual
pleasure	logical
salvation	loving
self-respect	obedient
social recognition	polite
true friendship	responsible
wisdom	self-controlled

Consumers' value systems can be divided into three groups:

1. Central values.
2. Domain-specific values.
3. Product-specific values.

Values which are only applied in a specific field are called domain-specific. Examples of domains include economy, religion, politics, work and consumer behaviour.[21] Values related to consumer behaviour are of interest when using value systems as an aid to strategy development. In using values to evaluate products and brands, the values of interest are product-specific values, applied to product categories or specific brands. Examples of values or attributes connected to product categories include the following:

Cars: safe, solid, modern styling, fast, comfortable.
Soft drinks: good taste, refreshing, low in calories.
Cosmetics: effective, safe, not too expensive.

A simpler approach to values was developed by Kahle *et al.* This is the so-called list of values (LOV).[22] LOV consists of nine values: sense of belonging, fun and enjoyment, warm relationship with others, being well-respected, sense of accomplishment, security, self-respect and excitement. This list was used to compare the values of students and their parents in Denmark, West Germany and the United States. It appeared that students value fun and enjoyment and self-fulfilment higher than their parents in all three countries; parents more often select security as their most important value. There were also cross-cultural differences: the sense of belonging seems to be primarily a German value. Kahle[23] grouped the LOV values into three categories: external values, endorsed by people who view life as being determined mainly by outside events, and internal values, endorsed by people who highly value control over all aspects of their own life. Internal values are further categorized into individual and interpersonal values.[24]

There are limitations to cross-cultural life-style research. Although some people in the advertising industry have high expectations of cross-cultural life-style research, others approach this kind of research with scepticism, maintaining that the life-style concept is only valid within a given country. The huge and relatively homogeneous US market was a natural place for the life-style concept to develop. Recently, life-style studies have also been carried out in Asian countries; these have been limited to specific countries, unlike the cross-cultural studies carried out in Europe.[25]

The most well-known survey instrument for measuring values, Values and Life-styles (VALS), has been developed in the United States and is based on Rokeach's instrumental and terminal values.

VALS

The VALS typology, based on the work of Maslow and Rokeach, was developed by the Stanford Research Institute (SRI) in 1975 and introduced in 1978. It was a pioneering attempt to describe how US consumers' personal beliefs shape their buying decisions. The original VALS was somewhat limited in its application to marketing, because it did not take account of how well consumers' motivations matched their ability to buy the goods and services they wanted.[26] Therefore, in 1989, VALS 2 was developed, which included an assessment of the consumer's ability to buy. The original VALS divided the American population into nine segments, organized along a hierarchy of needs. At the bottom were 'Survivors' and 'Sustainers'; at the top were the 'Integrateds'. Two separate paths led from bottom to top. One was externally-directed and included 'Belongers', 'Emulators' and 'Achievers'. These groups took their cues from the world around them.

The other was internally-directed – 'I am Mes', 'Experientials', and the 'Societally Conscious'. These groups made their own rules. These divisions reflected a population dominated by people in their 20s and 30s, as was the case in the United States in the 1970s.[27] In 1989, VALS 2 regrouped the population into eight segments.[28]

VALS 2 is built around the concept of 'self-orientation' and a new definition of resources. Self-orientation is the pattern of attitudes and activities which helps people to reinforce, sustain or modify their social and self-image. Three such patterns can be related to consumer behaviour: 'principle', 'status' and 'action' orientations. 'Resources', in the VALS 2 system, refers to the full range of psychological, physical, demographic and material capacities consumers can draw upon. This concept encompasses education, income, self-confidence, health, eagerness to buy, intelligence and energy level.[29] The self-orientation dimension captures three different ways of buying. Principle-oriented consumers are guided by their views of how the world is or should be. Status-oriented consumers are guided by the actions and opinions of others, while action-oriented consumers are guided by the desire for social or physical activity, variety and risk-taking.[30]

Thus, VALS 2 divides people into three basic categories: those who are principle-oriented, status-oriented and action-oriented. It also estimates the resources consumers can draw upon, including their education, income, health, energy-level, self-confidence and degree of consumerism. Most resources tend to increase from youth through to middle-age, and then diminish with old age. There are eight segments: 'Fulfilleds', 'Believers', 'Actualizers', 'Achievers', 'Strivers', 'Strugglers', 'Experiencers' and 'Makers'.

The psychographic groups in VALS 2 are arranged in a rectangle. They are stacked vertically by resources (minimal to abundant) and horizontally by self-orientation (principle, status or action-oriented).

At the top of the VALS 2 chart are the *Actualizers*, successful, sophisticated people with abundant resources. Image is important to actualizers as an expression of taste, independence and character. Their lives are characterized by richness and diversity. Their possessions and recreational activities reflect a cultivated taste for the finer things in life.

Next come three groups which are relatively affluent. *Fulfilleds* are mature, satisfied, reflective and comfortable people who value order, knowledge and responsibility. Most are well-educated. Fulfilleds are conservative, practical consumers; they are concerned about the functionality, value and durability of the products they buy.

The *Achievers* are successful career and work-oriented people. They value structure, predictability and stability over risk. Work provides them with a sense of duty and prestige. Their social lives are structured around family, church and business. Achievers live conventional lives. As consumers they favour established products and services that demonstrate their success to their peers.

Experiencers are young, vital and enthusiastic. They seek variety and excitement, and are politically uncommitted, with a disdain for conformity and authority. Their energy finds an outlet in exercise, sports, outdoor recreation and social activities. Experiencers are avid consumers and spend much of their income on clothing, fast food, music, movies and videos.

Down the resource-ladder there are three more groups. *Believers* are conservative, conventional people. They follow established routines, organized around their homes and families and around the social and

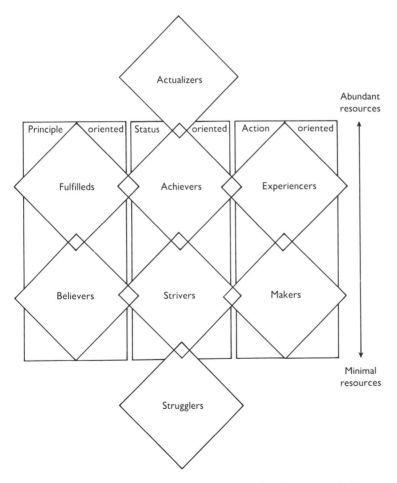

Figure 5.4 *VALS 2 (source: SRI International, Menlo Park, CA, USA)*

religious groups to which they belong. As consumers they are conservative and predictable, favouring established brands. Their education, income and energy are modest, but sufficient to meet their needs. *Strivers* seek motivation, self-definition and approval from the world around them. Unsure of themselves and low on economic, social and psychological resources, they are deeply concerned about the opinions of others. Strivers are sensitive to the tastes and the preferences of the persons with whom they live and socialize. *Makers* are practical people, who have constructive skills and value self-sufficiency. They live in a traditional context of family, practical work and physical recreation, and have little interest in what lies outside that context. Makers are politically conservative. They are unimpressed by material possessions other than those with a practical or functional purpose (e.g. tools or fishing equipment).

At the bottom of the scale are the *Strugglers*, who have limited social, economical and emotional resources. They are focused on meeting urgent, immediate needs. Strugglers are cautious consumers. They represent a very modest market for most products and services, but are loyal to favourite brands.[31]

Like all psychographic schemes, VALS 2 segments are most effective at linking consumer groups and buying patterns for products that engage the consumer's ego. Cars are a classic example. This type of analysis is less useful for small, relatively invisible items like toilet paper.[32] See Figure 5.4.

European life-style research

In Europe several life-style studies have described dimensions related to product use in an attempt to establish similarities in target groups across countries. Some have described or even predicted changing trends in society.

Anticipating change in Europe (ACE)[33]
This extensive study has been conducted by the research agency RISC. Since 1980 it has investigated social changes in twelve European countries, and in 1987 the study was extended to the USA, Canada and Japan. The objective is to try to understand how social changes influence market trends. RISC describes people in terms of dimensions, socio-demographic characteristics, socio-cultural profile, activities (sports, leisure, culture), behaviour towards the media (press, radio, television), political inclinations and mood, in order to better understand the individual as a whole. Each individual consists of a unique combination

of values, perceptions and sensitivities which are used, consciously or unconsciously, in interpreting the environment and interacting with it. The RISC research is based on the experience that when individuals share similar values, perceptions and sensitivities, their behaviour will also show consistent similarities. Those wishing to act globally must identify similarities between target groups in order to develop strategies with a common appeal. The differences must also be identified.

ACE has identified twenty-four Eurotrends based on a common core of seventy socio-cultural items, selected as most relevant for tracking changes in Europe. Using multivariate analysis, a socio-cultural map of Europe has been derived. The socio-cultural map is constructed on two axes. The first of these is termed North–South, although this does not refer to the geographical concept of North–South. The second is roots-flexibility. 'Roots' means belonging to one social unit, closed, static; this implies a structured society, explicit, life-long accepted values, and a hierarchical, authoritarian, normative approach. These are shown in Figure 5.5

Figure 5.6 shows the Eurotrends on the socio-cultural map.

The ACE Eurotypology is used to simplify the identification of sociological types. It consists of six Eurotypes, represented by the following overall percentages in Europe (percentages for individual countries vary):

Traditional	18%
Homebody	14%
Rationalist	23%
Pleasurist	17%
Striver	15%
Trendsetter	13%

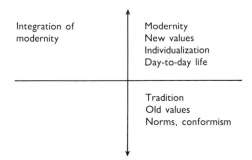

Second axis: social fabric, increasingly complex, uncertain and interactive

Figure 5.5 *Socio-cultural map (source: RISC, Paris)*

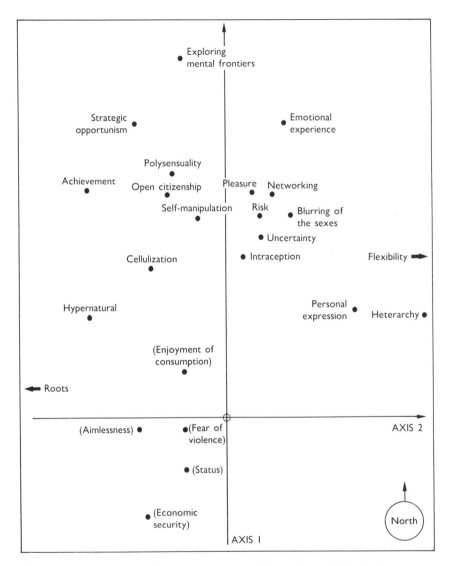

Figure 5.6   *Socio-cultural Euromap (source: ACE brochure, RISC, Paris)*

The *Traditionalist* is heavily marked by the culture, socio-economic history and unique situation of the country, with a profile reflecting deep-rooted attitudes specific to his or her country; consequently this is the least homogeneous group across countries.

The *Homebody* is mainly motivated by a strong attachment to roots in terms of physical and childhood environment. Less preoccupied with economic security than the Traditionalist, the Homebody is more concerned about feeling in touch with the social environment. The Homebody seeks for warm relationships, and has difficulty coping with violence in society.

The *Rationalist* is characterized by an ability to cope with unforeseeable and complex situations, and a readiness to take risks and start new endeavours. Personal fulfilment is seen more as a matter of self-expression than as a financial reward, and the Rationalist believes science and technology will help resolve the challenges facing mankind.

The *Pleasurist* emphasizes sensual and emotional experiences, preferring non-hierarchically structured groups built around self-reliance and auto-regulation and not around leaders or formal decision-making processes.

The *Striver* holds the attitudes, beliefs and values which underlie the dynamics of social change. The Striver believes in autonomous behaviour and wants to shape his or her own life and to exploit mental, physical, sensual and emotional possibilities to the full.

The *Trendsetter* favours non-hierarchical social structures and enjoys spontaneity rather than formal procedures. Trendsetters are not overly concerned with proving their own abilities. Even more individualistic than Strivers, they exemplify the flexible response to a rapidly changing environment.

The CCA Eurostyles[34]

The French agency CCA (Centre de Communication Avancée) embarked on a joint project with Europanel in 1988, using a US system adapted to the European situation. Multivariate analysis revealed sixteen European socio-styles. These socio-styles are supposed to reflect how the European consumer lives and thinks.

The first group of Europeans, living in socio-styles 1–4, can be characterized as 'socio-withdrawals'. The four socio-styles are called: Euro'prudents, Euro'defence, Euro'vigilante and Euro'olvidados. The next two styles represent the 'social dreamers': the Euro'romantics and Euro'squadra. Styles 7, 8 and 9 are characterized as 'socio-ambitious', and are called Euro'rockies, Euro'dandies and Euro'business. Styles 10 and 11 are 'socio-contestants', called Euro'protest and Euro'pioneer. 'Social militants', who emphasize helping others and social responsibility, consist of Euro'scouts and Euro'citizens. The last three styles represent the 'notables': the Euro'moralist, Euro'gentry and the Euro'strict. The CCA European life-styles are described in terms of three dimensions:

1. Progressive ⟷ Conservative.
2. Material ⟷ Spiritual.
3. Rational ⟷ Emotional.

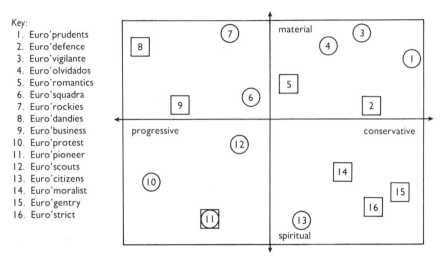

Figure 5.7   *Sixteen socio-styles in a three-dimensional map (source: CCA Presentation, 1989)*

The first dimension appears to be the most discriminating: on the left are the most modern and dynamic socio-styles, the Euro'dandies, Euro'business, Euro'protests and Euro'pioneers. On the right we find the most conservative styles: the Euro'prudents, Euro'vigilantes, Euro'gentry and Euro'stricts. The second dimension represents material versus spiritual. In order to create a three-dimensional map of socio-styles, this dimension is put on a vertical axis. At the top are the Euro'vigilantes, Euro'olvidados, Euro'rockies and Euro'dandies: they value materialism highly. At the bottom are the Euro'pioneers, Euro'citizens and Euro'stricts: they emphasize spiritual values. The third dimension is placed along a diagonal scale. Socio-styles 2 (Euro'defence), 9 (Euro'business) and 14 (Euro'moralist) are nearest to the rational pole. Socio-styles 1 (Euro'prudent) and 10 (Euro'protest) are nearest to the emotional pole.

The sixteen styles are depicted in a three-dimensional 'map', as shown in Figure 5.7, by depicting styles which are high on rationality in the third dimension in square boxes, while styles scoring high on emotionality are depicted surrounded by a circle.

Everyday-life-research

SINUS Gmbh of Germany[35] has developed an international approach to consumer research, describing so-called 'social milieus' in West Germany, France, the United Kingdom and Italy. Social milieus describe the structure of society in terms of social class and value orientations. They give distinctive clusters of values which define the social milieus in different countries and which provide a conceptual framework for cross-cultural comparisons. Two types of values can be distinguished: traditional values, emphasizing hard work, thrift, religion, honesty, good manners and obedience, and material values, which are concerned with possession and are often associated with a need for security. Everyday-life-research has developed a basic typology utilizing the concept of social milieus: this delineates groups of people who share a common set of values and beliefs about work, private relationships, leisure activities and aesthetics, and a common perception of future plans, wishes and dreams; together these determine the development of and changes in attitudes, values and patterns of behaviour.

Knowing the social milieu of a person can provide information about his or her everyday life, work likes and dislikes, and it helps in product development and advertising. It does not, however, say anything about how consumers relate to particular brands or markets. More detailed information on specific attitudes and behaviours may be required. This kind of information can be provided by product- or market-related typologies which are based on attitudes as well as product usage in a specific market.

The first social milieu study was done in West Germany, and from the start it was clear that the German model could not simply be grafted onto other markets. Therefore the social milieus for the United Kingdom, France and Italy were identified as a basis for identifying cross-cultural similarities and differences. The social milieus in West Germany (pre-1990) are described as follows:

1. *Konservatives-gehobenes Milieu:* traditional upper-class conservatives.
2. *Technokratisch-liberales Milieu:* technocratic-liberal milieu with a post-material orientation.
3. *Aufstiegsorientiertes Milieu:* social climbers and achievement-orientated white- and blue-collar workers.
4. *Kleinbürgerliches Milieu:* petty bourgeois milieu group mainly oriented to preserving the status quo.
5. *Traditionelles Arbeitermilieu:* traditional blue-collar workers.
6. *Hedonistisches Milieu:* pleasure-seekers, mainly young.
7. *Alternatives Milieu:* those pursuing alternative life-styles.
8. *Traditionsloses Arbeitermilieu:* those belonging to the uprooted blue-collar milieu and destitutes.

New emerging social milieus for the 1990s are the status- and success-orientated *Yuppies*, the *Neue Arbeiter* or neo-workers, often in advanced 'no collar' industries and the *Postmodernes Milieu* consisting of a post-modernist upper class.

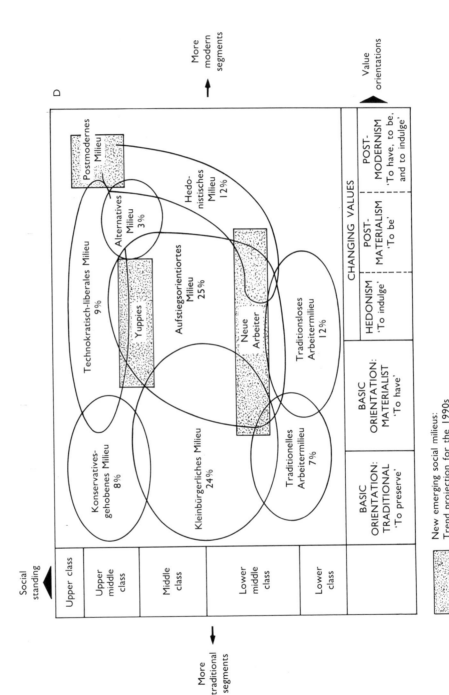

Figure 5.8   *The social milieus of West Germany (source: SINUS Gmbh, Germany)*

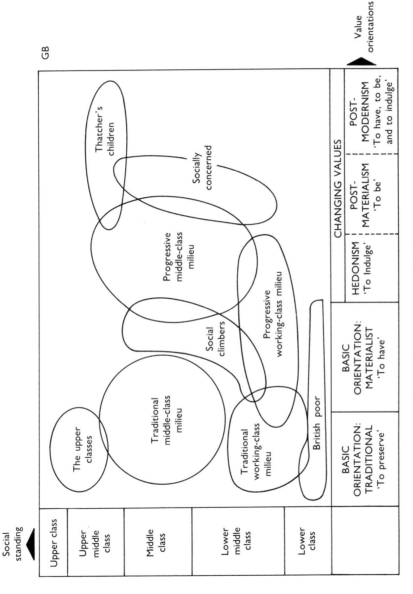

Figure 5.9 *The social milieus of Great Britain (source: SINUS Gmbh, Germany)*

For each society, these milieus may be plotted in a two-dimensional space, using values and social status as parameters. Figure 5.8 shows the social milieus of West Germany, with percentages. In order to provide a comparison with another European country, Figure 5.9 shows the social milieus of the United Kingdom.

By making a systematic comparison of values, attitudes and beliefs in each social milieu across the four countries, a map of multinational target groups was obtained. Each of these target groups represents a distinctive segment reaching across the different nations. Members of the social milieus within a multinational target group sometimes have more in common with each other than with many of their fellow

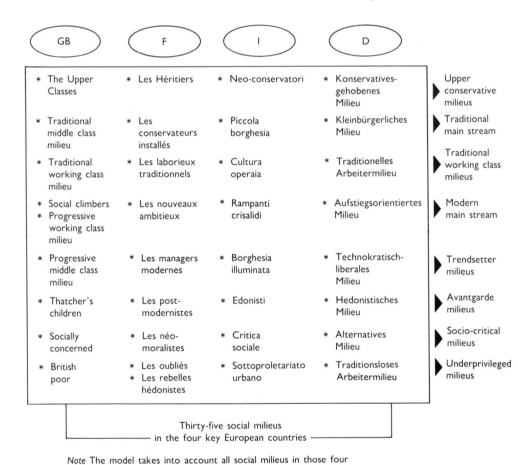

GB	F	I	D	
* The Upper Classes	* Les Héritiers	* Neo-conservatori	* Konservatives- gehobenes Milieu	Upper conservative milieus
* Traditional middle class milieu	* Les conservateurs installés	* Piccola borghesia	* Kleinbürgerliches Milieu	Traditional main stream
* Traditional working class milieu	* Les laborieux traditionnels	* Cultura operaia	* Traditionelles Arbeitermilieu	Traditional working class milieus
* Social climbers * Progressive working class milieu	* Les nouveaux ambitieux	* Rampanti crisalidi	* Aufstiegsorientiertes Milieu	Modern main stream
* Progressive middle class milieu	* Les managers modernes	* Borghesia illuminata	* Technokratisch- liberales Milieu	Trendsetter milieus
* Thatcher's children	* Les post- modernistes	* Edonisti	* Hedonistisches Milieu	Avantgarde milieus
* Socially concerned	* Les néo- moralistes	* Critica sociale	* Alternatives Milieu	Socio-critical milieus
* British poor	* Les oubliés * Les rebelles hédonistes	* Sottoproletariato urbano	* Traditionsloses Arbeitermilieu	Underprivileged milieus

Thirty-five social milieus
in the four key European countries

Note The model takes into account all social milieus in those four
countries except for the Italian *cultura rurale tradizionale* which has no
comparable counterpart in the United Kingdom, France and West
Germany.

Figure 5.10 *Multinational target groups (source: SINUS Gmbh, Germany)*

countrymen. In spite of these similarities within target groups there are, of course, differences. Similar values may translate differently at the local level. Depending on values and product use, there may also be some overlap with neighbouring target groups. Figure 5.10 shows these multinational target groups.

Everyday-life-research has shown that the up-market segments share a similar structure in all four countries; it has identified trend-setting milieus, containing heavy consumers with comparable attitudinal and socio-demographic characteristics. Important values shared by all these consumers include the following:

1. Tolerance, open-mindedness, an outward-looking approach.
2. Career and success.
3. Education and culture.
4. High standard of living.
5. Europe.
6. Hedonistic luxury consumption.
7. Individualism.

GLOBAL SCAN

This is a worldwide consumer study being conducted by the advertising agency Backer Spielvogel Bates Worldwide. The research has been carried out over six years. It originated in the United States and has been extended to France, the United Kingdom, Germany, Spain, Canada, Australia, Hong Kong, Japan and New Zealand. In 1990 it was launched in Belgium, Italy, Finland and Sweden. It is also being extended to Mexico and Venezuela.

One of GLOBAL SCAN's marketing discoveries is that there are five common consumer classes worldwide, called the 'Strivers' (26 per cent of the global population), the 'Achievers' (22 per cent), the 'Pressured' (13 per cent), the 'Traditionals' (16 per cent), and the 'Adapters' (18 per cent) with 5 per cent unassigned.[36]

This model is interesting as it covers more or less the whole world. However, it is considered rather superficial by many researchers, and does require careful scrutiny before use. However, it is an interesting phenomenon.

Life-style research in Asia

CORE, Japan

Kazuaki Ushikubo, president of Research and Development, Inc., Tokyo, describes[37] how CORE, his company's research system, studied people's wants in Japan. He believes that people's wants can be properly described in terms of a structure consisting of a variety of elements which change over time as people enter different life phases and situations. Wants or desires are considered to be a force which motivates specific behaviour. In contrast to Maslow's theory of a hierarchy of needs, Ushikubo describes an individual's wants as structured in a group with components which vary in importance according to the environment. These components can be categorized by the following process:

1. Two major social factors appear to be particularly relevant to human wants. One is 'chaos and order'. It is in the state of chaos that creation and innovation occur. The other is 'outer and inner direction', the interface between an individual and society. These two social factors are used as axes.
2. The most important personal factors are those of mobility and communication. Mobility is the degree of personal attachment to, or detachment from, the environment. Communication refers to the strength of the relationship with other human beings.

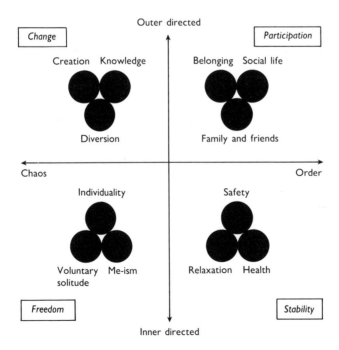

Figure 5.11   *Structuring of wants (source: Kazuaki Ushikubo, 1986: 'A method of structure analysis for developing product concepts and its applications', European Research)*

Table 5.1 Basic wants and wants factors

Basic wants	Wants factors	Meaning
Change	Diversion Knowledge Creation	I want to change my life-style occasionally I want to know more I want to do something to enhance myself
Participation	Family and friends (*Danran*) Belonging Social life	I want to have a pleasant time with my family and friends I want to be like others I want to keep company with many different people
Freedom	Me-ism Individuality Voluntary solitude	I want to live as I like regardless of others I want to be distinctive from others I want to have my own world, apart from others
Stability	Relaxation Safety Health	I want to relax and take a rest I want to keep myself safe I want to be healthy in mind and body

Source: Kazuaki Ushikubo, *European Research*, 1986.

3. These axes provide a framework for positioning the four basic wants of change, participation, freedom and stability.

Figure 5.11 shows a model for structuring wants.

In Figure 5.11 twelve factors from Murray's list of human wants have been integrated into the four quadrants.[38] These basic wants and wants factors have implications for the general life-style, as described in Table 5.1.

Similar explanations of life-styles are given for specific areas such as food and beverages, clothing, housing and leisure. The desire for safety, *danran* (having a happy time, enjoying communications with your family and the company of good friends), knowledge and creation seem to be crucial in the domain of food and beverages. For different domains of life, the expression of wants varies considerably.

The CORE system has been used mainly to study innovative products and services. Benefits and targets have been analyzed for the launch of such diverse products as word processors, fashion goods, the Tokyo Disneyland and a new type of shopping centre, called MARION, in the Ginza.

The INFOPLAN study – Japan

Japanese life-styles, attitudes to products and consumer behaviour have changed considerably during the last decade. Attitudes towards work and leisure time have changed, and personal wealth has grown. INFOPLAN[39] has conducted studies of changing life-styles within specific Japanese groups, such as 'the new teenager', 'the new singles', 'the new jitsunen (those in their 50s and 60s) and most recently 'the new rich'. This emerged from a study undertaken in 1989 among 1,000 Japanese males and females with a yearly income of over 10 million yen (US $80,000) – an interesting group as far as luxury products and services are concerned. The following sub-categories were found:

1. *The Quiet Rich:* 28 per cent of the total. This group is largely female, consisting of wives in traditional roles, who are becoming increasingly resentful of their roles and of the expectations forced on them.
2. *The Classic Rich:* 22 per cent of the total. This group represents the social and leadership elite of Japan. They are rather more flexible than the typical conservative Japanese, somewhat more male-oriented, and very well-educated; 53 per cent are university graduates. They tend to come from old, established families.
3. *The Conservative Rich:* 19 per cent of the total. These people are conservative; they are not sociable, nor are they interested in the pleasures of consumption. They are older and largely male.
4. *The Modern Rich:* one of the two New Rich types, and 15 per cent of the total. This is a new, younger, more independent,

Table 5.2 Major trends in Japan

Homogeneity ⟶	Variety
Traditional expectations ⟶	Personal preferences
'Large' (TV) (Superstores) ⟶	'Small' (Magazines) (Boutiques)
'The company' ⟶	'The works'
'Work-driven' ⟶	Balanced life
Things ⟶	Experiences

Source: INFOPLAN/Robert Wilk, 'The new rich: a psychographic approach to marketing to the wealthy Japanese consumer', ESOMAR conference, June 1990.

individualistic type, which is rather revolutionary in Japan. These Modern Rich are the youngest of all the types and the best educated; over 60 per cent are university graduates.

5. *The Overt Rich:* 16 per cent of the total, and the second New Rich type. The Overt Rich are into heavy consumption. They will buy and try anything. With the highest income of the five groups, these people are an important new category in Japan, and they also have the most fun.

INFOPLAN also found changes in attitudes towards tradition, marriage and relationships. One general observation is that the rich do not want to spend their money on 'things' but on 'experiences'. Table 5.2 shows the major changes among Japanese consumers which are of importance to marketers.

Four life models

Like other large advertising agencies, Dentsu[40] has also researched values and life-styles. The Dentsu Consumer Value Survey was used for this purpose from 1976 to 1988, with the aim of developing creative concepts for advertising. Four life models were found – 'Achievers', 'Intelligent', 'Group Merit' and 'Membership-dependent'. The attitudes and values attached to the four life models are as follows:

1. *Achiever:* enterprising; attaches importance to individuality and to human relationships.

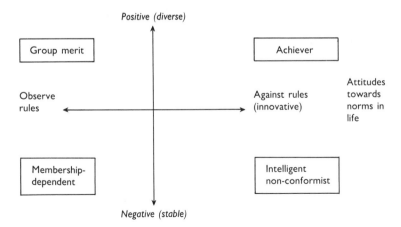

Figure 5.12 *Four Japanese life models: attitudes towards life changes (source: Dentsu/Hiroe Susuki, 'Japanese life-style, life models and applications to creative concepts', ESOMAR conference, June 1990)*

2. *Intelligent:* attaches importance to individuality in the area of intelligence, culture and arts; attaches importance to nature and communion with nature; lacking in collective heritage.
3. *Group Merit:* makes full use of the organization to own best advantage; attaches importance to human relationships; has a great interest in arts and culture.
4. *Membership-dependent:* highly loyal to the organization; family centred; has a deep interest in nature.

Figure 5.12 shows the four life models and the attitudes towards life change implicit in them.

Research in Malaysia, Singapore, Taiwan and Thailand

The Survey Research Group (SRG), which has offices in many Asian countries including Singapore, Malaysia, Taiwan, Thailand, Hong Kong and Indonesia, has conducted life-style surveys in Malaysia, Singapore, Thailand and Taiwan. This research will be extended to Hong Kong and the Philippines. In 1987, the first large-scale, quantitative psychographic research was conducted in Malaysia. This was the first research of its kind in Asia as a whole.[41]

Malaysia

In the Malaysian psychographic study consumers were clustered into seven psychographic segments: 'Yesterday People', 'Village Trendsetters', 'Chameleons', 'Loners', the 'New Breed', 'Yuppies' and 'Sleepwalkers'.

The 'Sleepwalkers' appear to be predominantly Chinese. They are relatively family-minded, moralistic, introvert, socially and physically inactive, conforming, followers, non-doers and neurotic. They are not religous, adventurous or houseproud, and are less community spirited and patriotic. In order to understand why 'Sleepwalkers' have such attitudes and values, it is necessary to understand Chinese culture and the influence on it of Confucianism, Yin and Yang and animism.

As an example, product buying behaviour of milk was compared for the Sleepwalkers and the Village Trendsetters, who are predominantly Malays. In the milk category, the penetration of fresh milk and evaporated milk on Sleepwalkers is only six per cent and two per cent, compared with seventeen per cent and thirteen per cent on Village Trendsetters. The relatively low penetration levels for the Sleepwalkers could be due to the Chinese belief in the yin–yang

Table 5.3 Penetration of fresh milk and evaporated milk among village trendsetters and sleepwalkers

Penetration	Village trendsetters %	Sleepwalkers %
Fresh milk	17	6
Evaporated milk	13	2

Source: Victor Kiu, Adasia conference, Lahore, Pakistan, 1990.

Table 5.4 Penetration of branded biscuits and sauces among village trendsetters and sleepwalkers

Penetration	Village trendsetters %	Sleepwalkers %
Branded biscuits	32	17
Branded tomato sauce	59	47
Branded chilli sauce	60	46

Source: Victor Kiu, Adasia conference, Lahore, Pakistan, 1990.

relationship. Refrigerated milk is still considered a 'yin' food which will soothe and still the spirit – not a good way to start the day! Table 5.3 summarizes the findings.

In the branded biscuits, tomato sauce and chilli sauce categories, the penetration levels for Sleepwalkers are again significantly lower than for Village Trendsetters, as Table 5.4 shows.

The Sleepwalkers appear to be more price-sensitive and more interested in what the product does for them. They buy to fit in, not to stand out. The Village Trendsetters in contrast prefer established brand names and focus on attributes, image and status – anything that will give evidence of success.

Singapore

In Singapore the Chinese and Malay population was clustered into ten psychographic groups.[42] The Chinese were clustered into four groups and the Malays into six.

Figure 5.13 shows typology names and percentages with a vertical axis representing high v. low drive and a horizontal axis representing Eastern v. Western value expectations.

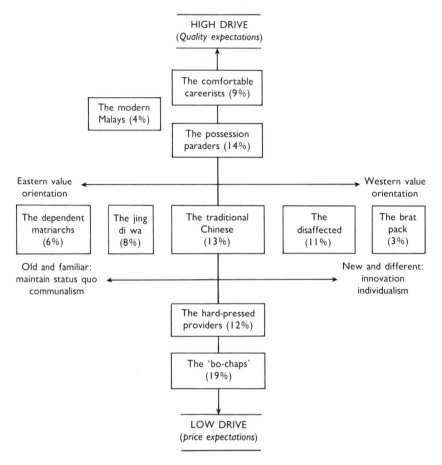

Figure 5.13 *Typologies found in Singapore (source: The Survey Research Group)*

The four Chinese groups can be described as follows:

1. *The Brat Pack:* aged 20–34, mostly single, with above-average education; Western oriented, youthful, individualistic and disinterested in most Eastern values; competitive, less materialistic, confident and quality conscious; light TV viewers, preferring English programmes; moderate radio listeners, preferring English channels; preferring English press to Chinese press.
2. *The Possession Paraders:* aged 20–44, married, well-educated; young optimists who have adjusted to the new society of Singapore; materialistic, status conscious, ambitious, upward striving; willing to spend on new and improved products; light TV viewers, preferring English programmes; moderate radio listeners,

preferring English programmes; prefer English press to Chinese press; visit the cinema regularly.

3. *The Comfortable Careerists:* aged 25–44, married, well-educated; leaders in professions, corporate executives; visible success and affluence; appreciate value of education, go for luxury goods/ services, like new and improved products; light TV viewers, preferring English programmes; moderate radio listeners, preferring English channels; avid English press readers, but also read Chinese newspapers.

4. *The Traditional Chinese:* aged 30–49 years, married, average education, mainly in Chinese; traditional, conforming, family-oriented, inward looking, religious and superstitious; rational buyers who are brand loyal, preferring established brands; cautious about new things and ideas; average TV viewers, preferring Chinese programmes; light radio listeners, preferring Chinese programmes, frequent cinema goers, preferring Chinese movies.

The Malays were clustered in six groups, which can be described as follows:

1. *The Modern Malays:* below 45 years, married, average education; belong to the new breed of non-Chinese who have adjusted to the new society; combine the materialistic trappings of today with their traditional, religious and moral background; family-oriented; success-oriented; believe in good education; relatively carefree about money; would respond to sales promotions; prefer to stick to reasonably priced, established brand names; light TV viewers on weekdays but heavy on weekends; heavy radio listeners; prefer the Malay press, but also read English press.

2. *The Jing Di Wa ('Frogs in a well'):* aged 35 years and over, married, primary education; traditional, family-oriented; narrow-minded, fatalistic and superstitious; follow norms; rational spenders, interested in what the product does for them, not what it says about them; heritage brand buyers; average on most things; heavy TV viewers and radio listeners; average press readership; low on cinema visits.

3. *The Disaffected:* age 20–34, mostly single, average education; come from traditional and conservative families but have been exposed to Western values through education; very status-conscious, materialistic; find life meaningless, do not know what to do with so much free time; bargain hunters, emotional spenders, seek new and improved products; heavy TV viewers especially at weekends; moderate radio listeners, average press readers.

4. *The Hard-Pressed Providers:* aged 35–39, married, primary education; law-abiding, good citizens; traditional and moralistic; family-oriented; materialistic, status-conscious; maintaining face is important; bargain hunters; image-oriented, but brand-loyal on established products; moderate TV viewers with low channel loyalty; moderate radio listeners; average readers of both English and Chinese press; go to cinema occasionally.

5. *The 'Bo-Chaps':* diverse age groups, married, primary education; indifferent towards attitudes and values imposed by society; self-centred; low motivation; followers; fatalistic; emotional spenders; low brand loyalty; focus on benefits and good value for money; light TV viewers, preferring Chinese programmes; light radio listeners, preferring Chinese programmes; read Chinese papers.

6. *The Dependent Matriarchs:* mostly women, aged 45 or over, married or widowed, primary education; out of the mainstream; resigned; relaxed, contented; hold oriental attitudes, values and aspirations; price is the dominant factor; heavy TV viewers on weekdays but moderate on weekends; light radio listeners; light press readers.

Taiwan

SRG found eight psychographic clusters in Taiwan.[43] These may be described as follows:

1. *The Traditional Homebodies* (16 per cent of the population): solid citizens who take a fairly traditional view of life; not interested in trends; value and money conscious, open to bargains; like television and especially soap operas.

2. *The Confident Traditionalists* (12 per cent of the population): middle aged with a traditional outlook on morals and social virtues; competitive nature; not impulse buyers or bargain hunters; highly developed self-image and a keen sense of social expectations and norms.

3. *The Family-centred Fatalists* (13 per cent of the population): a female, family-oriented, older group; fairly content with the status quo, not interested in trendy goods but in traditional women's and family products.

4. *The Lethargics* (14 per cent of the population): this group does not stand out in any way, either in behaviour or product usage; their overriding characteristic is 'ordinariness'. Their buying and media habits make them difficult to reach. The key to selling to them appears to lie in distribution and media weight.

5. *The Middle-class Hopefuls:* down-to-earth; optimistic; male and middle-class; reasonable spenders; interested in new things, and

willing to take a few risks with their money; important buyers of durables.

6. *The Discontented Moderns:* this group likes to follow new trends, but also retains a number of key traditional attitudes, and advertising should be careful not to offend these; heavy watchers of TV and cinema; looking for fun and a better quality of life.

7. *The Rebellious Young:* (7 per cent of the population): younger, discontented non-conformists; relatively affluent; seeming trend-setters in society; do not wait for a trend to be accepted; impulsive buyers; relatively individualistic, and therefore not impressed by any Western trend.

8. *The Young Strivers* (13 per cent of the population): a younger group of average affluence; competitive, materialistic; average TV viewers, but also users of cinema, radio, videos and magazines; not impulsive buyers or bargain hunters; look for specific goods that fit their self-image and needs.

Thailand[44]

In Thailand, psychographic research carried out in 1989 was restricted to Bangkok. A great diversity of life-styles and values was found. The results suggested nine distinct segments: 'Today's Women' (3 per cent), 'The Comfortable Middle Class' (11 per cent), 'We Got The Blues' (11 per cent), 'Mainstream Belongers' (17 per cent), 'Young Achievers' (11 per cent), 'Young At Heart' (8 per cent), 'Trying To Make It' (20 per cent), 'The Left Outs' (7 per cent), and 'Almost There' (12 per cent).

There are four groups which show brand loyalty and are readily influenced by advertising. *'Almost There'* consists of brand-loyal consumers, who are easily influenced by advertising. *'Trying To Make It'* is a group which is strongly conformist, but is also brand loyal and easily influenced by advertising. *'Mainstream Belongers'* support the status quo and the monarchy, are extrovert and brand-loyal, and, although they do not watch much television, are influenced by advertising. *'Young Achievers'* are materialistic, liberal and buy on impulse; they look for something new, and although they do not watch TV, they do pay attention to advertising. *'The Comfortable Middle Class'* consists of conformist, unambitious and unadventurous people who watch a lot of TV, but are neither greatly influenced by advertising nor very brand loyal. *'Today's Women'* are conformist, houseproud, family-oriented and watch a lot of TV, but are less strongly influenced by advertising. *'Young At Hearts'* are busy, socially-active people; they tend to be introvert, and are not impulse buyers; they watch less TV than others and are not greatly influenced by advertising. *'We Got The Blues'* are the least educated people of all segments. *'The Left Outs'* are the city's disadvantaged, low-income households.

■ Summary

This chapter has described some general theories of consumer behaviour which can be used in international marketing and advertising. Considerable attention was given to the values and life-styles, because these are a major tool for developing concepts in international life-style advertising. Examples of value and life-style research have been given, together with results. However, it must be remembered that this type of research does not always explain the relation between values and product usage, or changes in consumer values, product usage and brand preference. Nor does it really predict shifts in values. It tends to follow trends rather than predict them, although prediction is sometimes promised by some research institutes.

Value and life-style research can, however, be of help in structuring one's thoughts when developing concepts. In Asia, particularly, this research is expanding fast. This may be of help to the international advertiser.

■ Notes and references

1. Edward W. Cundiff and Marye Tharp Hilger, 1988: *Marketing in the International Environment*, 2nd edition, Prentice Hall.
2. Ernest Dichter, 1962: 'The world customer', *Harvard Business Review*, July/August, pp. 113–23.
3. Gabriele Morello and Elzo Boerema, '"Made in" and communication', ESOMAR Annual Congress, September 1989.
4. R. D. Schooler, 1965: 'Product bias in the Central American common market', *Journal of Marketing Research*, November.
5. D. Head, 1987: 'Advertising slogans and the "made in" concept', *International Journal of Advertising*, July, pp. 237–52
6. G. J. Bamossey and N. J. Papadopulos, 1987: 'An assessment of reliability for product evaluation scales used in country of origin research', in *World Marketing Congress, International Conference Series*, Vol. III.
7. Morello and Boerema, 1989: op. cit.
8. Everett M. Rogers, 1962: *The Diffusion of Innovations*, The Free Press, New York.
9. Morello and Boerema, 1989: op. cit.

10. Abraham H. Maslow, 1954: *Motivation and Personality*, Harper & Row, New York.
11. Geert Hofstede, 1984: *Culture's Consequences*, Sage Publications.
12. Ibid.
13. Ibid.
14. Geert Hofstede, 1990: 'Marketing and culture', Working Paper 90-006, University of Limburg, Maastricht, The Netherlands. We are greatly indebted to Professor Geert Hofstede, for allowing us to draw heavily on this Working Paper.
15. Hofstede, 1984: op. cit.
16. Hofstede, 1990: op. cit.
17. Giep Franzen and Freek Holzhauer, 1989: *Brands*, BBDO College Editions.
18. M. Rokeach, 1973: *The Nature of Human Values*, The Free Press, New York.
19. Ibid.
20. Franzen and Holzhauer, 1989: op. cit.
21. Rokeach, 1973: op. cit.
22. L. R. Kahle and S. Goff Timmer, 1983: *A Theory and Method for Studying Values and Social Change: Adaptation to Life in America*, Praeger, New York.
23. L. R. Kahle, 1983: *Social Values and Social Changes: Adaptation to Life in America*, Praeger, New York.
24. Klaus G. Grunert, Susanne C. Grunert and Sharon E. Beatty, 1989: 'Cross-cultural research on consumer values', *Marketing and Research Today*, February.
25. Hofstede, 1990: op. cit.
26. *New York Times*, 21 July 1989.
27. Martha Farnsworth Riche, 1989: 'Psychographics for the 1990s', *American Demographics*, July.
28. 'New Vals 2 takes psychological route', *Advertising Age*, February 1989.
29. 'The VALS 2 segmentation system', Information to VALS Subscribers, SRI International, 333 Ravenswood Avenue, Menlo Park, CA 94025, USA.
30. *Advertising Age*, February 1989: op. cit.
31. Farnsworth Riche, 1989: op. cit.
32. Ibid.
33. ACE Brochure, 1989: published by RISC, Paris, France.
34. CCA Brochure, 1989: Paris, France.
35. Norbert Homma and Jorg Ueltzhoffer, 'The internationalisation of everyday-life research: markets and milieus', ESOMAR Conference, 'America, Japan and EC '92: The Prospects for Marketing, Advertising and Research', Venice, Italy, 18–20 June 1990.
36. Jacqueline Silver, 'Turning tables: America and Japan, the market opportunities for companies of the EC', ESOMAR Conference on 'America, Japan and EC '92; The Prospects for Marketing, Advertising and Research', Venice, Italy, 18–20 June 1990.
37. Kazuaki Ushikubo, 1986: 'A method of structure analysis for developing product concepts and its applications', *European Research*.
38. Henry A. Murray, 1938: *Explorations in Personality*, Oxford University Press, New York.
39. Robert Wilk, 'The new rich: a psychographic approach to marketing to the wealthy Japanese consumer', ESOMAR Conference on: 'America, Japan

and EC '92; The Prospects for Marketing, Advertising and Research', Venice, Italy, 18–20 June 1990.

40. Hiroe Suzuki, 'Japanese life-style, life models and applications to creative concepts', ESOMAR Conference on: 'America, Japan and EC '92; The Prospects for Marketing, Advertising and Research', Venice, Italy, 18–20 June 1990.

41. Victor Kiu, 'How advertising people in Asia interpret psychographic data', Adasia Conference, 18–23 February 1989, Lahore, Pakistan.

42. From findings of life-style research done by The Survey Research Group, kindly provided by Victor Kiu, Ogilvy & Mather, Singapore.

43. Ibid.

44. Ibid.

Part Two

The worldwide advertising mix

Chapter 6
Marketing communication worldwide

■ Introduction

This chapter deals with marketing communication and advertising worldwide. A good starting point is provided by three definitions from distinguished authors, most of them defining international advertising or marketing communication rather than advertising worldwide.

> International marketing communications is the implementation of advertising, sales promotion and public relations activities that support the sale of goods or services in more than one country.[1]

> International advertising is advertising, created at, co-ordinated or directed from one central point, for execution, with or without local adaptations, in a number of countries.[2]

> International advertising is advertising designed to promote the same product in different countries and cultures.[3]

The first two definitions are rather execution-oriented, and the second implies a centralized organization. The third implies a more or less standardized product.

In Chapter 1 (page 6) the differences between international, multinational and global or transnational marketing, were pointed out, and these also apply to advertising. Definitions can be related to these differences. On page 11 a definition of 'advertising worldwide' was given.

The objectives

The communication efforts of a business influence all aspects of communication by that enterprise, including the corporate image, the product or service which the enterprise provides, the corporate culture, the customer perception of the product or service, the shareholders' view on the way the enterprise is being managed.

The development of cross-border communications, global media and advanced telecommunications have reduced the significance of geographical borders. However, the effect on psychological or perceived borders is perhaps less well marked. Two neighbouring countries can be stranger to each other than two countries situated on opposite sides of the globe. The English may have more in common with the Australians than they have with the Germans or the French. This makes international communications very complicated.

Global media hold an attraction for business enterprises because enormous savings can be gained by executing a single worldwide marketing and advertising strategy. In addition there is also the advantage of developing worldwide brands with worldwide quality standards. Global or regional brands are becoming the norm for large companies.

Michael Dowdall, detergents coordinator for Unilever, states that of Unilever's brands 35 per cent are fully European, 50 per cent are potentially European and 15 per cent are national or even local.[4] The widespread drive to European marketing will lead to lower production costs for harmonized products. Greater production efficiency will make it possible to reduce consumer prices somewhat, leading to the acceleration and intensification of competition. In the detergents market European brands exist and will increasingly become the norm; European marketing is a stage in the process towards true global marketing.

To be successful in global terms, the core proposition must be universally convincing. This requires outstanding advertising skills. When investing for global strategies, it is important to realize that the development of global brands takes time, as does the development of communication strategies for marketing such brands. The concepts which are developed must not only cross borders; they must also endure for long periods of time.

When devising an international or worldwide operation with global advertising campaigns and standardized products, two basic factors must be considered: the relative advantages and disadvantages of *standardization and differentiation* for each country, and the relative advantages and disadvantages of *centralized and decentralized decision-making and implementation*.

For the organization which adopts a standardized approach, the chances of success depend on how culture-bound a product or service is, the buying-behaviour of consumers, the competition, and national laws and regulations. Attention must be focused on two central points:

1. *What is being sold and to whom is it being sold.*
   First the choice between global or local brands must be made. Then research is needed to show the most appropriate messages and concepts, which can be targeted at similarities between different cultures or at specific cultural elements.

2. *How to link strategy with execution.*
   Everyone with some experience in advertising has at some time seen a brilliant strategy being ruined because of bad execution or a brilliant execution saving a bad strategy. Gearing strategy to execution is even more necessary in international advertising than it is in national advertising. Some appeals can cross borders, but only when they have been devised in the right way.

The choice between standardization and differentiation is not clear cut, as was outlined in Chapter 3. Products often have to be adapted to particular markets in terms of design or use. Communication strategies and/or execution will have to be adapted to the cultural environment.

Within organizations, there is a tendency, especially in Europe, towards centralization and standardization: marketing strategies are centrally planned at headquarters, and the marketing and advertising staff travel through the world or within a region, supporting local managers and learning from them. In this type of organization local management must transmit information on local trends to head office.

The extent to which standardization and centralization occur depends on the nature of the product or service, the level of service needed, the product category (rapidly changing or stable). It varies, too, from one industry to another. The extent of standardization and centralization is, of course, closely related to the corporate and marketing strategies.

■ Communication planning and strategy worldwide

International strategy development and planning are no different in principle to the development and planning of national strategy. The differences lie in the environmental factors and in the organization itself. The most important task in planning international marketing communication is that of establishing priorities. No enterprise is capable of seizing all marketing opportunities in all countries simultaneously. The task when planning is to decide which opportunities to pursue at what time. For this purpose an accurate analysis of the selected geographical markets and market segments is needed, on which is based selection of the right product or brand and of the right messages for the most promising target groups.

There are four fundamental strategies for multinational or global marketing communications:

1. *Standardized brand/product and standardized communications.*

This strategy involves a worldwide brand name and a uniform communication strategy. Examples include IBM computers, cameras, wristwatches, pocket calculators, perfumes and credit cards such as American Express. This type of strategy is only possible for culture-free products. Although food and beverages are usually culture-bound, Coca-Cola and Pepsi-Cola have been rendered more or less culture-free by means of the communication strategy. These are worldwide products with centrally-produced advertising, and only small local adaptations.

2. *Standardized brand or product and locally-adapted communications.*

Here different communication strategies are used for the same product or brand. This is appropriate where, for example, a bicycle is used in one country for recreation but in another as the basic means of transport. Biscuits and cakes are eaten at different times in different cultures. One brand can serve for different occasions. A new brand extension, though connected with a global, universal brand, may need different strategies in different countries. Cherry Coke never had the same associations worldwide as Coca-Cola: Americans were used to the taste because they liked to mix cherry/lemonade with Coke. For Europeans, the taste was new.

3. *Locally-adapted product or brand and standardized communications.*

Here the same communication strategy is used worldwide, although there are product differences across countries. An example of this strategy is provided by Esso with its tiger-in-the-tank campaign, which remained uniform although the octane solution differed in many countries. Complete standardization is rarely possible, however, and Esso had to adapt the campaign for Thailand, where the tiger is not a symbol of strength.

Branded fashion clothing also fits this category. Companies like Levi's, Esprit, Benetton or Mexx do not communicate the product but the life-style which it implies. Here the communication is the driving force in creating the international brand.

4. *Locally-adapted product or brand and locally-adapted communications.*
This is where a local product has a local brand name and a local communication strategy. Greeting cards are a good example, as they differ according to the public holidays in each country. Clothing also often fits this category. Where there are many competitive global brands, it can be worthwhile to create national brands or maintain existing ones.

There are only a few really global brands, and their advertising is rarely completely standardized, owing to cultural differences and legislation. There are limited possibilities for marketing global, standardized brands with uniform communications. Developing uniform communication strategies will only be successful where needs, feelings and emotions are similar. Experts in worldwide communication must be able to uncover both the differences between cultures and the similarities. Those similarities are to be found in the following aspects:

1. Basic needs – physical or biological needs such as those arising from hunger or thirst.
2. Basic emotions.
3. Basic frames of mind – people in every culture have the need to categorize and evaluate information.

There are less similarities worldwide, however, in the following areas:

1. Products and services which satisfy basic needs.
2. The extent to which emotions are expressed.
3. Ways of evaluating information – there are considerable differences between East and West.

Successful standardized advertising is most likely to be found in the capital goods industries or in business-to-business communication, not in consumer advertising, unless there are small homogeneous target groups. Considerable similarities can be found in groups such as the world's rich, at whom brands such as Cartier or Mercedes are directed. There are a lot of similarities too in the business-to-business market, because industrial products are generally bought for the same reasons throughout the world.

Common values shift so fast, however, that it is very difficult to find consistent similarities. Continuous research on trends in values and life-styles is necessary. If the forthcoming pan-European market is seen to too great an extent as an opportunity for standardization, this may be dangerous, as wide cultural differences are to be found in Europe.

Advertising will have to take these differences into account while also trying to develop overall concepts with a more or less standard output.

Basic emotions may be universal, but people in different cultures have varying opinions on the display of emotions in public. This has important implications for execution. The 'Reach out and touch someone' campaign by AT&T is considered too sentimental in Europe. The emotional behaviour shown in American television commercials tends to look ridiculous to Europeans. One example is the AT&T commercial showing the relief felt by an American businessman when he finds a telephone in a European country, and the telephone operator answers in English!

The communication strategy and execution

In the case of a worldwide brand or a product which shares the same concept and strategy in several countries, there are three possibilities for the execution of worldwide advertising:

1. A uniform, standardized strategy and execution, which is not adapted to each country. An example is an English language TV commercial transmitted on a European satellite channel, which reaches all European countries, and in which the message is put across in easy to understand English with few words and no colloquialisms, relying heavily on the visual aspects of the message.
2. Formal adaptation of message content. In this case the presentation is the same everywhere, but the copy is translated.
3. Situational and cultural adaptation of the message content. An example is Shell's message 'Shell helps'. Shell is represented as a company which helps motorists. This can be presented in numerous ways. Small booklets containing suggestions were handed out to consumers, and the contents differed in each country. There are many possibilities using this type of adaptation, and the extent of adaptation can vary considerably.

■ Worldwide standardization or differentiation

The decision to use a standardized international campaign is usually based on cost and creative advantages, even when campaigns have to be adapted to the local situation. One of the creative advantages is that provided by an international quality standard. However, there are several basic conditions which must be met.

1. There must be a consistent marketing objective and a consistent strategy which supports the rest of the marketing mix. Standardization also implies that the benefit which the product or brand offers to the consumer, imparted through the communication, is more or less identical in every country. The brand or corporate image must be consistent in all countries. For this to be the case it is important that the product or company concerned is equally well known in each individual country and exists in a similar competitive environment.

2. For each target group in each country the product or brand benefit must be equally important and interesting enough to make them buy the product or take the brand into the 'evoked set'. The consumers' expectations regarding the product must be the same. One example where this applies is that of airlines: businessmen's expectations of airlines are virtually the same in all European countries. For other services or products, the ways in which consumers evaluate them can differ considerably. Green, Cunningham and Cunningham[5] did cross-cultural research into the extent to which consumers of different nationalities use the same criteria to evaluate soft drinks and toothpaste, questioning students in the United States, France, India and Brazil. It appeared that in the United States as compared with France and India, more value was attached to emotional and less to functional criteria than was the case in France or India. However, in Brazil, even more value was attached to emotional criteria than in the United States. Consequently it was not appropriate to use the same appeal in these countries.

3. A third basic condition is a transnational homogeneous target group. A uniform target group is vital because this group greatly influences the presentation of the product and co-determines the product benefit. Moreover, this group forms the basis for media selection in different countries.

4. A fourth condition is that the product must be in the same phase of the product life-cycle in all countries. A different strategy is necessary where a product is innovative and in the introduction phase than in a country in which the product is already in the growth phase. Similarly, a different strategy is necessary in a market where a brand is market leader than where it caters for a 'niche'.

Consequently, there are three basic conditions which make a standardized advertising strategy impossible:

1. A brand's advertising cannot be universal if various national markets are in different stages of maturity.

2. A brand's advertising cannot be universal if the idea depends on a large budget but some markets cannot support a large budget.
3. A brand's advertising cannot be universal if it defies local customs and regulations and ignores the efforts of the competition.[6]

Hite and Fraser[7] examined the international advertising strategies of a sample of successful US multinational corporations to determine the levels of standardization being utilized and to identify those factors which are important determinants of the transferability of advertising. In their introduction they refer to earlier studies which suggest that international advertising should be standardized whenever cultural, demographic, governmental, competitive and infrastructural barriers are surmountable. The sample used for this study consisted of 418 of the Fortune 500 business firms which conduct international trade. One hundred and fifty usable responses were generated. The majority of firms advertised internationally (66 per cent) and used a combination strategy, standardizing some portions of advertising while localizing advertising for certain foreign markets (54 per cent). Only 9 per cent reported using totally standardized advertising for all foreign markets. A total of 37 per cent reported using solely localized advertising. Most (77 per cent) strongly agreed that it is important to change the language to blend with local culture. Firms tended to agree that it is also important to change models, scenic backgrounds, and product attributes. The majority rated acceptance of trademarks/brand names as very important in assessing transferability of promotional campaigns. A corporation with a well-known and accepted brand name is more likely to be successful using greater levels of standardization than a firm without such acceptance and name recognition. Transferability of slogans, levels of education of consumers and the degree of nationalism in foreign markets were also considered important.[8]

Arguments for and against a standardized international framework

The arguments for a standardized international framework include the following:

1. Cost – the most important argument for standardization. Empirical research by Jürgen Althans in 1983 found that one in every two people interviewed proposed 'economies of scale' as a reason for the standardization of their advertising at European level.[9]
2. A uniform brand image and corporate image worldwide avoid

confusion in areas where media duplicate heavily or where people travel a lot.

3. The globalization of media.
4. Advantages to the organization in terms of simplified planning through uniform objectives, and simplified coordination and control.
5. Maximum use of good ideas and transmission of know-how within the business. Through a continuous exchange of ideas, international plans can be developed faster.
6. The tendency for international enterprises to be centrally managed.
7. Better use of management abilities and of resources.
8. Universal guidelines and quality standards.
9. Better access to the stored know-how and experience of other countries, and improved ways of identifying global possibilities and problems.

Arguments against a standardized international framework include the following:[10]

1. The heterogeneity of the countries concerned in terms of culture, mentality and product usage.
2. The 'not invented here' syndrome: each country's desire to create its own campaigns and to prove its own creativity. David Ogilvy often said that: 'Each campaign adopted and not developed in the home country undermines self respect'.
3. Differences in the media scene.
4. Obstacles such as regulations regarding the product and its use, or advertising laws.
5. The nature of the competition in different markets.
6. Where the product is at different stages of its life-cycle in different markets.
7. The danger of being regarded as a foreign enterprise.
8. Reduced economic advantages due to higher coordination costs.

When developing international strategies, there are a number of dangers which confront management and which affect the quality of the strategies devised. These include the following:

1. Disputes of competence. While developing international campaigns, it is important to ensure that the positions of local or national managers are not being undermined. Treating them as servants to whom the terms of a campaign can be dictated is a fatal error. It is better to involve them in the campaign development at an early stage. Their local experience and their specific knowledge

of the market must be used to the full, and their input is needed particularly during the development of the strategy.

2. Pragmatism during the development process. In seeking similarities between countries, objective differences may remain unobserved, either consciously or unconsciously, because of the wish to communicate as efficiently as possible. The danger also exists that priority is given to larger countries and that the planning and execution are mainly aimed at these.

3. Bland creative strategy and weak execution. If the advertising strategy is developed with the aim of serving many countries at the same time, this can weaken the strength of the concept. Searching for a common denominator for a campaign may automatically mean that specific aspects of the message, relevant to the benefit expected by the consumer, are left out. Trying to please everybody often results in boring the target group.

Trends for the future

The question for the future is whether the trend of standardization will continue or not.

The assumption that standardization will increase is based on the theory that populations are growing more similar. This may apply to certain aspects of life, for example increasing divorce rates or the decline of the nuclear family. Little thorough research has been done on growing similarities, however. Probably the world will not become more homogeneous, but there will be more and more homogeneous cross-cultural groups with similar needs, which can be approached in the same way.

The present mass markets are disappearing. Currently the most important trend is not the merging of markets but the fragmentation of existing structures. The mass public no longer exists. New products only succeed by resolute segmentation. The necessity for segmentation has grown so much that one can speak of the regionalizing or even individualizing of products. There will be an increasing decentralization of existing markets in the form of socio-demographic and psychological diversification. This view is closely related to John Naisbitt's concept of the 'multiple option society', a society with an endless variety of propositions and choice, which will become manifest in diversified sub-markets and market segments.[11]

Satellite television also has its limits. Uniform advertising at the European level gives uniform products a uniform image. However, there is a limited number of product categories for which cross-border communication is worthwhile: examples include oil companies, airlines, cameras and the all-pervasive Coca-Cola. The possibilities offered by communication satellites might only be relevant for a few products. Moreover, satellite television does not solve the problem of language barriers: in Europe 75 per cent of German businessmen and 52 per cent of Swedish businessmen do not speak English.

Furthermore, as a counter to common markets and cross-border satellite TV programmes, it is possible that nationalistic feelings will grow.

■ The globalization of the media and worldwide advertising

The limitations of satellite television were described in the last section. Indeed, the existence of satellite television is not essential in order to make standardized campaigns possible. In Europe all the national TV stations can be used, for example. This is more expensive than using satellite television, but it does allow quite a large European coverage to be built up. Because of competition from satellite TV, more governments now allow advertising on national TV channels. There are other means of communication available which can help project a global image. Sponsorship and outdoor advertising are both possibilities which are developing internationally.

Ultimately differences in local demand, usage patterns and attitudes place the greatest restrictions on standardization, also for media. Food, for instance, is considered to be the most culture-bound. Even in the case of Coca-Cola, the product has never had the same popularity in England as it enjoys in the United States, due to the fact that the English habitually drink more tea and coffee. It is useless to try to give a brand a global image when it appears that habits differ considerably.

One other consideration is that advertising messages must fit the context of the media for which they are intended ('media-*umfeld*') and must be adaptable to those media. A TV commercial with lengthy copy will be difficult to adapt: translation of an English text into French requires on average, a 15 per cent increase in time; if it is translated into German this figure rises to 50 per cent.

In devising a worldwide campaign these media differences must be taken into account from the very beginning. More and more advertisers are developing regional campaigns and reach specific target groups via international media. 'International media' are the media which reach across borders and which are aimed at international target groups such as businessmen, those with a cosmopolitan life-style and the very wealthy. These media play a useful role for a limited number of consumer articles, but are more effective with the business-to-business market and for corporate image advertising.

In worldwide advertising related to articles of daily consumption, the national media, plays a more important role, although here too it is sometimes supplemented by the international media. The next section provides a brief description of the types of media used in international media planning.

The international media

Newspapers

Newspapers are increasingly being printed in several regional centres, and copy is transmitted by satellite to the printers. This allows faster and more efficient distribution, and the latest news can be circulated rapidly. The result is enormous savings in both transport costs and time. Investment in new technology is worthwhile even if it gains only half an hour.

NRC/Handelsblad in Rotterdam is also printed in Zwolle in North-East Holland. The daily newspaper *Yoiyuri Shimbun* in Japan is printed simultaneously in many Japanese cities. This development applies not only to national but also to international newspapers. The *International Herald Tribune* is printed simultaneously in Paris, London, Zürich, Rome, Marseille, The Hague, Hong Kong, Singapore, Tokyo and Miami. The *Financial Times* is printed in London, Frankfurt, Roubaix and New York. The *Nikon Keizai Shimbun* is printed in Tokyo and European editions are printed simultaneously in Heerlen, Holland. The *Wall Street Journal* is not only printed in New York; European editions are printed in Heerlen and the *Asian Wall Street Journal* is printed in Hong Kong.

Magazines

Certain national weekly journals, as well as international journals such as *Newsweek*, *Time* and the *Economist*, carry advertisements which are aimed at international, regional or global target groups of a specific social class. The Atlantic edition of *Time*, serving Europe and the Middle East, is printed in Europe. Also suitable for international use are a number of women's magazines such as *Cosmopolitan, Harper's Bazaar,* magazines like *Playboy* and *Penthouse,* and special interest magazines.

These so-called international magazines share the same editorial formula and reach fairly homogeneous international target groups, but are published by different publishers in each country. They are not all offered to international advertisers on an international scale with international rating cards. However, this situation is gradually improving.

Professional and technical magazines

There is a tremendous growth of professional and technical magazines. In Europe alone there are 15,000 different titles, and the number increases yearly.

Cinema

Although the importance of this medium has decreased considerably in the Western world during the last decade, it is still very important in a number of countries, such as India. However, it is difficult to measure the audience because of the variation in cinemas and in the films which are shown alongside the commercials.

A number of successful global brands give substantial attention to cinema as a medium. The best example is the famous Coca-Cola film 'I'd love to teach the world to sing'.

Television

There are only a few markets left in which television is not available. However, the role of TV advertising differs in each country. In a number of countries TV advertising is still forbidden. The rapid development of satellite television has accelerated the use of television as advertising medium.

In Europe in 1989, satellite transmissions were still relayed via existing cable systems. The situation will change, however, when larger-capacity satellites become operational, allowing transmissions to be received via a simple and affordable dish antenna. Uncabled regions can then be reached.

Videotext

In many countries this system is still under development, but in some countries it is already operational. In France, Minitel, the world leader in videotext, offers 3000 different services to its subscribers, from horoscopes to daily shopping. These services are often supported by newspaper promotions. This medium offers interesting prospects for large retail organizations or stores such as Harrods in London which want to operate in countries apart from their own by means of telemarketing.

Radio

The availability of commercial radio varies considerably. In the United Kingdom commercial radio is regional; only the BBC, which does not allow advertising, can run a national radio station. Within Europe there is one international station, Radio Luxembourg, which reaches the whole of Europe and sends out commercial messages in several languages. Its actual audience, however, is not known.

Outdoor advertising and transport advertising

Outdoor advertising is used all over the world. In some developed countries it is somewhat less prevalent than elsewhere, but it is gaining importance in these countries. Measured advertising expenditures on outdoor media grew considerably between 1986 and 1988. In developing countries in particular large advertising hoardings are often one of the most important means of advertising. This is true for example in India or the People's Republic of China.

Folders

Folders are used everywhere. The quality of printing varies depending on the stage of development a country has reached.

Point-of-sale material

This kind of advertising material is very difficult to produce internationally. It must be adapted to local conditions, taking into account language, distribution networks and local regulations.

Direct mail

This is mainly a local technique. It is difficult to apply internationally, because postal services vary in quality in each country. Only in countries or regions with an efficient postal distribution system or in regions with strong centralized mail organizations can direct mail be successful. Credit card organizations in particular use this system internationally.

Trade fairs and exhibitions

Regional or international trade fairs and exhibitions can be very useful media for international communications. However, large costs are involved for the building of stands, the crew and communication around them. Governments, in order to promote exports, are sometimes willing to offer subsidies to enterprises which wish to participate in a large exhibition.

Sponsorship

Sponsorship of sports and arts events can be a useful international means of communication. Sponsorship of major events like the Olympic Games or international football matches gives access to a vast audience. However, it is very difficult to measure the effectiveness of such initiatives. Awareness of a brand name is only a worthwhile target if the brand name already has substance. Sponsorship works best when it is encompassed by a number of related activities.

Reach

There is, at present, hardly any multinational research on audience profiles and sizes. In European countries, for example, about seventeen different research systems are used, and their results are not comparable. There is a trend towards harmonization of research techniques, but this has still to come into operation. This problem will be discussed further in Chapter 8.

■ The organization of marketing communication: centralization versus decentralization

The decision to centralize or decentralize the development and execution of advertising strategy is directly connected to the decision about standardization or differentiation.

There is no single answer to the question of whether it is better to centralize or decentralize. The ultimate goal of the organization must be to combine the best of the two elements: first, the efficiency and the possibility of better control afforded by centralization, and second the flexibility and adaptability offered by decentralization.

Several factors influence the degree of centralization which is necessary or desirable. They are directly linked to the choice of a standardized or differentiated advertising approach. The similarities and differences in the marketing situation of enterprises in different countries play a key role when making decisions on centralization or decentralization.

Factors influencing the choice include the following:

1. The corporate and marketing objectives.
2. The uniformity of the product.
3. The appeal of the product or brand and the product benefit.
4. Legal restrictions.
5. Cultural aspects.
6. Socio-economic aspects.
7. The competitive situation

The objectives

Most enterprises which participate in international marketing also have transnational corporate objectives. When global objectives predominate over national objectives, the marketing function and the organization of communications will be centralized. When the emphasis lies on short-term profits which can be obtained in certain countries, they will be decentralized. Long-term objectives for regions or parts of the world will then be sacrificed in favour of local or national objectives.

Product uniformity

The more similarities there are in production in the different countries in which a company operates, the more reason there is for centralized management of marketing. Even such things as packaging or user manuals can be centrally produced. Typical 'supermarket' products ask for a uniform approach. The shelves of supermarkets in developed countries are looking more and more alike.

The product appeal

Whether it is sold nationally or internationally, mineral water from a particular source remains mineral water. However, buyers use this product for different reasons. Although the consumer profile in various countries seems to consist of the same socio-demographic and psychographic variables, the reasons for using the product are different in different cultures: French women drink mineral water to remain slim and German women drink it to remain healthy. When products are sold for varying reasons, it seems sensible to allow local management to have a say in marketing decisions.

Legal constraints

For products and industries where strict regulations apply, such as the pharmaceutical and medical industry, it is necessary to decentralize responsibility, as enormous mistakes can result from a uniform approach. Consumer products and brands whose sale depends largely on promotional activities and on the relation to distribution, as in the case of food brands, tend to encourage decentralization.

Culturally-determined appeals

The more a product appeals to local tastes, habits, uses and ideas, the more decentralization is necessary. With such products, particularly food, a middle-of-the-road strategy must be devised which runs between the two extremes of central and local decision-making. In strategy and process control, local input and decision-making have to be considered with regard to specific cultural elements for each country.

Socio-economic factors

When the acceptance of a product depends on the socio-economic development of a country or territory, data can be obtained which clusters countries according to income, level of education, percentage of people working in agriculture, etc. For each country, buying behaviour must be related to these data in order to establish how disposable income is spent.

The danger of centralized marketing communication is that market research data and culturally determined attitudes can be interpreted wrongly if the information is interpreted from the frame of reference of the central organization. When socio-economic factors are mixed with factors like status and life-style choices, decisions on what and how to sell are best taken by the local management.

When similar countries are clustered according to marketing criteria and not geographic criteria, marketing communication programmes can be developed for each cluster, based on the similarities between the countries it contains.

The competitive situation

The competitors can be multinationals operating worldwide, nationally-operating multinationals or local enterprises. Advertising efforts must be adapted to the activities of the competition. The media budget in particular must be adapted to match the media-effort of the competition in order to have a comparable share of voice. For example, in countries where television advertising is heavily used for some products, it will be necessary to follow that practice and adapt the budget for similar products.

Three types of organization

The degree to which companies centralize depends on the factors described above, the countries in which they operate and their corporate culture.

There are three main organizational types: completely centralized, completely decentralized and a mixture of the two.[12] These three types show the following characteristics and advantages.

Centralized

Decision-making is done at head office. The flow of information is from head office to subsidiaries. Marketing decisions are made centrally.

The advertising and sales promotion departments of the head office supply their services to national as well as international departments.

Advantages include coordination, control, the use of specialists' skills at head office and little duplication of work.

Decentralized

The local manager of each subsidiary is responsible for the marketing functions of product design, pricing, market research, distribution, customer service, positioning, packaging, advertising and sales promotion. Head Office provides only general guidelines.

Advantages include flexibility in being able to react to the market, local knowledge of consumer behaviour and correct cultural interpretation.

Organizations which include both aspects

An organizational structure which is well balanced between centralization and decentralization can work for medium-sized as well as large enterprises which operate worldwide on the basis of a regional approach.

The organization of small international businesses

Smaller businesses with marketing communication specialists operate well when there is a balance between central guidelines and local input, with the help of local advertising agencies. The advertising agencies have to manage international coordination. When a smaller company has international ambitions including a certain degree of standardization of communications, it is important to choose an agency which has a network of associates in different countries, otherwise standardization will not succeed.

■ The international advertising landscape

The marketing communication landscape worldwide has three main aspects: total expenditure for marketing communication, expenditure per capita, and distribution of expenses across the various media. Countries vary strongly in all these respects.

The most important development in the last decade has been the shift in attention from media advertising to expenditure on 'below the line' activities such as sales promotion, direct marketing and public relations. In 1980 the approximate relative allocations for media advertising and below the line activities were 60 per cent and 40 per cent respectively. By 1988 this situation was reversed in several countries, with expenditure on below the line activities amounting to 60 per cent of the total communication budget.

Advertising expenditure

Advertising expenditure varies by country not only as a total, but also as a percentage per capita of a country's gross national product (GNP).

Starch Inra Hooper Inc. publishes annually a report on *World*

Table 6.1 Total advertising expenditures of seventeen countries in US $ millions

Country	Total reported advertising expenditures, 1988, in US $ millions
United States	118,050.0
Japan	34,471.3
United Kingdom	12,076.0
West Germany	11,750.1
France	6,936.5
Canada	6,058.8
Spain	5,880.3
Italy	5,051.5
Australia	3,475.0
Brazil	2,795.6
Netherlands	2,562.5
Switzerland	1,972.9
Finland	1,765.6
South Korea	1,747.9
Sweden	1,494.0
Belgium	1,173.4
Taiwan	1,091.7

Source: World Advertising Expenditures, 23rd edition, 1989, Starch Inra Hooper in cooperation with the International Advertising Association.

Table 6.2 Nine countries with advertising expenditures between US $500 million and US $1 billion

Country	Total reported advertising expenditures, 1988, in US $ millions
Argentina	944.4
Denmark	791.9
Austria	762.7
Norway	761.9
Venezuela	632.1
Hong Kong	629.6
New Zealand	627.1
Puerto Rico	572.9
Israel	524.7

Source: World Advertising Expenditures, 1989.

Advertising Expenditures, in cooperation with the International Advertising Association. In the 1989 edition, comparable data are given on fifty-eight countries.[13] In 1988 the total advertising expenditure for the countries researched was approximately US $228 billion. The United States, with an expenditure of 118.05 billion dollars, spent about twice as much on advertising as the next four countries combined. Table 6.1 lists the seventeen top-spending countries. Each of these countries spent over US $1 billion on advertising in 1988 (see Table 6.1).

Total expenditures include all print, television, radio, cinema, outdoor, transit, direct advertising and miscellaneous expenditures reported. The nine countries shown in Table 6.2 spent between 500 million and one billion dollars on advertising in 1988.

Per capita advertising expenditures

On the whole, the largest per capita advertising expenditure is found in the more highly developed countries of the world. The lowest per capita expenditure is found in the developing countries.

Table 6.3 shows per capita advertising expenditure in 1988. This averaged US $82.35 for the fifty-eight countries covered in the report of 1989; a total of twenty countries spent more than US $100 per capita on advertising. Seven of these, the United States, Finland, Switzerland, Japan, Canada, the United Kingdom, and Australia, spent over two hundred dollars per capita.

Table 6.3 Total per capita advertising expenditures

Country	Total per capita advertising expenditures, 1988, in US $
United States	480.2
Finland	357.2
Switzerland	301.5
Japan	281.6
Canada	232.2
United Kingdom	211.8
Australia	210.6
West Germany	192.5
New Zealand	187.9
Norway	181.2
Sweden	178.8
Netherlands	173.7
Puerto Rico	169.7
Denmark	154.3
Spain	150.8
France	124.2
Belgium	119.0
Israel	118.1
Hong Kong	111.0
Austria	100.8

Source: World Advertising Expenditures, 1989.

Advertising expenditure as a percentage of GNP

Both Puerto Rico and the United States spent more than two per cent of their gross national product on advertising in 1988. Table 6.4 shows, in rank order, those countries with advertising expenditures exceeding one per cent of GNP.

In general, growth of advertising expenditure per capita is positively correlated to the growth of a country's GNP per capita. The higher the GNP per capita, the higher the advertising expenditure per capita. In countries with a high expenditure per capita, possibilities for growth are limited in comparison with countries where advertising expenditure is in a developing phase. In developed countries additional communication expenditure gives a marginal additional yield, since a large number of commercial messages are already directed at the consumer.

As well as providing a complete survey of all countries, the Starch

Table 6.4   Advertising expenditures as a percentage of
GNP

Country	Advertising expenditures as a percentage of GNP, 1988 %
Puerto Rico	3.0
United States	2.4
Finland	1.9
New Zealand	1.9
Spain	1.9
Australia	1.6
United Kingdom	1.6
Dominican Republic	1.4
Israel	1.3
Canada	1.3
Japan	1.3
Bolivia	1.3
Hong Kong	1.2
Switzerland	1.1
Netherlands	1.1
Jamaica	1.1
Costa Rica	1.1
Argentina	1.1
Colombia	1.1
South Korea	1.1

Source: World Advertising Expenditures, 1989.

Inra Hooper report also presents a survey of the differences in
expenditure for the various media. There are significant differences in
the use of the three most important media – press, television and radio.

■ International corporate, business-to-business and consumer brand advertising

This section will consider some basic differences between three
types of communication. Some examples of the differences have already
been given. It is a fact that, in business-to-business marketing, buying
behaviour shows more cross-border similarities than does general
consumer behaviour for products. The following sections summarize the
main differences between international corporate, business-to-business
and consumer brand advertising.

Corporate communications

The objective is to communicate the corporate image internationally. When an international company wishes to convey a worldwide image it makes relatively more use of the international media. Along with this, a relatively high emphasis is given to sponsorship and PR. Corporate communications are characterised by centralized decision-making; communication decisions are made at a higher level than the decisions regarding product marketing.

Business-to-business communications

Communication is aimed at specific target groups within a great variety of industries. Decision-making about communications is usually centralized. For the buyer, selection and decision processes are more alike in different countries than is the case with consumer behaviour.

A wide range of communication media are used, with less emphasis on television and more on professional magazines and direct marketing techniques. It is important to use networks of local agencies who are familiar with the local situation in each country. Alongside this, centrally organized image campaigns have a part to play too. Usually media budgets are relatively low, and this is why it is necessary to make use of special interest media.

Consumer brand advertising

Target groups: buyers, users, influencers of consumer products, brands and services, which are offered in several countries simultaneously.

There are culturally-defined differences in consumer behaviour, and communication is likely to be more locally determined, except where it concerns a standardized international brand for which central guidelines are provided. The accent is on the integration of mass media, sales promotion and marketing PR. The coordination of communication efforts and cooperation with international agencies can result in considerable organizational complexity.

Corporate and business-to-business advertising

The earlier part of this chapter was mainly concerned with

international aspects of consumer brand advertising. The discussion will now focus on corporate and business-to-business advertising.

International corporate advertising

The possible objectives of international corporate advertising include the following:

1. To increase awareness, in order to improve penetration and acceptance in new markets.
2. To re-position in relation to the competition.
3. To change an existing or negative image, to cultivate understanding, or to remove misunderstandings.
4. To add new dimensions to a corporate image.
5. To voice the enterprise's viewpoint on political and/or social matters (advocacy advertising).
6. To sponsor a social interest (public service advertising).

Changing a negative image into a positive one is the most difficult thing to do, but it is sometimes very necessary in order to be accepted in other countries. ITT had to counter a negative image in Europe during the 1970s because of its supposed involvement with the Chilean Government.

Advocacy advertising aimed at social issues is a typical North American phenomenon; in many countries it is considered to be irrelevant or even harmful. It is only possible openly to support a particular social viewpoint in one country at a time, and often it is not possible at all. For example, equal treatment of men and women in the work environment, subject of many campaigns, is not considered appropriate in many cultures. The main function of advertising is to help sell products or services, not to change society. If advertising tries to adopt this role, it may receive a lot of criticism. This is not the case with public service advertising (advertising for good causes), which is sponsored by the total advertising industry.

Building goodwill and a long-term image is particularly important for global marketing. A sound reputation is necessary in order to penetrate new markets. An enterprise must choose a specific image and then substantiate it. Whether 'technologically advanced', 'the best quality', 'the best service', 'leader in the field of design' or whatever.

Typically top management are involved in corporate communications. It is necessary constantly to research existing and changing images in different countries. The costs are high but affordable research is possible by joining an existing research scheme in various countries.

International business-to-business advertising

Cultural influences on the buying process are less where industrial products are concerned, so a standardized approach has more chance of succeeding here than is the case with consumer products or services.

In devising a campaign, it is best to avoid mentioning the country of origin, as the effect may be more negative than positive. It is important to pay attention to the internationally accepted use of language and tone of voice within the industry; this also counts for illustrations. The environment should be kept as neutral as possible.

Budgets are usually relatively lower than for consumer products, and both direct marketing techniques and trade journals are frequently used; unfortunately, there is a lack of adequate information on the circulation of such journals.

The following steps are recommended for industrial advertisers wishing to internationalize:

1. Start communicating with representatives, agents, distributors, wholesalers. Use sales incentives and information conveyed in catalogues, product information and product specifications.
2. Intensify contact with existing clients; this is usually done by direct mail.
3. Cultivate any prospects which are known. Use professional and management magazines and trade exhibitions. When potential clients are unknown, concentrate on professional journals.
4. Use corporate advertising for overall positioning.

It is important to choose an agency that understands business-to-business communication and, preferably, one which has associations with a network of agencies in other relevant countries. For media selection, international media agents can also be used. This is preferable when there is a relatively strong marketing communications department in the enterprise.

■ Summary

This chapter has covered the whole field of worldwide marketing communications: strategy and planning, the issue of standardization versus differentiation, developments in the media, and the issues of organization: centralization versus decentralization. The international media landscape has been sketched, showing the different characteristics of three types of international advertising: corporate, business-to business and consumer advertising.

Further chapters will cover these issues in more detail.

■ Notes and references

1. Robert F. Roth, 1982: *International Marketing Communications*, Crain Books.
2. Rein Rijkens and Gordon Miracle, 1986: *European Regulation of Advertising*, North-Holland.
3. William Wells, John Burnett and Sandra Moriarty, 1989: *Advertising, Principles and Practice*, Prentice Hall.
4. Michael Dowdall, 1989: 'The challenge of the single market for company strategy', *Admap*, June.
5. Robert T. Green, William Cunningham and Isabella Cunningham, 1975: 'The effectiveness of standardized global advertising', *Journal of Advertising*, 41.
6. Barbara Mueller, 1987: 'Reflections of culture: an analysis of Japanese and American advertising appeals', *Journal of Advertising Research*, June/July.
7. Robert E. Hite and Cynthia Fraser, 1988: 'International advertising strategies of multinational corporations', *Journal of Advertising Research*, August/September.
8. Ibid.
9. Jürgen Althans, 1983, as quoted in Thomas Tostmann, 1985: 'Mondiale reclame: feit or fictie', *Harvard Holland Review*, Autumn.
10. Hite and Fraser, 1988: op cit.
11. John Naisbitt, 1982: *Megatrends*, Warner Books, New York.
12. Thomas Tostmann, 1985: 'Mondiale reclame, feit or fictie', *Harvard Holland Review*, Autumn.
13. *World Advertising Expenditures*, 23rd edition, 1989, Starch Inra Hooper in cooperation with the International Advertising Association.

Chapter 7
Creative development and execution

■ Introduction

Chapter 6 considered the choice between standardized and differentiated advertising strategies, and touched on the planning and execution of advertising campaigns. A growing number of branded products and services is being advertised and purchased globally, for example Coca-Cola, McDonald's, American Express, Toyota, Mercedes, Hertz, Marlboro, IBM, Philips. Not all such products, however, are advertised by way of a universal approach. Companies and brands are global, communications technology is global and advertising agencies are global, but most consumers still have a local perspective. It is their own neighbourhoods which influence their needs and buying behaviour and how they perceive advertising. Products and services can be standardized to a considerable degree but, most of the time, advertising cannot. Advertising, to be effective, must derive from and be part of a culture, sharing the language and values of the target audience.[1] When a standardized strategy is planned, the creative execution is a major consideration. That is the subject of this chapter.

■ The creative aspects of standardization and differentiation

The days when a centralized or standardized approach could simply be rejected by the creative team are over. It is arguable that a differentiated approach may be better because it is directed at specific cultural situations and consumer behaviour. However, in the case of multinational campaigns this advantage only applies if it is possible to achieve a consistent quality of creative execution in all the countries concerned. Unfortunately this is not always the case. Furthermore, a differentiated approach is not always the most effective choice from a media and organizational point of view.

It is not simply a matter of choosing between a sparkling international creative strategy and execution which neglects local needs, motives and buying habits, or a local campaign which strongly relates to local buying motives, but is inferior in terms of professionalism. The problem should not be seen in black and white terms. The best aspects of the two approaches must be combined. In order to produce an effective cross-cultural campaign, which can be easily adapted to local circumstances, the international advertiser must have the necessary cultural and professional know-how. Even then the results may vary, as success is influenced by the advertising styles prevalent in each country.[2]

Some appeals work well in all countries, especially when they are executed professionally and in the right tone of voice. For some product categories a coordinated but multilocal approach is more desirable. However, a standardized approach with local adaptations will succeed more often than one might expect, and must be considered as a first option.

Markets and people show similarities. The first goal is to find those similarities. From these, a basic appeal must be determined. There are certain feelings which are universal, such as happiness, fun or experience with a product, and these can be used cross-culturally in formulating a concept. However, the execution must ensure that these concepts fit in with the needs, attitudes and tastes of each individual market. For example, attitudes towards toothpaste are different in many countries. The French are less worried about cavities than the Americans. As a result, the selling proposition for toothpaste may have to be adapted in these countries, using a dental health appeal for the United States and a cosmetic appeal for France. It is possible, though, to overcome these cultural differences through successful marketing. Colgate was able to sell the 'Oral Care' concept in France and many other countries where earlier the dental health appeal had failed. Marketing and advertising can change attitudes.

Even where a uniform appeal is possible, the creative execution must still take account of cultural differences. The execution of advertising has three basic aspects:

1. Analysis of the most important cultural aspects of the appeal in order to prevent problems at a later stage.
2. Research into which approaches can be used across borders, and which cannot
3. Ensuring that the creative execution is such that the costs of adaptation for different countries are not prohibitive.

Today global advertisers are able to select worldwide, universal desires, emotions, wants or values around which the brand personality is developed. The desire for soft drinks, sports shoes or chewing gum is similar, whatever the nationality of the teenager. Having done this the next and most important step is to monitor the brand image and all relevant communications continuously. The most successful global brands have used advertising to create a culture around the brand; this is how large brands Coca-Cola, Marlboro, Martini and Pepsi-Cola ('The Choice of a New Generation') developed. It is possible to give a brand a certain identity in several countries simultaneously. A brand can also be introduced in one country, and gradually extended to other countries – this is termed 'roll-out'. Timotei shampoo is a good example of this; it started in Finland, where it in fact failed. After a few years the same concept was used for the Swedish market, where it was a success. Using the same appeal, it later became successful in many countries all over the world. Marlboro was not initially a global brand. The cowboy idea was developed by Leo Burnett, and the concept was intended for a re-launch on the American market. Later, however, the same concept was used to build a global brand.

Developing a good central idea

A good idea can come from anywhere. It does not necessarily have to come from head office, or from the country with the largest market. The creative idea for 'Cup a Soup' came from the United States, while the idea for Impulse originated in South Africa. In the case of Unilever's 'Cup a Soup', after the original idea was devised, the positioning was done carefully country by country.

Good ideas can work in many countries. Lux is advertised in about one hundred countries using the same concept executed by the same film star. Impulse is advertised in about thirty-five countries using the same creative concept.

There are substantial long-term cost savings in avoiding 're-inventing the wheel'. The communication strategy does not automatically have to be changed to cross borders, but it must change when the market situation changes. There are many good central ideas which can cross borders as long as they are properly adapted to the specific semantics and cultural environment of a country.

Three ways of developing and executing international concepts

Some advertising professionals prefer to centralize the 'what' and decentralize the 'how'. Their argument is that although people are similar with respect to basic needs, since environmental factors differ so much in the various markets, concept development can be centralized, but execution must be done locally. In other words, one basic concept is worked out for each region. This is called guideline advertising or concept-cooperation. A stronger form of control is termed prototype advertising. The most centralized approach is export advertising. This uses a centrally developed and executed campaign, which is either left in the original language or adopted in translated form.

Adoption or export advertising

Export advertising is imposed on the world unadapted, or simply with the copy translated. This is the ultimate form of centralization. Export advertising in some cases can be used as a strategy. For example, a product to which the country of origin is important, like French perfume, can gain by leaving the French copy untranslated, because this helps create the image of a typical French product. If this approach is taken, everything must remain French, from the packaging to the atmosphere of the advertisement.

Prototype advertising

In this approach definite instructions are given, usually covering numerous aspects of the execution. Prototype advertising provides better control than concept cooperation or guideline advertising. A successful execution of prototype advertising depends on the quality of local (and international) management of both advertiser and agency, the strength of the central idea and the quality of media execution.

Concept cooperation or guideline advertising

This is a more flexible way of standardizing a campaign which has from the start been developed for use in several countries. Guidelines are provided on concept uniformity, but not necessarily on execution. The head office usually circulates the concept guidelines. Instructions are given on product positioning, brand personality, logo use, etc. Such instructions may be given in the form of video tapes as well as written instructions, to achieve consistency in the audio-visual aspects.

One danger with this method is that the individual advertising agencies may prefer to do things in their own way, rather than complying with the extended concept. If this is the case the results will not look alike. It is therefore desirable for the execution to be done by international advertising agencies which have offices in many countries and central account coordinators who can supervise the overall quality.

The use of handbooks or manuals

For prototype advertising, as well as concept cooperation, it is helpful to develop handbooks or manuals containing instructions and guidelines on house style, logo, the kind of illustrations to be used, typeface, etc., in order to safeguard unity and maintain continuity.

Decentralization sometimes works better

Depending on the objectives, decentralization sometimes works better. This is mostly true for products which require different strategies in each country or region. Furthermore decentralization may be preferred where centralization simply does not fit in with the management philosophy of a company. Honeywell was an example of this. It has used very diverse campaigns with local strategies and execution, with the result that quality differed considerably from country to country.

An example of a product which seems to require different strategies for each country or culture is soup, which is eaten for breakfast in Japan, but not in the United States or Western Europe. In practice it may be preferable to develop another brand which suits the proposition better so that there is still one strategy per brand.

Creative impediments to centralization

On the creative side there may be factors which get in the way of attempts at centralization. These can include the following:

1. In each country creative people like to prove themselves. When they are not given the opportunity to do this, even if they receive strong directives to the contrary, they may feel that their jobs are at stake. After all, they were employed to be original.
2. Advertising agencies can also be obstructive because adapting campaigns pays less than developing campaigns from scratch.
3. The advertising managers of subsidiary companies can impede progress. If, for example they are not convinced that the concept imposed by head office will help to win the desired profits. Moreover, they may resist being dictated to as they do not want to run the risk of seeing their authority decline.
4. The NIH ('Not Invented Here') syndrome: the idea that a product which was not developed locally will not work in that country. A more positive approach is to consider that NIH stands for 'Now Improved Here'.

■ National and international appeals

Searching for similarities in cultures and markets

When determining basic appeals or propositions, a distinction must be made between the proposition (or appeal) and the execution. If a proposition is 'pleasure' and the execution shows people having fun, both elements can involve culturally-determined ideas which hinder internationalization.

Mueller[3] has researched the differences in cultural content of advertisements in the United States and Japan in order to try to find out whether differences in the two cultures were reflected in the advertisements used. Her assumptions were that well-known cultural differences, for example the emphasis on individualism in the West and on group norms in the East, would be reflected in advertisements. This was found to be largely true, although the assumption that the traditional Japanese reverence for the group over the individual would be reflected in advertising was not borne out, as Japanese advertisers found it more profitable to stress the emerging individuality of the Eastern consumer than to uphold the slowly declining traditional group orientation. This shift to individuality in Japanese advertising is reflected in the greater usage of individual and independence appeals. Themes such as 'be more attractive than the others' and 'stand out from the rest' are becoming increasingly popular in Japan. ONIDA TV's claim is 'neighbour's envy, owner's pride'. This is not a purely Japanese development; people are becoming more individualistic in other Asian countries too, and this is reflected in advertising.

Japanese advertising, however, tends to be less direct when compared to Western styles of advertising. Eastern advertisements appeal much more to the consumer's emotional state and rely on building a suitable atmosphere. Hard-sell themes are a rarity in Japan and there is little comparative advertising, because of the Japanese reluctance to cause a competitor to lose face. Reverence for nature is shown in images of blue sea, blue skies, sunrises, sunsets and flowers.[4]

There is a significant difference between East and West in attitudes to the elderly and to tradition. More than one in ten Japanese advertisements surveyed stressed tradition or respect for the elder generation, while only a minimal number of American advertisements contained such appeals. The use of youthful or modernity appeals differed little in the two markets. Status appeals were used in almost twice as many Japanese as American advertisements. The use of product merit appeals is considerably higher in American than in Japanese advertisements. No major differences were found in the use of nature-oriented appeals, but there was one subtle difference, US advertisements in this category focus on natural as opposed to man-made goods, while Japanese advertisements emphasize the individual's relationship with nature.

There were also differences in the approach adopted to promoting high-, medium- and low-involvement products. For high-involvement products, relatively expensive, infrequently purchased items, the appeal most commonly used by Japanese advertisers is the status appeal. In the United States consumers of higher-priced items are much more interested in information on product characteristics, comparisons and endorsements by satisfied consumers. For products in the *medium-involvement category*, like cameras, television sets and watches, the product merit appeal is most commonly used in Japanese advertisements, closely followed by soft-sell appeals. In the United States the most popular form of appeal for medium-involvement products is the product merit appeal. For *low-involvement products* such as food and haircare, the Japanese use product merit appeals and, to a lesser extent, appeals based on oneness with nature, status and group consensus. US campaigns rely predominantly on product merit and to a lesser extent on oneness with nature and status. There are similarities in the promotion of food products in the two countries. In Japanese advertisements, appeals draw a connection between the product and the traditional way of life, while in the United States the wholesomeness of nature is emphasized.

Mueller's research thus confirmed the thesis that advertising tends to reflect the prevalent values of the culture in which it exists. Of particular interest was the fact that the differences observed were greater for high- and medium-involvement products than for low-involvement products.

Market conditions

The perception and rating of advertising are always embedded in a network of values specific to each individual culture. Culture influences strongly both perception and rating. Where the advertising is executed in the same way and based on similar concepts, the message may be accepted in one country but not in another. Factors which decide this are the cultural environment, familiarity with the product category, familiarity with the brand, and product involvement. Identical concepts will only have similar effects if the position of a brand in different markets and the markets themselves are comparable.

Munzinger[5] describes a study which looked at the effects of a commercial for an established chocolate bar brand in France and Germany. The successful English commercial was adapted for France and was successful; however, it did not achieve the same effect when adapted for Germany. The reason was that the product was already established in France, but not in Germany; the brand name did not as yet convey anything about content and values to the German consumer. Another example described by Munzinger is a case where a commercial had similar results internationally. This was another confectionery commercial using both a video clip and life-style concept aimed at young people, who in Europe are a homogeneous group as far as cultural and leisure-time habits are concerned. An identical execution used different languages in France and West Germany, and the test results were comparable. The commercial was tested in Germany in two versions, one with English text and one with German text. The English text produced better results.

Categories of products and services

Clearly standardized concepts are possible with certain target groups and in certain market conditions. In addition, some categories of products and types of services are better suited for international campaigns than others. The product categories and types of services which are best suited for international campaigns include luxury consumer articles, business-to-business products and services – industrial, scientific and technical – and corporate and financial campaigns. Campaigns focused on the agricultural market and the pharmaceutical or medical industry can also be international in some cases. In general, though, this is rare, because of national differences in legal restrictions and the level of technological development. Considerable changes in this area are, however, to be expected in Europe after 1992.

Universal themes and concepts

Since advertising for packaged consumer goods and consumer durables is often planned and executed separately for each country, it is important to seek appeals which are either universal or easily adaptable to most countries. Several universal concepts which do well internationally are outlined below.

Case histories

This concept is difficult to execute, but very worthwhile if it succeeds. It works particularly well when the product or the enterprise offers different solutions to problems in different countries. The 'cases' must include a mixture of nationalities, landscapes and environments. Examples of advertisers using this approach are Hoechst and ITT.

Improved quality or productivity

In the business-to-business market, improved productivity is one of the most widely-accepted international concepts. This can result from improved process control, lower costs or other factors. British Airways have used this approach successfully.

Basic everyday themes

Themes based on appeals such as motherhood, taste, heat, thirst, pride, love, youthful appearance or jealousy are universal.

New products or services

The universal interest in anything new is an element which international advertising can make good use of. When introducing new products into a market, a campaign based on the novelty element is extremely suitable, provided there is a market for the product concerned in the country where the campaign is being run.

Service to the customer

Particularly where industrial capital goods are concerned, service is of vital importance. This must be emphasized in the communication.

Special expertise offered by a company

The special skills of an enterprise, for example in technology, often provide the core of an international campaign. A campaign may also feature areas to which the company gives special attention, such as quality, customer service, special product applications or innovation. This works particularly well where existing customers are acquainted with only one aspect of the enterprise, and other aspects are not well known in the country concerned.

The 'made in' concept

This is a useful concept which offers several possible approaches. These include the following:

1. Appealing to national pride; for example, KLM's 'Fly Dutch' campaign took this approach.
2. Using stereotyped characteristics of another nationality; this can be done verbally as well as visually.
3. Emphasizing the specific expertise of a country; this was done by Audi with the slogan *'Vorsprung durch Technik'*.[6]

Life-style concepts

Well-defined life-style groups such as young people, sports fans, businessmen or the very rich, can be reached using the same concept and often the same execution too. Examples include Camel, Martini and Pepsi-Cola. The execution of this approach may need to be adapted for different regions or countries, but the concepts tend to have universal appeal.

Heroes

Heroes can be used to link a brand to a certain sport, type of music, or whatever appeals to the target group. There are, however, very few worldwide heroes. If this concept is used, the advertising may have to be adapted locally or regionally, changing the hero to suit different markets. Coca-Cola used this concept in its worldwide campaign featuring a sports hero who offers his shirt to a little boy in exchange for his bottle of Coke. Different sportsmen were used in different countries. The original US sportsman was 'Mean Joe Green'. For several countries like Brazil, Thailand, Mexico and Argentina a different sport and a different star were selected. The Ford Fiesta commercial featuring famous motor racers was shot in one European location, but ten different drivers of different nationalities took part so that the commercial could be adapted for each country.

Culture-bound themes and concepts

Not all concepts are equally useful internationally. Campaigns which are based on fundamentally culture-bound buying motives, for example, are difficult to adapt. Campaigns aimed at culture-bound values are also difficult to internationalize. A number of culture-bound themes and concepts are detailed below.

Personal ideas and opinions

Themes based on personal ideas and opinions are usually culture-bound. In some cases, although a theme could cross borders, the execution itself is culture-bound. Opinions differ considerably from country to country on what a beautiful baby looks like; therefore the presentation of, for example, baby food and nappies is decentralized. Views of feminine attractiveness also differ; in many countries a slim figure is considered attractive, while in others, including some African countries, a plump figure is preferable.

Customers and moral values

When moral values differ considerably in different countries, affecting how a product such as, say, sanitary towels can be presented, it is better to advertise on a local basis. Otherwise the adaptations required will be too great.

The same is true where customs are concerned, although there are always exceptions to the rule. DeBeers managed to make the idea of exchanging engagement rings acceptable in countries where it was not customary to do so.

Humour

Humour is strongly culture-bound and can rarely be internationalized. Colloquial humour in particular does not travel well, especially the successful use of British humour used in British TV-advertising, for which many awards are won.

Motivation

Motivations vary from country to country. A classic example is the convenience of household products. This concept works better in the United States than in many European countries where, traditionally, women spend more time on household chores and cooking. For example, the change in South Africa, where more white women are keeping their homes clean and do the daily chores will make a convenience appeal now more successful than it used to be.

Individuality and the role of the woman

Individualism and personal relationships differ greatly in different cultures. Individuality is an element which must be treated carefully where Asian and Islamic cultures are concerned. The role of women in advertising, too, must be dealt with very carefully whether women are being targeted, or men. In China models must be well-clad, as sexual overtones and emotional appeals are considered decadent. In Islamic countries women are not generally shown in advertisements. In some such countries, where religious fervour is lower, women are shown, but only in the traditional role of mother and carer, not in any individual role. Within Europe the acceptability of sexual overtones varies.

■ Development and organization of campaigns

This section will start by giving some examples of how successful campaigns have been developed and organized.

Pepsi-Cola

Pepsi-Cola uses a series of basic commercials to convey a central advertising theme. The concept is 'the Choice of a New Generation' showing young people having fun at a party, on the beach or in a futuristic environment. The essence of the idea is, that people who set trends and are both on the leading edge of contemporary society and also young at heart choose Pepsi. Another campaign, the 'Pepsi Challenge', comparing Pepsi with Coca-Cola, runs mainly in the United States, as the concept is not accepted worldwide, and comparative advertising is not allowed in many countries.

Basically the 'Pepsi Generation' campaign can be used worldwide, though in some countries for legal and political reasons the commercial has to be shot locally, and it sometimes has to be dubbed. In some countries changes had to be made for cultural reasons. For example, one commercial shows a crowded, hot beach; a van arrives and from it a loudspeaker appears, relaying the sounds of someone pouring a drink into a glass, ice tinkling, and loudly drinking it. The van, it seems, is selling Pepsi, and everyone rushes over; the seller asks: 'who's first?' This was adapted for the Middle East to show men on a college campus. Another commercial shows a beach with very hot sand, where people trying to buy Pepsi are dancing on their toes so as not to get their feet burned. This was changed to feature solely men wearing shirts for use in the Middle East.

Alongside this campaign, Pepsi runs a music marketing campaign using famous singers like Michael Jackson, Lionel Richie, Tina Turner and Madonna, all worldwide stars who represent the leading edge of society. For Latin America the singer Chayanne, who is better-known there, was featured. The Madonna commercial could not be shown in the United States after the release of her video, which was considered offensive in a religious sense. The commercial was based on the same song, so there was a danger of confusion. The Tina Turner commercial was adapted for a number of countries by having a local singer join her. In fact the commercial was produced in one location for maximum efficiency, with all the local singers gathered together in one place.

Impulse

For Impulse deodorant, a whole-body perfume spray, a single concept is used around the world in locally adapted variations. A television campaign has been developed around the introduction of Impulse in thirty-seven countries. The campaign is based on one simple and very international idea, that of a brief romantic encounter. However, a number of different versions were needed. The Malaysian market required a Malaysian film with Malaysian actors. People with darker complexions were needed for the Italian commercials than for the Northern European countries. Cultural adaptions were needed too. Some versions imply that the male lead, after hastily buying a bunch of flowers for a passing, sweet-smelling girl, will subsequently start a relationship with her. In an Islamic country like Malaysia, it is considered very unrefined for a girl to accept such advances. She may show only a flattered smile. The Malaysian version indicates clearly that the encounter is just a single episode. In several versions the boy, in his haste to buy a bunch of flowers for the girl, runs straight through a park. In some countries it is strictly forbidden to walk on public lawns; in their versions, the boy stays on the paths. In the versions designed for some Western countries the boy does not even pay for the flowers, but some cultures would reject impulsive behaviour of this kind. Alternative versions show him paying with a high-denomination bank-note, which would be unlikely to happen in real life.

Ola's Cornetto

Ola's Cornetto had enjoyed twenty years of success in Europe, but the 'continental' approach to communicating its message did not go down well in Great Britain. A special campaign based on Italian romantic opera was necessary to force a breakthrough.

Captain Birdseye fish fingers

One example of a campaign which has been adopted year after year by various countries, is the television campaign for Captain Birdseye fish fingers. Starting in 1967, this campaign appeared on television in many countries under the name of 'Captain Birdseye'. Except for some editing differences, the commercials were identical in each country and only had to be furnished with the country's own voices. However, in all offices of Lintas, the advertising agency, minor elements were added, changed or omitted. West Germany, for example put in a children's choir as a background to the captain's heavy voice, and this change was also used in the Netherlands.

Marlboro cigarettes

Marlboro serves as one of the most famous examples of a successful international campaign. Although the campaign was originally made for North America, it has been successfully used in Europe. It has a basic strong idea which is interwoven with the brand image. A whole world was created around the brand and the approach has been consistent worldwide. Each creative execution of the advertising concept is related to the brand personality. This brand personality is not linked to fashion trends, so the long-term positioning has strengthened the brand. Because of the consistency of all the visual elements, there is no confusion for the consumer, who sees Marlboro ads in different parts of the world. Almost anywhere in the world, if someone is shown a picture of a cowboy and asked what product comes to mind, the response will be 'Marlboro cigarettes', even if the brand name is nowhere to be found. The cowboy has become a universal symbol of the world's best selling cigarette. Yet even this universal appeal has been supplemented by market-specific promotions. The Marlboro Adventure Team competition was started in Germany in 1984, capitalizing on a German interest in aggressive American-style adventuring. Marlboro badminton competitions in Malaysia and Indonesia reflect the local enthusiasm for that sport. Men's championship tennis and horse races have been sponsored throughout Latin America, and polo in Argentina. Marlboro country music concerts are popular in the United States and Switzerland.[7]

Long-term strategy

Only a few trademarks have really succeeded in being made into global brands. Marlboro, Coca-Cola, Sony and Levi's have become more than brands; they have become universal symbols of life-styles, images and satisfactions in which consumers all over the world want to share. For this kind of long-term strategy, commitment is needed. Marlboro has used the same package for thirty-five years and the same country imagery for twenty-five years. Throughout this period one agency, Leo Burnett in Chicago, has always had worldwide responsibility for execution.[8]

■ Guidelines on execution

Some kinds of artwork are understood immediately. Others are not, because insufficient attention is given to ensuring that the execution, as well as the concept, is appropriate. Many blunders in showing the wrong attributes or gestures ('props') in advertising have been made in the past.

A blunder like showing French cheese together with a glass of foaming beer is easily understood, but there are more subtle differences. American creative directors, for example, believe that a man kissing a woman's hand expresses something typically European. They forget that this is only customary in a few areas of Europe. When a couple enters a restaurant, it is not strictly necessary that the woman goes first. In Japan this is considered improper. Other differences are even vaguer: American advertising as opposed to European advertising is often harder and more direct. Tips and guidelines can be given for developing a feeling for these kinds of differences. Research is always needed.

In this section a few guidelines relating to organization and creative execution will be presented.

Organization

The following steps will help when working out a good standardized, centralized campaign:

1. Develop a system within the company which stimulates participation by all subsidiaries in central strategy development.
2. Create formats (prototypes or guidelines) by means of which standardized strategies, concepts and artwork can be communicated to the subsidiaries.
3. Avoid the 'not invented here' response through good management. Local creative teams may not accept ideas from others unless motivated to do so. This is the responsibility of management.
4. Organize a quality control system and a warning system for use where a subsidiary deviates from the central guidelines.
5. Allow creative work to circulate among the subsidiaries and the advertising agencies. Hold regular meetings involving key people in the subsidiaries and people from the agencies to discuss progress.

6. If possible, develop more than one approach and a number of examples of layouts, posters, etc., in order to give the subsidiaries and agencies the chance to make a choice.
7. Pay attention to the fact that local agencies may feel threatened when confronted with a standardized approach. International agencies will not be so worried about this, but local cultural input is essential.

Guidelines for creative development and production

Associations

If using associations, check that they fit in with local culture. For example, if the association is with 'fresh milk', it is important to check whether people know what the freshness of milk means. In many countries people are not used to drinking fresh milk. Associations with nature, too, must be checked; snow is not familiar in every country, for example, while in others it may be surrounded by different associations.

Language

Translations can be dangerous. Words often have a special and distinctive local meaning. If the local subsidiary is not involved, terrible mistakes can result, such as referring to the baby's 'arse' instead of its 'buttocks'. The People's Republic of China is one country where translations are being done on the cheap without proper controls. In many English-language advertisements screened in China inappropriate words, selected from a dictionary, are used; for example 'gestation' may be used instead of 'pregnancy'.

Copy for another country must be written by a copywriter from that particular country. Writing in a particular language requires the writer to think in terms of that language and the related culture. When planning a campaign for several areas each with a different language, this must be taken into account from the very beginning. It is best to avoid playing with words and using colloquialisms, and to keep the message simple, short and direct. On the other hand, it is important not to make the message so bland that it becomes boring.

Graphic design

In graphic design the latest ideas should be used and the highest possible quality achieved. Quality sometimes appears to be higher in Europe than in the United States. It is vital to convince the production people in the subsidiaries of the importance of following the guidelines and to show them that in most cases they will be just as creative by doing a very good adaptation job than if they started from scratch themselves. The end result must have a consistent style and tone of voice.

Layouts

Layouts should be left as flexible as possible. A translated text can well be much longer than the original. It is important too to watch out for deviations from the various standard formats such as A4 in Europe. Good quality materials should be used for full colour printing, and differences in printing quality should be borne in mind.

Photography

In shooting photographs and film for international advertising, neutral models, backgrounds and settings must be used. If a specific national setting is used, this may have to be adapted for other national environments. Landscapes, buildings, traffic signs, etc., must all be neutral. Dutch, Danish and Belgian houses may look similar to the Japanese or Americans, but they look different to the Dutch, the Danish and the Belgians! As soon as they cross each other's borders, they feel they are in a foreign country, not only because of the language, but because of the landscape, houses and churches. It is preferable not to use on-camera sound, except when this is strictly necessary for each home market. Dubbing is expensive and gives an unnatural effect.

Production

The measurements of paste-ups for international media should be scrutinized very carefully. It is also important to select the best place to do the printing work – the best place is where printing costs, including transport costs, are lowest and the quality is highest. This might mean that the printing has to be done in several places. International media standards should be regularly reviewed, and quality should be strictly controlled.

■ Summary

This chapter has considered creative development and execution. Topics discussed included how to appeal to the similarities in people's needs and wants, which type of execution works and which does not, and the difficulties of ensuring high-quality execution. This latter aspect is connected to the organizational aspects to be described in the next chapter.

The creative team consists of the people whose empathy makes the campaign happen. The product can be global, the advertising strategy can be global, but the advertising expression must be local. Local specialists all contribute to building the global brand image. Creative people are rarely global people. They get their rewards locally from their peers, and have little motivation to become global, unless management motivates them, and makes the environment and the organization rewarding for them. Clients can play a role in this process too!

■ Notes and references

1. Philip Geier, 1986: 'Global products, localized messages', *Marketing Communications*, December 1986.
2. Uwe Munzinger, 'Ad∗Vantage/AC-T International Advertising Research Case Studies', ESOMAR seminar on International Marketing Research, 16–18 November 1988.
3. Barbara Mueller, 1987: 'Reflections of culture: an analysis of Japanese and American advertising appeals', *Journal of Advertising Research*, June/July.
4. Barbara Sundberg Baudot, 1989: *International Advertising Handbook: A User's Guide to Rules and Regulations*, Lexington Books.
5. Munzinger, 1988: op. cit.
6. G. Morello and E. Boerema, '"Made in" and communication: a case history of "Made in Italy", in the Netherlands', ESOMAR Conference, Netherlands, September 1989.
7. Hamish Maxwell, 1989: 'Harnessing the power of global brands', *International Advertiser*, May/June.
8. Morello and Boerema, 1989: op. cit.

Chapter 8
The media landscape worldwide and media planning for worldwide advertising

■ Introduction

> Just think of it, there were ten viewers at the resurrection, 460 at the opening night of *Hamlet*, thousands at the first performance of Beethoven's *Missa Solemnis*, and there will be 1.5 milliard people simultaneously looking and screaming at the world championship football in Italy.
>
> George Steiner to Hans Magnus Enzensberger[1]

The changes in media technology, the development of mass markets, the standardization of brands and the changing life-styles of consumers all have an impact on the development of media and media planning, and vice versa.

Global business is growing, local business is decreasing. The advertising function is changing worldwide and the media are changing too. The media have not simply adapted to developments in communication; they have been the power behind them. McLuhan wrote in 1964 that

> the owners of the media always endeavour to give the public what it wants, because they sense that their power is in the medium and not in the message or the program.[2]

Indeed, media-owners, together with global business, have set the pace for worldwide developments.

Media planning for world brands, products or services consequently has some particular characteristics. The principles of international media planning are no different to those of national media planning: the objective is to make advertising effective by ensuring that it reaches the right people with the right frequency in the right environment at the right price. Media support brands, and play a crucial function in the marketing and advertising process. Decisions on standardization or diversification of brands have consequences for media planning. Choices will have to be made between the efficiency of using international media and the effectiveness of 'narrowcasting', or using highly selective media for special target groups. The media environment is changing to meet consumer needs: there is both a broadening and a narrowing of focus, meeting both global and micro marketing tendencies.

International media planning involves planning for several markets or countries simultaneously, and media which cross borders are termed international media. International media planning is more complicated than local media planning because of the varied media situations in different parts of the world. Moreover, in many countries there is no adequate research on audiences, while in others this research is in an early stage of development. In general, research into international media is not well-developed and still relatively expensive.

Depending on the advertising strategy, there are two main approaches for international media planning:

1. An international advertising strategy using mostly international media, supplemented by national media where the international media do not give enough coverage.
2. A more or less standardized advertising campaign based on the various national plans using national media supplemented by the use of international media.

The choice is strongly influenced by the nature of organization and by the way in which advertising responsibilities are delegated, as well as by the target groups and the budget available. An international advertiser with specific, highly-qualified target groups will find it more efficient to concentrate on international publications than would be the case with mass consumer goods. The differences in relative importance of each market or country also influence the choice. The final determining factor is the question of whether the target group can be reached by the international media.

This chapter will begin by outlining the differences in the media landscape in various parts of the world, and will go on to cover international media research and international media planning and buying.

■ The media landscape worldwide

The media situation differs in each country, and in addition there are differences in the availability of media to advertisers. It is only recently that television has become available for advertising in many countries, and it is not yet available everywhere. In the developed countries the press is more developed than in underdeveloped countries. In the least developed countries print media are for the happy few, and international publications are often more important than national ones. In such countries radio, outdoor advertising and cinema are the most important advertising media. However, in many less developed countries television is the pre-eminent medium. Smaller countries have fewer regional TV and radio stations and regional newspapers than large countries. Countries with more than one language often have a greater variety of newspapers and magazines.

Major changes

Important technological developments in the field of television and telecommunications have important implications for the media situation worldwide. In the developed world there have recently been some major changes which are of specific importance for advertising and the media. These include deregulation, diversification and consolidation.[3]

Deregulation

Governments worldwide are reducing their role in business. One of the impacts for advertising is the growth of commercial TV and satellite broadcasting. In Eastern Europe the fall of communism has acted as a deregulatory force, while in Western Europe the abolition of trade barriers among EC member states in 1992 will have a deregulatory effect. In other parts of the world, more free trade zones are emerging.

Diversification

Companies such as Philip Morris, Nestlé and Pepsi-Cola are diversifying their business horizontally in order to complement and supplement their existing portfolios. The Pepsi-Cola company, for instance, owns fast food chains like Pizza Hut, Taco Bell and Kentucky Fried Chicken. Mergers result in the development of megabrands, with concentrated media buying capacity; this in turn influences media development.

Consolidation

This is the age of the 'media barons' – such as Murdoch, Berlusconi, Maxwell, Filipachi and Bertelsmann – who own many kinds of media worldwide and who therefore have their own grip on developments.

Implications

These forces have resulted in the developments and changes in media which affect media planning worldwide. These include the following:

1. The increasing importance of satellite television.
2. The growth in international newspapers and magazines.
3. The growth in international business publications.
4. The development of an increasing number of specialized international professional publications covering trade and technology.

■ The media situation in different countries

This section will provide an overview of the media situation in different parts of the world. It is impossible to give a complete or even a fully reliable overview, since data are not available for all countries, and what data there are soon become outdated. Furthermore, because databases and reports are based on data from different sources data are not always comparable.

Table 8.1 shows data on the same countries from two different sources. These, and other sources used in this chapter, are listed in the Appendix on page 257. Both sources are valuable databases and it is not our purpose to criticize them. However, they do demonstrate that any given data should be viewed in perspective. The main differences can undoubtedly be explained by the fact that one set of data is based only

Table 8.1 Comparison of data from two sources

	Euromonitor 1987 data	World Advertising Expenditures 1986 data
	Number of mainstream consumer publications	Number of consumer magazines
France	50	1,339
Greece	27	20
West Germany	41	424
	Number of daily newspapers	Number of daily newspapers
India	1,334	1,722
Hong Kong	60	58
Australia	62	54
Japan	125	3,593

Sources: Euromonitor, European and International Marketing Data and Statistics, 24th edition, 1988/1989
World Advertising Expenditures, Starch Inra Hooper in cooperation with the International Advertising Association, 21st edition, 1987.

on national newspapers while the other includes all regional dailies. In contrast to the figures quoted in both these sources, *Benn's Media Directory 1990* (see Appendix) lists approximately fifty-four daily newspapers for India. No strict definition is given for consumer magazines, either; one data set may include special interest magazines while the other is restricted to general interest magazines.

The same problems arise in the case of data on the GDP of countries, translated into income per capita. Where such data are quoted in this chapter, an attempt has been made to select the most reliable data available or those most closely related to each other. Further on in this chapter the feasibility of harmonizing research data for international advertising will be discussed.

The aim here is to give an impression of how countries differ. For this reason we selected the most appropriate data. Exact data on local media should be obtained locally. For practical reasons it is not possible to cover every country. The selected countries are a representative sample of nations.

A number of countries will be compared in terms of population, population density per square kilometre, number of households, number of persons per average household, literacy rate, languages spoken and per capita income in US $. Data will also be provided for the same regions to indicate expenditure on different types of media as a percentage of total media advertising expenditure. This information is drawn primarily from *World Advertising Expenditures* produced by Starch Inra Hooper in cooperation with the International Advertising Association (see Appendix). The data are for 1988. This report does not cover all the countries mentioned elsewhere in other tables, as the relevant data are not available.

For the same regions overviews are given of the media available. Data are drawn from various sources, and therefore there are slight differences in presentation. Numbers of print media were obtained mainly from *Benn's Media Directory 1990*. The number of daily newspapers may include national and regional newspapers. Magazines are divided into several categories – family and home, general interest, men's magazines and women's or fashion magazines. 'Executive media' refers to the media used by international advertisers, intended for business people or high-income groups. These media cover business, management, commercial and economic affairs, and Benn's 'Current affairs' category.

TV households are given in millions, along with percentage cable penetration, VCR penetration, percentage of homes with radio and numbers of cinema screens. Unfortunately such data were not available for all continents; while numbers of TV households are available for most regions, for some countries only numbers of televisions in use are available. The same is true for radio. Numbers of TV channels per country change too quickly to be worth including here.

Data on television was taken from *TBI's World Guide 1990*, which gives very recent data. Data on Asia was taken from Zenith's *Asia Pacific Market and MediaFact 1990*, which also gives data on radio households and cinema screens. For other continents the Euromonitor report *International Marketing Data and Statistics 1988/1989* was used, which only gives data on numbers of radio sets. Most of its data relate to 1986–1987.

Data on Eastern European countries is at the time of writing unlikely to be reliable, but in some cases whatever data are available have been included. For demographic data it is necessary to rely on information provided by former governments, which is politically influenced. Data on the media is limited to whatever specialist sources were able to obtain in previous years. The availability of data from Eastern Europe is expected to increase rapidly.

In practice, the international advertising professional will need to go into greater depth, and should consult the sources listed in the Appendix.

Europe

Table 8.2 gives demographic data on eighteen Western European countries and eight Eastern European countries. Table 8.3 gives advertising data for Europe in the form of a breakdown of total advertising expenditures across media types. These data show how countries differ. Countries which do not allow television advertising, or where television advertising is limited, such as Norway, Sweden, the Netherlands and Belgium, use mainly press advertising. Less developed countries like Turkey, Portugal and Greece, as well as countries with a well-developed commercial TV network, such as Italy, make relatively greater use of television as an advertising medium. There is a great variation in the use of cinema and of outdoor media, but both are of less significance than television and the press.

Table 8.4 shows the available media in twenty-five European countries.

Eastern Europe

The extraordinary events that took place in the second half of 1989 have brought Eastern Europe into the media limelight. As a result, analysis of the television market in these countries has proved valuable. For this reason additional data is provided on a few Eastern European countries.[4] It is important to remember that the accuracy of data may be questionable.

Czechoslovakia

West German and Austrian television are watched by 27 per cent of the population. Channels from other Eastern European countries are readily available, and 66 per cent of the population used to watch East German television, which will now include the former West German channels.

Hungary

Satellite television can be seen by two million people. Thirty to forty cable networks offer up to ten channels which include Czech, Russian and Austrian terrestrial channels as well as Sky, Superchannel, TV5, MTV Europe and 3Sat.

Table 8.2 Demographics of eighteen Western European countries and eight Eastern European countries

	Total population (millions)[a]	Total no. of households (millions)[b]	No. of persons per average household[b]	Literacy rate (%)[b]	Language[b]	Income per capita (US $)[c]	Population density per km² (thousands)[b]
Austria	7.5	2.8	2.5	98	German	18,530	90
Belgium	10.0	3.6	2.6	98	French/ Dutch	17,165	325
Denmark	5.1	2.2	2.2	99	Danish	22,360	119
Finland	5.0	2.0	2.3	99	Finnish	23,833	15
France	55.8	21.0	2.5	99	French	18,636	101
Germany (West)	60.1	26.0	2.2	99	German	21,805	246
Greece	10.0	3.4	2.3	95	Greek	5,475	76
Ireland	3.7	0.8	3.9	99	English	10,090	50
Italy	57.4	18.0	3.0	98	Italian	16,281	190
Luxembourg	0.4	0.1	2.7	100	German/ French	n.a.	140
Netherlands	14.7	5.6	2.5	98	Dutch	16,702	357
Norway	4.0	1.6	2.5	100	Norwegian	23,134	13
Portugal	10.2	3.3	3.0	80	Portuguese	4,377	112
Spain	39.8	14.3	2.6	97	Spanish	10,353	77

Table 8.2 (*continued*)

	Total population (millions)[a]	Total no. of households (millions)[b]	No. of persons per average household[b]	Literacy rate (%)[b]	Language[b]	Income per capita (US $)[c]	Population density per km² (thousands)[b]
Sweden	8.4	3.7	2.2	99	Swedish	22,568	19
Switzerland	6.5	2.7	2.3	100	German/ French/ Italian	28,228	158
Turkey	55.3	9.1	5.3	70	Turkish	1,101	64
United Kingdom	56.6	21.0	2.6	99	English	14,300	233
Bulgaria	9.0	2.9	2.9	95	Bulgarian	n.a.	81
Czechoslovakia	15.6	5.5	2.7	99	Czech	n.a.	122
Germany (East)	16.7	6.6	2.4	99	German	n.a.	154
Hungary	10.6	3.9	2.6	98	Hungarian	n.a.	114
Poland	38.4	12.2	2.9	98	Polish	n.a.	120
Romania	23.0	7.4	3.0	98	Romanian	n.a.	98
USSR	287.0	67.0	4.0	99	Russian	n.a.	13
Yugoslavia	23.7	7.2	3.0	90	Serbian/ Croatian	n.a.	91

Sources: (a) *TBI's World Guide 1990*; (b) National accounts of OECD countries, main economic indicators, July 1987, from Euromonitor, *European Marketing Data and Statistics 1988/1989*; (c) GDP per capita in US $ at current prices (1989), pre-publication of Zenith *European Market and MediaFact 1990*.

Table 8.3   Advertising expenditure by medium in fifteen European countries

	Total media 1988 (US $ millions)	Print % of total media	TV % of total media	Radio % of total media	Cinema % of total media	Outdoor/ transit % of total media
Austria	762.7	52.7	26.5	12.1	1.0	7.8
Belgium	804.3	69.2	15.5	1.3	2.1	11.9
Finland	1,511.4	84.2	11.5	2.2	0.1	2.0
France	6,936.5	55.6	24.6	7.2	0.9	11.8
Germany (West)	10,477.6	81.5	10.0	4.3	1.0	3.2
Greece	299.2	41.2	44.4	7.1	—	7.4
Ireland	233.9	51.9	31.3	9.3	—	7.6
Italy	5,051.5	43.4	47.8	3.5	0.2	5.1
Netherlands	2,562.5	77.0	10.0	1.6	0.2	11.1
Norway	791.9	94.7	1.0	1.0	1.1	2.2
Portugal	240.9	32.3	49.8	12.3	—	5.5
Spain	4,472.5	52.6	30.9	11.7	0.7	4.0
Sweden	1,494.0	95.9	—	—	0.6	3.5
Switzerland	1,972.9	80.2	6.7	1.4	1.0	10.8
United Kingdom	12,076.0	62.6	31.4	2.1	0.4	3.6

Source: World Advertising Expenditures, 1989.

Poland
The two state-owned channels accept commercials. Silvio Berlusconi's Fininvest has contracted to supply commercials and programmes. A cable system is being planned, which will reach 1.8 million homes. Twelve satellite channels will be subtitled or dubbed into Polish.

USSR
Advertising has been permitted since 1988 when 700 commercials were shown. Silvio Berlusconi's Publitalia is responsible for advertising sales, and some bartered programming takes place.

Yugoslavia
MTV and Superchannel are available in almost all the quarter of a million cabled households in the Belgrade area. CNN is arriving.

North America: United States and Canada

Table 8.5 gives demographic data. Table 8.6 shows advertising expenditure by medium and Table 8.7 the available media.

Table 8.4 Available media in twenty-five European countries

	Daily newspapers[a]	Consumer magazines[a]	Executive media[a]	TV households (millions)[b]	Cable penetration (%)[b]	VCR penetration (%)[b]	Homes with radio (%)[c]	Cinema screens[c]
Austria	19	37	16	2.8	18	37	98	431
Belgium	59	39	13	3.6	92	45	99	450
Bulgaria	13	4	1	2.2	0	5	n.a.	n.a.
Czechoslovakia	19	24	4	4.4	0	3	n.a.	n.a.
Denmark	11	43	15	2.2	30	40	99	308
Finland	56	43	19	1.8	30	47	96	343
France	80	74	14	20	1	45	99	3,565
Germany (East)	37	16	7	5.9	n.a.	n.a.	n.a.	n.a.
Germany (West)	174	106	31	24.3	34	52	98	3,203
Greece	117	51	22	3	67	40	93	480
Hungary	7	10	7	2.8	9	11	n.a.	n.a.
Ireland	4	25	19	1	44	30	98	149
Italy	71	64	19	19.7	0	20	93	3,794
Luxembourg	4	5	2	0.2	0	54	98	n.a.
Netherlands	32	43	19	5.5	90	46	99	457
Norway	59	25	20	2	0	50	95	312
Poland	3	19	2	8.5	0	11	n.a.	n.a.
Portugal	22	36	12	2.4	0	28	88	360
Spain	71	45	19	10.7	6	40	93	2,309
Sweden	82	40	15	3.1	22	46	96	110
Switzerland	58	51	16	2.3	68	48	93	389
Turkey	50	11	9	6	0	37	n.a.	1,000
United Kingdom	95	112	74	21	1	66	97	1,215
USSR	43	5	4	93.5	0	1	n.a.	n.a.
Yugoslavia	18	13	3	4	0	7	n.a.	n.a.

Sources: (a) Benn's Media Directory 1990; (b) TBI's World Guide 1990; (c) Euromonitor, *European Marketing Data and Statistics 1988/1989.*

Table 8.5 Demographic information on North America

	Total population (millions)[a]	No. of households (millions)[b]	Average household size[b]	Income per capita (US $)[a]	Literacy (%)[b]	Population density per 1 km²[b]	Language[b]
USA	247.5	88.1	2.5	16,444	99	70	English
Canada	25.3	8.9	2.4	14,120	98	8	English French

Sources: (a) TBI's World Guide 1990; (b) Euromonitor, International Marketing Data and Statistics 1988/1989.

Table 8.6 Advertising expenditure by medium in North America

	Total media 1988 (US $ millions)	Print % of total media	TV % of total media	Radio % of total media	Cinema % of total media	Outdoor/ transit % of total media
USA	79,598.0	56.6	32.3	9.8	—	1.3
Canada	4,587.0	54.2	22.1	12.1	—	11.7

Source: World Advertising Expenditures, 1989.

Asia and the Pacific region

Table 8.8 gives demographic information on sixteen countries. Table 8.9 gives a breakdown of advertising expenditure by medium, while Table 8.10 summarizes the media available.

Latin and Central America

Table 8.11 gives demographic information on fifteen countries. Table 8.12 shows a breakdown of advertising expenditure by medium, and Table 8.13 summarizes the media available.

Middle East and Africa

Table 8.14 gives demographic information on seventeen countries. Table 8.15 gives a breakdown of advertising expenditure by medium, and Table 8.16 summarizes the available media.

Table 8.7 Available media in North America

	Daily newspapers[c]	Consumer magazines[a]	Executive media[a]	TV households (millions)[b]	Cable penetration (%)[b]	VCR penetration (%)[b]	Radios in use (thousands)[c]	Cinema screens[c]
USA	1,687	177	87	90.4	69	58	500,000	16,032
Canada	112	49	34	9.4	55	65	21,931	860

Sources: (a) *Benn's Media Directory 1990*; (b) *TBI's World Guide 1990*; (c) Euromonitor, *International Marketing Data and Statistics 1988/89*.

Table 8.8 Demographic information on sixteen countries in Asia and the Pacific region

	Total population (millions)[a]	Total no. of households (millions)[b]	No. of persons per average household[b]	Language[b]	Literacy rate (%)[b]	Income per capita (US $)[c]	Population density per km² (thousands)[b]
Australia	16.1	5.7	3.0	English	99	16,177	6
China, People's Republic	1,000.0	290.5	2.2	Mandarin	65	438	n.a.
Hong Kong	6.0	1.3	3.9	Cantonese	77	10,922	14,717
India	833.4	125.1	5.7	Hindi English 14 others	41	328	652
Indonesia	187.7	40.9	n.a.	Bahasa Indonesian	67	497	230
Japan	123.2	40.1	3.2	Japanese	n.a.	21,902	849
Malaysia	16.9	1.3	3.4	Bahasa Malay Mandarin	70	2,166	136
Nepal	18.8	3.0	5.8	Nepali	21	n.a.	340
New Zealand	3.4	1.3	3.0	English	99	11,889	33
Pakistan	110.4	19.2	5.9	Urdu	26	349	365
Philippines	62.0	10.1	5.2	Filippino English	83	728	526
Singapore	2.7	9.8	5.9	Mandarin Malay	83	10,114	12,058
South Korea	45.2	5.5	4.7	Korean	88	4,987	1,180
Sri Lanka	17.5	3.0	5.1	Sinhalese Tamil	87	n.a.	690
Taiwan	20.3	4.5	4.5	Cantonese	88	7,324	n.a.
Thailand	55.0	11.3	5.2	Thai	n.a.	1,154	281

Sources: (a) TBI's *World Guide 1990*; (b) Euromonitor, *International Marketing Data and Statistics 1988* (data mainly from 1986); (c) Zenith, *Asia Pacific Market and MediaFact 1990*.

Table 8.9 Advertising expenditure by medium in thirteen Asian/Pacific countries

	Total media 1988 (US $ millions)	Print % of total media	TV % of total media	Radio % of total media	Cinema % of total media	Outdoor/ transit % of total media
Australia	3,475.0	49.8	33.1	8.8	1.4	6.9
China, People's Republic	353.0	46.1	20.7	5.4	0.2	27.7
Hong Kong	629.6	39.3	53.1	2.7	1.3	3.5
Indonesia	123.1	78.7	—	17.5	3.8	—
Japan	27,520.1	43.0	37.5	5.3	—	14.1
South Korea	1,641.1	44.0	37.0	4.3	0.4	14.3
Malaysia	207.1	50.9	41.0	1.5	—	6.6
New Zealand	600.9	51.5	31.4	13.4	0.9	2.7
Philippines	138.0	27.0	52.4	19.6	0.2	0.8
Singapore	202.5	58.7	32.4	4.0	0.6	4.3
Sri Lanka	17.8	59.6	16.9	11.8	—	11.2
Taiwan	982.9	53.7	36.1	6.2	0.5	3.3
Thailand	318.4	32.1	48.1	15.0	0.7	4.0

Source: World Advertising Expenditures, 1989.

Table 8.10 Available media in fourteen Asian/Pacific countries

	Daily newspapers[a]	Consumer magazines[a]	Executive media[a]	TV households (millions)[b]	Cable penetration (%)[c]	VCR penetration (%)[c]	Households with radio (millions)[b]	Cinema screens[b]
Australia	39	49	25	5.4	0	68	5.4	619
China, People's Republic	28	n.a.	n.a.	121	0	3	n.a.	152,000
Hong Kong	30	18	22	1.5	0	57	1.5	115
India	54	55	9	20	0	n.a.	60	10,500
Indonesia	49	16	7	14.7	0	20	14	1,654
Japan	111	99	32	40	12	79	40	1,912
Malaysia	33	7	4	2.6	0	48	2.5	232
New Zealand	12	31	14	1	0	60	1.1	154
Pakistan	12	45	14	1.6	0	n.a.	9.5	444
Philippines	20	26	1	5.5	0	18	8.8	935
Singapore	7	10	10	0.6	0	62	0.6	45
South Korea	18	3	4	10.6	0	26	11	640
Taiwan	26	2	6	4.8	0	21	5	500
Thailand	18	12	4	6.9	0	18	8.3	312

Sources: (a) Benn's Media Directory 1990; (b) Zenith, Asia Pacific Market & MediaFact 1990; (c) TBI's World Guide 1990.

Table 8.11 Demographic information on fifteen countries in Central and South America

	Total population (millions)[a]	Total no. of households (millions)[b]	No. of persons per average household[b]	Language[b]	Literacy rate (%)[b]	Income per capita (US $)[a]	Population density per km² (thousands)[b]
Argentina	33.0	8.8	3.5	Spanish	94	2,331	31
Bolivia	7.0	1.6	4.1	Spanish Quechua Aymara	63	536	17
Brazil	145.0	36.6	3.0	Portuguese	78	1,523	46
Chile	13.0	2.6	5.0	Spanish	91	1,950	44
Colombia	31.8	5.9	5.0	Spanish	85	1,112	72
Costa Rica	2.9	0.5	5.4	Spanish	93	1,584	150
Dominican Republic	7.3	1.6	4.0	Spanish	69	1,221	370
Ecuador	10.5	1.9	5.0	Spanish	80	1,299	48
El Salvador	5.5	1.1	5.0	Spanish	67	700	798
Guatemala	9.4	1.7	4.7	Spanish	55	1,240	219
Mexico	88.0	15.2	5.5	Spanish	90	2,082	117
Panama	2.0	0.4	5.0	Spanish	88	1,970	81
Peru	21.8	3.9	4.6	Spanish Quechua Aymara	82	940	45
Trinidad and Tobago	1.3	0.3	4.5	English	95	3,731	645
Venezuela	19.2	3.7	n.a.	Spanish	85	2,629	56

Sources: (a) *TBI's World Guide 1990;* (b) Euromonitor, *International Marketing Data and Statistics 1988* (data from 1986).

Table 8.12 Advertising expenditure by medium in fourteen Central and South American countries

	Total media 1988 (US $ millions)	Print % of total media	TV % of total media	Radio % of total media	Cinema % of total media	Outdoor/ transit % of total media
Argentina	776.7	41.7	29.3	10.5	4.0	14.5
Bolivia	53.2	28.9	41.9	15.4	12.6	1.1
Brazil	2,781.6	30.0	61.2	6.6	0.3	1.9
Colombia	421.1	22.4	61.3	16.3	—	—
Costa Rica	52.3	35.9	53.3	10.7	—	—
Dominican Republic	67.7	32.5	34.6	28.5	0.3	4.0
Ecuador	35.0	35.4	56.9	4.9	—	2.9
El Salvador	37.5	32.3	48.0	18.7	0.5	0.5
Guatemala	39.0	38.2	34.4	24.4	—	2.8
Jamaica	30.4	49.3	17.8	26.6	—	5.9
Mexico	490.3	17.2	67.7	10.1	—	5.1
Puerto Rico	572.9	34.9	57.7	5.8	0.5	1.1
Trinidad and Tobago	24.5	32.7	40.4	21.2	2.0	3.7
Venezuela	632.1	32.8	60.7	3.0	—	3.5

Source: World Advertising Expenditures, 1989.

Table 8.13 Available media in fifteen Central and South American countries

	Daily newspapers[a]	Consumer magazines[a]	Executive media[a]	TV households (millions)[b]	Cable penetration (%)[b]	VCR penetration (%)[b]	Radios in use (millions)[c]	Cinema screens[c]
Argentina	63	14	9	9.7	8	0	20	921
Bolivia	27	11	6	n.a.	0	0	3.7	225
Brazil	80	31	23	22.1	0	11	53	1,410
Chile	32	8	5	3.5	0	10	4	177
Colombia	28	7	8	4.5	5	18	4	586
Costa Rica	4	8	2	n.a.	30	10	0.2	104
Dominican Republic	4	5	4	n.a.	43	0	1	83
Ecuador	16	5	4	n.a.	0	17	2.7	185
El Salvador	5	—	1	n.a.	5	12	1.9	79
Guatemala	5	—	4	n.a.	9	13	0.4	135
Mexico	245	45	13	9.3	1	17	15	2,241
Panama	6	—	—	n.a.	3	28	0.4	22
Peru	42	2	7	1.3	0	24	4	425
Trinidad and Tobago	3	—	2	n.a.	0	0	0.4	91
Venezuela	21	20	9	3.2	2	29	7.3	437

Sources: (a) Benn's Media Directory 1990; (b) TBI's World Guide 1990; (c) Euromonitor, International Marketing Data & Statistics, 1988/1989.

Table 8.14 Demographic information on seventeen countries in the Middle East and Africa

	Total population (millions)[a]	Total no. of households (millions)[b]	No. of persons per average household[b]	Literacy rate (%)[b]	Language[b]	Income per capita (US $)[a]	Population density per km² (thousands)[b]
Bahrain	0.5	0.1	6.4	70	Arabic	11,900	2,039
Egypt	54.8	9.5	5.1	44	Arabic	760	136
Iran	51.0	6.5	5.0	37	Farsi	1,667	81
Iraq	17.6	2.5	5.3	89	Arabic	1,740	112
Israel	4.4	1.3	3.9	92	Hebrew	5,995	576
Jordan	3.0	0.7	4.4	65	Arabic	1,540	114
Kuwait	1.9	0.4	5.4	68	Arabic	13,890	324
Lebanon	2.8	0.8	3.5	n.a.	Arabic	1,150	739
Morocco	25.4	3.8	5.5	21	Arabic/ Berber	630	143
Nigeria	115	24.1	5.0	42	English/ Hausa/Igbo Yoruba	790	318
Oman	1.4	0.2	4.5	n.a.	Arabic	n.a.	18
Saudi Arabia	12.7	1.7	5.5	51	Arabic	11,500	17
South Africa	35.6	8.1	4.5	78	English/ Afrikaans	4,000	78
Syria	12.2	1.7	4.9	40	Arabic	1,570	177
Tunisia	7.9	1.5	4.5	51	Arabic/ French	1,163	125
UAE	1.4	0.2	5.8	54	Arabic	23,000	49
Zimbabwe	10.0	2.0	4.5	n.a.	English	275	70

Sources: (a) TBI's *World Guide 1990*, (b) Euromonitor, *International Marketing Data & Statistics 1988/1989.*

Table 8.15 Advertising expenditure by medium in twelve African and Middle Eastern countries

	Total media 1988 (US $ millions)	Print % of total media	TV % of total media	Radio % of total media	Cinema % of total media	Outdoor/transit % of total media
Bahrain	7.9	44.3	55.7	—	—	—
Cyprus	19.3	36.3	50.3	13.5	—	—
Israel	450.6	81.8	3.3	6.5	1.6	6.8
Jordan	4.7	53.2	48.9	—	—	—
Kenya	15.9	62.9	12.6	19.5	3.8	1.3
Kuwait	56.4	69.3	30.7	—	—	—
Oman	5.9	61.0	39.0	—	—	—
Qatar	4.3	37.2	62.8	—	—	—
Saudi Arabia	54.8	78.1	21.9	—	—	—
UAE	26.1	70.1	29.9	—	—	—
Zambia	8.1	88.9	7.4	3.7	—	—
Zimbabwe	23.1	63.6	19.9	11.3	2.6	2.2

Source: *World Advertising Expenditures*, 1989.

Table 8.16 Available media in seventeen African and Middle Eastern countries

	Daily newspapers[a]	Consumer magazines[a]	Executive media[a]	Television sets in use (thousands)[b]	Cable penetration (%)[c]	VCR penetration (%)[c]	Radios in use (thousands)[b]	Cinema screens[b]
Bahrain	4	8	6	170	0	6	225	10
Egypt	10	11	6	3,860	0	12	12,000	185
Iran	5	6	4	2,500	0	26	10,000	294
Iraq	6	4	4	900	0	37	3,000	84
Israel	27	13	11	1,100	0	53	2,000	214
Jordan	4	1	3	240	0	31	791	41
Kuwait	7	7	7	426	0	58	497	12
Lebanon	10	9	10	800	0	66	2,100	n.a.
Morocco	13	15	9	1,150	0	28	3,850	284
Nigeria	30	31	38	500	0	n.a.	8,100	240
Oman	3	4	4	90	0	28	800	12
Saudi Arabia	13	9	10	3,100	0	41	3,700	n.a.
Syria	10	10	4	600	0	0	2,500	140
South Africa	20	36	11	3,000	0	24	10,000	n.a.
Tunisia	4	10	9	400	0	13	1,550	56
UAE	7	11	12	130	0	63	350	74
Zimbabwe	3	15	7	120	0	34	375	32

Sources: (a) *Benn's Media Directory 1990;* (b) Euromonitor, *International Marketing Data & Statistics 1988/1989;* (c) *TBI's World Guide 1990.*

■ The international media

All media can be used for international campaigns. However, international media are those which cross national borders. There are different ways in which media cross borders.

Local television channels may be seen by people in other countries, for example French TV in Belgium, German TV in Switzerland and the BBC (UK) in many other countries in Europe. This is termed 'incidental spillover'. In contrast, some channels may be created with the objective of broadcasting across borders; usually one common language is adopted. For example, Superchannel and RTL in Europe broadcast in English. This is termed 'deliberate spillover'.

Language may be a reason why media cross borders. German magazines are also read in Switzerland and Austria, because of the common language. For specific, global target groups a number of magazines have been specially developed, mostly in English. Examples are *Newsweek* and *Time*.

The media business is changing. Satellite television offers growing possibilities. In Europe the Astra satellite offers a number of cross-border channels. Figure 8.1 shows the various Astra channels.

Although much cross-border programming is in the English language, there is a growing number of channels broadcasting in

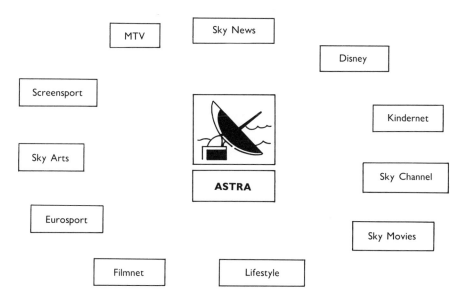

Figure 8.1 *Targeting via satellite in Europe (source: BBDO Worldwide)*

Figure 8.2 *Media diversification: the Rupert Murdoch Company (source: BBDO Worldwide)*

indigenous languages. The general increase in the number of TV channels implies a need for more programmes. This stimulates co-production, programme bartering, televising of sports events, albeit with higher rights fees, and the development of informal networks.

The effect of the media barons is to facilitate multi-media synergy and one-stop shopping, as well as multi-media discount opportunities.

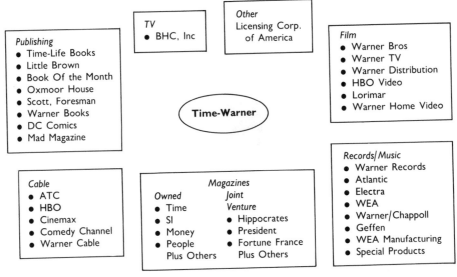

Figure 8.3 *Media diversification: Time-Warner (source: BBDO Worldwide)*

Some of the major media empires are:

Murdoch: television, newspapers, magazines.
Turner: cable television news on four continents.
Gannett: newspapers, outdoor media, radio, television.
Meredith: television, magazines, direct mail, real estate.
Time-Warner: television, cable, film, magazines.

Media diversification and the growth in satellite television are the major factors influencing media development. Figures 8.2 and 8.3 show the diversification of the Rupert Murdoch Company and Time-Warner.

This section will describe satellite TV, international executive media and international media addressed to specific life-style groups. First the development of cross-border TV and the international press will be considered.

International television

Cross-border TV is mostly of interest for international advertising where there is deliberate rather than incidental spillover. Incidental spillover only becomes interesting if large groups can be reached and if this can be measured; otherwise it is an inefficient method of media use. This spillover does not play an important role in most countries in the world.

In the USA there are hardly any cross-border channels; only in areas near the borders with Canada and Mexico might these play a role. In Europe, incidental spillover is used in some areas where neighbouring countries speak the same language.

Satellites have played a major role in creating deliberate spillover. In addition, the USA has a few television channels which can be seen all over the world, as other nations relay them by way of cable systems. An example is Cable News Network (CNN), which can be seen in over eighty countries. The fast-developing satellite system provides worldwide opportunities for advertisers, and Table 8.17 gives details of a number of satellites, with target groups and the number of channels, if available. Further information can be found in *TBI's World Guide 1990*.

In Europe developments in satellite transmission are greatly influencing international advertising practice and increasing its complexity. Direct To Home (DTH) transmission still plays a secondary role in most of Europe, as cable penetration is high in many countries, and terrestrial stations also provide a major input.

Technologically there are no limitations. The limitations result from language barriers and national legislation. Deregulation will gradually

Table 8.17   Satellites worldwide

Satellite name	Target	Number of channels
Europe		
ASTRA	West Europe	16
Eutelsat I and II	Full European coverage	17
Intelsat	West Europe	n.a.
TDF-1	Europe (mainly France)	5
Marco Polo	United Kingdom	n.a.
Olympus	Europe	6
Tele-X (DBS)	Scandinavia	n.a.
TV SAT I (DBS)	Germany	5
DFS Kopernikus	Germany	11
Asia		
AsiaSat I	China, Thailand, Pakistan, Korea, Hong Kong	24
Aussat A1, A2 (DBS)	Australia	15
Aussat A3	Australia, New Zealand/SW Pacific	n.a.
Gorizont	Asia	2
Insat (India)	n.a.	n.a.
Intelsat	Indian & Pacific Ocean regions	16
JC SAT	Japan	36
SCC:Superbird I and 2	Japan	20
Palapa	Indonesia, Thailand, Malaysia, Philippines, Hong Kong, Papua New Guinea	n.a.
Africa/Middle East/Southern Europe		
Arabsat	Arabia, Somalia, Sudan, Syria, Tunisia, Yemen, UAE	4
Intelsat: Ku band/ C band/V	Africa, Middle East, Southern Europe	n.a.
Intelsat I	Africa, Middle East, Southern Europe	n.a.
North America		
Satcom 3R	North America	23
Galaxy I	North America, Caribbean, Alaska, Hawaii	24
Satcom F4	North America	24
Telstar 301	North America	22
Galaxy 3	North America	20
Anik D1	Canada	18
Ku-band Satcom K2	North America	n.a.
Anik C-3	Canada	n.a.
ASC 1,2	USA	40
South America		
Brazilsat A1	Brazil	6
Brizalsat A2	Brazil	2
PAS-1	Latin America	36+
Intelsat (VAF 13 & 53)	Latin America	Spot beams to South America, Zone beams to Venezuela

Source: TBI's World Guide 1990.

remove legislative barriers, although many countries will try to protect their cultural heritage and may find new ways of preventing an influx of 'other-culture' programming. The language barriers will, for the time being, continue to impose limitations on the use of cross-border television and consequently advertising.

The language barrier

In countries like Sweden and the Netherlands there is a much larger audience for English language programmes than in countries like Germany and France, where there is less knowledge of English coupled with a wider choice of local channels. Lintas Worldwide research in Belgium, Germany, France, the Netherlands and Spain in 1987 showed that twice as many Dutch and Belgians understand English very well than nationals of the other three countries. In general a sound knowledge of the English language is restricted to younger or better educated people. This is true worldwide: it is the better educated people worldwide who can be reached by English language television and press. The Asian life-style research described in Chapter 5 confirms this.

Table 8.18 Understanding of English and German in Europe

	% Households per country which can understand:		Individuals in cabled households who understand English very or fairly well[b] (%)
	German (%)	English[a] (%)	
Austria	100	25	46
Belgium (Fr)	28	26	21
Belgium (Fl)	n.a.	n.a.	63
Denmark	48	51	76
Finland	5	25	47
Germany	100	30	37
Ireland	2	100	100
Netherlands	61	50	75
Norway	20	80	85
Sweden	20	80	71
Switzerland	81	26	30
UK	9	100	100

Sources: (a) Gallup 1985, quoted in *Marketing Week*, 4 November 1988; (b) PETAR 1989. Taken from Media Direction Nederland.

Table 8.18 shows understanding of German and English programmes for eleven European countries.

National laws

From the start of television in Europe there have been restrictions on commercial use in most countries. There is now a strong trend towards deregulation, with the result that Governments are permitting advertising on public television and, at the same time, an increasing number of commercial channels is emerging.

Satellite television in Europe

There have been dramatic structural changes in the broadcasting industries in most European countries since 1980.[5] The greatest increase in commercial television availability has occurred in Italy and France. In Italy in 1980 there were 27 commercial channels and approximately 350 private local channels, compared with 53 commercial channels and about 940 private local channels in 1988. France had two state-run commercial networks available in 1980 (TF1 and Antenne 2), increasing to six in 1988. Since 1980 new commercial channels have been launched in Spain, West Germany, the United Kingdom, Finland and the Netherlands. Denmark's first commercial channel was launched in 1987. In February 1989 the commercial channel VTM was launched in Belgium. In 1980 the maximum amount of advertising allowed each day on Europe's commercial channels was 897 minutes. This had increased to 1,963 minutes a day by 1988.[6] In general, the amount of time spent watching television differs substantially in each European country, as it is influenced by factors such as the quality of the programmes, the weather and scheduling. People in the United Kingdom spend more time watching television each day than people in other European countries. This cannot be ascribed entirely to the weather, as the Spanish come second! However, the Spanish spend less time reading newspapers than people in any other European country. It is in Switzerland, Scandinavia and Austria, where state-run public service networks have a comparatively low entertainment programme content, that the lowest level of viewing is observed.[7] Although satellite TV was perceived to offer opportunities for international advertising from the start, neither Sky Channel nor Super Channel was an unqualified success. Sky was driven from the European market place because of the failure of English language programmes to attract advertisers. In Europe it changed into Eurosport. In the United Kingdom and Ireland it reappeared as Sky One.

In comparison with US TV advertising expenditure – US $26 billion in 1988 for a population of 246 million – the European expenditure of US $12 billion for a population of 355 million seems meagre. The approaching European single market and new technological developments will influence this picture, and TV advertising expenditures in Europe have already increased relative to the United States. Another comparison with the United States shows that 117 million households in Europe watch an average of 16 hours' television per week against 33 hours per week in the United States.

Cable has been an indispensable means of bringing satellite TV into the living room. Cable will grow on a localized basis as new generation cable is laid. Depending on local willingness to accept international programmes on the cable networks, cable will be the major means of receiving satellite commercial television broadcasts. The anticipated growth of cable and satellite penetration in Europe is shown in Table 8.19. In 1989 viewing levels for satellite channels varied considerably in each country. The figures are by and large dependent

Table 8.19 European cable and satellite dish penetration: projection to the year 2000

Number of TV households: 131,280,560

	Cable connections (%)	Satellite penetration (%)	Combined penetration (%)
1988	12.3	0.1	12.4
1989	16.7	0.6	17.3
1990	19.3	1.2	20.5
1991	21.8	2.7	24.5
1992	24.8	4.2	28.9
1993	27.2	5.5	32.7
1994	30.0	6.8	36.8
1995	32.7	8.0	40.8
1996	35.2	9.0	44.2
1997	37.1	10.1	47.2
1998	39.2	11.3	50.4
1999	40.8	12.3	53.1
2000	42.2	13.4	55.5

Source: Television in Europe to the Year 2000, Saatchi & Saatchi Communications, February 1990.

upon the strength and number of the terrestrial channels in each country, the number of satellite channels available in the mother tongue and the understanding of foreign languages.

In 1989 the availability of cost-effective television advertising time throughout Europe is still highly restricted, but as audiences grow, further deregulation will take place. As satellite channels expand advertisers will exploit television increasingly. Over half of Europe's television households should be receiving multi-channel transmission by 2000.[8]

Table 8.20 shows the projected viewing shares of cable and satellite channels in Europe to the year 2000. These viewing shares reflect language barriers and other problems existing in 1989. Technological changes, better programming and changing levels of language knowledge are thought likely to increase viewing levels.

Data from the Pan-European Television Survey (PETAR) show the continuing importance of national terrestrial TV reception. The percentage shares of total viewing in cabled homes in eleven European countries, excluding France, are shown in Table 8.21.

Table 8.22 shows the percentages of mother tongue and foreign viewing.

Most of the satellite transmitters used prior to 1989 were low-powered. The strength of the transmitted signal was so weak that it had to be amplified on receipt to allow clear reception. A large dish antenna

Table 8.20   Viewing shares of cable and satellite channels in connected households %

	1989	1995	2000
Austria	39.3	50.4	59.0
Belgium	3.0	20.8	30.8
Denmark	16.0	27.0	30.0
Finland	9.7	29.2	38.6
France	3.4	21.4	31.8
Ireland	13.5	29.2	38.5
Netherlands	5.7	22.6	32.8
Norway	27.0	38.4	47.8
Portugal	1.0	21.6	31.7
Spain	4.2	22.6	32.7
Sweden	40.7	51.4	59.4
Switzerland	15.9	29.4	38.8
UK	25.1	36.4	45.7
W. Germany	37.3	48.0	57.4

Source: Television in Europe to the Year 2000, 1990.

Table 8.21 Percentage share of total viewing in cabled households in Europe

	% of homes receiving satellite via cable[a]	% share of total viewing in cabled homes:[b]			
		national terrestrial	spill in terrestrial	all terrestrial	satellite
Austria	18	45	16	61	39
Belgium	87	31	49	80	20
Denmark	27	73	11	84	16
Finland	25	88	2	90	10
Germany	20	61	2	63	37
Ireland	34	37	50	87	14
Netherlands	78	84	10	94	6
Norway	29	59	13	72	28
Sweden	22	58	1	59	41
Switzerland	69	40	44	84	16
UK	1	75	0	75	25

Sources: (a) Updated PETAR 1988; (b) PETAR 1988. Taken from Media Direction Nederland.
NB. Spill-in terrestrial includes all neighbouring countries' national services, in whatever way they are delivered.

Table 8.22 Percentage of mother-tongue and foreign language viewing in Europe

	Language	
	own	other
	% of all viewing	
Austria	99	1
Germany	99	1
Sweden[a]	85	15
Norway[a]	89	11
Denmark[a]	84	16
Ireland	100	—
UK	100	—
Netherlands	87	13
Belgium[b]	86	14
Finland	90	10
Switzerland[c]	94	6

Sources: (a) own language means Norwegian, Swedish or Danish; (b) Flemish and French language; (c) German and French together. Taken from PETAR 1989.

was required to pick up the signal. As this resulted in high costs, the existing cable infrastructure was used to provide central reception.

In 1990 there are four main satellites serving Europe: Intelsat, Kopernikus, Astra and Eutelsat. Intelsat and Kopernicus are low-powered satellites; programmes can only be received by large dish antennas; further transmission is by cable. Astra and Eutelsat are stronger transmitters, which allow households to receive signals directly via their own small dish antenna, with a diameter of around 60 centimetres. Future development of high-powered direct broadcast satellites will make reception even easier. These stronger satellites are of the DBS category (Direct Broadcast Satellite).

A few densely populated countries such as the Netherlands and Belgium have a high-level of cabling. In less densely populated areas cabling is relatively costly and relatively few houses are connected. High powered satellites will render cable unnecessary in these areas.

Figure 8.4 shows one of the strong 'footprints' of Astra. Astra is

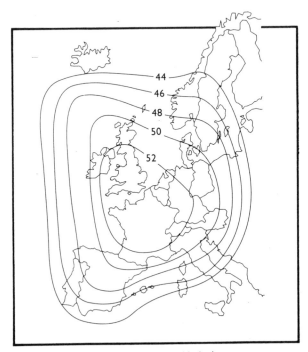

Vertical Polarization Mode I

Channel 4 Eurosport
Channel 8 Sky One
Channel 12 Sky News
Channel 16 Sky Movies

Figure 8.4 *Astra coverage*

the transmitter for twenty mainly English language channels. Eutelsat transmits twenty channels, the four Intelsat transponders twenty-one channels, and Kopernikus transmits eight channels.

It was always assumed that the launch of the Astra would galvanize the cross-border potential of television. So far this has not happened. The West German channels have not used the new satellite and the Astra channels are mostly targeted at the United Kingdom.

Instead, the satellite map has evolved into a series of supranational markets. Ironically, too, the relative success of international satellite channels has opened the gates to a flood of national television initiatives. However, the advent of high-powered satellites will open up possibilities for additional channels in areas such as Eastern Europe. The Direct Broadcast Satellite (DBS) system will lead to steady growth in satellite penetration in Europe, and this in turn will influence other developments such as cross-promotion – interaction between networks and retailers, linking programmes, advertising and in-store promotions.

Table 8.23   Audiences for major satellite channels in Europe

Channel	No. of countries reached*	Homes reached (millions)	Language	Satellite
Super Channel	14	17.9	English	Eutelsat
Eurosport	14	17.7	English	Astra
TV5	13	12.0	French	Eutelsat
MTV Europe	12	10.3	English	Astra
RTL Plus	7	9.9	German	Kopernikus
Sat 1	7	8.3	German	Kopernikus
3 Sat	3	6.8	German	Kopernikus
Pro 7/Eureka	1	6.0	German	Intelsat
Screensport	12	5.8	English	Astra
Lifestyle	12	5.8	English	Astra
Eins Plus	1	5.5	German	Kopernikus
Rai Uno	5	4.8	Italian	Eutelsat
BR3	1	4.6	German	Kopernikus
WDR3	1	4.6	German	Kopernikus
CNN	12	4.4	English	Intelsat
RTL4 Veronique	1	3.9	Dutch	Astra
TV3	3	2.1	Swedish	Astra
Galavision	1	0.9	English	Eutelsat

*Maximum of fourteen countries used.

Source: Television in Europe to the Year 2000, 1990.

This overview of satellite television in Europe concludes with Table 8.23, which shows the number of European satellite channels with over 900,000 homes connected.

CNN: the real global network

CNN was started in 1980 as a twenty-four-hour television news service in the United States. In 1990 it reached over 56 million US homes, more than 60 per cent of all TV households. CNN International is distributed via Intelsat and other systems to Europe, Australia and Asia. The North American satellite Galaxy covers Canada, the Caribbean and Central America. The Pan Am satellite covers South America. By the end of 1989 CNN was received in six million European homes.

Advertisers can select different options:

    USA: CNN – domestic feed
            CNN/Headline News (including Canada and the Caribbean)
    Asia: CNN – Japan, Thailand, Hong Kong
    Europe: CNN – Eurofeed, covers Europe, Middle East and Africa

Through a reciprocal arrangement with the China Central Television Network, CNN has two minutes per day available for sale in China.

By the start of 1990 CNN could offer a twenty-four-hour programming in over eighty countries worldwide. The objectives of CNN are to respond to today's life-styles, to cover worldwide news live, to stay with important stories as long as the situation demands and to cover developments in business. Sports, show business, fashion, travel, science and medical information round out the schedule. CNN offers different schedules for Asia and Europe. Although CNN International still has a predominantly American tone of voice and its reporters are mostly American, often talking about 'our country' or 'this country' without explaining where they are, there is an increasing tendency to give more news by 'locals'. CNN demonstrated its global importance in its coverage of the 1990 Gulf Crisis, and CNN is of interest to international advertisers, although many of the commercials shown are targeted at Americans living or travelling abroad, for example those for AT&T. Turner, the owner, obviously wants this channel to be global as its journalists/broadcasters get fined US $50 for every time they use the word 'foreign'.[9]

In Western Europe in 1989 CCN was available on 218 cable systems in 13 countries, with a total of 4,655,370 subscribers. Apart from this, CNN is available in the world's major hotels, businesses and government organizations and thus reaches those target groups who are

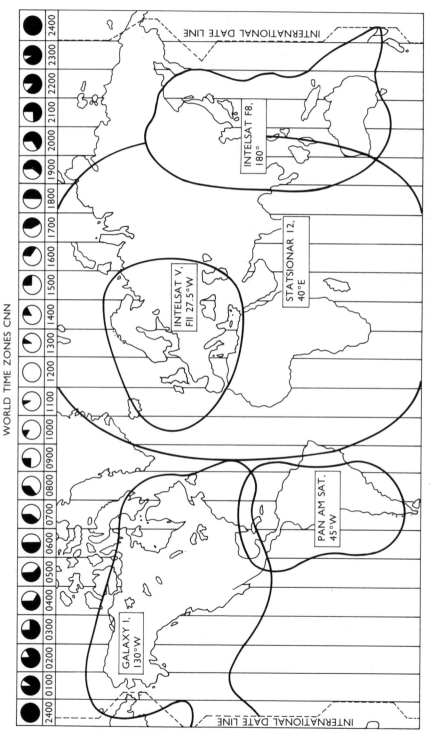

Figure 8.5 *CNN coverage worldwide via satellite (source: CNN International)*

frequent travellers or decision-makers in business or government. In Europe, CNN can be seen in 130,596 rooms in four- and five-star hotels. Figure 8.5 shows the extent of CNN satellite coverage.

International press media

International press media are based on the shared interests of specific groups, including international target groups such as business people, life-style groups and high-income groups. International media reaching these groups are mostly newspapers related to business, finance and management as well as the 'executive media' general interest magazines. Also relevant are inflight magazines and a few women's magazines. Most of these are in the English language and tend to be international editions of US publications. Until a few years ago these magazines were 'exported' to many other countries, in the original language; later, the formulae were sold to local publishers, resulting in multi-local magazines. For example, *Harper's Bazaar* has seven national editions. Women's titles such as *Elle, Cosmopolitan* and *Marie Claire* are now available in many markets. And Springer's *Auto Bild* motoring magazine format has established itself successfully in countries outside its native West Germany, such as Italy, France, Hungary, Norway and the United Kingdom. This process of exporting successful magazine formulae increased dramatically in the late 1980s, for a number of reasons:

1. Major publishers in European countries needed to tighten up their operation to counter the threat from Europe's deregulating TV industries.
2. Companies started to look outside their own borders when the launch of a new title became risky in a saturated domestic market.
3. Many publishers realized that similar life-styles and interests in the different European countries could be catered for using the same kind of publishing formula. The main benefit to publishers from launching multi-local editions is that costs are spread across several markets.

Table 8.24 shows a list of multi-local titles in Europe with the countries in which they are sold; many are also sold in other parts of the world. Originally these 'multi-local' publications were not so very international as far as the advertiser was concerned, as every local publisher offered local rate cards. In Europe this situation is rapidly changing: local publishers now mostly offer international rate cards.

The rapid growth in the internationalization of local media is exemplified by the growth of *Elle* worldwide. This is summarized in Table 8.25.

Table 8.26 lists the most important international business papers and their circulation. For most titles only circulation data are available. There are few reliable readership figures available.

Table 8.24   Multi-local titles in Europe

Women's magazines
Best/Femme Actuelle/Mizz	: France, Spain, United Kingdom
Cosmopolitan	: France, Germany, Greece, Italy, Netherlands, United Kingdom
Essentials	: France, Italy, Spain, United Kingdom
Harper's Bazaar	: France, Germany, Italy, United Kingdom, Netherlands
Hola!/Hello	: Spain, United Kingdom
House and Garden/Maison et Jardin/Casa Vogue	: France, Italy, United Kingdom
Marie Claire	: France, Greece, Italy, Portugal, Spain, Turkey, United Kingdom, Netherlands
Elle	: France, Germany, Greece, Italy, United Kingdom, Spain, Netherlands, Portugal, Sweden, Turkey
Prima	: France, Germany, United Kingdom
Vital	: France, Germany, Italy
Vogue	: France, Germany, Italy, Spain, United Kingdom

Men's magazines
Penthouse	: France, Germany, Netherlands, Spain, Turkey, United Kingdom
Playboy	: Greece, Germany, Italy, Netherlands, Spain, Turkey
Männer Vogue/L'Uomo Vogue	: France, Germany, Italy

General
Expression	: Belgium, France, Germany, Italy, United Kingdom, Netherlands, Spain, Switzerland
Geo	: France, Germany, Spain
Reader's Digest	: Belgium, Denmark, Finland, France, Germany, Italy, Netherlands, Norway, Portugal, Spain, Sweden, Switzerland, United Kingdom
Signature	: Austria, Belgium, France, Germany, Greece, Italy, Netherlands, United Kingdom

Other: Cars, Business
Auto Bild/Express	: France, Germany, Hungary, Italy, Netherlands, Norway, United Kingdom
Fortune	: France, Italy

Source: Media and Marketing Europe, March 1990.

Table 8.25 The internationalization of *Elle*

1945 – France
1968 – France, Japan
1985 – France, Japan, United Kingdom, United States
1988 – France, Japan, United Kingdom, United States, Italy, Spain, Hong Kong, Brazil,
        Sweden, Portugal, Germany, Greece, China.
1989 – France, Japan, United Kingdom, United States, Italy, Spain, Hong Kong, Brazil,
        Sweden, Portugal, Germany, Greece, China, Quebec, Holland.

Source: BBDO Worldwide.

Table 8.26 International business magazines

International business magazines	Circulation				
(W = Weekly; F = Fortnightly M = Monthly; B = Bi-monthly)	Europe	North America	(thousands) Asia and Pacific	Latin and Central America	Middle East and Africa
General					
National Geographic (M)	723	9,456	382	98	68
Newsweek (W)	248	3,288	319	55	—
Reader's Digest (M)	6,480	18,280	1,728	1,203	—
Time (W)	441	4,746	422	88	72
South (M)	9		24	12	27
Paris Match International (W)	136	35	2	3	34
Business					
Business Week (W)	46	900	28	21	7
The Economist (W)	159	161	41	6	13
Fortune (F)	51	672	40	12	8
Scientific American (M)	75	532	22	6	4
Newspapers (daily)					
Financial Times	257	21	9	1	3
International Herald Tribune	133	5	35	2	7
Wall Street Journal	44	1,836	37	—	—
USA Today	40	1,755	13	—	—
People's Daily	15	52	3,913*	13	7

* includes 3,850 in China

Source: 'Global media lineup', *Advertising Age*, 4 December 1989.

Inflight magazines

Air travel has increased tremendously during the last decade, and this increase is expected to continue. Growth is particularly strong among business people and high-income groups — target groups for luxury articles and professional services or products. Inflight magazines placed in the seat pockets of passenger airlines are a valuable medium for advertising products and services such as jewellery, personal computers, cars and luxury articles and also for duty-free goods such

Table 8.27 International inflight magazines

Airline	Title	Circulation (thousands)		Issues per year
Europe				
Aer Lingus (Ireland)	*Cara*	65		6
Air France	*Atlas*	300	(Low season)	8
		430	(High season)	4
Austrian Airlines	*Sky Lines*	150		6
UTA (France)	*Distance*	110		6
Alitalia	*Ulisse 2000*	180		12
British Airways	*Business Life*	250		6
British Airways	*High Life*	275		12
Finnair (Finland)	*Blue Wings*	92		6
Iberia (Spain)	*Ronda Iberia*	300		12
KLM (Netherlands)	*Holland Herald*	250		12
Lufthansa (Germany)	*Bordbuch*	570		6
Olympic (Greece)	*Motion*	150		4
Sabena (Belgium)	*Sphere*	78		12
SAS (Scandinavia)	*Scanorama*	150		8
		240	(High season)	2
Swissair	*Swissair Gazette*	490		12
TAP (Portugal)	*Atlantis*	110		6
Asia				
Qantas (Australia)	*Airways*	200		6
Cathay Pacific (Hong Kong)	*Discovery*	190		12
China Airlines (Taiwan)	*Dynasty*	60		12
Dragon Air (China)	*Golden Dragon*	30		6
Garuda (Indonesia)	*Garuda*	165		4
Philippine Airlines	*Mabuhay*	82		12
Korean Airlines	*Morning Calm*	175		12

Table 8.27 (*continued*)

Airline	Title	Circulation (thousands)	Issues per year
Air India	*Namaskaar*	50	6
Indian Airlines	*Swagat*	62	12
Air New Zealand	*Pacific Way*	90	11
Thai International	*Sawasdee*	100	12
Singapore Airlines	*Silver Kris*	220	12
Japan Airlines	*Winds*	280 (international)	12
		270 (domestic)	
Malaysian Airlines	*Wings of Gold*	80	12
Pakistan International Airlines	*Humsafar*	82	12
North America and Canada			
Pan American	*Pan Am Clipper*	350	12
United Airlines	*Vis a Vis*	450	12
Eastern Airlines	*Eastern Revue*	250	12
Northwest Orient	*Compass Reading*	500	12
TWA	*Ambassador*	360	12
Delta Airlines	*Sky*	410	12
American Airlines	*American Way*	280	24
Continental	*Continental E/W*	400	12
US Air (domestic)	*US Air Magazine*	475	12
Air Canada	*En Route*	145	12
Wardair Canadian Airlines	*Canadian Wardair*	150	12
South America			
Aerolineas Argentinas	*Revista Aerolineas*	50	4
Mexicana	*Caminos del Aire*	120	12
Avianca (Colombia)	*El mundo al vuelo*	70	12
Viasa (Venezuela)	*Aboard Viasa*	18	6
Varig (Brazil)	*Icaro*	130	12
Aeroperu (Peru)	*Tumi 2000*	20	6
Lineas Aereas de Chile	*Aboard Lanchile*	20	6
Middle East/Africa			
Cyprus Airways	*Sunjet*	50	4
Egyptair	*Horus*	100	4
El Al (Israel)	*El Al*	42	6
Gulf Air (Bahrain)	*Golden Falcon*	30	12
Kuwait Airways	*Sunrise*	45	6
Royal Jordanian	*Royal Wings*	50	4
Saudi Arabian Airlines	*Ahlan Wasahlan*	150	12
South African Airways	*Flying Springbok*	60	12
Tunis Air	*Marhaba*	200	1

Source: Inflight Media Marketing AG, Basel, Switzerland, 1990.

as cigarettes, perfumes and alcoholic beverages. Quality of editorial content, design and production has improved in recent years. A new addition to this medium is the inflight video.

Table 8.27 lists titles and circulation numbers of the inflight magazines produced by major international airlines as well as a few large domestic airlines who carry many international passengers.

Most of the inflight magazines are in the English language, but many airlines provide versions in other languages too. Further information on this, and on advertising rates can be obtained from IMM (see Appendix).

Outdoor media

Outdoor media can be an excellent means of advertising to international target groups with good planning and organization, since effective outdoor advertising is based largely on visual elements and rarely on copy. If the creative treatment is right, there is no translation problem. The disadvantages for international use lie in the different standard sizes and varying posting periods in different countries.

Posting periods in Europe range from seven days in France to ten or eleven days in Germany, fourteen days in the United Kingdom, fifteen days in Spain and a month in Italy.[10] However, outdoor advertising will develop into an international medium with the anticipated standardization of regulations and size. Specialized agencies are emerging which offer databases on various markets, coverage and frequency data, monitoring services and market research.

There are five main types of international outdoor advertising campaign. These are outlined below.

Posters and transport advertising

Posters can be displayed outdoors, on trains and in underground stations.

International airport advertising

Advertising in and outside major airport buildings reaches the same target groups as inflight media – business travellers and higher-income groups.

Outdoor Advertising International, an agency which specializes in international outdoor advertising and is represented in the United States and Canada, South America, Europe and Asia, offers a database with information on display positions and dimensions, rental costs, production and electrical requirements, passenger numbers and demographics, number of terminals and traffic flow in arrival, baggage and departure halls, piers, restaurants, lounges and duty free shops.

Advertising sites in large international airports are relatively expensive and the better positions are much in demand. One of the major companies specializing in airport advertising worldwide is Prime Sight.

Neon spectacular advertising

Neon spectaculars are seen in the busy centres of major cities, for example Piccadilly Circus in London, Times Square in New York and the Ginza in Tokyo, as well as in Paris, Moscow, Stockholm, Hong Kong, Rio de Janeiro and many other cities.

Hi-tech advertising displays

High-tech displays are similar to neon advertising, but more complicated, involving computer-driven matrices of light panels based on light bulbs or LED crystal displays. Advertisers frequently sponsor news bulletins, or weather, sport and financial results. This kind of advertising is also seen in the busy centres of major cities around the world.

Sports stadia advertising

Sports advertising and sports sponsorship is most effective when based on a year-round programme of sports events. Connecting the right outdoor advertising to the sponsored event worldwide can give greater leverage to any sponsorship campaign. Sponsorship will be discussed further in Chapter 9.

The growth of business travel across the world in particular will result in outdoor advertising in airports becoming an executive medium, as is the case with inflight media. Considering the two media together when planning a campaign will produce better results. Many types of display are possible, including revolving cylinders, vertical islands and two sheet posters. For example, Ackerley Airport Advertising Inc. offers displays such as these in more than 150 US airports.

■ Media research and research results

Availability of media research

In many countries in the world advertising space is bought and sold on the basis of circulation data, or on the basis of personal or business relationships between buyer and seller. This is changing. In the United States and Europe there is already a long history of press readership surveys, mostly done by the sellers of the media, and widely-used by media planners. In other parts of the world readership surveys are being set up.

Media research is a tool for media planning and for selling advertising space. Because research was done primarily by sellers of media to suit their own particular purposes, the fight for harmonization of research techniques in order to be able to compare data on different media within countries has been a long one. This is even more true as far as comparing media across national borders is concerned.

Comparing media research in different countries

When marketing world brands in local markets, comparison of media research data from different countries is necessary. This is, however, rarely possible. Most media research has been done by publishers or television corporations as a means of selling their own medium. In the past there was no reason to harmonize research techniques. Naturally, publishers prefer to pay for research which puts their media in a favourable light and which helps them sell space. Helping a 'harmonized international advertiser' has not been a high priority. [11] But advertisers are now demanding this help. [12] International advertisers require comparative research in order to define their markets in common terms across countries, evaluate each medium across countries and evaluate the effectiveness of different media.

The main problems of harmonization are the classification of consumers and the comparability of research techniques for establishing reach.

Socio-economic categories vary greatly across countries. There are great variations in the connection between income, life-style and interests. Age brackets vary in different national surveys (see Chapter 10). There are no standard definitions of 'businessmen', 'specialists' and 'affluent groups' or even standard age-groups. Even within countries, media surveys differ. In Spain the media survey EGM deals with individuals aged over 14, while ECOTEL works with individuals aged over 10 years.

Both definitions and sampling techniques vary across countries. Viewing and reading measurements differ: some surveys work with the interview system, others with meter systems. However, there is a trend towards harmonization here: most European markets have TV audience measurement systems using 'people meters'. Although there are a number of different people meters in use (for example, those produced by AGB, Telecontrol and Nielsen), they all do the same job and work in a similar way.

There are still a number of definitions, however, which are not standardized. Examples include sampling and panel control. In the absence of standardized practices it is difficult to assess whether a rating point means the same in all countries. One Gross Rating Point (GRP) equals 1 per cent of a specific audience, but this may be based on one of a number of audience measurement systems, for example diary, interview or meter. Furthermore audience definitions vary, for example in some countries viewers, in others guests and members of the family in-house and out-of-home are included. In Germany, for example, only German speakers are included, which rules out guest workers; in Spain, only telephone owners are included. As a result one GRP in the United Kingdom is not the same as one GRP in Portugal. Radio represents an even larger problem because radio listening is an even more diffuse concept than television viewing.

Press readership research also varies widely between countries. The main variations lie in the following areas:

1. How many titles are presented, rotation etc.
2. Use of filter questions.
3. Average issue readership questions.
4. Methodology (telephone, face-to-face).
5. Ad hoc versus continuous research.
6. Standardization of, for example, age and social class segments.
7. Recency and frequency questions.
8. Quality of reading questions.

The problems outlined so far lead to non-comparability of Gross Rating Points, which makes it difficult to assemble an international media plan and determine budgets for each country.

Media planners therefore develop 'standard GRPs'. BBDO Europe have developed a technique which gives a European Standard GRP (ESG). This method is based on rating definitions which are directly available in most of the countries involved and are as close to the advertising exposure as possible. For countries where the required rating definition is not available, a best estimate is provided based on the average between the existing method and the derived definition.

Knowing that it will take a long time to achieve real harmonization, media planners are increasingly using their knowledge of the differences in techniques to develop ways of comparing national media.

International media research

Research on international media is still very limited, mainly because of the high costs involved. However, most international media aim at specific target groups, which makes it possible to restrict the research to a part of the population.

International media research has been carried out in Europe for both television and for the business press. Research into the business press has also been done in Asia. Techniques and some of the results will be described for the following:

The Pan-European Television Audience Survey (PETAR);
The European Business Readership Survey (EBRS);
International Financial Management in Europe Survey (IFME);
The Pan European Survey (PES);
The International Air Travel Survey (IATS);
The Asian Businessman Readership Survey (ABRS);
Asian Profiles 5.

The Pan-European Television Audience Survey (PETAR)

PETAR, the Pan-European Television Audience Research organization, is an industry group composed of the BBC, CNN, IBA, MTV, McDonald's, RAI, Sky TV, Super Channel, W.H. Smith TV, RTL Plus and Sat 1. These television services are delivered via satellite to cabled households throughout Europe. Included in the study's measurement are cabled households in West Germany, the Netherlands, Belgium, Switzerland, Austria, Norway, Sweden, Denmark, Finland, Great Britain and Ireland. PETAR 1989 was the second consecutive study conducted by Research Services Ltd. of London, and the results from this study will be considered here. In 1990 the research agency Nielsen was awarded the contract for PETAR.

The 1989 PETAR study surveyed over 43 million individuals in eleven Northern European countries, capable of receiving commercial satellite television via cable. This represents the majority of the market but not its full extent, since France, Spain, Portugal, Greece, Italy and the Eastern European countries were not included. In a separate sample PETAR surveyed the direct-to-home (DTH) market in the United Kingdom. The survey also provided comprehensive details of respondents' sports and leisure activities, durables ownership and travel habits and a special booster sample of 356 businessmen across six countries.

The research population was defined as all individuals aged 4 and over living in households capable of receiving at least one commercial satellite station in the cabled areas of Austria, Belgium, Denmark, Finland, Ireland, Netherlands, Norway, Sweden, Switzerland, the United Kingdom and West Germany. A two-stage sampling procedure was used. First cabled areas were selected, and then diaries were placed with individuals in those areas. Recruited respondents were asked to record all their television viewing by quarter-hour time segments over a four-week period. All the available channels in each location were included in the diary, amounting to a total of 93 different channels. Replies were received from 4,206 individuals representing 89 per cent of all diaries placed. Fieldwork took place in April 1989.

The survey showed that since 1988 the potential audience for commercial satellite television had grown by 11 million, an increase of over 30 per cent. Over a four-week period, more than 32 million Europeans watched commercial satellite television, representing 75 per cent of all potential viewers. The average European viewer in a home receiving commercial satellite television watched 16 hours and 48 minutes of television a week, of which 20 per cent was spent watching commercial satellite television. Compared to 1988 time spent viewing commercial satellite television grew by 27 per cent, compared with a 1 per cent growth in overall viewing levels. The European viewer watched an average of 6.5 channels over a four-week period, over half of the average number of channels available. Germany was the largest single market for commercial satellite television, with the Netherlands second; both markets had over 10 million potential viewers. Table 8.28 summarizes the main results of PETAR 1989.

Since this research was conducted in 1989, the television situation has been changing continuously. Therefore, the reach figures given in Table 8.28 should be seen as an indication only. For actual media planning, the latest research data should be purchased.

The main changes which have taken place in 1989 and 1990 include the following:

1. Sky Channel, which until 1989 was available in several countries in Europe, remains available only in the United Kingdom and Ireland, including Sky Movies and Sky News

Table 8.28 PETAR 1989: main results

Four-week reach (%) by channel and country – Spring 1989

	Population (thousands)	CNN	MTV	RAI	RTL Plus	Sat I	SKY Channel	Super Channel
					All adults			
Total Network	36,300	0.6	8.3	3.2	32.6	32.4	22.2	19.6
Austria	1,074	—	—	—	83.7	81.5	17.2	10.8
Belgium	6,921	*	16.0	4.6	0.5	—	13.3	12.9
Denmark	1,224	2.7	13.3	—	16.6	7.7	18.6	30.2
Finland	848	0.3	10.1	—	—	—	47.3	33.9
Ireland	885	0.9	5.3	—	—	16.2	59.1	39.4
Netherlands	8,444	0.1	6.6	3.3	17.8	2.5	28.5	27.3
Norway	946	10.5	8.5	—	—	—	46.4	36.1
Sweden	1,027	5.1	32.1	—	—	—	34.2	39.1
Switzerland	3,567	—	0.9	15.7	0.7	47.9	31.5	25.5
United Kingdom	678	1.5	27.9	1.4	0.6	1.0	78.7	26.5
West Germany	10,506	0.1	3.7	—	87.2	84.2	8.5	8.3

* CCN was not included in Belgium

Source: Media Direction Nederland.

2. Sky Channel on the continent changed into Eurosport.
3. West Germany increased its use of RTL Plus and Sat 1.
4. In the Netherlands a new commercial cable station, RTL Veronique, was introduced. It later became RTL 4.
5. In Belgium VTM, a local, terrestrial commercial station, was introduced.

Initial findings from the PETAR 1990 survey announced by Nielsen in September 1990, indicate a dramatic increase in viewing figures for commercial satellite television. A daily audience of 24 million represents an increase of 103 per cent over 1989 levels. The share of total television audience held by commercial satellite television has increased from 20 per cent to 38 per cent.

European decision-maker surveys

The average European executive is male, over twenty-five, earns an average income of US $3,500 a month, works in industry or in professional services, has a university or college degree and plays a role in decision-making regarding important business purchases. He is a frequent traveller both privately and on business, uses one or more credit cards, rents cars and owns at least one in the upper middle or higher bracket, possesses all the usual home appliances and other durables, smokes and drinks but also practises sports actively. Many advertisers want to reach this type of executive, and there are many publishers producing business magazines aimed at this target group. This is the reason for the existence of several European multi-media business surveys. They are not comparable, but sometimes they can be used to supplement one another. Definitions of population differ. For example, the population for the Pan-European Survey (PES) consists of 'high status professional and executive men and women', providing a broad coverage of senior decision-makers. The European Businessman Readership Survey (EBRS) considers only top executives.[13] Short descriptions of the various surveys will be given below to provide a general impression. Readers seeking the latest results should contact the sponsoring publications or research agencies, which are listed in the Appendix. All the surveys are repeated at regular intervals.

The European Businessman Readership Survey (EBRS)

This survey was carried out in 1989 and was financed by twenty-four business publications, and covering seventeen European countries. The population consisted of heads of specified job functions in medium-sized and large industrial and commercial establishments, a total of 249,942 people. The sample consisted of 9,812 individuals in the EC countries plus Sweden, Norway, Finland, Switzerland and Austria. The survey is conducted approximately every three years, and covers 243 titles. The main interest lies in decisions related to work, such as business travel, car rental and use of credit cards. The research agency conducting the survey is Research Services Ltd in the United Kingdom. Table 8.29 summarizes the main findings of EBRS in 1989.

International Financial Managers in Europe Survey (IFM)

This survey was carried out in 1989 and sponsored by five financial publications covering fifteen European countries. The population consisted of international financial managers from Europe's 15,000 largest companies all with a turnover of at least US $325 million. The sample consisted of all relevant employees in 3,004 companies in Austria, Belgium and Luxembourg, Denmark, Finland, France, Germany, Ireland, Italy, Netherlands, Norway, Portugal, Spain, Sweden, Switzerland and the United Kingdom.

The survey is conducted approximately every three to four years and covers seventy-nine titles. The main objective is to obtain information on media use by top financial decision-makers in

Table 8.29 Main findings of EBRS 1989

Title	Reach (thousands)	Reach (%)
Financial Times	49.4	20
Frankfurter Allgemeine Zeitung	38.8	16
Le Monde	18.9	8
The Times	16.2	7
International Herald Tribune	10.7	4
Wall Street Journal Europe	10.6	4
USA Today	3.9	2
The Economist	28.6	11
L'Express	25.1	10
Business Week	23.6	9
Time	21.7	9
Le Point	18.2	7
Newsweek	16.0	6
L'Expansion	26.3	11
Fortune	17.0	7
International Management	18.8	8
Euromoney	10.9	4
Institutional Investor	9.6	4
Scientific American	4.8	2
Harvard Business Review	23.0	9

Source: The European Businessman Readership Survey 1989, Research Services Ltd.

international industry and services. The survey is conducted by Research Services Ltd in the United Kingdom.

Table 8.30 summarizes the main findings of the 1989 survey.

The Pan-European Survey (PES)

This survey was carried out in 1988 and covered thirteen European countries. It was guaranteed by five international business publications along with Research Services Ltd. The population consisted of men and women of high status living in good residential areas in thirteen European countries. This represented 5,371,000 top executive men and women. Economically active men and women aged 25–74 were eligible if they had achieved high status through their occupation and level of personal income or through educational achievement. Eligible men and women were defined as those living in good residential areas, in turn defined as those areas within each country in which 60 per cent of all men meeting the status criteria lived. In each country fewer than one in

Table 8.30   Main findings of IFME 1989

Title	Reach (thousands)	Reach of financial management (%)
Financial Times	1.5	50
Wall Street Journal Europe	0.5	17
International Herald Tribune	0.2	8
The Economist	1.0	33
Business Week	0.6	18
Time	0.3	9
Newsweek	0.2	8
Fortune International	0.4	14
Euromoney	1.0	34
Institutional Investor	0.8	27
Corporate Finance	0.7	22
International Management	0.4	12
The Banker	0.3	11
Global Finance	0.3	10
Global Investor	0.2	6

Source: IFM 1989, Research Services Ltd

ten of all adult males fell within the survey population; eligible men lived in about one-fifth of all possible areas. The proportion of adult women falling within the survey population varied according to the economic status of women in each country.

The Pan-European Survey is a source of data on the European elite as well as a readership survey. It is conducted once every three years, and reviews 328 titles.

Table 8.31 summarizes the main findings of PES 1988 relating to international media.

The International Air Travel Study (IATS)

This survey, carried out in 1989, was financed by airlines and four international media. It was targeted at frequent air travellers, with the objective of defining the profile of these travellers and what they read. The population consisted of frequent business travellers on international flights, interviewed at 18 large European airports. The sample consisted of 32,377 individuals from all parts of the world; in 1989 11,247 of these had made 6 business trips or more in the preceding period. The survey is conducted yearly, and covers 37 titles, 14 international publications and 13 inflight magazines.

Table 8.31 Main findings relating to international media, PES 1988

Title	Reach (thousands)	Reach (%)
Financial Times	264	4.9
International Herald Tribune	74	1.4
USA Today	10	0.2
Wall Street Journal Europe	34	0.6
Business Week	99	1.8
The Economist	210	3.9
L'Express (International edition)	60	1.1
Newsweek	177	3.3
Paris Match (International edition)	68	1.3
Le Point (International edition)	18	0.3
Time	261	4.9
Fortune	102	1.9
Euromoney	77	1.4
Institutional Investor	58	1.1
International Management	144	2.7
National Geographic	462	8.6
Playboy (English)	63	1.2
Reader's Digest (thirteen editions)	733	13.6
Scientific American	226	4.2

Source: Pan-European Survey 4, Research Services Ltd.

Table 8.32 IATS 1989: readership of thirteen inflight magazines

Airline	'seen' (%)	'read at least half' (%)
Aer Lingus	81.1	56.7
Air France	77.0	48.1
Air Inter	66.7	46.3
Alitalia	74.2	51.3
Austrian Airways	76.7	43.2
British Airways	78.4	48.5
Finnair	81.1	50.6
Iberian	77.0	44.8
KLM	80.9	56.4
Lufthansa	72.5	39.9
Sabena	73.3	42.0
SAS	80.2	52.4
Swissair	78.3	44.7

Source: Mediamarkt No. 1, 1990.

Table 8.32 shows the main findings of IATS 1989 regarding readership of inflight magazines.

Asia

In Asia there are two multi-media surveys for measuring readership of international media by businessmen. These are the Asian Businessman Readership Survey 2 (ABRS2) and Asian Profiles 5 (AP5). Asian Profiles 5 measures a much broader audience than ABRS2; in ABRS2 a greater proportion of the total population falls into the higher income brackets. Eighty per cent of ABRS2 respondents read English-language regional publications, in contrast with the Asian Profile 5 figure of only 25 per cent. In terms of methodology and population, the two surveys can be compared to PES4 and EBRS in Europe. Asian Profiles 5, like PES4, collects a broad range of readership, business and marketing data by means of personal questionnaire. ABRS, like EBRS, collects a much narrower range of data, and achieves a much larger sample size with a more elite audience.

The Asian Businessman Readership Survey

ABRS has been carried out twice; the findings of ABRS2 were presented in April 1989. The survey was sponsored by eight business publications, and covered eight countries in Asia: Hong Kong, Singapore, Indonesia, Malaysia, the Philippines, South Korea, Taiwan and Thailand. The population consisted of senior heads of function in 38,408 major business and industrial organizations and subsidiaries of multinational companies, and provided data on their readership, business and market behaviour. It covered major international media such as *Newsweek*, *Time*, *Asia Magazine*, *Business Week*, *Asiaweek*, *Asian Wall Street Journal* and *Fortune*, as well as local newspapers reaching the target group. Comparison of ABRS2 with ABRS1 showed that mass-circulation weeklies are losing out to smaller circulation titles.

ABRS employs a two-stage sampling technique. A sample of companies are contacted by telephone to establish eligibility for the survey in terms of the number of employees and the business activity of the establishment. In eligible organizations the names of the Chief Executive and heads of randomly-selected job functions are obtained. The eligible senior businessmen are then sent a postal questionnaire, in the appropriate language, to determine their reading, business and market behaviour. In each country eligible business and industrial establishments listed in the telephone directory are included for the following areas:

Hong Kong:	full coverage
Singapore:	full coverage
Indonesia:	Jakarta, Medan, Surabaya
Malaysia:	Kuala Lumpur, Penang, Johore Bahru, Ipoh
Philippines:	Metro-Manila
South Korea:	Seoul, Pusan, Daegu
Taiwan:	Taipei, Kaoshung
Thailand:	Bangkok

Restaurants, hotels, shops, government offices, retail/wholesale outlets, military, medical and educational institutes, farms, lawyers, accountants and personal services are all excluded. In Hong Kong and Singapore establishments with 50 or more employees are included as eligible; elsewhere establishments must have 100 or more employees.

In ABRS2 the total sample consisted of 13,800 individuals, of whom 6,100 returned their questionnaires, a response rate of 44 per cent. Fieldwork was conducted between December 1988 and March 1989. The research was carried out by Research Services Ltd.

Table 8.33 shows the main findings of ABRS2.

Asian Profiles 5

Asian Profiles 5 is the fifth in a series of surveys which started in 1976 and has been conducted at three-yearly intervals. The survey was carried out in the Spring and Summer of 1988.

Asian Profiles 5 is sponsored by *Far Eastern Economic Review, Newsweek, Reader's Digest* and *Time* Magazine, and purchased by six other magazines. The research was conducted in seven capital cities of Asia: Hong Kong, Kuala Lumpur, Jakarta, Manila, Singapore, Bangkok and Taipei. The population consisted of upper-class men and women aged 25 and over who are currently employed in senior positions in business, government and education. Previous surveys were restricted to men and the inclusion of women in Asian Profiles 5 was an important addition to the database. The research method was based on interviews with a high-quality multi-stage probability sample of qualifying men and women, together with booster interviews to enhance the sample size of the important top management group. All interviews were conducted in the language of the respondent's choice. The total sample size was 8,996 persons representing a population of 907,570 in the seven Asian cities.

Table 8.34 shows the main findings of Asian Profiles 5.

Table 8.33 Main findings of ABRS2

	Total	Hong Kong	Indonesia	Malaysia	Philippines	Singapore	South Korea	Taiwan	Thailand
				Average issue readership (%)					
Population	153,541	33,760	16,946	7,656	16,364	19,324	24,631	23,202	11,658
Dailies									
Asian Wall Street Journal	21	26	37	24	33	11	14	11	14
Financial Times	6	6	10	7	6	10	4	2	3
International Herald Tribune	6	5	11	4	9	8	3	3	5
USA Today	3	3	4	2	5	3	3	3	3
Weeklies									
Asiaweek	24	23	25	41	52	35	8	10	22
Business Week	26	20	31	25	31	30	20	33	17
The Economist	17	19	17	22	13	21	25	6	8
Far Eastern Economic Review	19	22	26	50	24	24	9	5	18
Newsweek	32	21	40	32	64	33	28	30	18
Time	30	25	40	30	51	27	23	31	18
Yazhou Zhoukan	3	5	1	2	1	4	1	4	1

Table 8.33 (*continued*)

				Average issue readership (%)					
	Total	Hong Kong	Indonesia	Malaysia	Philippines	Singapore	South Korea	Taiwan	Thailand
Fortnightlies									
Asia Magazine	27	19	22	60	36	61	10	10	27
Fortune	20	16	22	34	29	28	11	19	15
Monthlies									
Asian Business	17	16	25	30	18	26	12	10	11
Asian Finance	6	8	9	9	5	9	2	2	2
Asian Review of Business and Technology	5	4	10	6	3	8	5	2	2
Far East Business	11	9	15	18	12	16	8	16	11
National Geographic	13	10	14	25	15	17	7	17	12
Reader's Digest (English)	25	18	37	39	53	34	15	12	13
Reader's Digest (Chinese)	15	28	5	3	2	7	*	48	1
South	2	1	2	4	4	2	1	1	–
World Executive Digest	14	7	20	33	44	24	3	3	9

Note: * less than 1%

Source: Research Services Ltd.

Table 8.34　Main findings of Asian Profiles 5

		Average issue readership (%)						
	Total	Hong Kong	Singapore	Kuala Lumpur	Taipei	Manila	Bangkok	Jakarta
Population	907,570	192,797	100,897	88,476	146,068	163,398	146,472	69,461
Dailies								
Asian Wall Street Journal	3.3	4.9	3.3	5.5	0.9	4.3	0.7	3.9
International Herald Tribune	1.7	1.5	4.2	1.7	0.3	2.3	0.6	2.7
Weeklies								
Asiaweek	9.1	7.9	9.0	23.7	1.6	17.5	2.7	3.3
Business Week	3.9	4.9	3.7	6.3	1.3	6.4	1.1	3.1
The Economist	4.0	5.3	10.0	9.0	0.8	1.8	1.2	2.6
Far Eastern Economic Review	5.5	4.8	9.0	24.4	0.5	3.1	1.2	3.0
Newsweek	12.1	9.6	15.9	16.6	4.7	25.4	3.0	11.8
Time	13.0	13.6	13.8	18.6	6.9	20.9	4.2	16.5
Yazhou Zhoukan	1.0	2.2	2.8	2.3	0.2	—	—	—
Fortnightlies								
Asia Magazine	17.1	6.9	68.0	53.2	1.5	8.4	5.8	3.2
Fortune	4.5	4.4	8.5	9.4	1.5	5.3	1.7	2.6
Monthlies								
Asian Business	5.2	6.3	9.2	10.8	2.1	4.5	2.5	3.5
Asian Finance	2.1	4.7	2.3	2.9	0.6	1.5	0.6	0.6
Far East Business	2.3	3.3	4.7	3.6	0.7	1.3	1.3	1.8
National Geographic	5.1	3.0	11.2	8.7	2.7	7.4	1.9	4.5
World Executive Digest	5.2	1.5	9.4	11.7	0.8	11.5	1.2	3.8
Reader's Digest (English)	14.3	5.5	24.5	26.4	4.9	28.8	5.5	12.4
Reader's Digest (Chinese)	8.1	17.6	5.1	1.7	21.9	0.3	0.1	0.3
Triple A	0.4	0.4	0.8	0.8	0.2	0.4	—	0.3

Source: Asian Profiles 5, London.

■ Media planning for worldwide advertising

Any media plan, whether it is national or international, must be related to the marketing plan. Media objectives must be formulated in relation to the marketing objectives, and from this starting point the media strategy is developed and evaluated, and the plan made and implemented. Figure 8.6 summarizes the media planning process.

In translating marketing requirements into actionable media objectives, consideration must be given to target groups, geography, seasonality and scheduling, communication level and the copy and creative requirements. For international media planning decisions related to geography are particularly important: it is essential to establish where the advertising effort for a brand should be concentrated, and in which markets or regions opportunities exist to achieve the maximum return on advertising investment. The media availability in different regions and markets affects the amount of advertising needed to deliver the message effectively.

On page 184 the two main approaches to international media planning were outlined. The choice was between concentrating mainly on international media, which requires horizontal planning, and concentrating mainly on accumulated national media, which requires vertical planning.

Horizontal planning is mostly used with new products and brands intended from the start as global brands, and targeted at cross-cultural

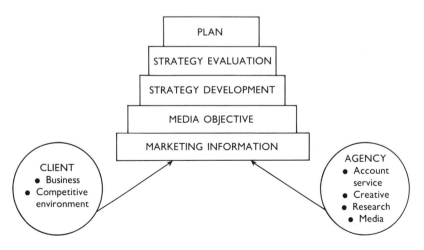

Figure 8.6 *The media planning process (source: BBDO Worldwide)*

groups like businessmen or young people. These products are culture-free. In horizontal planning those international media reaching the groups concerned are selected first; following this any additional requirements for local media are assessed. Horizontal planning is discussed further on pages 249–250.

Vertical planning is appropriate for culture-bound products or brands, delineating the demographics of specific countries. For international but culture-bound brands, the media plan should be multi-local. A good vertical media plan is the most difficult to establish. Some of the main difficulties are described below.

Three main issues for multi-local media planning

The three main issues for international media planning are. Setting the budget, both in total and split by market, defining GRP and comparing cost per GRP, and media spillover.

Budget setting

First the total budget must be decided, then it must be split between markets, taking into account the communication goals and objectives for the brand or company. For decentralized, multi-local companies with many local brands, a worldwide media plan will be made up entirely of local plans. Centralized companies marketing world brands often combine a top-down budget with bottom-up planning. The total amount to be spent is decided centrally, then each country comes up with a proposed budget. Depending on the kind of advertising needed (for example, launch of a new product or advertising for an established brand), the optimum budget for a region can be established by looking at the marketing and advertising goals, company profitability, the money available, and media availability in each country. The coordinating media planner must look at each region as the sum of individual markets, not at one standardized market which then can be split up. Depending on the marketing and advertising plan, a model must be developed for allocating money to markets.

For example, more money may be given to markets where the brand is not so strong. Alternatively the strategy adopted may be to concentrate first on large, high-potential markets with strong competition; only after profits are earned in these markets will additional markets be entered.

For each region and for each country it is necessary to establish the following information:

1. How each market is segmented.
2. The brand's share of the market in each country.
3. The phase of the life-cycle in which the brand currently resides in each country.
4. The advertising pressure in terms of competitive media expenditure.
5. The share of voice needed in the product category.
6. Specific use of media by the product category.
7. Available media, the cost of media and the cost per GRP in each country.

The key media budgeting issues for a global brand are as follows:

1. How to determine the optimum budget level for each region.
2. Deciding on the optimum allocation to each market within a region from a given media budget.
3. How to relate the media activity of one region, e.g. Europe, to another region, e.g. North America.

For a region such as Europe, the considerable differences in media availability and costs mean that it must be seen as the sum of the various national markets and not as a standardized whole. The optimum media plan can be standardized in terms of numbers of bursts, weeks advertised and type of campaign, but not in terms of opportunities to see (OTS) or to hear (OTH) and GRP.

Gross Rating Points (GRP)

Every local media planner is familiar with what, for example, 400 GRPs mean for his or her own country. However, the meaning differs considerably from one country to another. This issue was touched on earlier in this chapter (page 226). Comparison between GRPs across countries is a very complicated matter.

GRPs can be defined as the products of reach and frequency; they express the gross duplicated percentage of the audience that will be reached. GRPs describe total audience delivery without regard to duplication or repeat exposure, hence the word 'gross'.

Reach indicates what percentage of the audience at which the advertising message is aimed is likely to see or hear the advertisement at least once. *Frequency* indicates the average number of occasions on which the target audience has an opportunity to see or hear the campaign, measured in OTS or OTH.

In this chapter the term 'OTS' will be used to refer to television. However, it is important to note that in some countries the term is used for both TV and other media. Qualitatively TV and press media are very different, and if OTS is used for both media types, comparisons should be made with care. In some countries GRPs for television are referred to as television ratings (TVRs).

Rating is the statistically estimated percentage of persons or homes exposed to a particular print or broadcast vehicle in the survey area.

$$\text{Rating} = \frac{\text{Target audience exposed}}{\text{Total target population}}$$

The *average rating* is the percentage of persons or homes tuned to a specific programme during the average minute of programme duration. For print rating the word 'coverage' is used. *Coverage* is the percentage of the target audience exposed to an average issue of a magazine or newspaper. The concept of coverage is also used more generally to describe the percentage of reach in the target group.

Example
A campaign achieving 70 per cent coverage and 4 OTS would yield 280 GRPs.

Cost per rating point relates the cost of the message unit to the audience rating, allowing comparison of media vehicles.

The *cost per GRP* is the cost of purchasing one rating point.

$$\text{Cost/GRP} = \frac{\text{Average spot cost}}{\text{Average rating}}$$

Calculating cost per GRP makes it possible to estimate the total costs of a planned TV schedule within a market or country. To determine how many GRPs are affordable within a given budget, the cost per GRP is divided into the total budget.

Example
If the budget is $30,000 and the cost/GRP for the type of schedule required is $300, it is possible to purchase 100 GRPs.

The cost per GRP will differ for different countries. In order to calculate how many GRPs are needed for each country, the average cost per GRP for each country must be calculated; this indicates the optimum budget for each country.

Several methods have been developed which allow a rough comparison of cost per GRP for different countries. The input of local media experts is advisable when making cost comparisons, but for preparing rough budgets general estimates can be used.

Horizons Media International Group in London, part of Young & Rubicam, conducted a survey in thirty-eight countries in 1988 in order to estimate the approximate cost of translating a successful media programme from one market to another. Each country was asked to provide cost estimates for delivering 100 National GRPs against four broad target audiences (adults, men, women and housewives) in each of the four key media types (TV, radio, magazines and newspapers). Cost data was provided in local currency and converted into US dollars. The costs per thousand (CPMs) were computed by dividing the cost per 100 GRPs by the total population. These are not true CPMs in the purest sense as the figure does not reflect the penetration of each media type (e.g. TV households) and may not be directly comparable to specific market CPMs. The methodology used provides a reasonable base of comparison across markets for top-line estimating purposes only.[14]

Although there is a risk of overgeneralization, this research provided several interesting data. The variety of average cost efficiencies around the world is considerable – ranging from virtually nothing for radio in Colombia, Portugal and the People's Republic of China to over twenty US dollars per thousand in Italian newspapers. Asia is the most efficient region overall; Central and South America are close seconds.

Table 8.35 gives an example of the variety in cost per thousand adults based on 100 GRPs for high-demand television, high-demand radio, magazines and dailies recorded in 1988. Such data will, of course, rapidly become outdated, and are included only as an illustration.

To carry out an exercise such as this, the media elements to be compared must be standardized as far as possible. The Horizons research used for TV high demand, a peak evening 30-second spot in a heavy-demand month; for radio high demand, a peak morning 30-second spot in a heavy-demand month; for magazines a full-page, four colour bleed unit; for newspapers four columns × 250 mm black and white or equivalent. The unit of measurement was 100 GRPs, or the amount of commercial activity that approximately covers the entire demographic population.

Differences in the media scenes and in research methodologies in each country are the most difficult to incorporate in the comparison calculations. These differences create major problems in defining reach or OTSs.

Table 8.35 1988 international media cost comparison

Country	Cost per thousand adults based on 100 GRPs (US $)					
	Adults	% of region	TV	Radio	Magazines	Dailies
North America						
Canada	19,121	10	3.02	3.59	4.06	3.74
USA	176,870	90	6.60	1.33	3.61	16.96
Total region	195,991	100	6.25	1.55	3.65	15.67
Central America						
Dominican Rep.	898	2	2.24	0.18	—	2.83
Mexico	38,374	93	0.67	0.20	1.19	1.47
Puerto Rico	1,978	5	6.32	0.91	—	—
Total region	41,250	100	0.98	0.24	1.10	1.43
South America						
Argentina	7,090	5	0.85	0.84	9.90	3.10
Brazil	90,411	64	0.75	0.20	1.91	2.34
Chile	2,703	2	0.04	0.02	—	—
Colombia	29,991	21	0.15	0.01	0.04	0.25
Venezuela	11.254	8	0.28	0.23	2.28	0.17
Total region	141,449	100	0.58	0.12	1.90	1.72
Europe						
Austria	6,253	2	6.26	1.35	8.32	5.32
Belgium	7,877	3	13.89	2.65	6.42	6.04
Denmark	4,300	2	—	—	5.85	4.61
Finland	4,400	2	9.35	—	5.95	7.65
France	44,300	16	6.77	3.40	4.31	8.66
Germany (West)	48,220	18	6.68	5.61	6.47	8.32
Greece	7,859	3	2.95	—	—	—
Italy	44,975	16	7.27	1.87	6.06	22.50
Netherlands	11,123	4	10.04	1.12	4.74	5.18
Norway	3,269	1	*	*	6.72	5.24
Portugal	7,140	3			*	0.01
Spain	27,884	10	2.93	2.69	4.69	5.16
Sweden	5,934	2	—	—	5.62	3.87
Switzerland	4,476	2	13.39	—	19.88	20.21
UK	45,279	17	9.11	1.88	3.57	5.25
Total region	273,289	100	6.69	2.59	5.19	9.15
Africa						
South Africa	20,446	72	3.58	0.31	2.54	1.05
Zimbabwe	8,000	28	0.60	0.07	2.10	4.19
Total region	28,446	100	2.74	0.24	2.41	1.93

Table 8.35 *(continued)*

Country	Adults	% of region	Cost per thousand adults based on 100 GRPs (US $)			
			TV	Radio	Magazines	Dailies
Asia						
People's Republic of China	800,000	77	*	*	—	0.02
Hong Kong	4,291	0	1.25	0.05	0.47	1.19
India	59,546	6	0.44	—	0.66	0.92
Japan	85,994	8	0.99	0.20	12.09	2.43
Malaysia	8.821	1	1.45	0.05	2.49	3.17
Philippines	33,246	3	0.15	0.03	0.14	0.21
Singapore	1,997	0	4.05	1.10	8.00	1.28
Taiwan	11,482	1	0.81	0.61	3.62	2.14
Thailand	38,315	4	0.28	0.23	0.17	0.25
Total region	1,043,692	100	0.16	0.04	1.12	0.34
Pacific						
Australia	7,796	78	7.62	10.80	6.46	11.19
New Zealand	2,145	22	9.38	2.62	7.57	4.03
Total region	9,941	100	8.00	8.03	6.70	9.64

Notes: — = not available or not provided; * = less than 0.01.

Source: Young & Rubicam Worldwide Media Group.

For example Spain, with two TV stations, has a different reach curve from a country like France with six stations. Buying six spots spread over six stations will have different results to buying six spots on two stations. Figure 8.7 shows the different reach curves for the two countries.

The solution is to define a regional GRP by looking at the research methodologies used in the countries concerned and the differences in media scene, taking data from different sources in one market, finding an average and then comparing that with a comparable average from other markets. In order to make comparisons, prices must first be recalculated in comparable advertising units, and then converted to the latest, common research system (e.g. from the interview system to the meter system); media inflation must also be estimated. If pricing is not pro rata, the benefits should be removed when making comparisons. By following this method it may be possible to arrive at a European Standard GRP (ESG) for television, defined as 'reach per advertising block'.

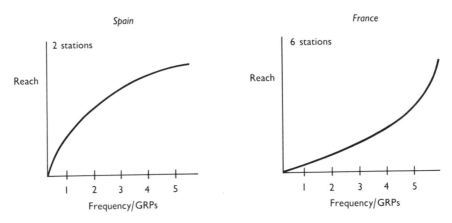

Figure 8.7   *Comparison of reach curves for Spain and France*

Such an exercise could result in the optimum plan for the launch of a new product for males over 16 described below. This originated from a US GRP level which, if recalculated and applied in every European market, would have cost too much while also resulting in under-delivery in some markets and over-delivery in others. Tables 8.36

Table 8.36   Unweighted comparison of US GRPs with GRPs of European countries

	Total GRP	Total US $000s
France	3,627	12,115
Belgium	3,627	5,465
Austria	3,627	15,754
Switzerland	3,627	1,493
UK	3,627	2,399
Ireland	3,627	16,929
Netherlands	3,627	472
Denmark	3,627	3,240
Norway	3,627	2,114
Finland	3,627	806
Sweden	3,627	1,689
Spain	3,627	5,606
Portugal	3,627	560
Italy	3,627	9,193
Greece	3,627	1,131
		$80,594

Source: BBDO.

Table 8.37 An optimum plan at lower cost

	Total OTS	Cover	GRP	US $000s
France	46	95	4,370	14,706
Belgium	30	90	2,700	4,099
Germany	35	90	3,150	13,786
Austria	31	95	2,945	1,222
Switzerland	27	85	2,295	1,909
United Kingdom	36	90	3,240	15,189
Ireland	36	90	3,240	423
Netherlands	20	80	1,600	1,440
Denmark	19	75	1,425	837
Norway	27	80	2,160	438
Finland	27	80	2,160	1,005
Sweden	24	95	1,920	1,125
Spain	62	95	5,890	9,173
Portugal	62	95	5,890	917
Italy	48	90	4,320	11,032
Greece	36	85	3,060	962
				$78,263

Source: BBDO.

and 8.37 show how an unweighted comparison can be converted into an optimum plan at lower cost.

The steps to take are as follows:

1. Establish a media strategy score for each country, based on agreed market variables, and define media weights for each country.
2. Allocate an OTS level for each media stage (e.g. launch, momentum, etc.) for each media weight.
3. Use the recommended OTS level to determine GRPs per month and per year.
4. Use a standardized currency – the dollar or ECU – to calculate cost per 100 GRPs and determine annual budgets by market.

Media spillover

There are two types of media spillover: incidental and deliberate (see page 205). Table 8.38 outlines the extent of TV spillover in Europe. It shows how a country receives broadcasts from other countries by relaying programmes by cable, by transmitting them from terrestrial stations or by individual reception by dish (satellite penetration).

Table 8.38 TV spillover in Europe – share of viewing by country

	Cable penetration %	Satellite penetration %	Terrestrial penetration %
UK	3.01	0.90	0.05
Germany	23.13	1.71	2.00
France	1.11	0.22	0.78
Italy	0.13	—	—
Spain	7.59	0.97	—
Switzerland	69.40	4.53	54.36
German		4.76	52.38
French		4.03	58.06
Italian		4.03	61.29
Belgium	90.80	1.60	27.04
Flemish		2.06	14.00
French		1.03	43.30
Ireland	36.00	5.90	25.90
Netherlands	77.27	6.70	21.60
Austria	19.68	0.44	11.29
Greece	—	5.94	10.32
Portugal	4.73	—	0.69
Finland	23.07	12.00	16.70
Sweden	31.83	11.26	4.00
Denmark	33.53	6.97	3.00
Norway	35.99	13.18	1.20

Source: BBDO UK.

Extreme examples are provided by the United Kingdom and the Netherlands. In the United Kingdom neither cable, nor the individual nor Government is interested in spillover from other countries, as the programmes are not in English. In the Netherlands cable penetration is high, as well as terrestrial reception from neighbouring countries such as Belgium and Germany.

The table shows that less than 5 per cent of viewing is of non-national channels, but spillover is important in markets such as Switzerland or Belgium and with target groups, such as businessmen. Spillover is increasing at an estimated 15 per cent, but there is little or no audience measurement so it is not easy to use for media planning purposes.

The horizontal international media plan

Horizontal plans are targeted at clearly defined, international groups, and use international media. The example below relates to a fictitious airline using international media and pan-European media research data:

Example: a media plan for a pan-European market for a fictitious airline company.

Starting points: Introduction campaign.
Product/service: Airline servicing various destinations within Europe.
Target Audience: Business travellers in Western Europe and Scandinavia, making six or more regular business flights annually.
Creative execution: Magazines – 1/1 page full-colour.
Timing: 4–6 months.

Media objectives:
To obtain a heavy introduction media pressure through current and authoritative media resulting in a high brand name awareness. To obtain a target reach and frequency level of at least 55 per cent or 10.0 OTS in the target group.

Candidate media evaluation: (cost 1990)

Evaluation of average reach per title in the target group is as follows.

Title	Cost US $	Coverage (%)
Time	38,036	13.6
Newsweek	22,915	10.1
The Economist	19,915	9.7
Harvard Business Review	13,500	7.9
International Management	12,522	7.5
Fortune	10,270	7.2
Business Week	9,540	6.8

Source: Pan European Survey
Total population target 544,000 persons

Due to the introduction character of the pan-European campaign, titles that generate a high actual reach are recommended. Weekly magazines will accomplish a strong media pressure during a relatively short period ('burst'), which optimally supports the building of brand-name awareness. An authoritative editorial stance should also be taken into consideration. Other relevant factors are cost per thousand and selectivity towards the target.

Media plan:

Titles	Frequency
Time	12
Newsweek	12
The Economist	12
Fortune	8
Business Week	12
Total indicative cost US $1,150,000	

Media performance:

	Net reach	OTS	GRP
Target audience	54%	10.0	540

Source: Pan-European Survey

Recommendation:
For the proposed media plan a budget of US $1,150,000 is required. This plan accomplishes a minimum reach of 54 per cent amongst the target audience through pan-European media vehicles.

■ International media buying

The world of media buying is changing rapidly. A decade ago, in most countries, the media planning and media buying functions were both located in the advertising agency. In some European countries the phenomenon of media buying and media broking as a separate function originated about twenty years ago. With the concentration of both advertising budgets and media owners, as well as the development of new media-related activities like sponsorship and barter syndication, there is now a vast range of possibilities. These include the following:

1. Qualitative buying, related to planning; this is usually still located within the advertising agency and closely linked with the advertising and media-planning process.
2. Financial buying according to client; combining budgets per client can lead to better negotiating possibilities.
3. Buying for a group of clients (bulking), usually done by independent media-buying agencies.

4. Buying for one's own risk (broking); this is also done by specialized media agencies.
5. Buying all pages/sites/spots.
6. Becoming a media owner.

The situation differs in every country, but all international agencies have one thing in common: large clients want large media pools, and a big buying centre can serve its clients' interests better by negotiating the best prices. This is why, in many European countries, the media buying function has been taken out of agencies and is now concentrated, sometimes merged with other buying agencies, into independent media buying shops.

In France, for example, advertisers working with different advertising agencies considered it necessary to centralize buying to achieve better conditions, harmonization towards media and brands and day-to-day optimization of TV advertising. This is why the French buying shops partly work for advertisers and agencies. The French market is an example of extreme concentration in terms of media buying: in 1989 three buying agencies represented 50 per cent of total media investment. In France everything is open to negotiation and rate cards are meaningless, but this is not the case in other European countries.

The fast-changing TV scene in Europe has created a new function in media planning and buying, that of TV optimization, where an international TV buyer with large TV budgets devotes all his or her time to finding out which commercial fits which TV programme at the lowest price. TV channel spot costs per GRP can vary enormously within countries, and to an even greater extent across borders.

Because of the concentration of advertising budgets and media owners, the situation is changing fast in Europe and the number of media buying agencies buying for international clients all over Europe is growing. The main reasons for this are as follows:

1. Major companies are developing power of scale, with revenues generated.
2. Media owners have the power of influence because of cross-ownership – across different media and countries.
3. Major companies have a growing power to communicate a range of opportunities from mass media to special interest media.

Table 8.39 gives data on the top ten European media companies. Table 8.40 shows the extent of cross-ownership of TV channels by media companies in Europe.

In Europe media buying agencies are entering into numerous new joint ventures. Among the largest of these are the French group Carat

Table 8.39   Europe – Top ten media companies 1988

	Media revenue $ million	As share of total % media revenue	Equivalent share of European advertising expenditure %
Bertelsmann (Germany)	1665	26	3.4
Reed International (UK)	1649	74	3.3
Fininvest (Italy)	1468	15	3.0
Axel Springer (Germany)	1425	88	2.9
Hachette (France)	1382	34	2.8
Havas (France)	1286	49	2.6
United Newspapers (UK)	1212	90	2.4
Hersant (France)	1176	100	2.4
Bauer (Germany)	1142	100	2.3
Rizzoli (Italy)	1092	100	2.2

Source: BBDO UK.

Table 8.40   Cross-ownership of TV channels in Europe

RTL Plus	%	BSB	%	La Cinq	%
CLT	46	Granada	16	Fininvest	25
Bertelsmann	39	Pearson	14	Hersant	25
WAZ	10	Reed	9		
Maxwell	2				
FAZ	1				

Source: BBDO UK.

(partly owned by media companies), the Media Partnership (owned by BBDO, O&M and JWT), Public Media International (owned by Interpublic, McCann Erickson, Lintas and Lowe), and Optimedia (owned by Publicis and FCB).

■ The organization of international media planning and buying

In whatever way it is organized, the function of media planning and media buying for international clients should offer the following services:

1. Tight control of regional budgets.
2. Consistent standard of media expertise in all markets.
3. Strategic media thinking related to the marketing goals.
4. Regional reporting and consolidation.
5. Evaluation of agency buying performance to improve planning.

Most often a company will employ a lead agency, either related to a large market or to the country where the client's headquarters is located. The role of the lead agency in media planning consists of coordination, planning and formatting, and implementation. Figure 8.8 shows an organizational model for the coordination of client, account management and media planning with the role of the lead agency.

When an independent media buying agency is involved, the organizational model becomes more complicated. Figure 8.9 provides an organizational model for this situation.

One of the major decisions when working with an independent media buying agency is where to locate the media planning function. Some agencies, in starting their separate buying agency, have moved the planning function to the buying agency. In most cases this has not worked well, as the link between account, creative and media planning is very important. On the other hand it is also important that media planning is closely linked to media buying, otherwise it will become out of touch with changing costs and new developments.

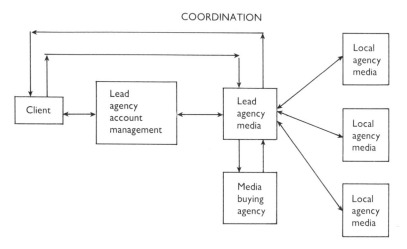

Figure 8.8 *Role of the lead agency (source: BBDO Worldwide)*

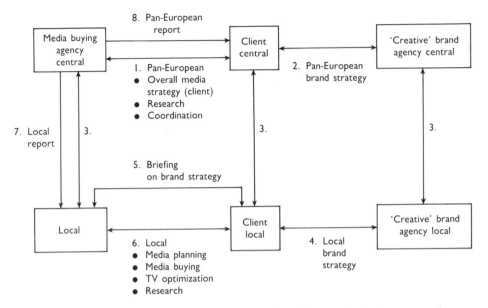

Figure 8.9 *Organizational system involving an independent media buying agency (source: BBDO Europe)*

Most buying agencies now specialize in the following functions:

1. Negotiating best rates.
2. Optimizing TV plans on a day-to-day basis for some brands; longer-term TV planning and searching for new availability.
3. Researching the audience.
4. Allocating time or space among the client's different brands.
5. Coordinating the media planning work of the client's agencies.

The coordination role taken by the lead agency requires knowledge of counterparts in local agencies and assisting with overall communication and understanding. The coordinator should know as much as possible about the media scene and about new developments in the countries involved in order to be able to interpret the plan and sell it to the client.

In the planning phase the coordinator's role includes the following aspects:

1. Providing a complete media brief and preparing a standardized media briefing form for feedback in order to be able to compare the response from the different countries.

2. Conveying the marketing and creative strategy for the brand to each country.
3. Agreeing on the target audience for each country.
4. Determining the budget by country, giving priority to countries according to their relative importance.
5. Determining overall strategy – whether the plan should take a top-down or bottom-up approach.
6. Preparing a model plan for other countries to use as an example.
7. Preparing a uniform presentation format.
8. Preparing summary plans and tables for the overall plan.

In the implementation phase the role will include the following aspects:

1. Examining a pan-regional media opportunity.
2. Looking for a common media owner among recommended vehicles for media rate negotiations.
3. Coordinating media deadlines for all countries.
4. Constructing regional and international plans and schedules.

In some cases a specialized international media planning team is set up to coordinate media planning. The team members provide strategic media supervision, develop a standard approach to budget-setting, give weights to key elements (such as marketing objectives, local market environments, category or brand development and competitive activity), act as experts on their region and on the local markets, coordinate local media planning, coordinate media overspill and adopt a regional perspective. Their task also includes regional financial reporting to the client's management.

International media planners, like international account managers, must develop an international perspective, even if they are working in a small market or country, which though part of a network plays only a minor role in it. People in this position often have to deliver data to their colleagues in lead agencies and hardly ever gain the revenues for themselves. Agency remuneration within a network should take this into account. There is another reason, too, for motivating the smaller markets or countries to play their role in the global game. As was stated in Chapter 1, any country may at any time change into a lead country, because of the shifting importance of regions or countries within regions. For example, a country's tax legislation may change with the result that important companies move their headquarters to a small country and need a lead agency there. Everybody working in an international agency network should adopt an international philosophy.

■ Summary

Global marketing and advertising developments influence media planning; to an ever greater extent, rapid developments in the media have stimulated the globalization of markets and provided opportunities for standardized advertising.

This chapter described the world media landscape and how the media scene is changing, locally and internationally. The issues and limitations of international media research were considered. The important issues for international media planning were outlined: budget setting, defining GRPs and media spillover. The media planning process for international advertising was discussed, and the kind of organization used for international media planning was described.

With the increasing concentration of advertisers and media owners, international media planning and media buying have become new, high tech skills. The international media planner and buyer needs a high level of education and experience to meet the enormous responsibility for massive global budgets.

For the global media planner, quantitative knowledge is not the most important asset. The global media planner must be creative in developing the best media plans worldwide, using all sorts of media, whether long-established or very new. He or she must also have close relations with the best creative media buyers. Advertisers must realize that this expertise is available within the large worldwide advertising agency networks and their related media buying companies.

■ Notes and references

1. George Steiner to Hans Magnus Enzensberger in an interview with *Haagse Post*, 3 March 1990.
2. Marshall McLuhan, 1964: *Understanding Media: the extensions of man*, McGraw Hill.
3. Arnie Semsky, Executive Vice President Media, BBDO Worldwide, unpublished presentation.
4. *Television in Europe to the Year 2000*, Saatchi & Saatchi Communications, February 1990.
5. *Media and Marketing Europe*, September 1989.
6. *Media and Marketing Europe*, December 1989/January 1990.
7. John Perris, 1989: 'Agencies and clients must find a common Euro research currency', *Media and Marketing Europe*, March.
8. Saatchi & Saatchi, 1990: op. cit.

9. Algemeen Dagblad, 20 March 1990.
10. Outdoor Advertising International, London.
11. Perris, 1989: op. cit.
12. Tony Twyman, 1989: 'Media research: a suitable case for harmonisation', *Admap*, July/August.
13. *Mediamarkt*, July/August 1989.
14. Young & Rubicam Worldwide Media Group, 1988: *International Media Cost Comparison*.

■ Appendix: Reference books and research agencies

Benn's Media Directory 1990, International Edition, 138th edition, Benn Business Information Services Limited, PO Box 20, Sovereign Way, Tonbridge, Kent TN9 1QR, UK.

European Marketing Data and Statistics, and *International Data and Statistics*, Euromonitor, 87–88 Turnmill Street, London EC1M 5QU, UK.

Inflight Media Marketing AG (IMM), P.O. Box 4628, CH-4002 Basel, Switzerland.

Nielsen – represented in 27 countries. Headquarters: Nielsen Plaza, Northbrook, Ill 60062-6288, USA.

Research Services Ltd, Station House, Harrow Road, Wembley, Middlesex HA9 6DE, UK.

TBI's World Guide, The Complete Television Yearbook, United States: ACT III Publishing, 401 Park Avenue South, New York, NY 10016; United Kingdom: TBI, 531–533 King's Road, London SW10 0TZ.

World Advertising Expenditures, Starch Inra Hooper, Department IAA, 566 Boston Post Road, Mamaroneck, New York 10543, USA.

Zenith Media Worldwide Publications:

Top Fifty European Media Owners, November 1989
Advertising Expenditures Forecasts, twice yearly
Television in Europe to the Year 2000, February 1990
Asia Pacific Market and MediaFact 1990, twice yearly
European Market and MediaFact 1990, twice yearly
American Market and MediaFact, 1990

Zenith Media Worldwide, 83/89 Whitfield street, London W1A 4XA, UK.

Chapter 9
Other means of communication used worldwide

■ Introduction

The use of other means of communication, such as sales promotion, direct marketing communication, public relations, trade fairs, exhibitions and sponsorship, is growing worldwide. Both in the United States and in Europe the allocation of marketing communication budgets has changed considerably, at the expense of the traditional advertising media. In 1976 the relative media/non-media allocation was 60/40; by 1986 this had reversed. There is a trend towards using a wider range of methods in both national and international communication.

Most other means of communication are much more culture-bound than media advertising, and for the majority of consumer products and brands they are mainly used locally. Particularly in the case of consumer promotions, different local retail situations and national legislation result in a much more local orientation than is found with media advertising. However, when promotions and direct marketing communication techniques are used in addition to advertising campaigns to strengthen brand image they can be very effective internationally.

Sometimes such means of communication are even used as a first priority – for example, credit card organizations do this. In business-to-business communication targeted at international groups, direct marketing techniques have been used for a long time.

Some large, annual trade fairs have always attracted an international clientele, and there is a growing trend towards internationalizing trade fairs, both for the advertiser and for the visiting public. Trade fairs and exhibitions are often a first step when going international, and are of continued major importance for international communication.

Sponsorship is growing in importance, especially when the objects of sponsorship are large global sports events like the Olympic Games and the soccer World Cup. As this kind of event is of major importance for global advertising, the appendix at the end of this chapter gives specific details of the 1988 Seoul Olympics.

Strengthening a global advertising campaign by sales promotion means that the brand awareness obtained through advertising can, with the help of point-of-sale material, be translated into direct sales. Image- or value-promotions, linked to international image campaigns, can strengthen the brand image. The global visibility of the brand can also be strengthened by a worldwide sponsorship campaign, combined with promotional activities. The result will be greater impact.

The future of client service and brand loyalty depends on approaching the client as directly as possible. The development of electronic marketing and direct marketing techniques will contribute greatly to this, both nationally and internationally. Therefore, promotions are usually linked to and integrated with other forms of communication such as direct marketing communication and public relations. More and more international companies are realizing the importance of public relations and paying greater attention to corporate communication activities.

This chapter will focus mainly on sponsorship, as this is internationally the most widely used of the means of communication outlined above. Since most large international companies now understand that it is necessary to link all the different means of communication together with advertising in one integrated communications campaign, presenting a single tone of voice worldwide, the chapter will end by stressing the importance of such integration.

■ Sales promotion

Sales promotion is directed towards the consumer by the manufacturer or the retailer, towards the sales force or towards the trade – in this case promotions are done by the producer for the retailer.

Sales promotion can be defined as:

> Those marketing activities that add to the basic value of the product for a limited time period and thus directly stimulate consumer purchases and increase sales-force and reseller effectiveness. [1]

Sales promotion offers an extra incentive for consumers to take action.

This extra incentive is usually in the form of a price reduction, additional volume of the product (volume plus), cash refund, coupon, contest, sweepstake or premium – all activities within the marketing mix which directly influence sales.

The concept of 'promotion' or 'promotions' has a specific connotation in the United States, which can sometimes lead to confusion in other parts of the world. When in the United States people talk about 'advertising and promotion(s)', the latter term is generally understood to imply a form of short-term stimulus, most often in the form of price-cuts. In Europe these short-term activities are called 'promotions' and the term 'promotion' is often used in the broader sense of communication.

In recent years, however, the term 'promotions' has also come to be seen in a broader context. In a society in which the volume of advertising is increasing and product differentiation is becoming less sharply defined, there would appear to be a need for promotional activities that not only give products and/or brands additional competitive advantages from a purely technical marketing point of view, but which also generate 'rumour around the brand' with tangible elements for the target audience. Therefore, in this sense, promotional activities are intended not so much to promote sales directly as to position for the consumer, in a tangible and accessible fashion, more aspects of the brand personality than might be possible solely with 'value' advertising.

It is therefore possible to distinguish two main categories of consumer promotions, 'classical promotions' and 'value promotions', or fleeting and loyalty-building promotions.

'Classical promotions' are action-oriented, short-term sales promotion techniques such as price reductions, on pack premiums, sweepstakes, bonus packs and coupons. These techniques have traditionally been used more frequently in the United States than in Europe or Asia. Their use has been stimulated by concentration in the retail and wholesale trade.

Leading up to 1992 a comparable development may be seen in Europe. The risk inherent in this development is that whenever profit margins come under pressure due to worsening economic circumstances or heavy competition, resulting in product surplus in relation to available shelf space, store promotions will be diluted to the level of generic propositions. However, in this situation, the brand manufacturer should stick to assisting his brand as best as he can by giving thematic support to the brand personality. Classical promotions are strongly nationally, regionally or even locally determined and are dependent on national need, competition or law. Sampling, for example where a sachet of perfume is inserted in a magazine, is an exception and can be used internationally.

The decreasing influence of the manufacturer has resulted in the creation of new types of promotions not primarily directed at the shop floor, but of a more thematic nature. The main objective is to influence the attitude of the consumer beyond the point-of-sale to the degree that he or she is sufficiently motivated to ask for the specific brand or product in the store. A thematic approach can also justify price differentials relative to competitors. Such promotions can be termed *'value promotions'*. Value promotions are image-oriented and are usually integrated with media advertising, direct marketing programmes, PR activities and sponsorship. The evolution of this kind of promotion makes sales promotion ideas internationally applicable.

Sales force promotion in an international company aims to motivate the sales personnel, whether international or in local subsidiaries. Organization and execution strongly depend on the corporate culture. In principle any kind of incentive techniques can be used. The emphasis is often on yearly or bi-yearly sales meetings, and on production of sales manuals and other materials.

For local sales force promotions, either cultural adaptations have to be made or else a tailor-made approach developed. Cultural differences, and differences in sales and distribution, have to be taken into account.

Trade promotion techniques are local, and depend on the way in which distribution is organized. The positioning of the sales organization becomes more important when producers and retailers internationalize.

Retail promotions, directed by the retailer at the consumer, are local where retailers operate locally. When retailers become international, their promotional activities also take on an international dimension, which can be a threat to the manufacturer of global brands. The retailer's communication strategy may conflict with the manufacturer's marketing strategy.

Trends in sales promotion

Sales promotion is being used more and more as a strategic instrument instead of merely a tactical instrument. Professor John Quelch of Harvard University outlined the following trends in the sales promotion industry in 1987:[2]

1. Expenditure on sales promotion will grow faster than expenditure on media advertising.

2. Expenditure on consumer promotions will grow faster than that on trade promotions.
3. Service industries and producers of luxury articles will lead in the development of new promotional techniques and will use these techniques more strategically.
4. Marketers of mass consumer goods, as well as those who aim at particular segments, will apply more electronic marketing techniques.
5. Sales promotion will become more international with a growing flow of information across borders.
6. The specialized sales promotion agencies will become even more specialized and will be able to advise their clients on a strategic level.

In 1990, it appears that these trends have become reality and will continue to grow. The exception is point 2: in the United States two-thirds of promotional expenditure is at trade level, but this is falling; in Europe, on the other hand, budget allocation for trade promotions are growing, due to increasing competition.

Promotions are continually being expanded with the objective of building a long-term relationship with the consumer and helping to develop brand loyalty. This means partially capitalizing on existing brand images which have been built by long-term thematic advertising campaigns.

Image or value promotions are usually connected to all types of entertainment, sponsored events and media. Mass media communication around the entertainment or sports event creates an association with a specific life-style. One of the better examples is Camel cigarettes with its Camel Trophy.

As well as using global mass media, there is a trend towards strong segmentation of specific consumer groups – niche marketing. The fast development of database techniques, together with the growing costs of mass media, encourage advertisers to aim at relatively small, homogeneous market segments which can be reached efficiently with direct marketing techniques. This applies mostly to products and services such as travel, credit cards, luxury consumer articles and cars, which are targeted at such clearly-defined target groups. More and more international advertisers are realizing that similar groups can be addressed with one concept requiring only small adaptations, and also via sales promotion activities.

A second trend is a growing need for regional/local or tailor-made activities for specific retailers, because local competition requires specific activities or incentives with communications support. The challenge for integrated marketing communications is to link these activities to the global approach. With international campaigns the first aim must be to harmonize and integrate the creative platforms for the thematic and promotional approaches to give optimum use of the budget and maximum communication effects.

An example of an integrated, thematic promotional campaign is the pan-European introduction of Natrel Plus, a deodorant from Gillette. A TV commercial was developed which was to be used for the whole of Europe. The promotional creative theme had to be linked to the advertising campaign. The message had to be the same in every country. Strict directives were given in order to ensure that the overall image would be connected to the advertising and the product positioning; the promotional material itself was developed on a local level, each market based on centrally-produced artwork. Give-aways for the business (wristwatches and clocks) were produced centrally because they were linked to the theme 'Round-the-Clock Protection'. The point-of-sale material was adapted to local circumstances, keeping in mind local restrictions. As far as the consumers were concerned, the most important objective was to get them to try the product, while at the same time strengthening the brand image. The most important promotion consisted of three elements:

1. A special trial can offer.
2. A test can in order to encourage the customer to smell the fragrance.
3. Folders offering the opportunity to win a trip to Club Natrel, a 'Club Med' village in Turkey, in keeping with the health positioning of the brand.

One of the most important aspects of the campaign was the creative consistency by means of which promotional activities supported brand positioning in the various countries.

Failures also occur when internationalizing promotions, most often as a result of the same kind of mistakes which are made when transferring advertising ideas to other countries, such as insufficient research. An example is furnished by Lego A/S, the Danish toy marketer who undertook American-style consumer promotions in Japan. Bonus packs and gift promotions were used, which the Japanese considered wasteful, expensive and not very appealing. Similar reactions were recorded in other countries.[3] Price reductions are a promotional technique that is generally not acceptable in Japan; in many other countries this technique is not as widely accepted as in the United States.

◼ Sponsorship

In an environment which is saturated with advertising, large advertisers have been looking for new means of communication to make themselves known. Annual sponsorship expenditure worldwide is estimated at US $4 billion. This is approximately 2–2.5 per cent of total worldwide advertising expenditure.[4] Reasons for the emergence and growth of this phenomenon include the following:

1. The increasingly prohibitive costs of media advertising.
2. The growth in leisure time which has led to a growing demand for sporting and cultural activities.
3. The necessity for a company to break through the media clutter.
4. The growth of both traditional and new media which has led to the need for more numerous and more attractive campaigns to differentiate brands from those of competition.[5]
5. The life-style relationship with target markets and the possibility of extending campaigns through personalities such as athletes.

These new means of communication were most necessary for products like cigarettes and alcoholic beverages, for which media advertising is forbidden in many countries.

Sponsorship can be defined as buying and exploiting a relationship with an event or organization of an event, or a person, or a team, club, group or institution, in order to achieve specific marketing communication objectives. This can be a sports, music or artistic event, education, or a good cause.[6]

Sponsorship has advantages both to the advertising company and to the public. The objectives of sponsorship include the following:

1. Enhancing corporate image.
2. Increasing awareness of the company.
3. Showing corporate responsibility.
4. Increasing brand or product awareness.
5. Increasing or improving brand image.
6. Accompanying the introduction of a new brand.
7. Circumventing advertising regulations for certain products.

Art and music

Art events are mainly sponsored by companies with the first three objectives, for example the following:

1. Companies whose activities are associated with unpleasant situations, such as insurance companies; companies who are associated with environmental pollution; companies, such as banks, whose activities are linked with money.
2. Companies whose products do not contribute to the general good of society, for example those whose products have negative consequences for public health, such as tobacco and alcoholic drink manufacturers.
3. Manufacturers who require a link with culture in order to position their products effectively, for example producers of photographic equipment or, hi fi equipment, or advertising agencies.
4. Manufacturers of computers and other hi-tech equipment who want to give their image a more human face.[7]

In Italy Fiat renovated the famous Palazzo Grassi, an eighteenth century palace in Venice, and made it into a museum. The Royal Shakespeare Company in the United Kingdom was saved by the Royal Insurance Company, who paid one million pounds to cover their losses. In 1988 Lloyds Bank sponsored 'The Age of Chivalry', the largest exhibition of medieval art ever organized in the United Kingdom. Peter Stuyvesant, L'Oreal, BASF, Philip Morris and many other companies have corporate art collections.[8]

In general, sponsoring the arts is used as a local rather than an international approach. However, Cartier was the first global brand to provide financial sponsorship of the arts, and Revlon sponsored the Rolling Stones' American tour. The Japanese company Suntory, the fifth largest distiller in the world, whose products include whisky, wines, beers, soft drinks and processed foods, had a diffuse image and used sponsorship to build a global corporate image. Suntory defines itself as 'a global life culture company, which enriches people's life through its activities'. In Japan Suntory operates an art museum and a concert hall devoted to the best classical music in the world. It sponsors a bird conservation campaign and golf and tennis tournaments, and maintains strong company teams in rugby, volleyball and badminton. It has been co-sponsor of the Hawaiian Open Golf for nineteen years and since 1979 it has sponsored the World Match Play Golf Championship in England. It is Patron of the Paris Symphony Orchestra, and organizes Baroque concerts at the Chateau Lagrange, a winery in the Medoc which it owns. As the name Suntory is not connected in terms of image to the company's products, it has to select the kind of sponsorship that is connected with these products, especially in Western countries, to achieve the aim of building a high-level corporate image.

Sports

For objectives like increasing or improving global brand awareness or global image, international sports events are a better medium.

Because of their ubiquity, large sports events, especially when connected to mass media, are a strong instrument. The relationship between the specific sport and the company's product is, when properly used, another strong instrument. ICI sponsors motor racing, which is relevant because it provides fibres used in the car industry. The Opel Omega was introduced with the help of sports events. Yardley had to encourage men to accept a name famed for feminine products and to educate a market, so it sponsored the MacLaren motor racing team.

Many advertisers purposely choose a particular form of sport, such as swimming, tennis, golf or motor racing. McDonald's sponsors FINA (Federation Internationale de Natation Amateur) and links as much as possible with television broadcasts showing swimming competitions, water polo and diving. In 1973 the Banque Nationale de Paris became sponsor of the Roland Garros tennis tournament. The first tournament was only visited by 50,000 people, and was on television in three countries. Seven years later Roland Garros achieved 120 hours of television in France, 56 hours in the United States and 20 hours in Japan. The tournament is shown on television in 70 countries. During one hour of television the name BNP is visible for about 45 minutes. Fuji Photo Film Co. was the official sponsor of the soccer World Cup in 1982 in Spain, in 1986 in Mexico and in 1990 in Italy. Fuji film is used for official records of the competition, and the Fujix Photo ID Card system is used to issue ID cards to some 25,000 players, officials and media representatives participating in the event.[9] The Trophée Lancome Golf Championship, sponsored by L'Oreal, led the company to develop a new brand with the same name.

Cause-related sponsorship

Sponsorship of good causes may serve various objectives, but it mainly enhances corporate image and brand awareness. It is mostly used locally, but large international companies also use it on a multinational basis. McDonald's sponsors all kinds of good causes on a local basis, for example housing for cancer patients linked to a children's hospital in Amsterdam. An international example is Reebok, the US shoe manufacturer who, with a budget of US \$10 million, sponsored the world tour of 'Human Rights Now' which included among others Sting and Bruce Springsteen.

Education

Educational sponsorship is mostly used on a local basis. The objective is mainly enhancement of corporate image and its main user is human resource management. Universities may be sponsored and in some cases even change their name. An example is the famous business school at North-Western University in Evanston in the United States, which is now called the Kellogg Graduate School of Management.

Sponsorship on a worldwide basis

The forms of sponsorship most widely used on a worldwide basis are:

1. Major sports events or sports organizations, which give scope for international exposure and coordinated promotion. For example, Visa sponsored the 1988 Olympics.
2. Music marketing, for example Pepsi-Cola with Michael Jackson.
3. Sponsorship of teams or individuals is used internationally, for example by Rolex, but has proved to be more effective in promoting national brands and less appropriate to a global strategy. One of the general dangers of sponsoring an individual is the risk of failure or a deterioration in the reputation of the individual sponsored. Ben Johnson, who was accused of taking drugs, had sponsorship contracts worth approximately US $20 million.

Sports events are the favourites of large international advertisers. In the long run, a coordinated international strategy of sports sponsorship, centred around one or two main sports, is very effective in supporting the corporate image or building brand awareness and brand image. By building up campaigns around a worldwide sports theme, like the Olympic Games, the advertiser has a good chance of controlling the communication activities.

There are numerous international sports events to choose from; for example between 1990 and 1992 in Europe the following major events all offer opportunities for advertisers: the FIFA World Cup (Italy 1990), the Rugby World Cup (UK, France and Southern Ireland, 1991), the Summer Olympic Games (Barcelona, 1992) and the Winter Olympic Games (Albertville, France, 1992).

Sponsorship of the Olympic Games

The costs of sponsorship differ with each type of product; the minimum is US $10 million, but the true costs including related promotional activities are estimated at US $20 to $30 million.

Sponsorship of the Olympic Games is controlled by TOP (The Olympic Programme). TOP offers a package of possibilities for using the Olympic symbols. By way of TOP it is possible to use Olympic symbols in most parts of the world without having to negotiate with each National Olympic Committee (NOC), as was the case before 1988. For the 1988 Olympics, Swiss-based ISL Marketing was appointed by the IOC as their commercial representative to enter into a series of complicated deals with the local organizing committees in Calgary and Seoul. TOP was the result. Under the TOP arrangement, sponsorship funds are channelled directly into the IOC, which then distributes them to all NOCs. ISL gets its share, the IOC receives some revenue as part of its aim to move away from television rights as a primary source of income, and many smaller NOCs, which formerly never received sponsorship support, now have access to this revenue.[10] In 1988 the following companies, among others, participated in the sponsorship of the Olympic Games: Coca-Cola, Kodak, Philips, Federal Express and Visa. A fuller list of sponsors is given in the Appendix. Sponsors for the 1992 Olympics in Barcelona will include: Coca-Cola, Visa, Kodak, Express Mail Service, 3M, Time Inc., Brother, Mars, Ricoh (fax machines), Philips (TV and audio) and Panasonic (video recording and cameras).

Exploitation

An appropriate product or sponsorship activity gives the greatest opportunity for image-enhancement. Thus, advertisers try to find a type of sponsorship that is related to their product or brand. Examples are breakfast cereals and athletics (natural energy), Pepsi-Cola and pop music (Michael Jackson), Cadbury and children's painting, or BP and the environment.[11] Michelin invests in all the important Formula One races in the world. Kodak is a large sponsor of graphic art. The sports or events selected should also fit in with the socio-economic characteristics of the target consumers.

Sponsorship which is relevant to the brand image, together with a promotional campaign based on that positioning, can offer an excellent platform for creative promotions. Sponsorship activities only have meaning when advertising campaigns and a good number of other promotional activities are organized around it. Sponsorship has to be supported by promotions, additional advertising, incentive programmes, sampling, publicity and community activities. It has to be integrated with the other types of communication, otherwise it would be a costly hobby. A sponsorship contract of US $100,000, when well-exploited, will normally amount to US $300,000. The effect will be greatest, if all sponsorship activities are effectively integrated into the total marketing communications mix. The more publicity a sponsored event is given, the greater the awareness of that sponsorship. Careful PR around sponsorship will increase the communication effects, and can, together with media advertising and promotional activities, reduce the importance of one disadvantage of sponsoring an event, namely the fact that it is a one-off. PR is also necessary in view of the possible negative results, for example when a sponsored athlete is accused of drug-taking.

Planning is essential. The sponsorship should be clearly visible before the sponsored event takes place so that, during the event, the maximum benefit can be obtained. The objective is usually to strengthen recognition.

Visa's sponsorship of the Olympic Games is a good example of how complete programmes can be built. Visa has taken into account all aspects of merchandising, including inserting the Olympic symbol on the Visa card. Fund-raising was another method used to obtain recognition: donations were given to the Olympic Committee for each transaction done through a Visa card. The card-holders themselves were also involved in this; they could donate via their Visa-card and those who did received a reward. Promotional activities were worked out within each market. Moreover, Visa also sponsored the Olympic Games for the mentally handicapped and the UK Special Olympics in which teams from eight European countries participated. A new travel product was attached to this. A pan-European advertising campaign was launched in order to make the promotion known, which also covered those countries where the promotion did not take place.

Originality

In a relatively short time sponsorship has become a communication instrument used by a large number of advertisers, who use basically the same mass media to accompany their sponsorship activities. This leads to more media clutter. Thus it is important to find the 'big idea', an activity related to the sponsored activity or event which stands out from the crowd. The exploitation must be original.

Programme sponsoring or programme bartering

Programme sponsoring is increasing in importance. The massive increase in the number of TV stations in Europe requires an equally massive increase in the supply of television programming. This is where programme sponsoring and bartering comes in. The barter company sources or commissions new programming and then sells the sponsorship rights and airtime to an advertising agency or client, effectively paying for the programme material. The programme is then offered to the television station free of charge, conditional on placement and on provision of airtime and credits or advertising time. In summary, the programme producer sells his product, the client acquires a powerful sponsorship campaign and the television station receives a high-quality programme.

The barter business is a multi-billion dollar one in the United States, representing $1.2 billion in 1990. Advertisers such as Colgate, Procter & Gamble, Unilever, etc., are leading participants in the industry. Warner, Columbia, MGM, Twentieth Century Fox are examples of American studios actively involved in the bartering business.

European examples of television sponsorship include Korean Air's sponsorship of golf on Super Channel, Coca-Cola's chart show on MTV and Ford's sponsorship of the ski report on Sky TV. These programmes are introduced by a full-screen introductory credit and in some cases there is a logo on-screen throughout the programme. Advertiser-supported programming will be a major feature of European television in the 1990s, and will help fund many of the programmes needed to supply the voracious appetite of the new stations. Music and sports programmes travel particularly well across European borders. [12]

When an advertiser produces his own programme and then offers it to TV stations in exchange for advertising time, this is called programme bartering. An example is Unilever's 'Wheel of Fortune'.

Sponsorship and bartering are costly and only worthwhile on a large scale, preferably global.

Measuring the effect

The greatest problem with sponsorship is measuring the effect, especially when a large number of different means of communication are involved.

Philips made an effort to study the effects of its sponsorship of the football World Cup in Mexico in 1986 and reported the results at the ESOMAR congress in Montreux in September 1987.

Via the international media a worldwide advertising campaign was conducted during the weeks before the World Cup. On the day of the opening match there was a campaign in the national and international media covering approximately forty countries, saying 'Good morning, you'll be watching Philips for the next four weeks', and showing the many Philips products such as TV sets and TV cameras, which were used to make the global broadcast of the World Cup a success. PR and promotion campaigns were conducted in each country.

A general research programme was conducted which tried to measure recall of the names of the sponsors, association with soccer in general, and with the Mexico World Cup in particular, and changes in awareness, imagery, brand recognition and brand content. As much information as possible was gathered about the audience and name-exposures from all over the world; results of private surveys were also used. The general conclusions were as follows:

1. When image and recognition are already well-established, a great increase cannot be expected; 'unknown' brands will achieve a relatively stronger effect. Modifications are gradual and also depend on other factors; therefore it is important to connect activities and to exploit them.
2. In many countries the campaigns created an association between Philips and the World Cup on the level of an active Philips brand (share of voice); this probably resulted on average in a small 'image plus' but the effect was not very significant. There was too much noise in the data.
3. There must be greater integration between event sponsorship and regular marketing communication programmes. Sponsorship must fit in with medium- and long-term planning, as only then can the exploitation be utilized to the best possible advantage.[13]

Other general research findings show a relationship with the amount of involvement which the audience has in the sponsored event. The higher the involvement, the greater the effects. Changes in image and awareness occur more slowly than changes in knowledge and attitudes.

Techniques for evaluating the effectiveness of sponsorship of sports and events include measuring the extent of media coverage, number of programme participants and increases in sales volume, and pre- and post-programme awareness studies to determine the effects of the event on corporate image, product or brand recognition and corporate objectives.[14] A research programme could consist of four stages:

1. Set measurable goals. For example, 'The goal of our sports sponsorship is to increase consumer awareness of brand X among young professional males in ten countries in Europe by fifteen percentage points'.
2. Research the sports interest of target consumers.
3. Measure the results. This could be done by three-way surveys (pre-event, event and post-event) of a designated audience, making it possible to measure changes in name awareness, corporate image, product use, etc., as a result of the specific sponsorship.
4. Re-evaluate the cost-effectiveness of the sponsorship.[15]

There are, however, numerous problems related to this type of research. These include the following:

1. How to calculate the dollar equivalent of 'free advertising'.
2. How to calculate GRPs for sponsorship in the various media used to communicate the sponsored event to the related thematic media-advertising in order to add up the total effort.
3. How to measure the level of involvement of the target group with the event.
4. How to compare and add up the effects of sponsorship in different countries to give a worldwide image effect.

These problems were discussed in Chapter 8, and will be dealt with further in Chapter 10.

■ Direct marketing communication

Direct marketing is a marketing system whereby the marketer establishes a direct, personalized and measurable relationship with the individual consumer through interactive communication. The instruments employed in direct marketing are intended to generate a kind of two-way communication.

Direct marketing involves using communication techniques such as direct-response advertising on television and in the press, direct mail or direct non-mail, telemarketing and the creation and use of marketing databases – all those techniques which make it easier to target in on, and generate responses from, the consumer or other audiences. These techniques were originally used by mail order and insurance companies, and these are typical examples of businesses which employ direct marketing in the purest sense of the word, where communication, sales and distribution are one.

Characteristics unique to direct marketing include the following:

1. Development of a relationship between the marketer and the customer or prospect.
2. The use of direct-response marketing communication.
3. Direct measurement and tracking of the physical response.
4. The possibility of creating and using a marketing database of customers and prospects.

Direct marketing is in fact a combination of three marketing techniques:

1. Advertising – convincing through non-personal media.
2. Sales promotion – action-oriented, creating a direct response.
3. Market research – direct feedback, tracking of individual information on prospects and customers.

The database is the crucial aspect of direct marketing communication: the company which knows its own customers, their names, addresses, ages, occupations and buying habits, can better satisfy their needs and wants and retain their loyalty. Databases can be built by using response-generating advertising, which in turn can be followed up by direct mail. The development of customer databases is not only done for small target groups. The cosmetics company Shisheido in Japan has a client database of 10 million names. There is a Shisheido club with reward programmes linked to dealers and stores. Shisheido knows what, why and where their clients buy and can communicate with them on a personal basis. Tobacco company Philip Morris has 14 million customer names in the United States and publishes a magazine for them.

Although direct marketing communication techniques and means are ideally suited to a number of specific goals, they can – as long as they are integrated with other communication instruments – contribute to the establishment of brand loyalty and to other general marketing communication objectives. Direct marketing communication techniques are ideally suited to the following goals:

1. The measurement of response.
2. The encouragement of prospect or customer requests for product information.
3. The encouragement of trial purchases.
4. Setting up a direct sales system.
5. Keeping in touch with individual customers and prospects (relationship building).
6. Helping the sales force in the establishment of contacts with prospects (creating sales leads).

7. Developing programmes to motivate intermediaries such as retailers, distributors, dealers, agents and sales staff.

Direct marketing communications media are as follows:

- Direct response advertising via press or television (coupon or telephone number in advertisement).
- Direct mail, direct non-mail.
- Telephone selling or telemarketing.
- Targeted print media such as magazines and newsletters.

These media can be used for both national and international communication. Use of these media has been growing worldwide: more than half of the $118 billion spent on advertising in the United States in 1988 went on direct response media. In Europe between 1981 and 1987 there was an average growth of 10 per cent in per capita expenditure on direct mail.

As far as execution is concerned, most direct marketing communication activities are strongly culture-bound and therefore locally-adapted. Legislation varies considerably around the world, for example concerning list usage, privacy and data protection, and telemarketing ('cold calling' is prohibited in Germany).

There are also differences in the organization and efficiency of postal systems in different countries. For example Italy has a poor reputation for postal efficiency, and so do many other countries. This is one of the reasons for the rapid growth in popularity of telefax. Postal rules also differ – for example, rules on maximum and minimum sizes and weights – and so do postal charges for national and international mail. In Japan, direct mail is not widely used and one of the main reasons is the fact that bulk postal rates are among the highest in the world.

International use of direct marketing

Direct marketing techniques are used internationally to reach business people, international travellers and high income groups.

Direct marketing communication is the pre-eminent means of communication for business-to-business marketing, which involves specific target groups. It is appropriate for all those markets where small segments can be distinguished and where it is possible to build up a database. With particulars like addresses, interest areas, purchase information, etc., direct marketing communication can be used as a supplementary means for special interest publications or professional publications.

Direct marketing communication methods are an excellent means of supporting export sales. The high costs of personal selling reach their peak when salesmen are travelling abroad. Furthermore, the actual time available for selling is even shorter than in the domestic market because of longer distances and time differences. In new, unknown markets, sales people also face problems such as the difficulty of obtaining correct information about companies and about the market situation. When a seller meets a potential client, there are immediately at least three unspoken questions: 'Who are you?', 'Where do you come from?' and 'What can you offer me?'. Many of these questions can be answered before the sales call. The target group can be selected using variables such as title, industry, company size, etc. The message can be personalized. Very few people do not open mailings or letters from abroad. After the sales call a continuous flow of information can be targeted at decision-makers, reinforcing the sales call and boosting client loyalty.

Enso-Gutzeit, a leading paper manufacturer, exports its wide range of products around the world. Sales offices and representatives of the paper division are located in more than forty countries. This company developed a new paper quality for the growing direct marketing industry, the wood-free, on-line bladed Ensomatt paper which guarantees top-class printing quality and durability in high-speed rotation printing. Excellent quality for laser printing and performance were a must. However, manufacturing for large rotary printers was new to Enso. Therefore direct mailing was first targeted at the technical and production managers and foremen of relevant companies to get qualified sales leads to the local representatives in certain European countries. The offer was a free test run on Ensomatt paper, so a very limited target group was selected. The addresses were chosen from Enso's own client database. A second mailing involved a package consisting of a laser letter, printed on Ensomatt, a thirty-two page brochure, three samples of different weights of paper and a reply card. This mailing was meant to encourage people from specialized laser printers and fulfilment houses as well as advertising agencies to visit Enso's stand at the annual direct marketing conference and exhibition in Montreux, Switzerland. An even more carefully selected group of conference delegates was invited to a cocktail party.

Using direct mail in connection with trade fairs is worthwhile, because it helps to target the right people and to obtain new addresses, and it serves as a reminder after the event.[16]

Although direct marketing communication techniques are not yet frequently used for international consumer campaigns, they can for instance be applied locally, under the umbrella of international mass campaigns. They must, however, be adapted as necessary. Often concepts which are successful in one country can easily be adapted to other countries.

Allo Diétique Nestlé in France developed a database of buyers of baby food, and provided a telephone service for customers who were having problems with feeding their children. This is a good way of instilling brand loyalty in mothers.

Local databases can be purchased for international mailings. Direct marketing databases are nowadays an important tool for hotels, travel agencies, airlines and business-to-business marketing. The international travel industry cannot ignore this development. The use of a combination of direct marketing databases and promotion techniques can stimulate repeat purchases and brand loyalty. This applies not only to international airlines and hotels, but also for large retail stores like Harrods in the United Kingdom, who sell to customers abroad.

Care must be taken in applying direct marketing techniques internationally, for the following reasons:

1. Decision-making units may be different in different countries: decision-making processes in offices differ even within Europe. In France, it is the boss who makes the decisions on what to buy, while in Scandinavia it is a much more democratic process.
2. The sophistication of the market varies: in some countries the consumers are not yet used to personalized messages. Consumers may think that their name has been misused. In other countries direct mail is seen as an intrusion and wasteful.
3. An incentive offered to the target market must be interesting for the prospects. An invitation for a test drive in the latest Volvo model, with the chance to win a series of Swedish detective books, is not really as great an incentive for the Dutch as it may be for the Swedish.

Because direct marketing media make particular use of the written language, the language problem is important. Correct translations are essential. It is best to use native copywriters. Text must capture the reader's attention immediately, which often means using particular words in a specific way, or even using colloquialisms. Care must be taken when the English language is used for international target groups: English and American are in some ways very different languages, but the English and Americans themselves are often least aware of this.

Direct marketing communication is, both nationally and internationally, an important instrument for the marketing of many products and services to specific segments. However, it is essential to be aware of a number of problems which can be expected in most countries:

1. Growing sensitivity of the public to unwanted intrusions on privacy.
2. Lessening acceptance of uninvited mail, strengthened by the environmental issues raised by using too much paper.
3. Abuse of telephone market research for sales objectives.
4. Poor standards generally can reduce the credibility of direct mail.

The future: new techniques for direct marketing communication

Telecommunications are now becoming interlinked with data processing. The age of worldwide direct marketing communications will begin with the introduction of Integrated Services Digital Network (ISDN). An analog world of the telephone is melting with the digital world of the computer. But this is a process only recently happening in the developed world. The ISDN network offers a wide range of possibilities for marketing communication, including more rapid transmission, value-added services and database applications.

Transmission speeds will increase between twenty and fiftyfold, and fax copies will be as good as photocopies. Value-added services will include store-and-forward services with interim storages, such as voice mail, telebox and registration of in-coming calls. Special facilities will include individual acceptance by the subscriber called, closed user-groups or subscriber segments and network information. Database services will include interactive videotex with more rapid transmission speeds. The success of Teletel in France may serve as an example: by mid-1987, some 3 million Minitels had been installed in France. There are roughly 2,000 professional and 1,000 private information-providers. In the store-and-forward service roughly 14 million calls are made per month. This corresponds to 30 per cent of all Teletel activities. The electronic information service showing a complete address is used by 93 per cent of subscribers. This kind of service will become international as regional ISDN networks are developed in Europe and other areas. It will provide quicker and easier access to information such as telephone numbers, travel timetables and lists of special offers, and will allow access to special fields of knowledge. Possibilities will include telework, teleschooling, teleadvertising, teleshopping with rapid order confirmation, mass sample surveys together with TV and radio commercials and promotional letters.[17]

◼ Public relations

The following general description of public relations was endorsed by the National Assembly of the Public Relations Society of America in 1986:

> Public relations serves a wide variety of institutions in society such as business, trade unions, government agencies, voluntary associations, foundations, hospitals and educational and religious institutions. To achieve their goals, these institutions must develop effective relationships with many different audiences or publics such as employees, members, customers, local communities, shareholders, and other institutions, and with society at large.
>
> The managements of institutions need to understand the attitudes and values of their public in order to achieve institutional goals. As a management function, public relations encompasses the following: Anticipating, analyzing and interpreting public opinion, attitudes and issues which impact, for good or ill, on the operations and plans of the organization. Counseling management at all levels in the organization with regard to policy decisions, courses of action and communication, taking into account their public ramifications and the organization's social or citizenship responsibilities. Researching, conducting and evaluating, on a continuing basis, programs of action and communications to achieve informed public understanding necessary to the success of an organization's aims. [18]

Philip Kotler, in his definition of PR, stresses the business aspect:

> Public Relations exists to produce goodwill in the company's various publics so that these publics do not interfere in the firm's profit-making ability. [19]

The aims of public relations as a management function are to create positive opinions about the organization, promote products and services, raise operating funds and capital, and generate support. Its audiences may be external (customers, the trade, the general public) and internal (employees, stockholders).

As with advertising, public relations messages are often presented via mass media channels. Public relations practitioners, however, rather than buying space or time, have to persuade the media 'gatekeepers' such as journalists, talk show coordinators, etc., to carry their information. Advertisers can control the message content for the space they buy and select appropriate frequency and reach. Public relations practitioners cannot.

The advantage of public relations messages (often called 'free publicity') are credibility and message length. Information conveyed through the non-advertising portion of a journal is usually more disarming and more believable. Usually, too, a news or feature treatment of an issue is longer than a television commercial or an advertisement. A high proportion of press and television content originates from PR activities. A newspaper is 50–75 per cent PR-driven.

In order to get publicity, there must be news. If there is no news, it can be created, but news is a prerequisite for publicity. The term publicity is often used in the sense of 'free publicity'. However, to gain publicity by creating events or news requires a PR investment. One of the problems of PR is that its effectiveness is difficult to measure in the short term. Its costs cannot be compared with advertising media expenditures.

Two main kinds of public relations can be distinguished: corporate PR and marketing PR.

Corporate public relations

Global corporations worldwide have realized that the success of their corporate strategies depend on how they are seen by the outside world – on their corporate image. The importance of the corporate image worldwide, as well as that of the local corporate image, has become more important than ever before. As a result most international corporations nowadays have public relations departments at corporate level, both internationally and locally.

Corporate public relations are internationally of great importance when corporate cultures have to cross borders, for example when companies merge. In such cases internal PR or internal motivation programmes are also an important instrument. Often the communication aspects of internal motivation programmes are executed by the public relations department. An emerging use of PR is to identify and manage issues which are important to the company or organization, such as environmental issues, which are a big concern for the 1990s.

As the scope of public relations is widening, the profile of the PR manager is changing. PR managers are no longer predominantly ex-journalists; instead they usually have a management background and a business education. Managers are needed to manage the image of large corporations!

Local problems are usually different to global problems. Public relations for a stock market flotation requires a different approach and expertize than does dealing with an environmental action group. However, many national problems are no longer isolated problems, especially when they concern global issues such as the environment or racism. The world press has seen to it that such problems have become universal. Even when there is a local aspect, problems recognized worldwide should be handled on a worldwide basis.

After the oil spill in Alaska, Exxon did not communicate at all. Exxon obviously thought it could solve the communication problems raised by this tragedy with just a telephone number in Texas. Following the incident in which capsules had been poisoned, killing several people, Tylenol expressed their concern for the families. Later they brought back their brand in a different form and were accepted as a responsible company.

Local PR becomes global without people realizing it: Ron Kidmore, president of Pepsi-Cola South in the United States, had to offer his apologies for the fact that a PepsiCo employee, conducting a recruitment seminar, had said that Southerners were 'cowtippers', obviously intended as a slur against Coca-Cola. This typical US event was shown as the latest development in the 'war between the cola giants' on the CNN network all over Europe. Stupidity as well as failure gets into the global communication networks very fast, with unmeasurable effects.

The globalization of the information industry has contributed to the internationalization of the public relations function. Because media opportunities are becoming alike, PR is also becoming more similar around the world.

When attempting to win attention from the media in different countries, it is essential to realize that one is competing in an information market. The supply of news often exceeds the demand, and this demand is mainly aimed at politics. The legitimacy of either political information or image improvement will not be challenged here, but it must be recognized that the objectives are not always those of enhancing harmony between countries.

Generally speaking, economic and technological news have a more positive effect on relations between businesses in different countries than political news. News about a joint venture between an American oil company and the Chinese authorities for oil production in the South China Sea does more for international understanding than the exchange of viewpoints at a conference table.[20]

A global public relations plan often has to be adapted for every country. As with advertising, the different cultural aspects have to be taken into account. Multinationals with subsidiaries all over the world tend to appoint local public relations officers. These meet once or twice a year to exchange experiences and to become better-informed about the relation between local and global objectives.

The organization of the PR function in an international company is related to the structure of the company, and may be either centralized or decentralized. Selection of and cooperation with public relations agencies will reflect this. Like advertising agencies, PR agencies are organizing themselves into international networks. These networks can be based on full ownership by the head agency or they can be much looser networks, based on an exchange of information.

The globalization of enterprises and growing cooperation between large multinationals have the following consequences for the PR discipline:[21]

1. It is essential to know about the relevant positions taken by foreign governments and international organizations as well as reactions from the national and international press.
2. Good contacts must be maintained with the authorities in foreign countries. Sometimes this means that one's own efforts must be supplemented by those of external advisors.
3. Special attention must be given to building the image of the multinational, as this may need to differ from country to country. Establishing corporate image in a foreign country is inconceivable without professional preparation.

Marketing public relations

Marketing public relations concerns the marketing of the company's product, service or brand. Marketing PR is an activity which, when well-organized, can make an important contribution to the following:

1. Introducing new products or brands.
2. Upgrading or rejuvenating existing brands.
3. Strengthening the brand image.
4. Generally contributing to the effectiveness of international image campaigns, particularly when integrated with promotions and direct marketing communication.
5. Supporting dealers and distributors.

There is usually a strong relationship with corporate PR; corporate elements are often used in introducing new products, communicating product improvements, or upgrading brands. Even existing products can be put into a broader context by placing them in the context of the corporate environment or a part of it, such as R&D.

Many activities need to be executed locally because they must capture the interest of the local media. Therefore, marketing PR is often under the jurisdiction of the local management of an international enterprise.

The means of communication by which marketing public relations can be effected are growing because of the increasing flow of information. New media and new target groups require new approaches. Marshall MacLuhan said as early as 1964 that:

> The owners of media always endeavour to give the public what it wants, because they sense that their power is in the *medium*, not in the *message* or the program.[22]

With the growth in the number of TV channels it will be easier to get product-related news or events on television. The video news release is the instrument for news programmes: some channels are too small to cover everything themselves. Videos giving statistics, visuals and a picture of the spokesperson, without voice over, which can be used in a news programme, are found to be very valuable.

Besides the usual PR instruments like news releases and media conferences, there are a number of methods which can be used internationally. These include the following:

1. Media tours – 'John Jones is on the road, today in Madrid, tomorrow in Barcelona, talking about . . .'
2. Expert spokespersons – for example a motor racing driver who speaks on behalf of Audi.
3. Tie-in promotions.
4. Research studies or surveys – for example an international survey by *National Geographic* uncovering the fact that young people in many countries lack a basic knowledge of geography.
5. Video news releases.
6. Trade show exhibits.
7. Annual/quarterly reports.
8. Internal publications, or video journals for in-company use.
9. Video brochures.
10. Event PR, related to sponsorship.

Public relations campaigns can be very international: the Gillette Sensor, a new type of razor, was launched on 3 October 1989 in nineteen countries simultaneously. This was an innovative product, at that time not even in the shops. In the same year it became one of Fortune's ten products of the year.

It is, however, the combination of public relations and advertising which generates the most effect. Public relations and advertising should also work together with trade and consumer promotions.

■ Trade fairs, exhibitions and congresses

International trade fairs have many functions, including the following:

1. They are very important for companies which are in the early stages of international business, mainly aiming at export.
2. They are important also for international companies wishing to penetrate new areas, particularly developing countries. Many countries offer subsidies to companies which participate in joint sales efforts. Exhibiting at a trade fair provides the chance to explore market possibilities before making a commitment to export to a country.
3. When introducing products, trade fairs have the advantage that the products can be seen, tried and tested.
4. Trade fairs are also useful in maintaining relations with the trade.

There are two main types of fairs. One is the broad, general type of annual fair. The two annual Hanover fairs in Germany serve as examples – Hanover Messe Industrie for seven major industrial categories and Hanover Messe Cebit for office equipment and automation – which both attract five to six thousand exhibitors and five to six hundred thousand visitors from all over the world. There are also trade fairs which specialize in certain fields, for example agriculture, cameras and related equipment, cars, packaging industries, etc. Examples of this type of fair are the annual Paris Air Show and the Fotokina (photo and video) in Cologne, Germany. Congresses are often connected to these specialized trade fairs or exhibitions.

An important reason for participating in trade fairs is that all the important competitors are usually there, and most important international buyers visit the fair both to gain information and, often, to place orders directly. The cost of participating must be weighed against the potential loss incurred by not participating. Fairs which are well attended by buyers in the particular country may also be worth attending.

Especially where trade fairs are connected to congresses, it is important to implement a total, integrated, correctly-timed communication effort. This must take into account direct marketing techniques for reaching clients and prospects, inviting them to the congress and luring them to the fair, presentation of the stand, the personnel who will be present, advertising in the trade journals, events, sales and trade promotion, public relations, hand outs, etc. The visitor will have to be convinced that it is worthwhile putting the stand on his or her list of stands to visit.

Measuring the effect

Both the exhibition industry and the exhibitors themselves need to put more effort into measuring results than has been done up to now. The more advanced trade fairs now offer data on numbers and profiles of visitors, their behaviour and effects of their changing knowledge. Individual exhibitors research these aspects and compare the findings with the data offered by the exhibition industry to see whether they are in line with the general outcome.

In Western Europe the exhibition industry acknowledges the lack of uniform, independent statistics about exhibitions. Only the Germans, and to a lesser extent the French, have an established system for providing independent data on numbers and types of visitors, exhibitors and other basic information. The United States has such a system, and so does the Asia-Pacific Rim.

In July 1989 about forty European exhibition organizers agreed to set up a pan-European representative council in order to work towards harmonization of data and thus help exhibitors select the most effective show at which to exhibit their products. Global companies which participate in fairs in different European countries should be able to make proper comparisons between exhibition venues as a result.

The high quality of statistics in Germany is one reason why its exhibition industry has maintained European market leadership, particularly in international fairs. About half a dozen European countries have brought in independent audit systems, but the classification of exhibitions within product groups varies from country to country.[23]

International trade fairs and exhibitions will remain a growing vehicle for international trade and communications, as existing trade fairs spread around the world. The furnishing fabric exhibition of the German Messe Frankfurt ('Heimtextil') is also organized in Japan. 'Interstoff', the German clothing trade fair, is organized in Hong Kong. In 1991 the first 'Frankfurter Messe ASIA' will be held in Tokyo.

■ Integrating other means of communication with advertising

With the use of a greater variety of communication instruments there is a greater need to integrate the planning and execution with thematic advertising. Brand image is built up through a number of channels, and uniformity and one tone of voice are required; brand image is influenced by all communications relevant to the brand which reach the target group. As the consumer changes and adopts a broader world view, the expectations of consistency increase. It is increasingly necessary to coordinate style, tone of voice and timing of the various selected means of communication.

The consumer experiences a unique combination of contacts with the product or service. He or she hears about it from a friend, reads about it in a newspaper column, sees and hears about it in a television show, sees promotions for it in the mail, attends a concert sponsored by its producing company, sees the package and the display in the store. The list can be very long. All of these contacts contribute to the consumer's perception of the brand, and to his or her relationship with the brand. All the contacts and impressions are merged in the consumer's mind. Each one influences the others and affects the whole.

Communicators, however, all too often fail to integrate communications. Everything about the brand speaks to the consumer in an array of fragmented bits. Consciously or unconsciously a consumer absorbs this information and files it by category and brand in her/his memory. When the consumer becomes confused, he or she is unlikely to become or stay a loyal customer if there are other competing brands with consistent communications.

Marketers must guide the process so that the total impression is favourable to the brand. It stands to reason that planning and coordinating many individual contacts with the brand increases the likelihood of creating the desired favourable impression. This is one way of looking at integrated communications: multiple messages, organized and coordinated to provide the desired overall impression to a specific audience. This leads to a broader definition of integrated communications:

> Integrated communications are tuning target groups, goals, messages and means of communication in such a way that they complement and reinforce each other so that the overall effort yields more than the sum of the parts.[24]

The advantages of integration for the advertiser include the following:

1. Consistency in building a strong brand.
2. Synergy of efforts and budgets.
3. Possibility of greater impact.
4. The total effect of integrated communications is larger than the sum of the parts.
5. More effective use of the budget leading to lower costs.
6. Assists in developing and maintaining brand loyalty.

For the agency the advantages include the following:

1. Diversification through specialized agencies can lead to increased turnover and, if efficiently organized, to a higher income.
2. An integrated approach can lead to a greater involvement on the part of the client, and can thus improve the relationship between client and agency.
3. Integration creates enormous growth potential both for expanding into related disciplines and for acquiring new clients.
4. Better understanding of the client.

The organization of integrated communications is a complicated matter, particularly for global organizations where the question of centralized or decentralized control also arises.

Therefore the following points should be borne in mind:[25]

1. Strong central direction and authority are absolutely necessary for full integration, whether this is across national borders or within a single country.
2. The CEO must organize his company in such a way that integrated marketing communications can be executed without being sabotaged by the little empires of sales, advertising, PR and sales promotion that exist in most companies. That means giving the appropriate executive power and budgets to the person responsible for integration. Fragmented budgets do not encourage integrated work.
3. The advertising, promotion and other specialized agencies, such as those dealing with direct marketing, must be motivated to recommend a balanced approach to a marketing problem or opportunity. An advertising agency is not going to recommend the use of other disciplines for which it receives no commission as it then will rob itself of revenue and profit. For this reason it may be best to select one agency which can offer a range of other disciplines apart from media advertising. Alternatively, an experienced, well-trained staff is needed to coordinate and manage all the different specialized agencies. Somewhere along the line, coordination must be paid for.
4. Both clients and their agencies must find and train professionals with a broad outlook who are able to diagnose a marketing problem or opportunity and prescribe the right solution – whether it is advertising, a travelling road show, a direct mail campaign, a dealer promotion, a trade press approach or whatever.
5. Better ways must be found of measuring the effectiveness of marketing communications and the results in terms of sales.

■ Summary

This chapter has given a short description of means of communication other than media advertising. For global and international campaigns, television has in the past been the most obvious medium, together with the international press. However, the use of new media and other means of communication has been growing. These means are used across borders for reaching specific target groups, and also locally, alongside other media.

Because of this growing use of other means of communication or 'below the line' media the global advertiser needs to know about the opportunities they offer, and also about the importance of integrating all means of communication.

■ Notes and references

1. William Wells, John Burnett and Sandra Moriarty, 1989: *Advertising: Principles and Practice*, Prentice Hall.
2. Gerry Postlethwaite, KLP International, in a presentation for the IAA Education Conference, Amsterdam, 3 March 1988. John Quelch's ideas can be found in John A. Quelch, 1989: *Sales Promotion Management*, Prentice Hall.
3. Kamran Kashani, 1989: 'Beware the pitfalls of global marketing', *Harvard Business Review*, September/October.
4. Ton Otker, 1988: 'Exploitation: the key to sponsorship success', *European Research*, May.
5. Ibid.
6. Ibid.
7. Claude Wolton, 1988: 'Arts sponsorship: harmony or discord', *European Research*, May.
8. *FEM*, Europese editie, 25 March 1989, pp. 45–6.
9. Ibid.
10. Kevin Cote, 1986: 'How sport ties reshape big-time marketers', *Focus*, 1986.
11. Mike Hopkins, 1990: 'The mixed medium – adding value through sponsorship', *Sponsorship News*, January.
12. Peter Dodds, 1990: 'Barter and pan-European sponsorships', *Sponsorship News*, January.
13. *Tijdschrift voor Marketing*, October 1987.
14. Russell Abratt and Pieter Schalk Grobler, 1989: 'The evaluation of sports sponsorships', *International Journal of Advertising*, no. 8.
15. Ibid.
16. Jarmo Kuisma, 'Supporting export sales with direct marketing methods', Eighteenth Montreux Direct Marketing Symposium, April 1986.

17. Dr Bernd Kroger, 'New marketing approaches with the international communications network', Twentieth Montreux Direct Marketing Symposium, April 1988.
18. Public Relations Society of America, 1986: 'Official statement on public relations', *Public Relations Journal*, Public Relations Society of America Register Issue, June, p. 6.
19. Philip Kotler and William Mindak, 1978: 'Marketing and public relations', *Journal of Marketing*, 42, October.
20. E. Denig, 1987: *Public Relations en Voorlichting*, Samsom, Chapter 10.
21. Ibid.
22. Marshall MacLuhan, 1964: *Understanding Media: the extensions of man*, McGraw Hill.
23. Sean Milmo, 1989: 'Europe's exhibition industry seeks new data', *Business Marketing*, October.
24. BBDO College.
25. Charles Francis, Charles Francis Consulting, New York, Third European Advertising and Media Conference, 24–26 February 1988, Management Centre Europe.

■ Appendix

The Seoul Olympics, a mammoth marketing event

As the Olympic Games are the example of a global sports event offering many sponsorship possibilities, this Appendix tells the story of the Olympic Games from the point of view of the last host country, South Korea. This section is an abstract of a presentation given by Mr Ki-Hung Lee, Executive Managing Director of the Korea Broadcasting Advertising Corporation (KOBACO) at the *Adasia Conference* in Lahore, Pakistan in February 1989. Further data collected by KOBACO in 1990 for the purpose of this book have also been included.

Linking the Olympics and marketing

One of the characteristics of the modern Olympics is the merging of the Olympics and marketing. This sports event has become a marketing event for several reasons:

1. The Olympics are a prime marketing opportunity for corporations because the attention of the entire world is focused on the Games, which attract participants from more nations than any other event.
2. The Olympics represent excellence and corporations which link themselves with the Olympics benefit from this association with excellence.

It was at the Los Angeles Olympics in 1984 that the marketing concept was first introduced. The Coca-Cola Company had already distributed free cola to athletes at the ninth Olympic Games in Amsterdam, and since then many corporations have increased their marketing activities during Olympic Games. However, the LA Olympics and the Calgary Winter Olympics were turning points in the history of the Games in that they introduced marketing concepts to the Olympic operations themselves.

With the impetus from the two preceding Olympics behind them, the Seoul Olympic Organizing Committee (SLOOC) drew up a plan of potential revenue sources to meet its budgetary needs, and the Seoul Olympics, held from 17 September to 2 October 1988, now stand as a successful example of the profitable linking of the Olympics with marketing.

The Seoul Olympics was the largest sports event in human history, with 160 nations from five continents participating. The Seoul Olympics were also a cultural event with various cultural exchanges and festivals. All kinds of events such as public music and dance performances, street festivals and exhibitions enriched the Olympics. The Seoul Olympics were also a communication Olympics, more advanced than the LA Olympics in terms of communication equipment and technologies. More than 5,000 journalists from 1,583 mass media, including press, broadcasting stations and news agencies, competed with one another to report on the Games. Many types of new hi-tech media were used, such as mobile studios, IBS and audiotex. A variety of hi-tech developments resulted from these Olympics, such as the computer network which incorporated the official results system, which was seen as setting a new technological benchmark. Finally, the Seoul Olympics were business Olympics. The total income raised through SLOOC's marketing efforts was about US $730 million. The main revenue sources were rights, sponsorships, licensing and advertising business. The total income of the Seoul Olympics was US $719 million, which compares with US $167 million of Montreal and US $669 million for Los Angeles.

The sponsorship of the Olympics consisted of official sponsors, official suppliers and official licensees. A total of 142 firms participated as the official sponsors and licensees of the Olympics. The total income generated by them was US $138 million. SLOOC devoted itself to raising advertising revenues from the official sponsors. The main media used in Seoul were TV, transit advertising, outdoor advertising, advertising on Olympic tickets and advertising at venues.

One of the great success stories of the Olympics was the commemorative coin business. It accounted for 17.5 per cent of the total Olympic income, much higher than the previous levels of 8 per cent in LA and 8.8 per cent in Moscow.

Advertising expenditures in Korea during the Olympics in the four mass media amounted to approximately US $86 million. TV advertising accounted for 50 per cent of this. Advertising hours were sold in packages combining popular and less popular events. The expenditures for newspaper advertising reached US $35 million.

Sponsorship programmes and sponsors

Official programmes in which private companies could participate included official sponsorship, official supplier, and licensing.

Official sponsorship was given to the companies which supplied money, products or services valued at more than $2 million to the Olympic Committee. The companies who were given official sponsorship status could use the Olympic flag and mascot and the official name of the Games in their advertising, PR and product promotions.

Table 9.1   Official sponsors, Seoul Olympics

Company	Product categories
Eastman Kodak	Film, photographic products except 35 mm cameras
Coca-Cola	Soft drinks, fruit juice
Federal Express	Courier services
IBM Korea	Information processing systems
Visa International	Credit card
3M Company	Video/audio tape
Time Inc.	Publishing
Philips International	TV and audio
Nikon	35 mm cameras
Matsushita Electric	Video equipment
Xerox Group	Copiers
Dentsu Inc.	Agent for sponsorship and licensing programme in the region of Japan

Source: TOP.

Table 9.2   Official suppliers, Seoul Olympics

Moojyo Rubber Ind.	Balls for volleyball and water polo
Toledo Scale Reliance Electric	Scale and measurement
Mizuno Corporation	Swimming equipment
Asics Corporation	Equipment for volleyball and handball and badminton net
Bat Taraflex	Volleyball and handball court
Senoh Corporation	Equipment for gymnastics
Cooper Group	Rulers
Backstrand Company	Wrestling mat
Campagnolo SPA	Bicycle technology
Molten Corporation	Balls for basketball
UCS Inc.	Equipment for track
Uesaka Iron Works Co	Equipment for weight lifting
Brother Industries	Typewriters
Nutrexpa NV	Cocoa mix
EF Colleges Ltd	Foreign language training
ARA Services Inc.	Consultancy on catering services
Infortron Systems Co	Electric equipment
Cuno Inc.	Water purifier

Source: TOP.

Official supplier status was accorded to those who supplied less than $2 million in money, products or services.

The official licensing programme gave selected companies the exclusive right to produce and sell souvenirs or convenience products with the Olympic flag or mascot emblem. The Olympic committee collected royalties from the companies with exclusive rights according to the size of sales revenue.

Tables 9.1, 9.2 and 9.3 list some of the companies who were official sponsors, official suppliers or licensees. The lists are not complete, but they give an impression of the companies involved in the Olympics and the products they market. Table 9.1 lists official sponsors, Table 9.2 official suppliers and Table 9.3 licensees.

Table 9.3 Olympic product licensees for foreign countries, Seoul Olympics

Company	Product categories	Region
Adidas USA Inc.	Bags, caps, T-shirts, cloths, towels, socks	Worldwide except Korea
Lloyd Shin Fine Arts Inc.	Art posters	Worldwide except Korea
Atlas Advertising International Ltd	Maps	Worldwide except Korea
Olympic Collections Ltd	Imitations of postage stamps	Worldwide except Korea
HoHo Art & Craft International Co.	Badges, Buttons, Keyholders and Teaspoons	USA
PP & K Trading Co.	29 items, including stickers	USA
KOL Synthetics Ltd	14 items including badges	Canada
Korean Merchandise Centre	All merchandise except for KOL products	Canada
J.H.M. Engineering Trading	All merchandise	Iceland
Deutsche Sports Marketing Gmbh	Licensing agent	West Germany
Romagosa International Merchandising SA	Licensing agent	Spain
Serem International Co. Ltd	All Olympic products	Belgium and 7 other countries
Al-Khalidiah International Est.	All Olympic products	Saudi Arabia and 7 other countries
Ken Planning	Golden Poster Plate	Japan
Ho Chun Emblem & Dies Corp.	Licensing agent	Taiwan
Hippo Books	Olympic Fun Book	Britain

Source: TOP.

Part Three
Managing worldwide advertising

Chapter 10
Research for worldwide advertising

■ Introduction

As the international scope of advertising broadens, financial risks will multiply; consequently up-to-date and relevant marketing data on global developments will be increasingly important. [1]

Elements such as product quality, design, technology, marketing and advertising must be seen in relation to the global competition. Global developments can give a different perspective to the company's strategic position. Business environment and competitive strength play an important role in the trend towards further globalization. In the case of advertising, the needs of the target audience must be assessed through both quantitative and qualitative research data.

Advertising research covering international target groups is more complicated than research involving only local target groups. It also needs to be organized in a different way. The organization of marketing and advertising research is changing both within companies and also in advertising agencies. The account planning system, for example, is now more widely used in advertising agencies producing international campaigns.

International marketing research is responding only slowly to the changing strategic positions and environments of global and international companies. Slow progress is being made in the harmonization of data and standardization of research techniques which will allow comparison of data across borders.

This means that better use will have to be made of secondary data. Knowing where to look and how to compare data for international use is a new and important skill.

The basic theories and techniques of international marketing research are no different to those of research in general. However, internationalization gives rise to a number of complications which will be discussed in this chapter. These factors are incorporated in the following two definitions of international marketing research:

> An activity initiated by an entity in one country which wishes to gather information from a number of countries simultaneously or sequentially in a coordinated multi-country marketing effort.
>
> Frederick A. Goldstein[2]

> Internationalized means for research the extent to which harmonized research procedures exist across national borders.
>
> Mario van Hamersveld[3]

The complications are as follows:

1. 'Gathering information' means assessing the information requirements, knowing where to look and knowing how to interpret data in relation to the culture of origin.
2. 'Number of countries' and 'multi-country' imply problems like language differences and incomparability of data, techniques and reporting.
3. 'Harmonized research' implies a certain uniformity in defining the problem, setting up procedures, selecting uniform research techniques and reporting methods as well as finding ways of working with secondary data which are not directly comparable.
4. 'Coordinated effort' and 'procedures across borders' imply that both the producer and the buyer of research require an international organization.

The major problem in international marketing research is the incomparability of data, both secondary and primary. International standardization of research techniques and interviewing procedures is being given a high priority, but it is not a simple matter. Complete uniformity will be impossible in the near future, but cooperation between researchers is growing.

It is not yet possible to use one single methodology across the world – for example, it is impossible to conduct telephone interviews in every market. However, a common interview design is possible. Comparability also depends on the topics being investigated: simple data on usage or penetration are reasonably comparable, as are data from some consumer diary panels and Nielsen data are also comparable, but more specific cross-border data such as indications of intention to buy are difficult to collect in a comparable way. Cross-border data on attitudes are difficult to compare for several reasons, for example because responses to attitude scale questionnaires may be culturally determined. As a result, most of the cross-border studies are mainly usage studies or very simple attitude studies.

The task of the skilled international researcher is not to eliminate country differences but to understand, manage and control them. To stimulate this process it is essential for commercial management to give careful attention to specifying exactly what marketing information is needed and the role this will play in the decision-making process. There is an increasing readiness on the part of management to do this.[4]

The problems of international research can be divided into two major areas: marketing issues and communication issues. These can be summarized as follows:

1. Marketing issues include:
   (a) environment analysis for each country or region;
   (b) competitor analysis;
   (c) product testing;
   (d) differences in price elasticity;
   (e) distribution patterns;
   (f) consumer trends in general;
   (g) trends in the product category;
   (h) sales measurement via retail audits or consumer panels;
   (i) buying behaviour and usage patterns;
   (j) strengths and weaknesses;
   (k) measuring the effect of marketing.

2. Communication issues include:
   (a) analysis of competitors' advertising;
   (b) brand image measurement;
   (c) clients' profile;
   (d) communication behaviour;
   (e) communication barriers;
   (f) advertising reader, listener and viewer surveys;
   (g) measuring the effect of advertising;
   (h) concept testing

This chapter will describe these issues and the related problems of international research. It will consider how best to organize international research and finally it will focus on some of the methods and techniques used for marketing and advertising research worldwide, such as sampling, questionnaires, interviews and group discussions.

■ Market analysis and sources of information

The first step is to find out how much information, or secondary data, is already available on which to base an analysis of one's own situation and the environment. Then one must decide what primary data is needed in addition, whether this is carried out by the company or bought from research institutes.

Environment analysis

In scanning the international environment the issues which should be considered include economic conditions, demographic trends, the physical environment and climate trends, the political environment, the legal/regulatory environment, the competition, technology, socio-cultural trends and the financial environment. Three levels of information can be distinguished:

1. *Macro-information*: cultural, demographic and economic trends and environmental analysis. These trends must be investigated because they influence the business, although the business cannot influence them.
2. *Meso-information*: developments in the areas in which the business operates, and over which it has influence, for example competitors, distribution, suppliers, buyers, entries and exits to and from markets.
3. *Micro-information*: information about the effectiveness of the business activities, including communication (brand awareness, top-of-mind awareness, evoked set and willingness to try the product or brand), sales, distribution and pricing.

Entering new markets

When entering new markets in other countries, there are three basic market opportunities which must be assessed.[5] These are existing markets, latent markets and incipient markets.

Existing markets

Existing markets are markets in which consumer needs are being served by existing suppliers. The size of existing markets can theoretically be measured by estimating consumption or by measuring the extent of local production of a particular product plus the amount imported minus the amount exported.

Assessing a market opportunity requires a measure of both the overall size of a market and the competitive conditions in the market. It is the combination of total size and competitive conditions that determines sales opportunity and profit.

Global marketing companies focusing on existing markets must first estimate the size of these markets and then assess their own overall competitiveness in terms of product appeal, brand values, price, distribution, advertising and promotional coverage and effectiveness.

Latent markets

Latent demand is demand which would be expressed if a product were offered to customers at an acceptable price. Because nobody has yet offered a product which satisfies these latent needs, there is no market, and demand is zero. After such a product is offered there is existing demand. Personal computers are an example of a product for which there was enormous latent demand.

If the objective is to identify and exploit latent markets, the challenge is different to that posed by existing markets where competition is the main factor to consider. The challenge here is the identification of market opportunity, and success depends on the ability to identify opportunity and launch a marketing programme to meet the latent demand. If there are other companies producing the same or equivalent products, it is important to assess the likelihood and expected timing of competitive entry into latent markets. Examples are innovative products like Sony's Walkman and the videorecorder.

Incipient markets

Incipient demand is demand which does not yet exist but will emerge if present trends continue. If a product is offered to meet incipient demand before the trends have had their impact, there will be no market response. After the trends have had a chance to unfold, the incipient demand will become latent demand. An example of incipient demand is the impact of rising income on demand for consumer durables or cars. As per capita income rises in a country, the demand for cars will also increase.

Incipient international markets are those which will emerge as a consequence of known conditions and trends. These are important for planning purposes. In advanced countries, because of high wages, there is a ready market for any product that saves labour and therefore reduces costs. There is also a ready market for household labour-saving devices. The same pressures and forces operate throughout the world. Companies marketing labour-saving products can predict with reasonable accuracy when demand will emerge in a country as wages and incomes rise, and can plan to deploy their sources to tap these markets as they emerge.

Information needs

For global marketing and advertising strategies a range of information will be needed.

The product

When a product or brand is to be marketed in additional countries, information is needed on the product and market situation in each country, growth potential, strengths and weaknesses of the markets, buying patterns, existing alternative products or brands, and the level of service which can be given in each country. It is necessary to consider whether the product will need to be adapted in some countries. Price levels in the various countries and the strategic brand positioning must be determined.

The distribution

Analysis of distribution patterns in the various countries should indicate distribution intensity and sales methods in each country, and give an idea of how to approach the distribution in each country.

Market shares

Sales analysis is needed to show the market shares of products and brands in each country. It will be useful to know the number of clients that account for 80 per cent of sales, details of heavy users, the number of prospects and the relative proportions of repeat purchases and initial purchases.

Competitor analysis

When competing globally a systematic monitoring system should be available which makes it possible to anticipate competitors' moves. There should be a dossier on each competitor in each country with data on their product range, individual products, brands, market shares, prices, packaging, obtainability, operating strengths and weaknesses.

Advertising activities

In order to decide on the advertising strategy a range of data must be assembled. These include analysis of one's own advertising activities in all countries, past and present, share of voice held by one's own brand and by competitors' brands, changes in brand awareness, brand image and attitudes, media use by competitors, competitors' budgets, advertising ratios in the product field, types of advertising concept adopted, and the use of other means of communication.

Main problem when analyzing markets

Later in this chapter a number of problems in international research will be considered. This section outlines a few general problems encountered when analyzing markets.

The basic problem when analyzing markets and assessing market opportunities in different countries is the limited information available in many markets and the doubtful reliability of the data. Political reasons may influence the presentation of data. In any case, most demographic and economic data are incomparable for most countries. Furthermore, many markets are not big enough to justify a major investment in assembling primary data by conducting marketing research. The absence of known, reliable marketing research agencies in many countries adds to the problem.

The existing large international research agencies who publish data often describe markets in a producer-oriented rather than a consumer-oriented way. For example, dividing a market into 'sauces' and 'mayonnaise', is a producer-oriented distinction which may not be reflected in customers' perceptions, distinguishing ketchup-based sauces and mayonnaise-based sauces.

Research must look at markets from a consumer viewpoint, reflecting differences in consumers' perceptions. The question 'Do you drink wine?' would, in the perception of the French, include all wines, but the Dutch would think only of red wine, as white or rosé wine is generally thought of as an aperitif. In response to the question 'Do you drink alcoholic beverages?' both the French and the Dutch would think only of distilled alcoholic drinks, not of wine or beer.

▣ How to deal with international research

Five rules for international research

Five rules for international research can be outlined. Experience shows that if these rules are followed, they will contribute to the preparation of research reports which act as effective management tools. The rules are as follows:

1. Before beginning the research, ask yourself these six questions:
   (a) what information do I need? What will I do with the information when I get it?
   (b) where can I get this information? Is it available in files, a library, or on line from a database?
   (c) why do I need this information?
   (d) when do I need the information?
   (e) what is this information worth to me in money?
   (f) what would be the cost of not getting the information?
2. Start with desk research. Use the available information in your own files, libraries, on-line databases, trade associations and so on. Quite often the information you are looking for is in your own files or in an easily obtainable public source.
3. Identify the type of information that is available from local sources. Just because the information is or is not available at home does not mean that it is or is not available abroad. The general rule is that the more developed the country, the greater the information available.
4. Know where to look. If you do not know, go to someone who does. Ministries, public libraries and marketing or export consultants will know.
5. Do not assume that the information you get is either comparable to information from other countries or accurate. Check everything. Use common sense and logic to evaluate the comparability and accuracy of the information obtained from sources in other countries.[6]

The sources

Too often market research which mainly comprises the processing and interpretation of consumer interviews is seen as the most important source of marketing information.

The freely-available published demographic and other relevant marketing data is at least as important. In national markets this tends to be taken for granted, but once marketing moves outside national boundaries into less familiar surroundings, obtaining this information fast is essential. In Europe it is relatively easy to obtain such data quickly. This is important as there are major demographic differences. For example, across the whole of Europe 35 per cent of the population is aged under 25, but this varies from 50 per cent in Ireland to 40 per cent in Spain and to 32 per cent in Germany.[7]

Secondary data

A range of publications provide useful secondary data. Some of these are outlined below.

Eurostat, the Statistical Office of the European Communities, produces *Demographic Statistics*.

London-based Euromonitor produces two publications, one covering the European market and the other the remaining countries in the world. Euromonitor also provides information on advertising expenditures and media access.

The *Economist* (Economist Intelligence Unit Publications Ltd) in London publishes the *EIU World Outlook* detailing industrial developments in more than 160 countries. *Marketing in Europe*, a quarterly edition, gives reviews on specific markets in Europe under various product categories.

The World Bank publishes statistics on 124 countries, giving basic data on population, GNP per capita, inflation, literacy, food production, growth of the production per sector, consumption growth, etc. The country economic reports give extensive information on each country, both for macro-economic and industry-specific trends.

The *United Nations Statistical and Demographic Yearbook* and the *UNESCO Statistical Yearbook* are valuable official sources of demographic and social statistics on income, population, birth rates, death rates and marriages, literacy levels, levels of education, unemployment, incomes, consumer prices and production.

In the United States, Business International publishes information on national incomes, gross national product, population, remuneration, prices, foreign trade, production and consumption for 131 countries. Predictions for future development are included for seven countries, the United States, the United Kingdom, Japan, France, Brazil, West Germany and Italy.

Also in the United States, Worldcasts and Predicasts publish worldwide data on regions such as North America, Latin America and the EC.

In each country the Ministry of Economic Affairs or institute for trade promotion in a country will know what information is available from other industries and organizations and how to set about obtaining it.

Furthermore, there is a host of other sources of information about specific markets and countries, such as economic manuals or reports of economic surveys; such information is issued by the national authorities.

Relevant published data do not, of course, cover only demographics: there are many non-confidential sources of industrial and product information that may provide a better starting point for new ventures than commissioning research.

The International Office of Cocoa, Chocolate and Sugar Confectionery (IOCCC) in Brussels, for example, has a first-rate European database on the confectionery business which gives information on country-by-country market shares by value and by volume and the relevant importance by country of chocolate and sugar confectionery. The database also holds many other vital confectionery statistics.[8]

International marketing and market research organizations

International organizations such as the European Society for Opinion and Marketing Research (ESOMAR), the American Marketing Association (AMA), the World Federation of Advertisers (WFA), the International Advertising Association (IAA), the Advertising Research Foundation (ARF) and the Japan Marketing Association (JMA) hold a wealth of information, publish reports and can refer to the national offices which are members of their organization.

International research organizations regularly organize conferences, where delegates gather from all over the world to exchange experiences, and present papers. Often these papers are published and are available for sale after the conference. ESOMAR especially, together with AMA and JMA, offers a vast array of conferences on marketing and advertising research.

International market research agencies

There is a growing number of market research agencies which have a worldwide network and which can conduct or coordinate international research. Examples are Nielsen, Research International, AGB, INRA, Gallup and Burke. Nielsen is one of the largest, with offices in twenty-seven countries. A survey of all market research agencies in most countries of the world is published in the yearly ESOMAR directory. The appendix to this chapter lists a number of international research organizations which can provide addresses.

Primary data

If secondary data are not sufficient, primary data must be obtained. The main categories of research which market researchers carry out for international marketing include the following:

1. Business-to-business research.
2. Media audience research.
3. Brand image measurement.
4. Sales measurement using either retail audits or consumer panels.
5. Advertising research.
6. Usage and attitude studies.
7. Product testing.

A study carried out by AGB in 1989 showed that key marketing personnel in Europe considered brand image measurement the most useful aspect in non-national marketing, with attitude and usage studies second. The third most useful aspect was thought to be product testing.[9]

The future of cross-border research studies

The need for research using identical research techniques on a country-to-country basis is growing. With this growing need there is a growing demand for the following:

1. Standardized techniques.
2. Better modelling and fusion techniques.
3. On-line computer access to European and global market research data.
4. Centralized cross-border interviewing; with the growth of telephone penetration and linked communications in Europe, studies can now be conducted from one central source by multi-lingual interviewers or locally by telephone with all the data being sent down the line to a central point for processing.[10]

◼ **Research for world brands**

Earlier chapters have discussed the choice between standardization and differentiation. The choice of whether to launch a world brand or gradually change regional or local brand ranges into world brands depends on whether it is possible to find similarities in cultures on which to base an international or global campaign.

It is important to identify those aspects of the marketing mix which will have to be the same between countries because of communal distribution lines. Design, package, price, quality and communications play an important role.

The weight attached to the different aspects of the marketing mix will vary according to the type of product. Consumer durables have often succeeded in becoming world brands because of their technical quality, combined with a relatively low price. This was the basis for Sony's success: innovative, high-quality products and good service. On the other hand, the success of Coca-Cola was based on communications combined with an efficient global network of bottlers and distribution.

Fast-moving consumer goods rely more heavily on expressive values, created by advertising. The successful global fast-moving consumer brands have achieved their leading position on the basis of added-value consumer benefits; they are 'image-intensive' global brands.[11] These brands often have three important characteristics which have to be taken into account when researching acceptance in new markets:

1. They often originate from a particular culture: Levi's are American jeans, Johnny Walker is Scotch whisky, Buitoni is Italian pasta, Chanel is French perfume.
2. The package is the same worldwide; it serves as a global advertising medium and radiates the brand personality. The major role played by the packaging in determining the success of a global brand makes researching on this aspect crucial. However, a negative result from a pack-test in a minor market must be weighed against the communication effects of a globally standardized package.
3. The majority of these brands are based on life-style marketing and related communication techniques. Most brands for which the communication is based on life-style research, however, are 'adoption' brands, based on a life-style concept belong to the home country. The result is that their positions with respect to competitive brands are not the same in the different countries.

When launching a new global brand, a lead country is often chosen as the starting point. Research is done, and the outcome compared with details on the countries in which a roll-out is being considered. Countries are often grouped according to priority, size, language, phase of the product life-cycle which has been reached or comparability of product/market combinations or distribution structures. Methodical assessment of all the variables is necessary. All too often decisions are taken based solely on demographics, income levels, age or ownership of products. These can differ more than one might think in different countries. For example, in Europe, the United Kingdom has the highest level of microwave ownership (43 per cent), compared to only 3 per cent in Italy. However, the United Kingdom has a below-average penetration of dishwashers (11 per cent), with Germany leading at 33 per cent.[12]

Although common trends are identifiable across countries, national differences will not disappear. The growing similarity in consumer trends is shown in the following ways:

1. The relationship that consumers have with the brands they buy is changing; brands offer values such as longevity, reliability and quality.
2. New forms of self-expression, excitement and personal fulfilment are appearing.
3. Time is becoming a scarce resource amongst affluent urban majorities.
4. The roles of the sexes are shifting.
5. There are broad demographic shifts; for example, the youth market is in steady decline while the older population is growing.
6. Awareness of environmentalism is increasing.[13]

International consumer differences which influence consumer needs, problems and usage habits include the following:

1. Differences in population trends in different countries. In Europe Germany's population is declining, while those of the Netherlands and Spain are increasing at three times the rate of the United Kingdom.
2. Income distribution varies greatly between countries.
3. Language differences will continue to play an important role.
4. Markets differ in the level of ownership of durables and consumption of food.
5. Attitudes may differ towards products made in other countries; however, national stereotypes can also be used positively.[14]

The development of pan-European or global brands and advertising make it necessary to look for both similarities and differences in markets.

If the differences do not dominate they can be used to fine-tune the marketing effort on a country-by-country basis.

The right kind of research is needed to find these similarities and differences and present them to marketers in a way which enables them to make the right decisions. How to organize research which covers a number of countries is an important question; the larger the number of people involved, the more risk there is of having to make concessions. Structures for cooperation will have to be designed and the methodological problems of cross-country research will have to be overcome. Input from the consumer is essential, and providing a structure which allows for consumer input is essential.[15]

■ Organizational and methodological problems

There are a number of conceptual, methodological and organizational problems which hinder international research. These include the following:

1. The complexity of the research design.
2. The lack of secondary data and the quality of the secondary data which is available.
3. Difficulties in establishing the comparability and equivalence of data from different countries.
4. The lack of harmonization of data.
5. The high cost of collecting primary data.
6. The availability of and differences in the use of techniques.
7. Non-standardized research techniques.
8. The customer orientation of researchers and research organizations.
9. The changing organization of research in companies.

Complexity of research design

When setting up international research it is not enough to add together the results of individual surveys. Each project should be seen as one piece of a puzzle contributing to an overall picture.[16] While countries are convenient units of analysis due to the existence of political, organizational and language boundaries, and also because secondary data are mostly available by country, they may not be the appropriate units from a marketing standpoint. Management might prefer to look at, for example, teenagers all over the world. The relevant respondents may differ from country to country; while in the United States children may play an important role in decisions about buying sweets, in other countries mothers may be the relevant decision-makers.[17] Defining children as a communication target group may not be practical as local rules may prohibit showing children on television.

Lack of secondary data and poor quality of data

Sophisticated researchers in developed countries are confronted with the fact that the same type of information they are used to in their own market is not available in all markets in the world. Where data are available they are often inaccurate or unreliable, or at least not comparable with data from other countries. There is a variety of local practices in data collection worldwide, and the question is to what extent it will be possible in the future to maintain control over the quality of data collection.

Data on population are collected in different ways and data on income or product sales are often absent. Data on media access are available but not comparable because of different ways of defining the kind of media or readership. Thus factors which influence consumer buying decisions may have to be estimated in a different way than is usual in the home country. This requires a considerable degree of creativity on the part of the researchers, and appropriate training will be necessary.

Establishing comparability and equivalence

It is very difficult to determine the equivalence and comparability of both secondary and primary data and of the methods used for data collection. Sometimes data appear comparable but in fact are not. An example is the registration of motor vehicles. In some countries company cars which are also used for personal transport are registered as commercial vehicles. Many research methods have been developed in the United States or other Western countries, and may be of limited relevance for other countries. For example response data may differ largely for written questionnaires or personal and telephone interviews in different countries.[18]

When comparing groups or subgroups, data may also differ considerably. Local sources are firmly rooted in the local market; this can be a strength, but it is not necessarily an advantage for internationalization.[19]

Lack of harmonization

Harmonization of both primary and secondary data is necessary but rarely occurs. Each country uses its own system of grouping information; this is demonstrated by the examples outlined below.

Age brackets differ in various countries; some use five-year intervals and others ten. Even if the intervals are the same, there may be different brackets, for example 25–29 or 26–30. The level of adulthood may also start at different ages: in Germany it is at age 18, in Japan it is the age of leaving the parental home. In Japan a young person still living at home is defined as a child. In some countries media research defines adults as those over 18 years; in others adults are defined as those over 12 years.

Definitions of main income earners vary, as do definitions of income: monthly net income, monthly gross income, annual income, personal income, total amount of household income are all used.

Social class scales differ. The British scale 'ABC1C2DE' is one of the most widely-used classifications, but it is made up of ten components, and depends on details of occupation and educational qualifications which are not comparable throughout Europe. Companies in other countries who work with UK companies often use the system, but adapt it for other countries. In Germany the definition of social class is done on a point scale roughly consisting of income, profession and education. The French classification consists of data on what people do and where they do it – for example, whether they work for public or private companies.

Life-cycle groupings differ.

Definitions of 'household' differ, depending on the culture of the country. It may just mean 'everybody living in the same house'. As a result in some Western countries classifications consist of one-person, two-person and three-person households, and households with three or more members. However, one has to look at the family structure in each country; in some cases it may be usual for grandparents, aunts and uncles to live in the same household, or there may be other criteria. In one African country the definition is 'those eating out of the same pot'. In some countries children leave home relatively early, to live by themselves, while in others they stay with their parents till they marry. As a result the average number of people in a household may not have much meaning unless the structure of the family is also taken into account.

Standard household equipment differs widely. In some countries a washing machine is considered a necessity and almost everybody owns one, so in France, for example, it might not be thought worth mentioning in answer to questions about household equipment. In other countries, such as Greece, a washing machine is still a luxury.

Education systems differ, despite apparent similarities.

Research methodologies differ. In Southern European countries more focus group discussions are widely used while in Northern European countries more individual interviews are conducted. In the United States there is more quantitative research. Sampling techniques and questionnaire design also differ, and there are problems in equating values, concepts and expressions.

Differences in budgets can lead to differences in outcome. The same budget spread over several countries will give a different research outcome than if it is used in a single, more homogeneous market. Different budgeting customs also play a role: usually in the United States a budget for research is included in the communication budget, but this is often not the case in Europe.

High costs of collecting primary data

Research for a company with a global approach should be conducted on a worldwide basis. However, researching every topic across all countries in the world where one might want to market the product or brand would be costly and time-consuming, especially since not all countries have a market research infrastructure or experience in conducting market research.

The costs of research vary widely in different countries. Belgium is known as a country where low-cost research is possible, while in Germany the costs are very high. Some people argue that concessions can be made, for example by extrapolating from secondary data or varying research techniques where certain techniques are not available in some countries. For example, costs can be reduced by grouping together certain European countries, for example, Benelux, the Iberian peninsula, countries with a Germanic culture or countries with a Latin culture.[20]

Availability of and differences in the use of techniques

Group discussions are used everywhere. However, in some countries they are considered sufficient, but not in others. This also varies according to advertiser and agency. Groups vary in size from eight to fourteen persons, and in length from one and a half to five hours, depending on the country. Depth interviews are common practice in others.

Telephone interviewing is a well-developed interview technique in some European countries, and for business-to-business research it is even done on a Europe-wide scale. Its usefulness depends on telephone penetration, so it cannot easily be used on a global scale; this might be possible for business-to-business research, but certainly not for consumer brands.

The response percentages for written questionnaires differ very much by country; needless to say this kind of interview can only be used in countries with a sufficiently high literacy rate. Culture, and especially religion, has an important influence on response rates in general. People often give answers to questions on buying behaviour which do not mirror their actual behaviour. These differences vary according to country and culture.[21] An example of this is given by Table 10.1, which lists the differences in concept test responses for a food and drink product in nine countries. Overstatement of intention to buy within Europe is noticeably higher in Catholic countries such as Spain and Italy than in countries such as Germany or the United Kingdom. Among the Asian countries, the Japanese tend to make less overstatements than the Chinese, whether in Taiwan or China.[22]

In Europe there is an increasing reluctance to participate in

Table 10.1 Concept test responses in nine countries

Purchase intention	Germany %	UK %	France %	Italy %	Spain %	US %	Japan %	Taiwan %	China %
Definitely would buy	25	26	24	41	61	28	3	4	8
Probably would buy	38	48	35	42	34	32	38	51	34
Might or might not buy	17	12	17	6	1	18	28	30	39
Probably would not buy	10	8	12	2	2	7	23	10	15
Definitely would not buy	10	6	12	9	2	15	8	5	4

Source: Burke International Research Corp., USA and Burke European Research Center, Germany and Italy.

personal interviews. An increasing number of people do not want to be bothered in their homes by an interviewer they do not know.[23]

Increasing regulations and legislation on privacy in developed countries are placing more limitations on the use of research techniques.

Non-standardized research techniques

If there is no such thing as a standard global consumer or even a standard Euro consumer or Euro company, then needs cannot be met by standardized research. However, a growing number of companies want to look at the world or at a continent like Europe as a whole, and therefore need the research industry to deliver an overall perspective.[24] Some progress has been made in this area.

International research agencies are gradually setting up comparable *ad hoc* or continuous research activities and individual researchers are adopting a more international outlook. Databanks are becoming more international and research products are being offered on an international scale. The possibilities offered by information technology are playing an important role in this process.[25] Large international advertising agencies are also offering standardized research techniques to their clients.

John Clemens[26] describes a pan-European image study which measured the European image of the leading German car brands, conducted by Sandpiper International Ltd. This study used identical techniques country by country and produced data for most of Europe on the images of German car brands. The data could be cross-analyzed in many useful and informative ways. It compared six makes of German car, measuring their image on eight dimensions identified as critical in car choice. It was possible to position any car brand on any dimension, for example image, reliability or dependability. Alternatively the data could be used to position all the German cars on one dimension in one country. Not surprisingly, on the sporting dimension Porsche and BMW were in the lead in the United Kingdom. Looking at all eight dimensions in Italy, Volkswagen scored high on reliability.[27]

International professional organizations like ESOMAR play an important role in the standardization and harmonization of research data. For example the ESOMAR Working Party on Harmonization of Demographics has put forward a number of recommendations on standard definitions for use in Europe. The following are a few examples:[28]

1. *Household*: 'Group of one or more persons living together, in the same main residence.' If a more precise definition is needed, it includes all those having most of their meals together.

Table 10.2 Recommended classification of European occupational groups

E1 : General management, six employees or more (Chief Executive Officer, President, Chairman, Executive vice-president, Managing Director, Senior Manager, etc.)
E2 : Self-employed professional (doctor, lawyer, accountant, architect, etc.)
E3 : Employed professional (in actual profession)
E4 : General management, five employees or less
E5 : Middle management, six employees or more (department group head, branch manager, junior manager, etc.)
E6 : Middle management, five employees or less
E7 : Businessman, six employees or more (owner of large shop/company)
E8 : Office employee (non-management staff working in office)
E9 : Businessman, five employees or less
E10: MIE: retired   resp.: Student
E11: Out-of-office staff (shop-keeper, salesman, nurse, etc.)
E12: Farmer
E13: MIE: unemployed   resp.: 'Housewife'
E14: Manual worker (to be further assessed as 'skilled' or 'unskilled')

Source: ESOMAR, *Progress Report June 1990*, Working Party on Harmonization of Demographics.

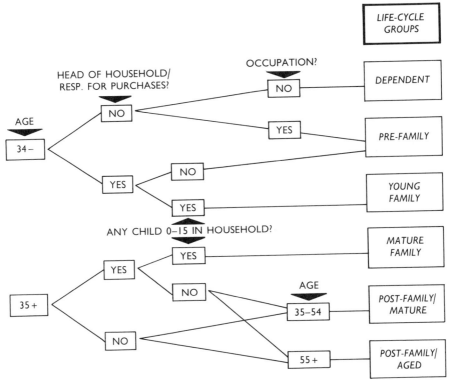

Figure 10.1 *Recommended life-cycle classification of individuals in six groups (source: ESOMAR)*

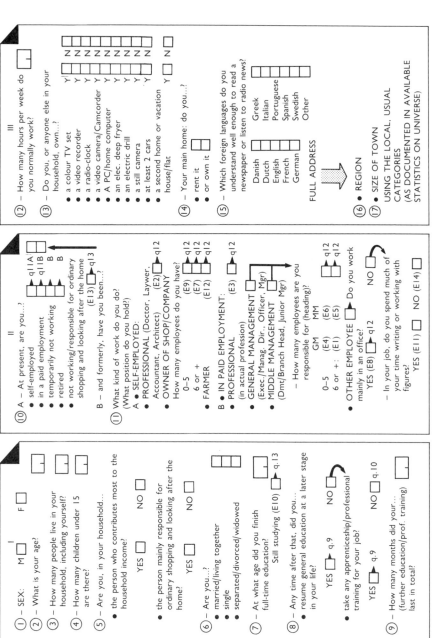

Figure 10.2 *Recommended demographic questionnaire (source: ESOMAR)*

2. *Housewife*: 'Person responsible for ordinary shopping and looking after the home.' This person can be male or female, and may eventually be the Main Income Earner as well.
3. *Main Income Earner* (MIE): 'The person, in the household, who contributes most to the total income, irrespective of sex, age, or working status.' 'Income', unlike 'Wages', includes all types of revenues.
4. *Terminal Education Age* (TEA): 'The age at which the respondent (or the MIE) finished his/her full-time education.' This measure is recommended as a substitute for 'level of education', because of the difficulty in establishing equivalence between a great variety of diplomas and certificates across countries.

The working party has also produced a recommended classification of occupational groups based on fourteen categories. This is shown in Table 10.2.

A preliminary suggestion on life-cycle classification has also been presented. This is shown in Figure 10.1.

Figure 10.2 shows the recommended questionnaire produced by the ESOMAR Working Party.

Customer orientation of researchers and research organizations

Not all researchers, whether in research agencies, advertising agencies or in the research department of the company itself, are sufficiently customer-oriented. Often they are too much in love with their own techniques and methods and it is difficult to persuade them to make concessions for the sake of internationalization.[29] For decentralized international organizations this is a major problem, as data from specialized proprietary research techniques are difficult to compare with those produced by the research agencies used in other countries.

Changing organization of research in companies

Mario van Hamersveld, Head of Marketing Research and Support for Philips Consumer Electronics in the Netherlands,[30] notes an additional obstacle:

Many large companies have in the last years substantially changed the organization of the research function. Amongst other things, this has resulted in the externalization of research. There is often only an 'information buyer' left in the company. Head Office probably regard this as a favourable situation – but it is doubtful if this has a positive effect on continued research quality. It means that many research agencies now have to accustom themselves to dealing directly with the organization's commercial management.

The effect of this will be enhanced by the limited vision typical of marketing managers in the 1980s, who are used to seeking short-term success and profit. When they fail in one company, they move to another, believing that their principles can apply to any product category.[31] Research for a long-term global brand strategy should be a continuous effort. Some international market researchers in large multinationals – where these still exist – have to defend their research strategies every eight months or so to a new marketing or brand manager.

■ Organization and coordination of international research

In order to develop a well-coordinated research plan and carry it out in various countries, there must first be agreement on the research objectives in every country in which research is conducted. Design and data collection must also be harmonized.[32] The best way of doing this depends largely on the organizational structure of the company. Coordination costs can be limited if only the translation and the fieldwork are done in the individual countries: research design, sampling, data processing, interpretation and project management can be done centrally with greater efficiency.

International research agencies which provide full resources and equal skills in each country, especially those owned by a central coordinator, will be better placed to serve international clients than more informal associations of independent local agencies.[33]

One negative aspect of using a centrally-organized international research agency is that the conceptual framework of the research design may be dominated by one cultural perspective. Problems with analyzing and interpreting the data result. However, if the client is heavily involved in research design and interpretation, the bias of the research institute should not be such a problem.

In an international or multinational company with regional and local subsidiaries, the research function may be centralized at company headquarters, or it may be to a large extent delegated to the operating units of the company. This depends largely on the way in which the organization is structured in general and on whether marketing is organized by geography, product category or brand. The main objective should be to obtain the best information to support decisions on specific goals.[34]

Organization and coordination of research activities will be different where the aim is to develop and execute a largely standardized marketing and advertising effort than when a decentralized local or regional approach is preferred. This section will concentrate on the former. If the objective is standardization, this will demand an orientation which seeks out consumer similarities and manages the differences. Usually this requires at least a central coordinator. Where the objectives are more localized, this may be because such an approach suits the marketing and product category.[35] In this situation it may be justifiable to leave marketing research totally in the hands of local subsidiaries.

The main objective of the organization must be to let the 'consumer voice' be heard in the management decision-making process. Centralization and decentralization should not be seen as opposites. An integrated effort should be made to combine the advantages and disadvantages of both systems.

An important aspect of international research is the coordination of multi-country studies: research done in different countries yields local market knowledge which must be coordinated to support decisions about multi-country brands. How to coordinate the results depends largely on the organization of the company; this can be done by the company itself, perhaps together with an advertising agency, or by a product category specialist, or by a local coordinating agency.[36]

In real life, many companies have both central or regional research departments and decentralized local ones. Their relative importance depends on corporate philosophy. Their importance determines their size and budgets, which in turn determine the scope of the research each initiates and conducts.[37]

As is the case with the organization of advertising, centralization and decentralization have both advantages and disadvantages. These are considered below.

Advantages and disadvantages of a centralized and decentralized approach

Advantages and disadvantages of centralized and decentralized approaches have been presented by Hawkins,[38] Grobe,[39] Kalim,[40] and

Origlia.[41] Table 10.3 summarizes the advantages and disadvantages of a centralized approach outlined by these theorists.

The advantages and disadvantages of decentralization are the reverse of those for centralization. The greatest advantage of decentralized research is the local flavour and the commitment of local

Table 10.3 Advantages and disadvantages of centralized research

Advantages	Disadvantages
Control over detail and techniques	Limited local usefulness
Wider perspective of the international researcher	Lack of sensitivity to local conditions:
	— language mistranslations
Uniformity of data and data processing	— local customs
Standardization of methodology, consistency:	— local research practices
	Study design may be impractical for specific market, local needs sacrificed to international consistency
— target audience definition	
— sampling procedures	
— eligibility criteria	Difficult/inaccurate data interpretation
— questionnaire	Danger of too much compromise for the sake of homogeneity
— interview administration	
— analysis procedure	Surveys repeat local studies
— report format	Limited local acceptance:
Better coordination	— because not locally 'owned'
— within the client company	— central reporting may fail to take account of local situation
— if one coordinating research agency, greater efficiency, central reporting and accessibility	If research is not used by local managers its value to headquarters is diminished
Comparable results for different markets	
Building up expertise	
— managing country differences	
— cross-country fertilization	
— unbiased analysis of country differences	
Closer to the decision-making centre for long-term issues	
Often greater financial resources	

Table 10.4 Trade-offs between centralization and decentralization

Favours Centralization	Favours Decentralization
Ability to instil more uniformity, and to collect and analyse data that are truly comparable	Ability to optimally understand needs and peculiarities of local markets

management. Lack of standardization and harmonization of data are the greatest impediments for international use.

Grobe[42] gives a summary of the trade-offs between the two approaches. This is shown in Table 10.4.

Integration

There are different ways of combining the advantages of both the centralized and the decentralized approaches. Ideally the two approaches should be integrated. Some multinational companies are therefore looking at the concept of 'core questions'.[43] This implies including certain key measures as standard features in local surveys. The results of these key questions may then be forwarded to central or regional headquarters as input to a central or regional database. It sounds simple, but there are problems involved, such as how to fit the core questions into the questionnaire, how to administer them in order to provide comparable results and so on.

Hawkins[44] describes the organization of the research function at Braun as an example of a good balance between centralization and decentralization. The Braun market research department consists of six researchers; all are multi-lingual and have several years of international research experience. These researchers have specific product line responsibility, and so mirror the product divisions. Additionally four of the dozen most important subsidiaries each have a small research department. These researchers are responsible for providing continuous data relating to their own countries (such as retail audits) and for conducting studies in their own countries to assist the central department. The main part of Braun's research programme is conducted in Europe and North America. The company has central research departments in both continents, who get involved in the different countries within their region. Translations are checked, briefings are given personally and in writing, and whenever possible researchers make field visits and get involved in discussion about the analysis. They are also involved in the selection and assessment of agencies.

Unilever[45] has a number of local products for which research is done locally. In the case of an international brand, masterminded by a lead country, the latter will often carry out much more intensive consumer research than will a receiving country. The lead country, when developing a new brand, will call for considerable concept, product development and marketing mix research before other countries become heavily involved with the new product, especially where technical development work is an important element. Nevertheless at an early stage a broader geographical picture of consumer habits, needs and responses to formulation variables may be needed. This may necessitate habit surveys across a number of the major countries. If the new development goes well in the lead country, then research elsewhere will begin by checking the reactions to the mix already developed. Only if problems arise will more basic studies be done in the receiving countries. Unilever's decentralized structure means that allocation of funds for market research, as well as relevant decisions, take place primarily at the local level.

Sara Lee/DE[46] is an example of a fast growing international organization. The group has been expanding very rapidly in recent years as a result of take-overs. After an initial integration, the group is now developing a more multinational strategy for the different divisions and product groups. One of the divisions markets coffee and grocery products and has subsidiaries in five European countries. The organization in the Netherlands – the original home-base and headquarters of the Douwe Egberts company (DE) – has a department of eight researchers. In the other countries the independent research function is filled either by just one person or not at all. The head of the Dutch research department spends half his time on international operations. His first task is to harmonize research techniques, definitions and reporting. He has to motivate and stimulate the researchers in other countries to cooperate in this process. His function is not formalized and he has no official authority, but must depend on the respect his colleagues have for his expertise. This is not an uncommon situation in developing international organizations.[47]

Grobe[48] describes an integrated approach with the following main objectives:

1. Make everyone aware of:
   (a) why the project is being done;
   (b) what is the fundamental objective;
   (c) how the results will affect management decisions.
2. Give the subsidiaries all relevant details if they are expected to participate or if the study is done in their territory.
3. Assess rationally the subsidiary's feelings that a 'special situation' in their country warrants a different study design. The subsidiary would have to ensure that findings could still be integrated in the international study.
4. Define precisely:
   (a) who will do what;
   (b) who will check what;
   (c) who will approve what;

(d) deadlines for each activity to which HQ, subsidiary and agency must adhere;

(e) specific functions to be delegated to the international or local agency.

A continuous flow of information between all parties involved is a prerequisite.

The organization of the research function in the advertising agency

The role of the research function in the advertising agency has changed in recent years. Advertising agencies took the lead in conducting research for advertising and marketing in the 1950s. As the research function within major companies grew during the 1970s, the research function in advertising agencies diminished. Research, being a separate function, and not closely integrated with the advertising campaign process, was increasingly seen as a threat by the creative team in the advertising agency. In the 1980s, the growing number of research agencies has created a need for the advertising agency to play an intermediary rate in coordinating and initiating research.

Research personnel in advertising agencies counsel management and clients. Their major function is pulling the consumer into the process by conducting research. Researchers in advertising agencies may form a service department, with a title such as 'Marketing Services', or function in the role of strategy director or account planner. Account planners are a new breed of researchers who often have advanced degrees in psychology, and specialize in areas ranging from cognitive science to semiotics.

Account planning

The account planning function serves to channel the consumer's viewpoint to the agency's creative staff during the process of creating the campaign. With their research input, account planners or strategy directors are better able to bring the consumer background into the creative brief.

Account planners are most often found in international agencies, and they are more common in the United Kingdom than in the United States. A local client of an advertising agency will less often ask for research input to strategy planning than an international client for whom more is at stake. The role of the account planner will vary for each client: it may involve receiving and implementing the client's research needs or just coordinating the client's research activities.

The way in which the account planner works with a client relates to the way in which the agency works with the client: centralized or localized control will affect the way in which research is handled. Thus, an account planner in a lead agency may play an important role in the cross-cultural research needed by the client, while in the local agency, the account planner may play a minor role.

The type of researcher needed for international research

The ideal international researcher is a smart, strategic thinker, multilingual, well-travelled, competent and experienced, and with a strong methodological background. Most important, he or she must have a marketing-oriented, open-minded and problem-solving approach.[49]

■ Research methods and techniques

This section will cover certain research techniques to which special attention must be given when used for international research.

Sampling

Advanced sampling methods have been designed for use in developed countries. These methods cannot be easily transferred to other countries. Thus, the researcher in less developed countries may have to rely much more heavily on judgement samples than on random samples. The researcher must also design the sample to be representative only of that portion of the population which is part of the potential market. In some countries, city residents operate in a money economy while rural residents may be self-sufficient or use barter to meet their needs.[50] Sometimes asking for a representative sample in all the countries where one wants to market a brand is too costly. In some cases one can rely on a few countries to provide a sample for a quantitative research.

If there is a clearly-defined target group of people with shared characteristics, for example businessmen who travel a lot, sampling is not the greatest problem. For an industrial product it is feasible to deal with a small number of highly knowledgeable people in twelve countries than with a large sample in two or three countries.

Questionnaire design

Three central issues in the design of survey questionnaires are scaling, measurement and wording. Common scales in marketing questionnaires are the semantic differential and Likert scales. When developing an instrument for use in another culture, the researcher should take care to ensure that such scales are understood and responded to in the intended manner; otherwise, any interpretation of the responses is meaningless.

For example, Latin Americans are more likely to use the extreme points on a scale to express their individualism, while Indians may express similarly intense opinions using points near the middle of the same scale.[51] In Northern European democratic and socialist countries a four-point scale is preferred to a five-point scale, to force a choice: people do not want to stand out from the crowd, and tend to give average opinions when attitudes are concerned.

With attitude or brand loyalty measurements it is necessary first to verify the meaning of a concept in the other culture. Some concepts just do not exist in some cultures and the words for them are not even translatable. The concept of *gezelligheid* in the Dutch culture or *hyggelig* in Denmark is of great importance for associations between certain products like coffee and moments of 'togetherness'. The concept is not directly translatable into other languages and does not exist in all the other European countries. Concepts like this are not fit for international use.

The same counts for associations with other products. Comparing powdered milk with fresh milk can only be done in countries where fresh milk exists and has a certain connotation. In most countries in Asia fresh milk is not consumed as it is in the United States. Even within Europe there is a great variation in perception, attitudes and drinking habits as far as fresh milk is concerned. When researching usage of coffee as a morning drink, there are many different alternatives to compare in each country, from instant coffee to chicory-related products.

Translating questionnaires for multi-country use is not enough. First the concepts have to be checked. Another useful approach is retranslation: questions can be translated back into the original language by someone who has not seen them before to see how they are interpreted.[52]

When formulating questions which will have to be translated the following principles should be observed:[53]

1. If any associations with other products are made, check the existence and use of those products in target countries.
2. Formulate single-element questions.
3. Have the questions checked for conceptual meaning related to the culture in the target countries.
4. Use no ambiguous questions.
5. Avoid leading questions.
6. Do not use personal or embarrassing questions. What is considered personal or embarrassing in the target country should be checked.
7. A pretest may help avoid mistakes.

Interviews and group discussions

Within Europe there are considerable differences in the way in which qualitative research is done. The United Kingdom is notorious for its heavy dependency on group discussions, whereas in Germany and Holland individual interviews are more common.[54]

There are many important reasons why postal surveys are often unsuitable for international research, making it necessary to rely on personal interviews. Telephone interviewing is growing, but in many countries a low percentage of telephone availability in homes makes this approach unsuitable.

Personal interviews rely heavily on the expertize of the interviewer, who has to deal with cultural differences. The interviewer should be a national or a long-standing resident of the country. Different cultures may be more or less open in their answers on certain matters. In many Islamic countries women cannot be interviewed by men, and women interviewers are not easily available because it is not common practice for women to work outside the home. Other solutions have to be found; in this situation women often do not do the actual buying outside the home. This is done by men who can be interviewed instead. The acceptance of women being interviewed by other, indigenous women is increasing.

The way in which group discussions and in-depth interviews are set up and run vary widely from country to country. A client in one country might ask for six group discussions on a particular product field, while a client in the United Kingdom or Germany will consider one two-hour session enough.

Recruiting participants for group discussions and interviews poses more problems. There must be standardization in representation of, for example, working women and mothers, which poses problems in countries where women work and do not want to be interviewed in the evening. Holiday seasons must be taken into account: the French go on holiday for the whole of August and the Swedes in July.[55]

■ Research for advertising

Tracking studies

With the development of the global brand strategy and accompanying global advertising campaigns, advertising tracking research has emerged as an important technique. Tracking studies are based on continuous monitoring of brand awareness, trial, usage and image (these are all partially advertising effects). Even in the most sophisticated markets in Europe, with similarities in brand and advertising strategies, this kind of research has encountered cross-border problems. Varying conditions in different countries even make comparison of tracking study results difficult. These varying conditions include the following:

1. The size of the advertising expenditures in each market.
2. The nature of the brands: share of market, share of voice.
3. The differences in advertising cultures in countries: different styles of advertising.
4. Media differences in advertising practice: in the United Kingdom television accounts for 33 per cent of advertising expenditure, while in Germany there is more emphasis on print advertisements and television accounts for only 11 per cent of expenditure.
5. Differences in legal restrictions.

When tracking an international campaign which utilizes a different media strategy in each country, the different levels and qualities of awareness have to be taken into account. Levels of awareness will vary according to media use. An advertising tracking study of a comparable international campaign in six countries in Europe showed that the lowest level of advertising awareness was in Germany and Holland and the highest in Spain and Italy, because of greater use of television. Mean levels of advertising awareness in Europe tend to climb as one moves further south in mainland Europe, corresponding to the degree of freedom from restrictions experienced by local TV advertising.[56] With the rapidly-changing media conditions in Europe this should not, however, be seen as static.

Life-style research

In the United States, Europe and Asia, life-style research is developing. The results can be useful for defining life-styles across countries as the basis for selecting a communication concept and positioning a brand. Life-style research can only be used in combination with more discriminatory variables such as socio-demographics. Life-style research helps describe a state of mind, but it does not work as a discriminatory variable.

Concept testing

When planning a global or pan-European advertising campaign it is important to discover at each stage of the creative process whether the message will be viable in the individual markets. Whether the campaign is developed in a lead country and then spread to other countries, or simultaneously introduced in a series of countries, this kind of research must be done.

The usual methods are focus group discussions or in-depth interviews. Variables to measure include the following:

1. Target reactions: does the target group understand the message and the product benefit? Is the desirable key response effected?
2. If life-style advertising is used: does the projected life-style fit with the life-style and values of the target group? Are the values conveyed recognized by the target group? Are they valid in the target culture?
3. If there is an element of problem-solving or product benefit in the concept, are these problems or benefits perceived as such?

Pretesting and copytesting

When there is agreement on the concept, the execution must be considered. The key question is whether the execution will work equally well across the markets.[57]

Pretesting must be done at the local level. One example may be sent to the various countries, giving each the chance to make amendments.

In the end a central decision may be taken on what to adapt and what to leave. Again, focus group interviews or just local expertize may be used.

Large companies which have been used to one large home market and are now spreading out to regions with many different markets will have to realize that the costs of pretesting are relatively much higher in a number of small countries in other continents than they are in the United States. Research costs are not comparable, for example, to those in Europe. It is not possible to test all details in the different European countries as it would be in the United States. Compromises have to be made. As television is a major medium for global advertising campaigns in many markets, copy research may concentrate on this medium, while relying on local expertise to estimate the viability of the additional print campaign.

As much standardized advertising relies heavily on visuals, it is ideal to test the concepts of commercials visually, and not to make people respond verbally, since this gives rise to possible problems of misunderstanding and misinterpretation.

Experiments have been done involving testing the cross-border use of television commercials in order to be able to change elements which may not be appreciated or accepted in all the countries where the commercial will be used. One example of an experiment of this kind was done by Pegram Walters International, using the PEAC system.[58] Other research institutes have either experimented with the system or are already using it.

The system works as follows. Focus groups are selected consisting of people belonging to the target group, who are shown the commercials to be tested. Electronic hand units the size of a television remote control pad are used to collect the information. Each unit is essentially a microcomputer with a memory and a clock calibrated to a time code contained on the reel of commercials investigated. Respondents are asked to enter their reactions to the ads on a second-to-second basis, by pressing five keys (A–E). For the purpose of the study the five point scale adopted was as follows:

Very positive
Positive
Neutral
Negative
Very negative

It is therefore possible to monitor changes in consumer reaction on a moment-to-moment basis, synchronized to the material they are seeing. In a forty-five second commercial it is not unusual to find that a

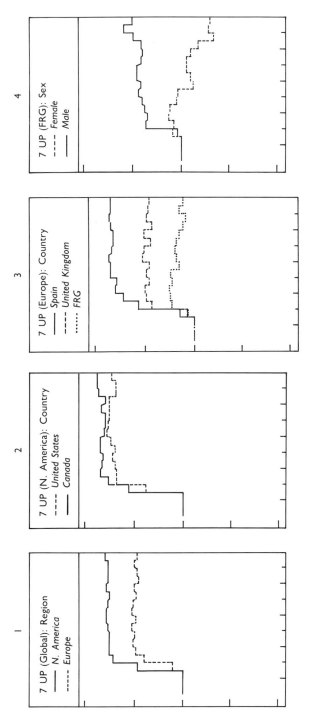

Figure 10.3 Test results using the PEAC system (source: Pegram Walters International, United Kingdom)

respondent has entered twenty key presses, describing how he or she is feeling about what he or she is seeing and hearing at any given point in time. The respondent is requested to react in real time and thus lacks the opportunity to give a considered logical response. In this way a spontaneous measurement is collected of how positive or negative the consumer feels about the advertising he or she is watching.

As an example the testing of the Seven Up 'Fido Dido' commercial, in which the character Fido Dido paints a lady ('Eraser'), will be described. It was tested in five countries: the United States, Canada, Spain, West Germany and the United Kingdom, using local versions. The graphic results are shown in the four graphs of Figure 10.3. The first graph shows two lines for North America and Europe: it indicates a high level of overall acceptability both in North America and Europe, which implies a degree of similarity across continents. However, analysis by country indicates that major regional differences occur. Consistent reactions are seen in the North American continent, where both the United States and Canada demonstrate strong positive reactions to the commercial (graph 2). In Europe both Spain, and to a lesser extent the United Kingdom, react warmly to the film. West German respondents, on the other hand, are considerably cooler in their overall reaction, particularly to the character itself (graph 3). Further examination reveals that it is West German girls who find the film least interesting and motivating (graph 4).

Examples using other commercials have shown that often the reactions diverge at a certain point. Therefore the system can help in finding out which parts of a commercial are, overall, universally accepted, but may have to be adapted slightly in order to achieve the best standardized execution.

Post-testing and effect measurement

Continuous monitoring of image and awareness is a costly business, but it is a necessary investment when building a global brand. Ideally the total image of a global brand should be measured in the different countries. This total image is a compilation of all aspects of the brand: brand name, package, advertising concept and execution. All the variables have their influence on the total effect.

Tracking studies, as discussed before, are a useful instrument for continuous monitoring. Changes in awareness as a result of advertising can also be measured by participating in omnibus surveys. These surveys are usually not particularly fine-tuned to the individual advertiser's wishes, but extensive changes will be revealed.

Earlier the differences of awareness in tracking studies as a result of different media situations were mentioned. Different advertising styles in countries also have different awareness effects. The level of rating of commercials in different countries is influenced by the advertising styles prevailing in those countries.[59]

Selecting an international research agency and building a relationship with this agency is one way of setting up continuous research. Another possibility is to delegate this to the international advertising agency or to the agency network with which the company works. This choice depends largely on the organization of the advertiser's company.

■ Summary

Investment in world brands and worldwide advertising campaigns requires investment in research. International marketing research aimed at devising long-term strategies for global, competitive brands must be seen as an investment, not as an expense. The right techniques must be chosen and the organization must be tailored to carry out the task effectively.

Not all research agencies are yet prepared for this development; nor are their clients. The techniques currently available are not yet ready to cope with a truly global approach.

The standardization of research techniques and harmonization of research data are gradually taking place. New technologies such as point-of-sale scanning systems, computerized data storage and improved communication systems will help accelerate this process.

However, it is the human factor which is the most important: global advertising needs creative researchers, whose experience and way of thinking enable them to break down national barriers by developing and executing research for worldwide marketing and advertising.

■ Notes and references

1. Mario van Hamersveld, 1989: 'Marketing research, local, multidomestic or international?', *Marketing and Research Today*, May.
2. Frederick A. Goldstein, 1987: 'International research – myth or reality?', *European Research*, May.

3. van Hamersveld, 1989: op. cit.
4. Ibid.
5. Warren J. Keegan, 1989: *Global Marketing Management*, Prentice Hall.
6. Ibid.
7. John Clemens, 1989: 'What information does the "single market" marketing chief need?', *Admap*, 5, July/August.
8. Ibid.
9. Ibid.
10. Ibid.
11. Ivor Shalofsky, 1987: 'Research for global brands', *European Research*, May.
12. Linda Caller, 'Effective management of international research and planning in brand and advertising development', ESOMAR Congress, September 1989.
13. Ibid.
14. Ibid.
15. Ibid.
16. Lex Olivier, 1989: 'International marketing research: will 1992 arrive before 2005?', *Marketing and Research Today*, May.
17. Susan P. Douglas and C. Samuel Craig, 1983: *International Marketing Research*, Prentice Hall.
18. Ibid.
19. van Hamersveld, 1989: op. cit.
20. Olivier, 1989: op. cit.
21. Lynn Y. S. Lin, 'Comparison of survey responses among Asian, European and American consumers and their interpretations', ESOMAR Conference on 'America, Japan and EC '92: the prospects for marketing, advertising and research', Venice Italy, 18–20 June 1990.
22. Ibid.
23. Paul A. Robert, 'International telephone research: an interesting *intermediate* stage between the inefficiency of large-scale personal field research and the future direct dialogue with the consumer', ESOMAR Seminar on International Marketing Research, 16–18 November 1988.
24. Shalofsky, 1987: op. cit.
25. van Hamersveld, 1989: op. cit.
26. Clemens, 1989: op. cit.
27. Ibid.
28. ESOMAR, June 1990: 'Getting ready for single European sample surveys', Progress Report, Working Party on Harmonization of Demographics.
29. van Hamersveld, 1989: op. cit.
30. Ibid.
31. Goldstein, 1987: op. cit.
32. Douglas and Craig, 1983: op. cit.
33. Olivier, 1989: op. cit.
34. Shalofsky, 1989: op. cit.
35. Ibid.
36. Ibid.
37. Jane Kalim and John Rutherford, 'Which dog, which tail?' ESOMAR Seminar, November 1988.

38. David A. Hawkins, 'A review of pros and cons of centralized research in manufacturing companies', ESOMAR Seminar, November 1988.
39. Bernd E. Grobe, 'Centralized and decentralized marketing research – how to find the optimal balance in a multinational pharmaceutical company', ESOMAR Seminar, November 1988.
40. Kalim and Rutherford, 1988: op. cit.
41. Clara Origlia, 'Coordinating methods in multinational qualitative research: is what we get better than what we miss?', ESOMAR Seminar, November 1988.
42. Grobe, 1988: op. cit.
43. Kalim and Rutherford, 1988: op. cit.
44. Hawkins, 1988: op. cit.
45. John Downham, Head of Market Research, Marketing Division, Unilever PLC, London, adapted from Keegan, 1989: op. cit.
46. We are indebted to Leo van Deutekom of Sara Lee/DE in the Netherlands, for producing this description as well as making many suggestions for improving this chapter.
47. Ibid.
48. Grobe, 1988: op. cit.
49. Origlia, 1988: op. cit.
50. Edward W. Cundiff and Marye Tharp Hilger, 1988: *Marketing in the International Environment*, Prentice Hall.
51. Ibid.
52. Ibid.
53. Keegan, 1989: op. cit.
54. Shalofsky, 1987: op. cit.
55. Anne Ward, 'Circumventing Babel – making real sense of multinational qualitative research', ESOMAR Seminar, November 1988.
56. Lucy Purdy and Astrid Carl-Zeep, 'International advertising tracking – some lessons learned in the UK and Germany', ESOMAR Seminar, November 1988.
57. Joseph T. Plummer, 1986: 'The role of copy research in multinational advertising', *Journal of Advertising Research*, October/November.
58. Bill Pegram, 'Making sense of global advertising – from a consumer perspective', ESOMAR Conference, June 1990.
59. Uwe Munzinger and Karl-Georg Musiol, 'Ad*Vantage/AC-T International Advertising Research Case Studies', ESOMAR Seminar, November 1988.

■ Appendix: international organizations

This appendix gives addresses of international organizations which can provide further information on international data collection.

International Advertising Association (IAA): 342 Madison Avenue, Suite 2000, New York, N.Y. 10017, USA.

World Federation of Advertisers (WFA): 54 Rue de Colonies, Box 13, B-1000 Brussels, Belgium.

European Society for Opinion and Marketing Research (ESOMAR) J. J. Viottastraat 29, 1071 JP Amsterdam, The Netherlands.

American Marketing Association (AMA): 250 South Wacker Drive, Suite 200, Chicago, IL 60606, USA.

Japan Marketing Association (JMA): Wako Building, 4-8-5 Roppongi, Minato-ku, Tokyo 106, Japan.

World Association for Public Opinion Research (WAPOR): 1500 Stanley, Suite 520, Montreal, Quebec H3A 1R3, Canada.

The yearly ESOMAR directory gives descriptions of research agencies in Europe and the addresses of research agencies which operate internationally.

Chapter 11
Organization of advertising worldwide: advertiser and agency

■ Introduction

Many parties are involved in the organization, planning and execution of global advertising campaigns.

Organizations which have become international, multinational or global usually began by exporting. The way in which this growth takes place depends on a number of factors, including the company's country of origin. Corporations which originated in the United States may have a different type of organization from those which originated in Europe or Japan. However, the major global organizations are today evolving a common type of format, one which has proved the most effective. Organizational structure is a means of conducting effective competitive strategies.

A company's approach to worldwide marketing and advertising depends first on its overall business strategy and organization. As a result of the tendency towards global strategies, many companies have been restructuring their organizations in the 1980s and that process will continue. This restructuring is a long-term and continuous process. The evolution of international companies was described in Chapter 1, and it is of particular relevance to the subject of this chapter. Some aspects of organization structures will therefore be discussed here. Variations in approach to marketing and advertising – standardized or differentiated – require different degrees of centralized and decentralized control. Finding the best balance depends on the following factors:

1. The present organizational structure of the company and its objectives.
2. The stage of international development reached by the company.

3. The developments in the product or market.
4. The degree of brand image globalization.
5. The history and corporate culture of the company.
6. The skills and money available.

The Coca-Cola company had been in international business before the Second World War. Headquarters made all strategic decisions then and is still doing so now. Local bottlers control local marketing. Nestlé was also prompted by the war situation in Europe to grant its managers considerable autonomy. However, Nestlé headquarters in Vevey, Switzerland, has since increased its central decision-making power. Both Coca-Cola and Nestlé are considered to be global brands or concepts, but their corporate organization and the style of their cooperation with advertising agencies are very different.

The real management issue for advertising agencies in the 1990s is to ensure their capacity to work effectively with the client's organization and procedures. Advertising agencies tend to organize themselves for each of their clients. Many of them have also become global corporations in their own right.

Global developments such as the wave of mergers at the end of the 1980s have also affected the advertising industry. These developments have not always been favourable for advertisers, but they seem to have come to terms with the situation. In the relationship between advertisers and agencies, too, a balance must be found. It is not always most effective simply to copy the client's organization. Often it is better not just to follow the client's organizational structure, but also to cooperate in developing it. Many advertisers who enter the international arena have not had much experience of organizing their communications effectively. International agencies with organizational experience may sometimes be able to develop models which will help the client structure his organization appropriately.

■ Organization of the advertiser's marketing communication function

Historically companies growing internationally have developed organizational structures which enable them to respond to relevant differences in markets in different countries while at the same time extending valuable corporate knowledge and experience from national markets to the entire corporate system. It is this pull between the value of centralized knowledge and coordination and the need for response to the local situation that creates a constant tension in the international marketing organization.[1]

There is no single correct organizational structure for international marketing. Types of organizations differ according to the stage of international development the company has reached, the extent of geographical dispersion, the type of product or service and various other factors.

The three main types of organization are multinational, international and global.[2] The multinational company builds a strong local presence through sensitivity and responsiveness to local differences. The strategies of the international company reflect the pattern of worldwide exploitation of knowledge; parent company knowledge and capabilities are exploited through worldwide diffusion and adaptation. The global company treats the world market as an integrated whole. It builds cost advantages through centralized global operations. The newest type of organization to evolve is one which can combine all the advantages of these three main types: the transnational company.

Although there is no one single organizational solution, some general patterns have emerged. In the first stages of international expansion there is *central control by headquarters*, including the marketing function, and there are a series of foreign subsidiaries, often clustered in regional groups. Corporate structure may be functional or divisional, with central control.

The next stage is marked by an *international division structure*: a staff group takes responsibility for coordinating and directing the organization's growing international activities. The corporate staff may or may not be involved in managing marketing activities at this point. If the staff of the international division is small, there is a tendency for services such as market research to be supplied by the corporate staff organization.

The next stage of organizational evolution is the emergence of an *area or regional headquarters* as a level of management between the country organization and the international division headquarters. There are two main reasons for creating regional headquarters. One is the scale of complexity of a company's operations within a region. Size generates revenues that can cover the cost of regional headquarters, and complexity creates a pressure to respond at the regional level. A second reason is the nature of regions. A geographical region is by definition a group of countries related to each other by geographic proximity. When a region is additionally unified by tariff reduction, by shared communication media, by the development of intra-regional transport systems, by moves towards economic, social and political cooperation and a common culture, then the development of the region itself puts pressure on the company to create a regional headquarters which will guide corporate activities. Europe is often seen as a region, but the diversity of cultures means the need for local advertising agencies is greater than, say, in the United States.

The major disadvantage of a regional centre is the cost. Whenever operations are under financial pressure, these costs become quite apparent and have led many companies to abandon a regional headquarters. For example, in 1990 Saatchi & Saatchi has been reducing the number of its regional offices.

As companies develop the ability to operate in foreign markets with an international division, this leads to the creation of a geographical structure for a single-product company and a worldwide product division for the multiproduct company.

The geographical structure involves assigning operational responsibility for particular geographical areas to line managers. Corporate headquarters retains responsibility for worldwide planning and control, and each area of the world, including the home or base market, is organizationally equal. Thus, for a company with US origins,

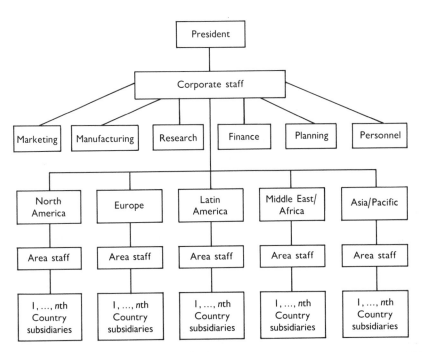

Figure 11.1 *Geographical corporate structure (source: Warren Keegan, 1989: Global Marketing Management, Prentice Hall)*

North America is simply another geographical market under this organizational arrangement. Figure 11.1 gives a model of the geographical corporate structure.

Figure 11.2 provides a model of the divisional corporate structure.

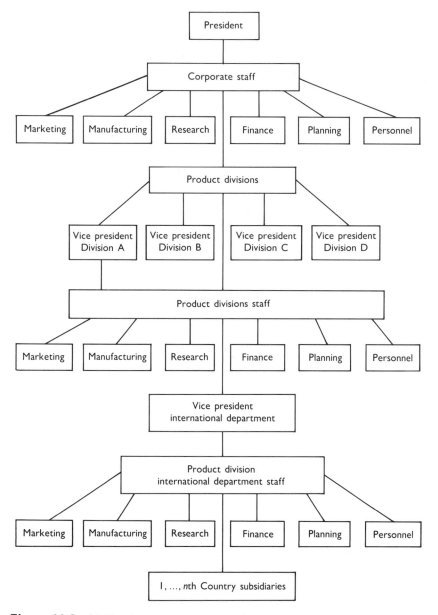

Figure 11.2 *Divisional corporate structure for a multiproduct company (source: Warren Keegan, 1989: Global Marketing Management, Prentice Hall)*

The matrix structure

The most sophisticated organizational arrangement, the matrix structure, brings to bear four basic competences on a worldwide basis. These competences are as follows:

1. *Geographical knowledge.* The country subsidiary has the best knowledge of the local economic, social, political, governmental and cultural conditions.
2. *Product knowledge.* A duplication of the product management function in domestic and international divisions increases competence in both organizational units.
3. *Functional competence* in such fields as finance, production and especially marketing. Corporate functional staff with worldwide responsibility contribute to the development of functional competence on a global basis. In a handful of companies, the appointment of country subsidiary managers is reviewed by the corporate functional manager who is responsible for the development of his or her functional activity within the organization on a global basis. What has emerged in a growing number of multinational companies is a number of relationships between corporate, regional and country staff as dotted lines. These relationships are illustrated in Figure 11.3. The dotted-line relationship ranges from a situation where nothing more than advice is offered by corporate or regional staff to regional or country staff to a situation where staff activities at a lower organizational level are directed and approved by higher-level staff.

    These relationships can become a source of tension and conflict if top management does not create a climate that encourages organizational integration. Headquarters staff will probably want to extend its control or influence over the activities of lower-level staff. For example, in market research, unless research design and activity is coordinated, the international headquarters will be unable to compare one market with another. If line management, instead of recognizing the potential contribution of an integrated worldwide staff, wishes to operate as autonomously as possible, the influence of an integrated worldwide staff is perceived as undesirable. In such a situation the stronger party wins. This can be avoided if the level of management to which both line and staff report creates a climate and structure that expects and requires the cooperation of line and staff, and recognizes that each has responsibility for important aspects of the management of international markets. The climate can be improved by regular job rotation programmes.

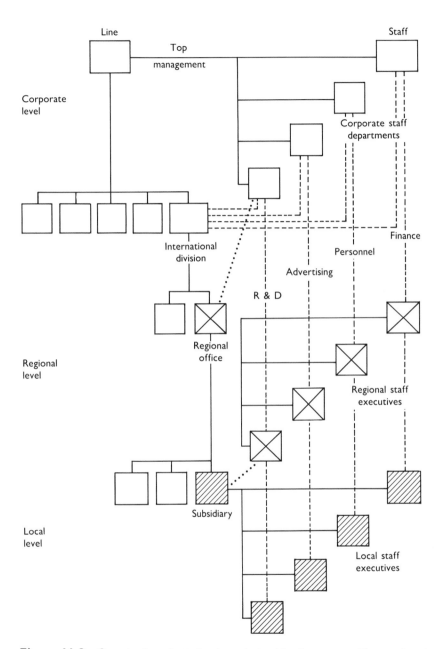

Figure 11.3 *Organization chart showing relationships between staff executives in corporate departments, regional office and subsidiary (source: Warren Keegan, 1989:* Global Marketing Management, *Prentice Hall)*

4. *A knowledge of the customer or industry and its needs.* In certain large and very sophisticated international companies, staff who serve particular industries on a global basis are available to assist line managers in the country organizations in their efforts to penetrate specific markets.

In the fully developed, large-scale international company, knowledge of the product, function, area and customer are simultaneously focused on the organization's worldwide marketing objectives. This total competence approach is that of the matrix organization.

In the matrix organization the task of management is to achieve an organizational balance that brings together different perspectives and skills to accomplish the organization's objectives. Under this arrangement, instead of designating national organizations or product divisions as profit centres, both are responsible for profitability: the national organization for country profits, and the product divisions for national and worldwide profitability.

The key to successful matrix management is the extent to which managers in the organization are able to resolve conflicts and achieve integration of organizational programmes and plans. In a matrix, influence is based on technical competence and interpersonal sensitivity, not on formal authority. This is one of the generators of conflict. In a traditional hierarchical structure there is a choice: either the country or national organization or the worldwide product divisions may act as the profit centre. In the matrix both locations are responsible for profits. Another problem with the matrix structure is that it requires a substantial investment in control systems: dual accounting, transfer pricing, corporate budgets and so on.[3]

For most companies the matrix structure has not produced the expected results. Bartlett and Ghoshal[4] have this to say about the failure of the matrix structure:

> In theory, the solution should have worked. Having front-line managers report simultaneously to different management groups (such as area and business, area and function, or function and business) should have enabled the companies to maintain the balance among centralized efficiency, local responsiveness and the building and leveraging of functional competencies . . . Matrix companies developed a management process that was slow, acrimonious and costly. Communications were routinely duplicated, approval processes were costly and time-consuming, and constant travel and frequent meetings raised the company's administrative costs dramatically.

Nevertheless, there is a need to find an organizational structure which allows global integration, which can meet the need for efficiency and responsiveness to different environments, and which makes it possible to develop and diffuse worldwide innovations internationally.[5]

Global competition requires organizations which can play 'global chess'. Companies which have operated their local companies as independent profit centres have found themselves at a disadvantage compared with competitors who have used funds generated in one market to subsidize its position in another.

The transnational

Bartlett and Ghoshal[6] describe the transnational as the winning organization as far as global competition is concerned:

> The transnational company seeks efficiency not for its own sake, but as a means to achieve global *competitiveness*. It acknowledges the importance of local responsiveness, but as a tool for achieving *flexibility* in international operations. Innovations are regarded as an outcome of a larger process of organizational *learning* that encompasses every member of the company. This redefinition of the issue allows managers of the transnational company to develop a broader perspective and leads to very different criteria for making choices.

The transnational centralizes some resources at home, some abroad, and distributes yet others among its national operations. The result is a complex configuration of assets and capabilities that are distributed, yet specialized.[7] The organization of the transnational is characterized by an *integrated network*. There are many communication links, work interdependencies and formal and informal systems. Companies that are in the process of becoming a transnational organization start reducing the control of headquarters over local operations, and flatten their organizations. Headquarters staff will be reduced, and specializations are established in those parts of the world where the best resources are available. Top management in the transnational retains the clarity of line authority, but pays a great deal of attention to the allocation of responsibilities. Figure 11.4 shows a simple organization chart of a decentralized organization with local control and authority, and a small central staff function with specialized consultants.

The aim in flattening marketing organizations is to enable them to respond faster to changing markets. Procter & Gamble changed its renowned brand management system when they realized it had become too complex. To secure an important decision, brand managers often

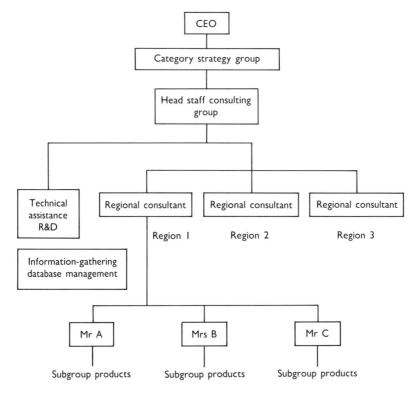

Figure 11.4 *Organization chart of a central staff function for a decentralized organization*

had to go through three or four layers of management. With up to fourteen brand managers in each division, getting the attention of the division chief was not easy. Another difficulty was that brand managers were so focused on a single product that they lost sight of the market-place. There was a lot of cannibalization. Coupons were issued at the same time for both liquid and powdered detergents. To solve these problems a new level of management was introduced, called 'category manager'. The company was broken into thirty-nine product categories with twenty-six category managers. Brand managers now report to the category manager, who acts like a small business unit. The category manager has total profit-and-loss responsibility for an entire product line, for example all detergents. The category manager will think in terms of product groups and will make sure that the brand managers are not sabotaging each other. The system has helped Procter & Gamble to effect a rapid international expansion. The company now markets its products in 140 countries. International (non-US) sales increased from 29 per cent to 40 per cent in three years.[8]

IBM, Coca-Cola and PepsiCo have also flattened their organizations in order to increase the ease and speed of decision-making and to become more reactive to the market.[9]

In this stage headquarters reduces its role in the subsidiary's decision-making process and concentrates on global scanning of the international operations. As a result, for example, the R&D department may be located not necessarily in the country of origin but instead in a region which offers the greatest resources, or in more than one region. Efficient local plants may be converted into regional production units. Creative subsidiary marketing groups may be given a lead role in developing global marketing strategies. When developing global or regional brands teams from different countries can be involved. When Procter & Gamble started developing Euro brands, Euro Brand Teams were created for each key brand to analyze opportunities for greater standardization of products and marketing programmes. Chaired by the brand manager from a lead country, each team includes brand managers from the other European subsidiaries which market the brand, managers from P&G's European technical centre and one of P&G's three European division managers, each of whom is responsible for a portfolio of brands as well as for a group of countries. Concerns that the larger subsidiaries would dominate the teams and that decision-making would be paralysed or produce results based on the lowest common denominator have proved groundless.[10]

Philips' consumer electronics division created a World Policy Committee and a World Strategy Council to provide a forum in which functional managers from headquarters could resolve strategic and operating differences with managers from key national operations.[11] Colgate-Palmolive, with manufacturing operations in nine countries, has appointed a pan-European board. Unilever's detergents unit opted for a multi-subsidiary structure to coordinate brands in Europe. The European Brand Group (EBG) is a decision-making body which includes executives from a number of large national subsidiaries.[12] Since the spring of 1990 these European Brand Groups report directly into Lever Europe, a regional company with offices in Brussels, responsible for all aspects of Unilever's detergents business in Europe. Nestlé locates product directors as well as support groups at headquarters. Together they develop long-term strategies for each product category on a worldwide basis, coordinate market research, spot new product opportunities, spark the field launch of new products, advise the field on how headquarters will evaluate new product proposals, and spread the word on the performance of new products so that other countries will be motivated to launch them.[13]

There are two main ways of coordinating a global marketing

programme through and after its launch: from headquarters or from the office in a lead market or lead country.

When headquarters is in control, the formal authority for a programme rests with a central line or staff function, such as world or regional product management or international marketing coordination.

Under lead market control, a subsidiary is assigned responsibility for defining and managing a given programme for all the participating or 'follower' countries. The choice of a lead market is usually a function of its expertise or experience with a particular product or service and the availability of external resources such as market research.

Both systems have their weaknesses. Headquarters may lack the knowledge to keep the programme fine-tuned to changing subsidiary market conditions. The lead-market structure may lack a global perspective.[14] A central programme manager or management team with international overview must have the responsibility for consistent implementation of an international marketing programme. Decisions on local adaptation are best left to subsidiaries or country organizations.

In developing marketing and advertising strategies for a cross-national brand the lead country is not necessarily the country where headquarters or regional headquarters is located, or the country with the largest market. It may be the country where the subsidiary is most enthusiastic about the product, or the country where the advertising agency has the strongest expertise regarding the specific brand. For example, Rowntree Mackintosh (owned by Nestlé), is based in the United Kingdom but has its European regional headquarters in Paris, while the lead advertising agency for KitKat, one of its European brands, is in the Netherlands.

Centralized or decentralized control

Most companies with an international business sell a mix of products, some of which may be sold in only one national market, while others may be multinational and a few may be global. When a company is growing more international the percentages of sales and profits from the various categories will change. As a result the organization itself will change. The issue of standardization versus differentiation varies for each category of products. Likewise the need for centralized control will vary. Continuous analysis is necessary to establish the level of existing standardization or adaptation of all elements of the marketing mix as well as the desired level. This can be done by completing a matrix like that shown in Figure 11.5.

The same analysis can be made for advertising. Copy strategy may

	Standardization		Adaptation	
	Full	Partial	Full	Partial
Product design				
Brand name				
Product positioning				
Packaging				
Pricing				
Advertising				
Sales promotion				
Distribution				
Customer service				

Figure 11.5 *Marketing mix: analysis of standardization and adaptation (source: John A. Quelch and Edward J. Hoff, BBDO Worldwide network meeting, 1985)*

be the same worldwide, but copy execution may need to vary from one local market to another. Some aspects of research can be centralized while other elements must be localized. The location of the decision-making process regarding agency selection, evaluation and process control should be determined. Decisions on standardization or differentiation affect decisions on how to organize the company's advertising, and to an even greater extent decisions on how to select and work with the advertising agency. Again, a matrix can be completed; an example is shown in Figure 11.6.

Central control will be at one or other end of a continuum, depending on the organizational structure and corporate philosophy of the company, on corporate objectives and strategies, and on the level of standardization of the product or brand concerned. This continuum can be described as follows:

inform – persuade – approve – decide – enforce

The strength of the company's local subsidiaries and their size and staff capabilities, the brand mix, the relationship with the advertising agency and the strength of the advertising agency's organization will all play a role in determining the extent of central control or local authority. A moderate influence exerted by headquarters can result in a form of

	Standardization		Adaptation	
	Full	Partial	Full	Partial
Product positioning				
Copy strategy				
Copy execution				
Media planning				
Media buying				
Advertising research				
Performance tracking				
Production				
Account management				
Agency selection				

Figure 11.6 *Advertising programming: analysis of standardization and adaptation (source: John A. Quelch and Edward J. Hoff, BBDO Worldwide network meeting, 1985)*

consultation. In this scenario subsidiaries are separate profit centres; they take advice from headquarters, but do not have to live up to it if they have good reasons and good bottom lines. A strong influence by headquarters can result in a standard high level of quality, but requires a high degree of discipline. In this scenario headquarters imposes central strategies on the subsidiaries. The degree of control needed, or the degree of freedom possible, must be decided for each instrument in the marketing mix. Central decision-making does not necessarily mean standardized marketing. It can imply differentiated marketing strategies with strong guidance and quality control.

Factors which decide the level of influence exerted by headquarters include the following:

1. The function of the subsidiary; whether it is fully-owned with production and marketing functions, or a sales or distribution centre.
2. Tradition; whether the subsidiary is a long-established organization with a long history of independence, its own sales and bottom line responsibilities, long experience and high profits.
3. The product/brand mix; what proportion of sales comes from international brands and what from local brands. The larger the

Participation in decision-making

	Head office	Local office
Selection of advertising agency and evaluation	x	Consultation
Product/brand positioning	x	
Concept development	x	x
Execution	x	x
Media planning		x
Media buying		x
Marketing research	x	x
Effect measurement	x	

Figure 11.7 *Involvement of head office and local office (source: John A. Quelch and Edward J. Hoff, BBDO Worldwide network meeting, 1985)*

proportion of sales derived from international brands, the greater the influence from head or regional offices will be.

4. The role the subsidiaries play in the organization and the quality and quantity of the staff.

When developing global strategies decisions will have to be made about the appropriate level at which to involve the local managers: whether to consult them in a role of global brand development teams, or just to give them responsibility for their local brands and locally adapted brands while using the centrally-directed international brand coordinators or teams for developing and coordinating international brand strategies. Figure 11.7 shows how advertiser and agency can be involved centrally and/or in a decentralized way in the decision-making process for a multi-local campaign.

The role of head office

The role of head office covers both management and the professional aspect, the 'creative conscience'. The management aspect involves among other things guarding the international climate of cooperation and evaluation both within the company and with the agency. The professional aspect involves creating and executing advertising.

The most important professional areas in which a central marketing communications staff must be involved are as follows:

1. Positioning.
2. Strategy development.
3. Creative concept development and judgement.
4. Assisting local management in selecting the right target groups.
5. Giving an insight into the degree to which specific products and product attributes must be emphasized in local campaigns or in adapted campaigns.
6. Providing an insight into what kind of advertising is most effective in which country.
7. Selecting the media types to be used, both locally and internationally.
8. Drawing up procedures for reporting and internal communication between subsidiaries and head office.
9. Cultivating a feeling for cultural differences and thus increasing the possibilities of standardizing a creative approach.
10. Evaluating international media.
11. Coordinating advertising research and measurement of effect.

The aspects of management in which involvement is necessary include the following:

1. Providing worldwide planning systems including worldwide production outlines or guidance.
2. Organizing worldwide coordination of local advertising plans.
3. Setting global budgets, dividing them according to region or country, evaluating country budgets and checking whether they meet the company's requirements.
4. Assisting with the selection of local advertising managers.
5. Developing documentation systems for registering successful multinational campaigns in order to help local subsidiaries developing their own campaigns.
6. Selecting advertising agencies (local, multinational or global).
7. Evaluating agency relationships and remuneration arrangements.

Internal communication and coordination

Coordinating a centralized approach with strict guidelines is relatively more simple than coordinating a decentralized approach. Process control and methods of communication are much more complicated when local subsidiaries have a large degree of autonomy.

Process control is of great importance when developing and executing global campaigns: the quality of global communications are a crucial factor in establishing the brand and corporate image.

There are various means of internal communication. These include the following:

1. Marketing communication workshops.
2. Travelling coordinators or teams.
3. Exchange programmes.
4. Education.
5. Meetings at head office for subsidiary personnel.
6. Contests or other incentives for quality advertising adaptation.
7. Reports, newsletters or an in-house magazine.
8. Formal guidelines and standardized planning systems for achieving a consistent quality of communication.
9. Manuals with guidelines and specifications regarding the use of logos, concepts and central themes, indicating the degree and manner of adaptation, and covering budgeting, reporting, presentation etc.
10. Allowing the advertising agency to control communication
11. Electronic mail systems and databases.
12. A clear corporate culture.

■ The international advertising agencies

As multinational corporations developed around the globe, advertising agencies followed their example. The reason why advertising agencies went international was the international growth of their clients. Most of the international advertising agencies originated in the United States. Those were the agencies with the large international accounts for products like cigarettes, cars and soft drinks, who wanted their agencies to serve them in the countries into which they expanded. Large agencies such as J. Walter Thompson, Masius, McCann Erickson, Young & Rubicam, Ted Bates, Ogilvy & Mather and DDB originated in this way.

However, this was not solely an American phenomenon because Unilever originally owned Lintas (Lever International Advertising Service), which later became an independent agency network. Fortune Advertising originated in Australia and started expanding by setting up a network in Asia. Due to the mega-mergers in the 1980s many of the agencies have become less American, and therefore more international,

Table 11.1 The ten largest advertising agencies and their worldwide gross income, 1989

	Worldwide gross income, US $ millions
Dentsu Inc.	1,316.4
Saatchi & Saatchi Advertising Worldwide	890.0
Young & Rubicam	865.4
Backer Spielvogel Bates Worldwide	759.8
McCann-Erickson Worldwide	715.5
Ogilvy & Mather Worldwide	699.7
BBDO Worldwide	656.6
J. Walter Thompson Co.	626.4
Lintas Worldwide	593.3
Hakuhodo Inc.	585.5

Source: Advertising Age, 26 March 1990.

as a result of merging with large agencies in other parts of the world. Table 11.1 shows the ten largest global agencies with their worldwide gross income. In 1984 the top five agencies controlled roughly one-tenth of worldwide billings. In 1989 it was one-fifth, and the proportion is growing.

A series of advertising mega-groups has emerged. Table 11.2 shows the gross income of the five largest advertising mega-groups.

The new conglomerates or mega-groups argue that their business

Table 11.2 Five advertising mega-groups and their worldwide gross income, 1989

	Worldwide gross income, US $ millions
WPP Group PLC (JWT, O&M, Lord Geller Federico Einstein, Conquest Europe, ScaliMcCabe Sloves)	2,404
Saatchi & Saatchi PLC (Saatchi & Saatchi Advertising, Backer Spielvogel Bates)	2,300
Interpublic Group of Cos (McCann, Lintas Lowe Marschalk)	1,355
Omnicom Group (BBDO, DDB Needham, Diversified Agency Services, Tracy Locke)	1,210
FCB Publicis	689

Source: Advertising Age, 26 March 1990.

is different; there are opportunities for synergy and for muscle to count.[15] These groups can offer many other marketing services alongside advertising, as they have aligned with all sorts of other communication specialists in order to be able to offer an integrated communications service.

A growing proportion of advertising budgets will be concentrated in the hands of the international or bigger local agencies, and an even greater proportion of advertising budgets will be decided and spent on a supranational level. Consequently growth in the advertising market will increasingly occur through aligned, integrated agency networks.

There are quite a number of differences between individual groups. However, in general, the advantages of large international agency groups are as follows:

1. Being a large-scale operation can save money; running more agencies within one group can lead to economies of scale and can offer a way around client conflict.
2. Size also counts when securing commodities: a big media-buying unit will be able to command attention in the national and international media markets.
3. The alignment of most mega-groups with other communication services can offer a more wide-ranging service, although not all large international agencies manage to offer an integrated marketing communications service.

The effectiveness of large international agencies in handling international accounts may depend on the way in which they are structured, which in turn largely relates to how they were originally set up, whether as fully-owned subsidiaries, joint ventures or partnerships.

Advertising agencies have used and are still using various ways of entering other countries. These include the following:

1. Opening a local office, staffing it with expatriates and training locals.
2. Acquiring a full or partial interest in existing agencies.
3. Forming a joint venture which may later develop into full ownership.
4. Networking: forming a federation of local agencies for exchange of information and *ad hoc* service in other countries.

When developing large international networks, agencies found that it was not always possible to find an agency in each country which could deliver the required quality. One solution was to adopt a system of international account coordinators or 'commando teams', who travel around the world to examine the local situation and coordinate the development and execution of international strategy.

One of the disadvantages of the original large agencies was the predominance of the head office culture; this was often solved by appointing intercultural management teams, setting up regional headquarters, or giving local management more autonomy.

With improving levels of advertising education fewer expatriates were needed in local offices and local management could, in most developed countries, handle the international accounts locally just as well as, or even better than, their American counterparts.

Another change in emphasis in the deployment of human resources in international agencies is that whereas in the past the people with the highest potential were not sent abroad, this is now becoming more usual. In the old days being sent abroad was to a large extent seen as degrading; the international jobs were considered to be for the 'bimbos'. Most of the real global agencies now have management development programmes with exchange arrangements for their most talented people in order to create real internationalists and future global managers.

Global agencies are questioning whether it is preferable to own 100 per cent of their local offices or to leave some equity in local hands.[16] Traditionally, agencies like McCann Erickson, Young & Rubicam and J. Walter Thompson have owned nearly all their offices in countries where local laws allow it. They use their ownership as a benefit in selling to clients by claiming that they can control the client's work better than agencies with only fractional ownership. Those not owning 100 per cent, like BBDO and Grey, claim that local partners with a stake in the agency will be motivated to produce superior work. A few agencies, like Ogilvy & Mather, have sold shares to local employees to motivate and improve productivity.

In the 1990s, with the increasing concentration of clients and the tendency for clients to select only a few major agencies worldwide for each product category or brand, with more centralized control, it may be doubted if local control of partnership agencies will remain an advantage. However, news on this may change again, as global companies become more organized and more stable. The trend at present, though, is towards centralized ideas and strategies combined with local execution.

Centralization has led marketers to reduce the number of agencies used to one or two worldwide. Some advertisers are moving towards using just one agency for their entire business, while others use specific agencies for specific brands. At the end of the 1980s, 3M reviewed its association with sixty assorted agencies and decided to concentrate its attention on three. Philip Morris uses Leo Burnett exclusively. Philips has selected Ogilvy & Mather and DMB&B as its major agencies around the world. The computer company Apple works with BBDO on a worldwide basis. Unilever works with Lintas, Ogilvy & Mather, McCann Erickson and J. Walter Thompson. Nestlé works with Ogilvy & Mather, McCann Erickson, Lintas, J. Walter Thompson, Publicis and BBDO. Henkel now uses only four agencies: TBWA, BBDO, HDM and Lowe International.

Organization and coordination

Whether agencies fully or partly own their local offices, there is usually a central head office, together with a number of regional offices. The role of head office may fall into one of five categories:[17]

1. *Those who command*: some agencies believe that success means top-down direction and control. These groups make all decisions centrally and local agencies have none or little input.
2. *Those who persuade*: headquarters makes decisions, and will then persuade local agencies that these are for the best. This is a softer approach, and the main difference lies in the fact that the locals do have a choice in using centralized work. However, the reasons for not using it must be strong.
3. *Those who interact*: an interacting headquarters exchanges ideas and information with local agencies. The philosophy is cooperation. Therefore the concepts developed are often a combination of central and local contributions.
4. *Those who coordinate*: headquarters coordinates the flow of information between the agencies and ensures concept consistency, but local agencies enjoy autonomy.
5. *Those who ignore*: local agencies have complete autonomy and are often poorly linked with other national agencies. Creative teams are happy because they have complete freedom and responsibility.

International agency networks with fully-owned local agencies tend to have stronger centralized control, fewer of the problems resulting from too much local autonomy than is the case with local ownership. Strong local ownership in an international network has some disadvantages for winning international accounts; for example, conflicting accounts may be held locally and there may be difficulty in persuading the local creatives. The local agencies may have a mixture of international and local accounts, with a predominance of local business. Gaining a conflicting international account may force them to let go of the local account, which may be much more profitable and/or attractive than local adaptation of international accounts.

Another problem is the enthusiasm of the creatives, who tend to be motivated by their local environment. It is well known that creatives prefer developing their own campaigns to adapting those developed by others. Solutions to these problems may include compensation for letting go local clients, or mixing the local and international work for creatives. Adaptation work can be made into a challenge, changing the NIH philosophy from 'Not Invented Here' to 'Now Improved Here'.

The choice of which tasks are best done by headquarters and which are best done by the local offices depends on the client's organization, the geographical planning relating to the brand and the need to keep a balance between interdependency of local agencies and stimulation of local creativity.

There is no single right way to organize the agency to serve international clients; every client asks for a different approach. Most international agencies try to give the best service by following the client's organization: customized control. The agency's organization often mirrors that of the client, and works with international account coordinators or 'Euroteams' to coordinate the client's advertising for international brands.

Some agencies have set up international training schemes to produce the network's internationalists. At some agencies top management is personally involved in multinational account service. Only a few agencies have career planning systems for their international personnel.

Lintas has international client directors, international creative directors with worldwide responsibilities and European account directors for Eurobrands, all working from different countries. Leo Burnett has international directors who lead international accounts. Each international account is led by an international account director and a creative director. At Ogilvy & Mather an executive committee allocates business to different regions. There is a team of worldwide management supervisors, working out of different offices. McCann Erickson has regional directors (three in Europe) and regional executive committees whose members each take personal responsibility for international clients. Each international account is managed by an appointed coordinator. A creative resource consisting of several creative teams of internationalists develops transnational campaigns. BBDO has a 'Euroteam' for the coordination of European clients, and worldwide and European account directors. JWT has in 1990 begun working towards stronger centralized control, giving international account managers line responsibility. Saatchi & Saatchi has worldwide account directors, who ensure that local work on major multinational accounts is in line with overall strategy. All international agencies will continue adapting their structure during the process of change in Europe and other parts of the world.

In general, the American agencies have developed further, as far as organization and coordination systems for international advertising are concerned, than their European counterparts. These are originally mainly French or British – agencies like Publicis, HDM, FCA!, BDDP and RSCG in France and Lowe, Dorlands and Saatchi & Saatchi in the United Kingdom. The Japanese agencies are strongly centrally controlled.

One of the account handling decisions which must be made in international agencies is whether to have international and local specialists or to mix the type of clients handled by an account manager or client service director. In international agencies where a lot of not very inspiring adaptation work has to be done, it is sometimes a solution to give account managers and creative specialists the responsibility for a mixture of local and international clients.

Some international agencies offer proprietary research techniques to their international clients. Most international agencies offer international media planning and buying services; if these are not provided by the agency itself, they are offered by the related media buying unit.

Internal coordination can be ensured by using the following means of communication or motivation:

1. Central information systems and databases.
2. Central training and education.
3. Consistent agency philosophy and planning systems.
4. International account meetings.
5. Proper international accounting systems.
6. Uniform systems for briefing, planning and reporting

The most important thing, however, is a spirit of cooperation: advertising is a 'people business'. If there is no sense of solidarity and no willingness to cooperate, then no coordination system will work, neither for the advertiser nor for the agency. People must learn to like each other and respect each other. It is the responsibility of top management to design a corporate culture which brings people together.

■ The relationship between advertiser and agency

An international advertiser will prefer to work with an agency that can help it organize its international advertising efficiently. The agency needs to create an organizational structure which can match that of the advertiser. Such structures have been changing rapidly during the last decade.

In the 1980s marketing decisions in large multi-brand corporations have changed from being country-driven to being headquarters-driven, and this has changed the relationship between the advertiser and agency. Yet there is still a variety of ways in which the company's advertising function can be organized, depending on what type of product and brand the company markets, and whether it is a multi-product or multi-brand company or a one-brand company. The historical background plays an important role in how organizations and their advertising function are organized and in the changes which occur.

The choice of an advertising agency is closely related to the question of organizational structure. Other factors play a role: qualitative or emotional reasons, mergers, high turnover of marketing managers or CEOs, family and/or private businesses which turn into public companies – all these can provide reasons for reassessing the relationship with the advertising agency. However, a few generalizations can be made.

Selecting agencies for international advertising

The *centrally-organized international advertiser* may want a centrally-driven advertising agency, with the lead agency in the home country, and possibly regional offices matching the advertiser's organization. An alternative is to use a local, independent agency which operates internationally and controls everything from the home base.

A *multinational advertiser* with a strongly differentiated approach or with many local brands which require local campaigns or a high level of local adaptation may not need strong central control and may prefer to work with a looser network or federation of agencies in which strong local offices can offer a full service and a high level of local creativity. On the other hand, the looser the coordination within the company, the stronger may be the need for coordination skills at the advertising agency to manage the differences across the relevant markets.

A *global organization* with a strong central communication function may impose its creative strategy on its own subsidiaries, while allowing them autonomy in selecting local agencies. In this situation headquarters leaves execution and media planning and buying to the local offices. IBM in the past has followed this kind of organizational strategy.

Global organizations which market global packaged brands will, on the other hand, prefer to use strongly organized global agencies with ubiquitous knowledge of the relevant market situations in all their markets. Coca-Cola uses McCann Erickson, Lux soap and Kodak use JWT and Colgate uses Young & Rubicam.

The development of global brands and Eurobrands has changed the criteria for selecting advertising agencies. Mergers and the growing number of global or regional brands have led to an established trend for large international advertisers to select a small group of advertising agencies offering a full service, thus increasing concentration in the advertising agency business. The number of major pan-European client/agency alignments has doubled between 1983 and 1988. However, there are general criteria that can be used in selecting an international agency. These include the following:

1. The organization of the advertiser, whether centralized or decentralized; quality and quantity of marketing communications staff and where they are located.
2. The balance of local brands the advertiser wants to maintain and new product or brand introductions planned by the advertiser.
3. Whether the agency network has strong local agencies in the advertiser's home market and in other major markets.
4. The extent to which the organization and corporate cultures of advertiser and agency fit together.
5. The product category of the advertiser and the related target groups.
6. The type of brand: product brand, range brand or umbrella brand.
7. The extent to which the agency is familiar with the type of brand and its markets.
8. The quality of this market knowledge and experience.
9. The extent of the full service which the agency can deliver; whether or not it can provide not just creativity and media planning expertise, but also marketing research and expertise in the other areas of communication such as sales promotion, direct marketing communications and PR, either within the agency itself or via an aligned international network.
10. Whether adequate international account management and account handling personnel are available everywhere.
11. Management and internal communication systems in the agency: whether there is one philosophy worldwide, one process of reaching the correct decision which is applied everywhere, one common discipline; whether there are international human resource management for international personnel, intercultural training and exchange programmes.
12. Whether there is a good international account handling and remuneration system.
13. Whether there is a good balance between local and international

accounts (local accounts to ensure expertise on local culture, international to ensure international experience).
14. Whether top management are involved in handling international advertising.
15. Whether both the expertise for developing a central international campaign and the willingness to adapt central ideas from other countries are available.
16. Whether suitable expertise is available to coordinate marketing and advertising research internationally.
17. Ownership: if the agency is not centrally owned, how central or regional control and authority is organized; if it is centrally owned, how local personnel are motivated.
18. Whether a central media buying unit is available.

The more complicated the product and the greater the number of local cultures involved, the greater the degree of local advertising expertise required. The more additional means of communication are involved, the more difficult it becomes to operate centrally from a distance. Agency selection and the choice of how to cooperate depends on more factors than those listed above: every situation is different. There is no one way of working together; usually the cooperation between advertiser and agency is adapted to the specific situations and countries involved.

Conflicting accounts

Advertisers demanding a full service from agencies in each country may encounter increasing problems with conflicting accounts. Many of the largest advertisers now operate in many markets, often unrelated to their traditional core business. Mergers and diversifications can be expected to make matters worse. Advertisers will in future have to accept that their agencies may work for a competitor in a non-conflicting product field.[18] Distinctions will have to be made between corporate conflict, category conflict and brand conflict. For each kind of conflict, the risks will have to be considered. Corporate conflict is becoming less important. Category and brand conflicts, however, remain important.

There are two major risks: confidentiality and the blocking of talent. The blocking of talent cannot be controlled in any case because of the high turnover of personnel at advertising agencies. That leaves the question of confidentiality. It must be remembered that, with the growing data transmission industry, information may in any case be public knowledge.

Cooperation and coordination

Depending on the organization of the advertiser there are several possible formats which cooperation can take. Four main types of situations in the advertiser's organization for which international cooperation between advertiser and agency may differ are as follows:

1. Central planning and execution of a standardized approach.
2. A worldwide standardized approach, locally adapted.
3. From a multinational to a global or transnational approach.
4. Global advertising strategies for world brands originating from a multi-local situation.

Central planning and execution of a standardized approach

Client headquarters provides a framework and gives strong directives which must be executed by the local agencies. In the subsidiaries there are local managers who have no say in a direction of change except perhaps for those additional activities which are specific to a particular country, such as promotions. Figure 11.8 provides a model of this approach.

A variation of this is a centralized approach in which the local manager has more input with respect to local adaptation of the campaign, if this is necessary. Contact between the local manager and the local agency takes place only on a local basis. The local managers of the client's subsidiaries as well as those of the local advertising agency report to their respective head offices. The local manager informs his or her head office and provides feedback, but the decisions are made at head office.

Figure 11.8 *Central planning and a standardized approach*

A worldwide standardized approach, locally adapted

The client's head office determines and manages strategy while local managers control the execution of campaigns in their own markets following the directives of head office. This model is used by international airlines with local subsidiaries. It is shown in Figure 11.9.

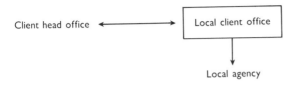

Figure 11.9 *A worldwide standardized approach, locally adapted*

There is no absolute need for a worldwide international agency. For each brand, the local manager may choose his own agency. This system is mainly used for execution, while strategy development is done by head office, together with its own agency.

A recurring problem in this system is that the local agency – consciously or unconsciously – may try to go beyond local execution and to take a firm grip on strategy development. After all, an agency's objective is to be original and creative. Local offices of international agencies have learned to cope with and harness this urge. Even so, they too sometimes fail in controlling the international client's strategy.

This model is also applicable to the brand for which a worldwide standardized strategy and worldwide execution is used, while leaving local managers free to a certain extent to execute their own campaigns on top of the international campaign.

From a multinational to a global or transnational approach

This reflects a situation in which a multinational which markets culture-bound products and is aiming towards a global approach may find itself. There is usually one R&D department, but the product and market strategies are worked out by a few regional head offices, for example for each continent or major group of countries. This is a top-down approach. Local brands are developed for each region or country. The advertising strategy is developed at regional level and local managers adapt strategies to their own market. These local managers play an important role in selecting and working with an agency. The marketing staff at head office monitor the relationship with the agency as far as strategy development and maintenance of global brands are concerned. They often work with international agencies for each brand or category. Such an agency has worldwide or regional account directors at the agency head office or lead agency dealing with the marketing communication for each brand. In such a situation the leading input does not necessarily come from the agency's headquarters. In an international agency network a lead agency may be appointed which can be anywhere: in the client's home country, in the largest markets or in the market where a new product is first being launched. Alternatively there may be lead agencies for each region, located in the countries where the client has regional headquarters. Local account managers report to the lead agency account director. The local agency staff naturally work together with local marketing managers when adapting campaigns to local conditions.

Depending on the situation of each client, authority can be delegated to a regional or local level; the choice relates to the extent of regional or local cooperation with the advertising agencies. The agency organization adapts to the way the client is organized, stressing the authority of head office, regional office or local subsidiary.

Global advertising strategies for world brands originating from a multi-local situation

This is an organizational framework with a bottom-up approach for developing regional or world brands: local managers provide the input on which development of international brands and related communication strategies is based. The local managers have decisive power regarding national brands. They work with the local agency, which is usually owned by, or a partner in, an international agency network. Local agency people are selected to develop strategies in regional teams together with the client company's marketing director or regional marketing team. In the agency there is an international account director who coordinates the efforts and works together with the client and controls the quality of the output from local agencies.

The client's strategy determines the agency's organization. The lines of communication are as shown in Figure 11.10.

For a global brand, local agency personnel report directly to the international account director for that brand, and also to the manager of the advertiser's local subsidiary. This creates double reporting, a common problem in the matrix organization.

Client:	Country managers	→	Head office
Client/agency:	Country managers	→	Local account managers
Agency:	Country managers	→	Lead agency/head office
Client/agency:	Head office	→	Head office

Figure 11.10 *Lines of communication in the international advertising agency*

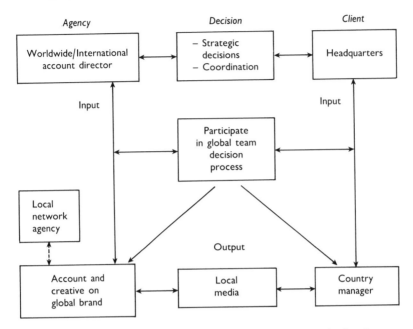

Figure 11.11 *International cooperation between agency and advertiser*

Figure 11.11 shows an organizational chart for international cooperation between client and agency at the different decision-making levels.

There are a number of conditions which must be met in order for this kind of organization to work. There are always at least four parties involved. Lead agencies and local agencies often play games; a common problem is that local agencies do not want to follow lead agencies. On the other hand local clients do not always have the necessary communication expertise. The team charged with developing global strategies should consist of participants from both client and agency, working in unison, perhaps together with appropriate specialists – for example, in media or research. Local agencies must be asked to provide information needed to help head office or the team. It is difficult to control the flow of information between local client and local agency. The local client may, for example, demand things from the local agency and think that headquarters will pay for it. This must be controlled, or else the roles of local client and agency must be limited.

Any layer that can be eliminated must be eliminated in order to avoid difficulties in communication and unnecessary cost. If a client's organization is centralized, the worldwide account director must have direct lines of communication with the client's headquarters.

The organization becomes even more complicated when more means of communication are involved; the various disciplines must then be integrated in local markets so that timing and implementation are coordinated. Only if the specialized work is of a very local and decentralized nature is it better to let local client managers do it their way. If the other disciplines need to be integrated in an international campaign, a relationship manager can assist the international account director, or the international account director can add this role to his or her job of international coordination.

To achieve coordination within the agency network, one key point must be remembered: at all times make clear who is doing what and what the cost will be for the client.

Trends for the 1990s

The tendency towards centralization of advertisers will result in a preference for centralized agencies. The role played by the headquarters of those agencies is becoming less relevant. The role of lead agencies will be to act as a 'centre of excellence', the place where central strategies are developed; they will have less day-to-day contact with clients. Media, research and other related services may well be centralized, with the result that there will be less need for an international agency chain providing a full service agency in all markets.

People at headquarters or in lead agencies have often held staff functions. Although the main function of the centre should be as a source of information, inspiration and motivation, the role of international coordinators will be important for international client service. Therefore international coordinators will have line responsibility. Until now, international jobs have been staff functions, which are not the most interesting functions for those who want to make a successful career. There will not necessarily be one head office centrally or one for each region. There may be more agencies in the regions with the potential to become centres of excellence. Those agencies which are the potential lead agencies or centres of excellence will be the ones which have always had the most interest in international affairs.

There is also a growing tendency to train people internationally and eventually pull the best ones to the centre at least for a certain amount of time. Mobility will grow; responsibility and authority for servicing clients will be centralized. Those agencies which do not invest in international human resources will be the losers.

International agency remuneration

Worldwide the most frequently used agency compensation system was formerly that which allowed the agency to keep the 15 per cent of media expenditure paid as a commission by the media to the advertising agencies. Other compensation systems were based on a percentage of the advertising budget; the level of the percentage depended on the size of the market.

The following basic agency compensation systems are still used worldwide:

1. The commission system, usually 15 per cent of media expenditure, but sometimes lower or higher, depending on the size and the complexity of the client. The percentage may be lower if adaptation work alone is done. Additional income can be generated by charging additional fees and/or production surcharges. The percentage depends on the size of the market. The bigger the market, the lower the percentage may be, since the agency functions will be covered to a greater extent by the commission income.

2. The fee system. An advertising agency determines the team that will be working directly on the client's work, and determines what proportion of each person's time will be spent on the account. An overhead figure is determined which will yield the income necessary to pay for non-direct work such as general management, accounting and administrative services. Allowing a suitable profit margin, the agency can determine the total amount of compensation it requires to undertake the client's work. This is called a 'fixed fee'; the agency charges a fixed fee and takes the risk of profit or loss. Another version is the cost-plus arrangement or a straight hourly charge arrangement. The agency strikes an hourly rate for each person working on the account, including overheads, and simply bills the client for the hours spent. In this case the client pays for all the work done and there is no risk for the agency. When the agency works on a fee basis only, it will not keep any media commission.

3. A variation of the fee system in which the fee necessary to make the account profitable is determined and any media commissions earned are credited against that fee.

The situation varies in each country: levels of commission differ and some countries, like Sweden, do not work with commission at all. In general there is a trend away from commission-based remuneration towards hourly rates and fees.

The development of media buying centres has changed most of the remuneration systems in many countries. As a result of using media buying centres, advertising agencies no longer pay the media, so there is no direct basis for media commission. The media buying agency gets paid for its services by the advertiser, by the advertising agency or by the media. The agency gets paid on the basis of a fee or a percentage which may be related to the budget or to media expenditure.

Figure 11.12 shows how the system used to work when it was based on receipt of 15 per cent media commission by the agency.

When a media buying agency is involved the system is different. Media buying agencies negotiate media rates and other conditions of placement, not the remuneration. Figure 11.13 shows the situation when a media buying agency is involved.

For multinational advertisers, who allow their local subsidiaries to work with local agencies without central coordination by the agency concerned, the situation is different from the one where centrally organized clients work with international agency networks.

In the former situation, the local client subsidiary makes arrangements with the local agency, which may or may not be part of a network. The client must realize that compensation for small agencies in small markets needs to be different to that given to large agencies in large markets where the same kind of work is expected from them. A rigid 15 per cent agency commission system is impossible if countries vary greatly in size. Fifteen per cent of $30,000,000 gives an agency in a large country $4,500,000 in gross revenue. An agency in a small country with a billing of $70,000 would have an income of $10,500. The same service

Figure 11.12 *The media commission system*

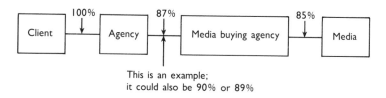

Figure 11.13 *Remuneration where a media buying agency is involved*

cannot be expected from all agencies if one sticks to this rigid commission system.

In 'smaller' countries like Denmark or Finland, the 15 per cent commission system is used, but it is acknowledged that a part of the agency costs is not covered by this media commission. For example, creative work is paid for by additional fees. For multi-local advertising with a non-centralized agency network or independent agencies, one must realize that not all agencies are the same; some may be able to give better service than others. Clients, too, differ in the service expected and some clients are more complicated to handle than others.

No agency should be expected to handle an account at a loss. There must be a healthy relationship between the advertiser and the agency, and realistic remuneration is one of the starting points.

For an international agency network, the situation is easier if it is centrally owned than when there is local ownership. A fully owned international agency can play 'global chess', invest where it wants and use the profits of one agency to invest in other agencies. Yet, on a country-by-country basis, profitability must be controlled; this requires inter-company compensation systems. If the centralized agency considers the local agencies as separate profit centres, there can be similar problems to those encountered with partially locally-owned agencies.

A local agency that is part of a network often has a very dualistic attitude towards that network, especially if it is one of the smaller agencies. It will have to position itself in the local market if it wants to attract the top local talent, on the other hand it has to deal with the problem of conflicting accounts. It will have to deliver inter-agency services to the network, including local data, research and adaptation work. It may also have to let go of a profitable local client, if the network wins an international account which conflicts. As a result there must be some sort of compensation system within the agency. On the other hand the local agency receives local media income from international clients, for whom the campaigns have been developed by headquarters or a lead agency. The lead agency then has to do the creative development and coordination, the cost of which cannot always be recovered from its media income. Local agencies therefore sometimes pay the lead agency a percentage of local media-related income (commission plus fees for work done on media advertising, including commission on production) for creative work and/or coordination.

The way this is done depends also on the country in which the lead agency is situated. The lead agency may be in one country and the media may be bought in another. The percentages vary for coordination and/or creative work, for centrally-originated creative work and for the whole package.

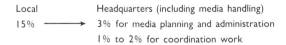

Figure 11.14 *International inter-agency compensation*

As an example Figure 11.14 shows a possible system for internal compensation in a large agency based on guideline advertising, without creative development in every country. The locals keep 8 to 10 per cent for their local work, but headquarters may not receive enough for central creative development, for which separate remuneration arrangements will then be made with the client. The amount will depend on the budget, and may be paid by a fee or on a commission basis. Depending on local negotiations, local agencies can be paid extra fees or production surcharges.

As far as the inter-agency services rendered by local agencies to headquarters or lead agencies are concerned, a system can be set up to cover specific aspects such as out-of-pocket expenses, hourly rates that can be charged to the client or hourly rates for internal work.

Making good arrangements within an agency network is very difficult if the network does not have a uniform system for time recording and accounting. Such a system is, in turn, very difficult to set up for many reasons, both technical and cultural.

The role and organizational structure of the client also influence the process: if the client is well organized, getting an agreement on international compensation is much easier than it is where the client's organizational structure and lines of communication are not clear. If local clients want to have more input and the client's organizational structure is not clear it is also difficult for the agency to structure an efficient organization.

There is a tendency for clients to give agencies incentives in order to improve the efficiency of their relationship and make the creative teams more committed to the client's account.

◼ Summary

The trend towards globalization has changed the organizations of many advertisers and agencies. During the last decade both have been struggling to adapt their organizations for global integration, to achieve greater efficiency and responsiveness and to spread international knowledge and innovation.

Large global enterprises consisting of portfolios of national businesses have emerged, and advertising agencies have had to follow this development in order to serve their clients. This chapter began by describing the changing organization of the advertiser. One of the major issues for international and global advertising is the question of whether control should be centralized or decentralized. International advertising agencies have been organizing themselves to adapt to international developments. The possible organizational structures were outlined in this chapter. Working for international clients requires different procedures and sometimes even different people than when serving local clients. Last but not least, the relationship between the advertiser and agency in the global context was discussed.

One major conclusion must be drawn: both networking within an agency and cooperation between clients and agencies involve a people-oriented undertaking for which mutual trust and respect is needed. If there is no mutual trust, it is very difficult to develop good international advertising. Organizations must be well structured, not only in order to achieve efficiency but also in order to create openness towards each other, which will result in mutual trust and respect.

When all is said and done, another definition of 'advertising worldwide' might be 'Managing people and resources in advertising worldwide'.

■ Notes and references

1. This section draws heavily on Warren J. Keegan, 1989: *Global Marketing Management*, Prentice Hall.
2. Christopher A. Bartlett and Sumantra Ghoshal, 1989: *Managing Across Borders*, Hutchinson Business Books.
3. Keegan, 1989: op. cit.
4. Bartlett and Ghoshal, 1989: op. cit.
5. Ibid.
6. Ibid.
7. Ibid.
8. Brian Dumaine, 1989: 'P&G rewrites the marketing rules', *Fortune*, November.
9. Don E. Schultz interviewed by Laurie Freeman, 'Why markets change', *Advertising Age*, 22 February 1988.
10. John A. Quelch and Edward J. Hoff, 1986: 'Customizing global marketing', *Harvard Business Review*, May–June.
11. Bartlett and Ghoshal, 1989: op. cit.
12. Kamran Kashani, 1989: 'Beware the pitfalls of global marketing', *Harvard Business Review*, September/October.

13. Quelch and Hoff, 1986: op. cit.
14. Kashani, 1989: op. cit.
15. John Micklethwait, 1989: 'What fate awaits the supergroups?', *Campaign*, 30 June.
16. Julie Skur Hill and Julia Michaels, 1987: 'Rethinking global buys', *Advertising Age*, 6 April.
17. This is adapted from John A. Quelch and Edward J. Hoff, Harvard Business School 'Serving client needs in the era of multinational marketing', BBDO Worldwide Network Meeting, September 1985.
18. Ogilvy & Mather brochure: 'Marketing to Europe: opportunities and threats of 1992'.

Chapter 12
The worldwide advertising plan

■ Introduction

This chapter focuses on the planning of international marketing communications. The planning and decision-making process in international marketing communications is very complicated for a number of reasons.

An analysis must be done for each market and/or country, to establish differences in, for example, infrastructure and culture. Decisions about whether to adopt a centralized or a decentralized organization will have to be made, and these will depend in turn on whether brands and their advertising are to be standardized or differentiated. Some markets will have to be given priority over others. Decisions on target groups may have to be made on a global, regional or local basis.

Because of the complicated decision-making-process, timing also becomes more difficult. Usually a continuous flow of information from headquarters to subsidiaries and continuous feedback from the subsidiaries to headquarters is necessary for proper decision-making, by both advertiser and agency. The right organizational structure and lines of communication are a prerequisite for planning, developing and implementing an effective international campaign.

■ Ten steps in planning worldwide advertising

One of the decisive factors in determining the organization of the worldwide advertising plan is the way the company itself is organized.

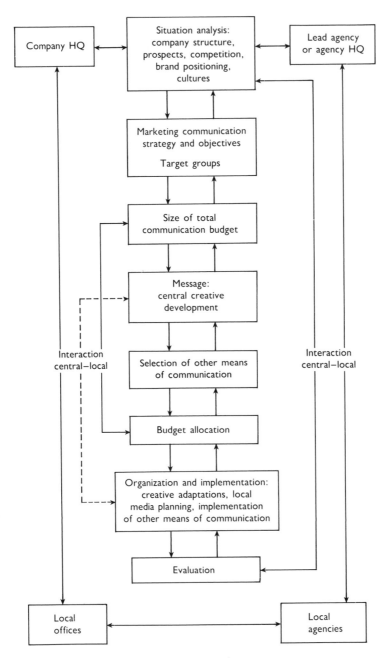

Figure 12.1   *Model for planning international marketing communications*

This is often historically determined. However, changing structures and changing strategies may influence the organization. This chapter will therefore address the centralization/decentralization aspects inherent in several of the stages in planning.

The ten steps in planning worldwide advertising are as follows:

1. Situation analysis.
2. Marketing communication strategy and objectives.
3. Deciding on the target groups.
4. Setting the total communication budget.
5. The message.
6. The means of communication and their integration.
7. Centralized or decentralized control of the means of communication.
8. Budget allocation.
9. Organization and implementation.
10. Control and evaluation.

Figure 12.1 shows these ten steps and the interaction between them.

The ten steps will be described in the sequence in which they are shown in the model. However, it is not necessary to follow the steps in the sequence shown; it may be appropriate to start at any point, depending on the actual situation.

◾ Situation analysis

This step involves analyzing the forces which influence decisions.

The company's structure must be considered. Whether it is a multinational, international, global or transnational organization will make a difference, as will the question of whether it is a multi-brand company or a one-brand company. The structure of the company's international brand portfolio is important – whether the company has many established brands, or whether it is very innovative, focused on new brand introductions? The extent of representation in other countries or markets must be considered, together with the following aspects:

1. The degree of brand standardization.
2. The percentage of each market currently derived from domestic/ national, multinational or global brands.
3. How long the company has marketed brands with the current geographical mix.
4. The market share in each category which the company expects in the future?[1]

The internal structure is relevant – the level of involvement by headquarters, the degree of centralized control, the clarity of the organizational structure and whether this is understood by all concerned so that everyone involved knows each other's responsibilities and authorities in the decision-making process.

The structure of the market must be understood too – the geographical or cultural boundaries, who the customers are, the actual and potential market size, potential for growth, market trends and threats.

The market situation should be analyzed for each country or region. The analysis should indicate the size and potential of markets, the competitive share of markets, total market size, and own company's share, the competitors and their strengths and weaknesses relative to those of the company itself, the market's media situation and the availability of media.

As well as deciding who the customers or prospects are, it is necessary to establish the nature of their needs and wants, the availability of disposable income, the general economic conditions which affect this and the buying patterns for the products or brands concerned.

The brand's positioning in the various countries or markets must be clearly determined. The analysis will cover product or brand awareness, perceived benefits of the brand and willingness to try the product. The brand must be viewed in relation to the product category, product usage, product brand associations, consumption behaviour (time and place of usage) and market segmentation (which social classes use it). Pronunciation or perception of brand name, symbols and local relevance must be clear.

The company's communication should be compared to that of the competition. Here the analysis will consider the value of company and brand names and trade-marks. It will ask how the brand is differentiated vis-à-vis the competition, and whether the market is one of brand parity or brand differentiation. Any communication problems will be pinpointed.

■ Marketing communication strategy and objectives

The key strategy decision is whether to develop a brand globally or multi-locally. A company's interest in turning a brand into a global one depends upon its relative importance in the company's international product portfolio.

New brands are often more easily globalized than established brands, because the marketer does not have to worry about investments already made or consumer franchises already built.[2] However, introducing and maintaining global brands needs large communication budgets, especially in the case of fast-moving consumer packaged goods or brands.

Advertising is the means by which perceptions are differentiated and mental images are created. In a world of brand parity, parity-breaking advertising involving a large share of voice is necessary in order to differentiate a band from that of the competitor. If there are not sufficient funds to secure the necessary share of voice, it would be better to restrict the markets and set priorities, starting with certain regions.

When deciding whether to globalize or not, the company should first consider the brand portfolio to assess in which category each brand currently fits – whether global, purely national, or somewhere in between.[3] It should ask in which direction the brand can be developed, and which brand is most suitable for development into a global brand. The company must consider what are the desired communication effects, whether the communication objectives are to generate knowledge, attitudes or behaviour, whether there is a need to change attitudes and, if so, of which target groups?

In practice there is often a gap between analysis and setting the objectives. It is not unusual for objectives to be set first and later checked against the analysis. Also, when developing a global strategy, an overall vision – a rough strategy with an emphasis on the brand personality – can be communicated to the various countries to check its creative feasibility. After feedback is received, the definitive strategy can be decided upon and fine-tuned in the countries concerned.

▣ Deciding on the target groups

When targeting groups which are similar worldwide in relation to culture-free products or services, these target groups can be described in terms of values and life-styles to assist in creative development. Further fine-tuning in connection with socio-demographic factors will be necessary for local media planning. This can be done on a local or regional level.

Useful criteria often include age and brand usage, but criteria vary according to the particular communication problem. For creative development, and especially for image advertising, the profile of the target must be described realistically and not in too abstract a way. Describing the target individual or person solely in socio-demographic terms will lead to bland, unfocused advertising.

Target groups for differentiated culture-bound products, using multi-local campaigns or adaptations of standardized campaigns, should be described by local subsidiaries in terms of consumer values, brand usage and attitudes, buying habits, etc.

For practical reasons markets or countries will often be grouped into regions. Numerous approaches to grouping world markets have been made, using for example geographical and linguistic criteria. For example, Chapters 5 and 8 mentioned the fact that one common characteristic of high-income groups and businesspeople is the ability to read and speak English. Other criteria may include climate or religion. Each company needs to come up with its own grouping for planning and operating purposes. Such a company-specific grouping needs to take into account not only the market characteristics but also company characteristics. In General Electric, for example, several countries have multi-product manufacturing affiliates. These countries are different from all other countries for GE because of these affiliates, and therefore they must be taken into account in both planning and execution.

The general criteria used in grouping countries include market size, market accessibility, stage of market development, present and future prospects for growth, economic risk and political risk.[4] A grouping can also be based on the availability of some communication services within a region. For example, some countries have better developed direct marketing communication services than others; the Netherlands is very well organized in this respect, while in Spain there is minimal development of the use of these techniques.

■ Setting the total communication budget

The total communication budget is either centrally determined, or a compilation of local budgets, depending on the degree of centralization. The total budget in a campaign for an existing brand may be based on past experience, advertising-to-sales ratios used in the industry, or the objectives set for each country or region, or worldwide.

Priority may have to be given to certain geographical regions or target groups. The most widely-used method for setting budgets is the objective-and-task approach, although advertisers frequently also use methods based on a percentage of sales or simply rely on executives' judgement. These practices differ in different countries.[5,6]

There are also variations in advertising-to-sales ratios in different countries. Advertisers in the United States have comparatively lower expenditure than their counterparts in other countries, which may be attributed to economies of scale in US advertising.[7] However, these ratios also differ within Europe and from market to market.

Many factors influence the level at which the budget is set; these include the phase of the product life-cycle which the product has reached in each country, the media scene in each country, the competitive share of voice, and local rules and regulations.

When comparing share of voice it is important to check the definitions carefully: people in various countries may have different things in mind when using the term 'share of voice'. Some countries include only thematic media advertising, others include media advertising related to sales promotion as well, while still others include all communication efforts, even the costs of sponsorship.

Exchange rates can be a complicating factor. Budgets must be set in the currency of the country where the costs are incurred. This is particularly important in areas of high inflation, such as Latin America.

The costs of translation and adaptation are often underestimated, and bad timing can also increase costs.

When introducing a new brand, a relatively high share of voice is usually necessary to make a good start. When introducing, for example, a new brand of soft drink, it may be necessary to start with a 30 per cent share of voice to win a 5 per cent share of the market. The advertiser will lose money in the beginning, but may well win in the end. If the budget is not sufficient to make this possible on a worldwide basis right from the start – only the very large, global companies have sufficient funds to be able to do this – it is better to start with a few countries or a single region and then roll out into other countries. As described in Chapter 8, p. 240, careful planning and media buying in regions like Europe help in deciding the optimum budget.

If the intention is to use other means of communication, the costs should be taken into account from the start. Pepsi-Cola paid US $5 million to Michael Jackson for his first commercial, but this developed into a strategy of music marketing albeit very successful – with spiralling costs.

'Free' publicity also requires a budget. Planning sponsorship needs to be accompanied by planning media campaigns, and the related additional costs must be taken into consideration. When planning a Direct Marketing Communication campaign, money must be available to set up databases in other countries.

Setting the total budget should be an interactive process, whether it is assembled bottom-up (subsidiaries send in their budgets which are consolidated and negotiated at headquarters) or top-down (tentative budgets are set at headquarters and feedback is received from the subsidiaries). Interaction can be achieved in a centrally-organized budget-setting process by asking local offices or subsidiaries to set their own budgets within guidelines provided; these budgets are then consolidated and fine-tuned at headquarters.

■ The message

There are two main possibilities: a multi-local campaign with different messages for each country, locally developed and executed, or a more standardized campaign. The latter is appropriate for a more culture-free brand or a brand which is made into a global or regional standardized brand by the communication. Careful research and good coordination across countries will be needed to identify the cultural similarities necessary in developing a global brand. This will provide a basis for developing an idea which will successfully communicate the desired message.

Consumer goods have cultural significance, and consumers can be seen as seeking out the meanings of consumer goods and using them in creating their notions of themselves and the outside world.[8] McCracken describes five steps in identifying the cultural properties of consumer behaviour:

1. Determine the symbolic elements and cultural meanings that are currently important to a market segment, and those that are emerging as potential matters of concern.
2. Undertake product development to ensure that the product is given the physical properties it needs in order to carry the cultural meanings that have been chosen for the brand.
3. Devise a promotional campaign that brings the brand into contact with carefully controlled symbolic elements and their cultural meanings and values.
4. Test the copy to see if transfer of meaning has taken place.
5. Carry out research: track the meanings and values into the life of the consumer to see whether the consumer has been able to absorb the meanings and values of the brand.

It is not only the message content which is important in determining the effect of a cross-cultural campaign: the execution and/or adaptation is often of even greater importance. A brilliant idea which is poorly adapted or executed may result in a less effective campaign than an average but well-executed message.

■ The means of communication and their integration

Planning and organizing integrated communications for an international campaign is even more complicated than for a local campaign.

Every specialist means of communication has its unique characteristics, effects and costs. Before selecting a combination of specialist means of communication, it is important to look at each type in turn to determine its own specific merits with regard to the communication objectives. Each has advantages in terms of one or more of the three areas at which communications are targeted – knowledge, attitude and behaviour. The appropriate means of communication for each of these three areas are summarized in Table 12.1.

The choice of an appropriate combination of marketing communication instruments is related to the product/market combination, the type of strategy (push or pull), the phase of the product life-cycle reached by the product or brand, whether it is a high or low involvement brand or product, the consumer's decision-making process and a number of other factors. The criteria may differ for different markets.

The key to integrating marketing communications lies in precise communication with all the different target groups and precise use of all the different instruments.

Table 12.1 Appropriate means of communication for changing knowledge, attitudes and behaviour

Knowledge:	Sponsorship
	Media advertising
	Public relations
	Exhibitions
	Direct marketing communications
Attitudes:	Media advertising
	Sponsorship
	Design
	Public relations
Behaviour:	Sales promotion
	Packaging
	Direct marketing communications
	Personal selling

Table 12.2 shows a number of audiences and the possible media and other means of communication which can be used to reach them. In principle all media can be used for all target groups, but some are more appropriate than others and will thus be given priority. Messages in the various media must be harmonized.

Translation of the central message into a format appropriate to the different means of communication requires strong coordination. It will be necessary to set up an organization to manage the integration process, giving guidelines for administration, and to appoint leaders, both in the agency and in the client company. The key elements of the overall strategy can then be worked out, establishing what messages are to be communicated to what prospects in which media. There is an optimum combination of prospect-message pairs that will work to accomplish the objectives. It is important to decide from the start which activities should be centrally coordinated and which should be planned and executed locally.

Table 12.2 Audiences and media to be integrated

Audiences:	Media and other means of communication
Customers	All elements of
Prospective customers	the product:
Dealer or agencies	– design
Sales force	– price
Wholesalers	– performance
Retailers	– package
Suppliers	Advertising
(Shareholders)	– mass media
(Government	– trade press
officials)	– direct mail
	– special publications
	Publicity
	– horizontal media
	– vertical media
	Direct marketing
	– mail
	– non-mail
	– telemarketing
	Sales promotion
	– all printed matter
	– trade show exhibits
	– travelling road shows
	– product demonstrations

■ Centralized or decentralized control of the means of communication

The decision to leave control to the local offices depends on the nature of the target groups and on the types of communication involved.

Sales promotion, direct marketing communications and to a certain extent sponsorship and public relations are often better handled locally, provided guidelines are given to control the overall image. At the very least it is necessary to safeguard the consistent use of company logos; ideally consistency of the brand image and of the corporate image should be maintained.

However, cultural differences, changing infrastructures and local regulations may require the sales force, wholesalers and retailers to adopt different approaches. The rapidly-changing situation of the retailer, in particular, may call for tailor-made promotional activities and other incentives. Often these are best developed and executed locally.

Central coordination and control can be appropriate for both these and other means of communication, if carefully planned. An example is the way in which Océ copiers formulated its communication plan for the years 1986–1990, incorporating the use of direct marketing techniques.

Océ's Communications masterplan 1986–1990[9]

1986: Start using one strategic message for our products in all communications to all our target groups. Océ: reliable performance in making quality documents.

1987: Plan and control advertising and promotional activities together with local companies and earmark at least 50 per cent of the actual yearly expenditures for advertising and for direct mail in order to build awareness and to generate leads for conversion to sales.

1987/1988: Introduce the concept of direct marketing communication techniques to the local organizations. Set up and start with the organizational implementation of promotion-oriented databases. Learn from pilot projects.

1988: Increase expenditures on marketing communications from the current 2.4 per cent of sales to 3 per cent of sales in 1988.

1989: Temporarily increase, within the budgets concerned, the share of advertising expenditures from the current 20 per cent to 30 per cent in order to improve brand awareness and brand image and to create leads to improve sales force efficiency.

1990: When brand awareness and image have been improved, bring the 30 per cent back to 20 per cent and put more money into direct communication activities, once promotion-oriented databases are operational and well implemented in the local organizations.

■ Budget allocation

First of all the budget has to be divided between consumer and trade advertising.

The mean percentage of total advertising budget spent on consumer advertising worldwide is 88 per cent.[10] Percentages vary for each country. Advertisers of non-durable products spend more on consumer advertising than advertisers of durable products. The breakdown of advertising expenditure across media also differs for each country. In some countries television is the major medium, while in others it is the press.

The importance of other means of communications such as direct marketing communication and promotions has grown throughout the world. However, a comparison of expenditure on media advertising and expenditure on other means of communication is very dangerous, as different criteria and definitions are used in different countries. In the United States, for example, data on sales promotion expenditure include price-cuts, but in other countries these are not included, and figures are based only on the costs of the promotional activities. Often budgets for means of communication such as sales promotion are not included in the advertising budget; instead they are considered to be part of the sales department budget.

Budget allocation for media advertising and other means of communication is something that every company must decide in the light of its own strategy and objectives. This should be done in an early phase, in order to make integration possible.

Allocating the funds available to the different media types in various countries is the specialist role of the media planner. Decisions are made relative to the target groups, the media scene in each country, the share of voice needed and the specific campaign objectives.

The methods for allocating budgets to countries were described in Chapter 8. Local expertise is needed to allocate local budgets to the available media types in each country.

■ Organization and implementation

The development of an effective international campaign, standardized or adapted, requires careful management and good communications. If a standardized campaign fails, this is often because the implementation was not effective. However well the objectives have been worked out, however appropriate and well-executed the creative strategy, the campaign will fail if the implementation is poorly organized. Likewise, non-standardized campaigns have failed to achieve corporate worldwide objectives due to a *laissez faire* management philosophy. Some multinationals seem to have taken the attitude that conducting a non-standardized campaign simply involves relaxing all controls over the subsidiaries and letting them go their own way.[11]

There are a few basic rules for successfully controlling an international campaign: know the markets and travel in them, work with an international agency network, get to know the (account) people at the various offices, use long planning lead times, and maintain central budget approval.[12]

To ensure good coordination, guidelines for creative development and execution should be devised. It is a good idea to use a standardized briefing format, both for the client to brief the agency and for the account team to brief the creative team within the agency. Standardized briefings should also be used when gathering research data on different countries, and particularly when collecting media data, in order to be able to assemble one master plan.

Frequent contact between everyone involved in developing an international campaign is vital from the phase of strategy development right through to implementation. This should not be restricted to inter-office communication using the telephone, telefax or electronic mail; it should also involve meetings and visits to local offices. Coco-Cola has adopted this approach; every year a coordination team consisting of company personnel and staff from the agency, McCann-Erickson, makes three trips around the world to discuss strategies and concepts and present new campaigns.

◼ **Evaluation**

Methods of measuring advertising effectiveness differ in various countries. The two most popular methods are sales and recall.[13] Chapter 10 described the incomparability of research methods in different countries. In order to measure the effects of international or global campaigns, image and awareness must be continuously monitored by tracking studies. If the target groups are international, homogeneous life-style groups, research can be tailor-made. Tracking the effects of a multinational campaign in each country in order to measure the total effect is only possible when research techniques are harmonized.

■ Summary

This chapter described the ten stages in planning worldwide advertising. These ten steps do not differ fundamentally from those involved in domestic marketing communication or advertising planning. However, there are a number of factors which make the process more complicated, and these were outlined.

■ Notes and references

1. John E. Quelch and Edward J. Hoff, 1985: 'Serving client needs in the era of multinational marketing' BBDO Worldwide Network Meeting, September.
2. Ibid.
3. Ibid.
4. Warren J. Keegan, 1989: *Global Marketing Management*, Prentice Hall.
5. Charles F. Keown, Nicholas E. Synodinos and Laurence W. Jacobs, 1989: 'Advertising practices in Northern Europe', *European Journal of Marketing*, March.
6. Nicholas E. Synodinos, Charles F. Keown and Laurence W. Jacobs, 1989: 'Transnational advertising practices: a survey of leading brand advertisers in fifteen countries', *Journal of Advertising Research*, April/May.
7. Keown, Synodonis and Jacobs, 1989: op. cit.
8. Grant McCracken, 1989: 'Culture and consumer behaviour: an anthropological perspective', *Journal of the Marketing Research Society*, Volume 32, No. 1.
9. D. van Buuren, 'De opbouw van Océ als internationaal merk', Studiedag Internationale Communicatiecampagnes, Studiecentrum voor Bedrijf en Overheid, The Netherlands, 22 November 1989.
10. Keown, Synodinos and Jacobs, 1989: op. cit.
11. Dean M. Peebles, John K. Ryans Jr. and Ivan R. Vernon, 'Coordinating international advertising', in Norman Govoni, Robert Eng and Morton Galper, 1988: *Promotional Management, Issues and Perspectives*, Prentice Hall.
12. Ibid.
13. Keown, Synodinos and Jacobs, 1989: op. cit.

Chapter 13
Constraints, rules and regulations

■ Introduction

The forces that constrain worldwide marketing communications are manifold. Cultural and social influences have always played an important role in local advertising.

Global communications have not made the world into one homogeneous culture; on the contrary, they have caused countries increasingly to assert their own cultural identity. 'Foreign' advertising has given cause for special legislation in a number of countries. Some of these countries have adopted specific laws restricting the use of foreign languages and materials. Furthermore, they may require that all advertisements originate in the receiving country and employ local people, customs and expressions.[1]

Global communications have also made some national cultures more inward looking, with a growing concern for moral issues and ethics, and growing religious fundamentalism. Fundamentalism which was formerly implicit in some cultures has now become explicit.

Technological developments have diminished technical constraints, because of the harmonization of techniques. Technological developments have also led to deregulation, for example in television, which in turn generates other types of constraints – more rules and regulations concerning the content of advertising targeted at specific groups or, in the case of some products, a total ban on advertising.

Global communications have made certain issues global, for example environmentalism. The advertising industry uses – and also misuses – some of these issues ('environmental whoring'), again with the result that there are growing global constraints on advertisers.

Common markets, like the EC, will harmonize their laws on advertising; the new laws are likely to resemble the strongest laws of the member countries. Developing countries will follow.

The overall result is that in some countries advertising is no longer protected by the principle of freedom of speech embodied in the national constitution.

Professional ethical considerations must also be taken into account. In those regions or countries which do not have a long-standing tradition of advertising, the advertising techniques familiar elsewhere are often viewed in a different way. People in countries which are not yet used to persuasive advertising claims are more ready to believe them and consider them to be true than the consumer who has long been used to advanced advertising techniques and is therefore more sceptical.

The international advertising industry must be aware of all these developments, and must adapt its professional behaviour accordingly.

This chapter will describe the cultural and technical constraints, the underlying issues for the international regulation of advertising, the main regulations and laws which apply, and the regulatory bodies.

■ Cultural and technical constraints

A country's culture determines behaviour patterns, values, tastes, fashions and so on. These are permanently subject to change, and therefore it is important to conduct systematic research into cultural changes both within countries and internationally. The type of research data available was described in Chapter 5.

Global advertising has influenced some cultural phenomena to a certain extent. Advertising for Maxwell instant coffee has made a few select target groups in China aware of the fact that there is something more than a tea-culture. This serves as an example that it is possible to market and advertise a product which is not endemic to the country's specific culture.

However, the execution of advertising often gives rise to the most constraints. Advertising has to take into account the behavioural patterns of a culture, which often leads to constraints in the execution of advertising.

Constraints on execution

Music

Although music is universally accepted by specific target groups (Michael Jackson, Lionel Richie by the youth), this certainly does not apply for all kinds of music. Sometimes the music in a commercial must be changed for different cultures. Translating song lyrics is even more risky. A classic example of a situation where music failed to act as a universal language comes from Canada, where a company in the car business produced a well-received English language commercial, playing on a theme from a hit Broadway show. Although well known to English-speaking Canadians, the music was essentially unknown to French Canadians.[2]

Humour

Humour generally does not travel well: what is thought to be funny in one country may be considered stupid or misunderstood altogether in another. Slapstick humour in particular is very much culture-bound. In some countries humour is used very well in advertising, in others it is not. Humour is an important element in many British commercials, but is less prevalent in US or Canadian advertising.[3]

Religion

Some cultures have much stronger religious feelings than others. A Pepsi-Cola commercial featuring Madonna had to be withdrawn in the United States because people were offended by Madonna's video which came out at the same time, and which was considered offensive in a religious sense. As the same music was used as for the commercial, people confused the commercial with the video. In most European countries people were not offended.

Sex and erotic scenes

In some countries scenes are felt to be erotic, or even pornographic, while in other countries the same scenes are considered perfectly acceptable.

Sex role stereotyping

Sex role stereotyping should be of serious concern to advertisers. In many developed countries female consumers reject the 'perfect (advertising) woman'.

Relationships between men and women

In segregated societies it is impossible to show men and women eating at the same table. This is an extreme example, but there are more subtle variations which should be taken into account when adapting advertising to different cultures.

Patriotism

A cultural issue which should be carefully considered is patriotism. United States commercials in particular appear to suffer from excessive patriotism – not in the sense of waving of the Stars and Stripes but, for example, emphasizing 'centuries of tradition'. This appears to annoy the British, who see such commercials as aggressively nationalistic.[4]

Language

It seems obvious that different languages impose restrictions. However, the 'same' languages often impose still greater restrictions. Afrikaans and Flemish, though basically the same language, are not the same as Dutch. Canadian French is not the same as the French spoken in France. Americans often do not understand the British accent. In some countries it is forbidden to advertise in the English language, while in others certain accents will not be taken seriously. The language problem highlights the importance of non-verbal commercials which use music alone in worldwide advertising.

The importance of local knowledge

In general, societal behaviour gives rise to conflicts which may require regulation. These may focus on custom and tradition, religion, informal negotiation procedures or social convention. All these fields are relevant to the communication industry, and particularly to commercial persuasive communication or advertising.

The company's subsidiaries and local advertising agencies should be consulted on local cultural differences. Headquarters do not always have open ears, and the results may be disastrous.

Professional and technical constraints

Professional and technical constraints vary according to the type of media used. National characteristics can affect what is possible or appropriate. Constraints also arise as a result of time pressure.

Television

The main constraints where television is concerned are as follows:

1. The permissibility or acceptance by the public of dubbing or subtitling films.
2. The availability of a given medium.
3. Differences in transmission and receiving systems.
4. Acceptance of spot lengths by TV stations.
5. Accepted technology – the type of film or video.
6. The country of production of the commercial – some countries will not accept a commercial produced elsewhere. Local law may state that a commercial must be produced locally.
7. Style or pace: the faster pace and quick cutting of North American advertisements are less appealing to British audiences.[5]

Press and print media

With the press and other print media the main constraints are as follows:

1. Format differences in, for example, writing paper sizes, poster sizes and measuring systems.
2. Differences in skills in countries, advanced machinery, quality of printing.
3. Laws that prohibit the import of printing done elsewhere.
4. Differences in quality of printing techniques of magazines, for example for food advertising.

Time planning

The main constraints imposed by time planning are as follows:

1. Differences in delivery production times.
2. Differences in time planning where different phases of the product life-cycle have been reached.

National characteristics

The main constraints resulting from national characteristics include the following:

1. Typical landscapes vary and thus may necessitate adaptation.
2. Facial appearance, hairstyle and clothing vary for different countries. For example, North American businessmen wear their trousers shorter than European businessmen, and North American businesswomen dress more formally than European business-women. Korean women always wear stockings, even in the hottest weather, while Scandinavians do not.
3. National pride.
4. Changing attitudes towards product use, the environment, etc.

■ Issues underlying regulation

Although the term 'advertising' has many personal meanings, everyone will agree that it refers to the use of society's mass information systems for economic purposes. Individually or in groups, people want access to the use of a society's mass information systems in order to offer or receive information and eventually, to buy or sell a variety of things. As societies have become more complex, and as the technology of mass communications has improved, more and more individuals and groups have begun to use mass communication for economic purposes, to buy or sell goods, personal services or ideas.[6]

Advertising is intrinsically related to the mass information system in a cultural, economic and technological sense. It interacts with all other uses of the system and shares all the related problems, including the problem of regulation.[7] In looking at the forces underlying advertising regulation worldwide, advertising can be considered in two different ways:

1. *As a business function*. It is a company's way of communicating economically with those consumers who might be interested in its product or service.
2. *As an institution*. It is all the people and activities concerned with the sending and the seeking or receiving of information for economic purposes. This includes the producers of the advertising message (advertisers and agencies), the media, the regulatory bodies and the message itself.[8]

Advertising as a business function

Advertising, as an instrument used by business, employs persuasive techniques. In the 1960s and 1970s, when consumerism became an important influence on marketing and advertising practice, this persuasive element meant that advertising was increasingly seen as manipulative, forcing people to do things they would not ordinarily do.[4] Vance Packard epitomized this view, describing advertising as follows:

> large scale efforts being made, often with impressive success, to channel our unthinking habits, our purchasing decisions and our thought processes by the use of insights gleaned from psychiatry and the social sciences. Typically these efforts take place beneath our level of awareness; so that the appeals which move us are often, in a sense, 'hidden'. The result is that many of us are being influenced and manipulated, far more than we realize, in the patterns of our everyday lives.[10]

The consumer movement of the 1970s, which originated in the United States, based its criticism of advertising on this manipulative model:

> advertising uses deceptive practices, misleading messages, and exploits vulnerable consumers. It promotes so-called unhealthy, unsafe or useless products. Its advertising messages take advantage of the ignorant, the illiterate or the young. Thus, it is supposed to have negative effects on health, personal values and economic decisions.[11]

Another criticism levelled at advertising is that it makes people buy things they do not need or want. D. M. Kendall, Chairman and CEO of PepsiCo Inc. commented on this in the following way:

> It is often said that 'advertising sells people things they don't need'. The best answer I've heard to that criticism was in a house ad run by the Young & Rubicam Agency. It went in part like this: 'Yes, advertising does sell people things they don't need...things like television sets, radios, automobiles, catsup, mattresses, lipstick, and so on. People don't really need these things. They really don't need art or music

394 Managing worldwide advertising

or cathedrals...they don't absolutely need literature, newspapers or historians. All people really need is a cave, a piece of meat, and possibly a fire.'... So when I'm told that people don't really need certain kinds of products – I have to agree very quickly. Marketing is a process that satisfies wants and desires most of which are not fundamental needs.[12]

By now, experience and research have proved that in developed societies advertising cannot make people buy things they do not want. There may be some doubts about this in developing societies. By showing new goods and alternative life-styles, consumption patterns of developed countries are transferred to developing countries, and the result is a shift from local staples to luxury or prestige items, either imported or produced locally by multinational affiliates. Furthermore, the idyllic picture of people and the world painted in advertisements presents a distorted view of health and happiness, suggesting these are dependent on the consumption of certain foods and other products. On the other hand, the appeal of new goods to the consumer has always been a powerful factor in economic development.[13]

Growing literacy and better education in developing societies will make consumers more assertive as far as advertising is concerned. Nevertheless, developing countries are seriously concerned about the economic consequences of foreign advertising, including the displacement of local advertisers and the increase in imports of consumer goods. In many countries the threat posed to social and religious values and cultural traditions by international advertising is an important issue.[14]

Irritating the audience in advertising both attracts criticism and makes advertising less effective. Research has shown that irritating advertising may sometimes achieve a relatively high impact. In the long run, however, especially where there is a high frequency of advertising in the same medium, irritating the audience will be counterproductive. Irritation may result from showing people acting in a dumb or stupid way, hype, certain types of humour or, often, just bad advertising.

There are two main arguments as to why advertising should not manipulate, mislead or irritate consumers:

1. Advertising will lose its effectiveness if it misleads by false claims or irritates by portraying people as stupid. Offending customers has never helped sales. Neither is it possible to go on fooling all of the people all of the time.
2. Deceptive or irritating advertising will eventually damage the credibility of the advertising industry, leading to increased regulation worldwide. For this reason those who are involved in international advertising must be sensitive to cultural differences.

Better education in the advertising industry, and the resulting higher professional standards, have made advertisers aware of these unwanted side-effects.

The consumer, too, has changed. Consumers in the 1980s and 1990s are different to those of the 1950s and 1960s, and buying behaviour has changed. Consumers are better educated; they perceive advertising as part of their lives, something which gives them information on products, but is also part of the accepted mass communication system. People have accepted advertising as part of their daily life instead of seeing it as a threatening phenomenon which might make them do things they do not want to do. Twenty years ago it was unthinkable that people would provide 'free advertising' for brands by wearing a T-shirt with a brand name on it. By the end of the 1980s T-shirts bearing the names of some major brands were selling well, and sometimes they were even status products. In 1986 there was only a mild protest when the Crown Prince of the Netherlands – where the Royal family is not supposed to engage in commercial activities – was seen wearing a Marlboro shirt while participating incognito in a major Dutch skating race, which was shown on national television.

Advertising creates successful world brands which are perceived by the consumer as quality products. However, advertisers have adapted their style, and their current consumer policy is based on the prevailing regulatory set-up. As a result, enthusiasm for consumer protection has waned in most developed countries.

Advertising as an institution

The advertising institution encompasses the senders and producers of advertising messages, the media, the receivers of messages, regulatory bodies and the messages themselves.

The main issues concerning the institution of advertising are the social, cultural and economic factors which generate criticism of advertising as a phenomenon. These aspects mostly have to do with the content of the message. They vary with the type of society, and change over time. Both message and media play their role. The general effects on society are said to be increasing materialism at the cost of more spiritual values and discrimination against certain groups in society. Some of the main aspects of advertising which supposedly influence cultural and social patterns are as follows:

1. Truthfulness in advertising
2. Values and life-styles.
3. Stereotypes.

Truthfulness in advertising

Truthfulness in advertising is a concept which is very difficult to define. Barbara Sundberg Baudot[15] has this to say about truthfulness in advertising:

> Underlying the advertising controversy is the elusive nature of human truth; variations in human personalities reflected in different thresholds of credulity, persuasibility, and comprehension; and the large part played by emotions in purchasing decisions. Thus, while deliberate dishonesty with the intention to defraud generally is considered a crime, the acceptability of many other practices may depend on prevailing social philosophies and values on the elusiveness of human truth.
>
> The following are examples of contentious questions: What are the criteria for determining false advertising? What is deception? To what extent is exaggeration permissible? What is the link between disclosure and truth? Truth is relative to the perception of the audience. Literal truth can be misapprehended or misleading to some audiences.

Many regulatory bodies have tried to define the concept of truth in advertising. However, the concept must always be seen in the context of the message and the audience. One example of what may be considered untruthful is 'puffing' or gross exaggeration. This will not be misleading to a literate audience used to the prevailing advertising techniques in a specific country. It may be misleading in countries which are not yet used to the role of advertising in society or to techniques based on the principles of persuasive communication.

Persuasive communication implies giving the kind of information which will persuade people to buy, and leaving out other, often more negative information, with the result that the information is incomplete. Incomplete information may mislead, but is rarely based on deliberate dishonesty.

Deliberate dishonesty has always existed in advertising and will always be there, just like bad business practice. Laws, rules and regulations have been made to restrict deliberate dishonesty, and the advertising industry itself has developed into a more responsible industry. Global companies cannot afford the negative effects of deliberate dishonesty, as this would damage their global reputation. What was possible in the past is no longer possible today. Daniel Boorstin[16] writes:

> Never was there a more outrageous or more unscrupulous or more ill-informed advertising campaign than that by which the promoters for the American colonies brought settlers to North America. Brochures published in England in the seventeenth century, some even earlier, were full of hopeful overstatements, half-truths and downright lies, along with

some facts which nowadays surely would be the basis for a restraining order from the Federal Trade Commission. Gold and silver, fountains of youth, plenty of fish, venison without limit, all these were promised, and, of course, some of them were found. It would be interesting to speculate on how long it might have taken to settle this continent if there had not been such promotion by enterprising advertisers. How has American civilization been shaped by the fact that there was a kind of natural selection here of those people who were willing to believe advertising?

Values and life-styles

Critics of advertising claim that advertising exploits values and can reinforce them or accelerate their development. The question is, however, whether advertising creates or reflects the values of society. Attempts to connect advertising with materialism seldom recognize anthropological evidence that analogies to modern society's use of products for ego-enhancement existed in almost all primitive cultures.[17]

The area of interpersonal relationships is different: the manner of portraying women and minority groups has always been criticized. From a business point of view the portrayal of women in a particular manner may be defensible. However, the cumulative effect of showing women as housewives, mainly relating to household products, may not reflect the complete role of women in society. In many societies, a majority of women work in service industries, with the result that in their working roles they are most often portrayed as subordinate to men. Examples are the stewardess in the airline advertisement who is serving a businessman, or the hostess of a car rental service who leads her male client to his rented car. In societies with a strong women's liberation movement, this kind of advertising is less widely accepted than in countries where this reflects the actual pattern of the rules adopted by men and women.

Research has shown that new media and advertising have changed life-styles and values in certain societies. An example is the change in leisure activities brought about by television, together with the fact that television has failed to broaden children's interests. A few general conclusions may be drawn from research into the effects of mass communication:[18]

1. Mass communication confirms and reinforces existing attitudes, following the process of selective perception, by which people only absorb those elements which they want to see or hear.
2. When mass communication influences people directly, those whom it influences are those who are most often confronted with the mass media, the poor, the less well-educated and children.

3. If any type of social change is taking place, mass communication can accelerate it.
4. Mass communication is the product of those who control the process and the techniques. These people are not neutral and will always influence the outcome of the process.

Stereotypes

Using stereotypes when portraying people is a normal, human habit. Erving Goffman[19] states that the human race has always focused on a number of religious and social rituals.

Human beings have always tended to portray themselves at the best moments of their lives. Photographs are testimonies of the best social moments. This is a form of stereotyping. One picture cannot portray a whole society, since a society consists of a series of sequential activities. The more an activity is recorded in a stereotype, the easier it is to guess the consequences and effects of the activity shown.

Advertising does this to the extreme. It portrays ideal activities, with ideal effects. All types of persuasive communication use this technique. Using stereotypes is necessary when the content of the message, in the right context, must be perceived and understood at one glance. The effect is an artificial portrayal of reality. Stereotyping is strongest in life-style advertising.

Economic aspects

Advertising which gives information to consumers on the basis of which they can make better buying decisions is seen as economically useful. Advertising which provides only emotional added value in order to differentiate brands from the competition is seen by critics as wasteful.

The counter-argument is that free competition, with business having the freedom to select the appropriate advertising techniques, will prevent monopolies. It will thus reduce prices and lead to higher quality branded articles. The recent concentration through mergers of both producers of mass consumer goods and media companies may lead people to doubt this. However, mergers between major producers of branded articles has resulted in the creation of more different, competing brands rather than in a concentration of brands.

Another economic aspect of advertising is that it subsidizes the media. Without advertising there would not be such a diversity of media. Again, the large media mergers provide a counter-argument;

the media barons have a strong grip on the creation and operation of the media.

The critics

Criticism of advertising and marketing practices started in the 1960s, as the marketing concept was more widely adopted. The most influential critics in developed countries are the consumer interest groups, the driving force behind consumerism. Consumerism is defined by Greyser and Diamond as

> the organized movement to increase rights and powers of buyers in relation to sellers in an imperfect market.[20]

Consumerism has come to mean the activities of those who promote or protect consumer interests from real or perceived abuses by sellers in the market-place.[21]

Some consumer organizations continuously monitor consumer-related issues; there are also looser groups of activists which tend to focus on specific issues.

The consumer movement has made demands in three main areas:

1. *Consumer information* – data about products and services offered for sale and information to assist specific buying decisions, especially comparative data.
2. *Consumer education* – the development of the knowledge base necessary to be an intelligent consumer, to know how the economy operates, how buyers and sellers interact, and how to deal with the people and institutions one encounters.
3. *Consumer protection* – the call for governments and regulatory bodies to safeguard consumer rights, protect against deceptive practices or set health and safety standards.[22]

On 15 March 1962, US President John F. Kennedy, stimulated by the consumer movement and the rapid growth of international advertising, formulated four fundamental consumer rights:

1. *The right to safety* – to be protected against the marketing of goods hazardous to health or life.
2. *The right to choose* – to be assured access to a variety of products and services at fair and/or competitive prices.
3. *The right to be heard* – to be assured that consumer interests will receive full and sympathetic consideration in the formulation of government policy.

4. *The right to be informed* – to be protected against fraudulent, deceitful or grossly misleading information and to be given adequate information.[23]

On 17 May 1973 the Assembly of the Council of Europe adopted a European Consumer Protection Charter, which included the same basic rights as those formulated by President Kennedy. On 14 April 1975 the Council of the European Communities formally adopted a European Consumer Protection and Information Policy incorporating the following five basic consumer rights:[24]

1. The right to protection of health and safety.
2. The right to protection of economic interests.
3. The right of redress.
4. The right to information and education.
5. The right of representation.

Originally the right to choose was not included. Later the following statement was added:

> These rights are seen within the context of a general consumer right to the primary satisfaction of basic needs and freedom of individual choice for the expenditure of discretionary income.[25]

Major categories of criticism

The social, cultural and economic issues already described have generated all kinds of criticisms of advertising practice. There are, however, a few major issues which underlie the increasing regulation of advertising.

Rijkens and Miracle[26] define three major categories of criticism:

1. Advertising is sometimes unfair or harms competitors – or at least it is seen as unfair by competitors.
2. Advertising sometimes injures the competition, or precludes the maintenance of workable competition.
3. Advertising sometimes provides less than adequate, or even false, deceptive or misleading messages, and therefore harms consumers.

Rijkens and Miracle state that truthful and accurate advertising which harms competitors ought *not* to be regulated. However, advertising which is false, deceptive or misleading ought to be regulated not only because it harms competitors, but more importantly because it can harm consumers both directly, if they make poor purchasing decisions on the basis of such information, and indirectly by harming efficient competitors who serve consumers well.

Comparative advertising, even if not misleading, is an example of the kind of advertising which is forbidden by many local advertising regulations. This is changing, since truthful comparative advertising benefits the consumer by providing information which can help in making buying decisions.

■ Laws and regulations

The principal sources of advertising regulation are national governments, international governmental organizations (global and regional), and non-governmental institutions, including associations of individual advertisers, advertising agencies and media.[27]

Most industrialized countries with a free market economy initially began to regulate advertising with the aim of maintaining fair competition. Over the years the protection of consumers also became a major goal. The social mores of each society are reflected in the substance of restrictions regarding truthfulness, decency and use of language.[28]

Many countries now have laws on misleading advertising; these mainly come into the category of civil code or common law. A third, Confucian, antilegalist tradition is very relevant for Japan. All European countries except the United Kingdom follow the civil code system. Common law countries include the United Kingdom, United States, Canada, Australia and New Zealand.[29]

Self-regulation started in the United States at the beginning of the twentieth century with the foundation of local clubs consisting of agents, advertisers and media representatives. The American Advertising Federation (AAF), American Association of Advertising Agencies (AAAA) and the Association of National Advertisers (ANA) joined to form a central organization for the regulation of advertising. This is the National Advertising Review Board (NARB). The NARB, together with the Federal Trade Commission (FTC), has helped in setting standards for developing the regulation of advertising in other parts of the world.

In 1919 the International Chamber of Commerce (ICC) was established to promote international business interests. The ICC in 1930 established the International Code of Advertising Practice with the support of advertisers, agencies and media. It was first published in 1937.[30]

General laws and regulations often deal with misleading advertising, false claims and unfair practices concerning the competition. Most countries also have laws relating to sales promotion practice or regulations concerning the incentives used for sales promotions, such as contests, free offers, etc.

Special target groups such as children are protected by law in many countries.

In many countries, too, a number of *product categories* are subject to specific laws or regulations, for example pharmaceutical products, tobacco, alcoholic beverages, cosmetics and children's products.

The media have long been a special target for laws and regulations: many countries have in the past banned advertising from television. However, this is changing fast, due to satellite television and the resulting deregulation.

Foreign advertising has given cause for special legislation in a number of countries. Some countries have adopted specific laws restricting the use of foreign languages and materials.

Laws related to direct marketing communication techniques are emerging to protect the consumer's privacy.

Many countries, in establishing their own self-regulation, have followed the guidelines of the ICC Code of Advertising. Since its establishment in 1954, the International Advertising Association has worked to help improve standards, practices and ethical concepts of advertisers, advertising agencies and allied services.

International law

International law may be defined as the rules and principles which states and nations consider binding upon themselves.

International law has two unique characteristics. First, those areas covered by international law have always belonged to individual states or nations – property, trade, immigration and so on – and the law exists only to the extent that individual states are willing to relinquish their rights in these areas. Secondly, there is no adequate international judicial and administrative framework and no body of law that would form the basis of a truly comprehensive international legal system. In this situation multinational marketers face a complex legal situation. They will discover that simply finding out what the law is, or whose law prevails, in a given situation is a difficult task.[31]

The EC is the first area in which true international regulation is emerging: the EC Directive on misleading advertising was formally adopted in September 1984 after years of complex negotiations. The directive is the first inter-governmental attempt to regulate advertising through binding international legislation. The directive establishes minimum standards for the regulation of 'misleading advertising' in the twelve member countries of the European Community.[32]

International self-regulation

Self-regulation in advertising has three basic objectives:

1. To protect consumers against false or misleading advertising and against advertising that intrudes on their privacy through its unwanted presence or offensive content.
2. To protect legitimate advertisers against false or misleading advertising by competitors.
3. To protect the public acceptance of advertising, so that it can continue as an effective institution in the market-place.[33]

There are three different levels of self-regulation:

1. Pure self-regulation, where advertisers, advertising agencies and the media together decide what is acceptable.
2. Negotiated codes of practice, drawn up between the industry and a governmental body.
3. Agreements or conventions, where self-regulation is suggested to, or is imposed on, the advertising business by an outside body.[34]

International codes and guidelines can contribute to the harmonization of national laws. They provide direction for policy-makers in national governments, and may form the basis for legislation in areas which are inadequately covered under national law.[35]

The first formal international self-regulatory code for advertising practice was the International Code of Advertising Practice of the International Chamber of Commerce (ICC). This was designed as an instrument of self-discipline, but it has also been used as a reference for national self-regulatory bodies as well as in devising national laws and government regulations. The ICC has become the most important non-governmental, independent and global organization representing the interests of international business, especially in the sense of defending private enterprise and the market system.[36] The original Code of Advertising Practice has been extended with special guidelines on advertising to children.

Misleading advertising

Just as it is difficult to define what is meant by truth in advertising, so it is equally difficult to define the concept of 'misleading' advertising. Misleading advertising is the main issue addressed by self-regulatory codes. Other issues covered by many national regulations are good taste, safety, health issues, guarantees, ethical issues, comparative advertising, discrimination, racism, and the protection of special groups such as children and young people, the poor and the elderly, especially where specific products are concerned, for example cigarettes.

With regard to misleading advertising, various definitions have been attached to the concepts 'misleading', 'deceptive' and 'false'.

The US criteria for defining deception and considering an advertisement false, misleading or deceptive can be described as follows:[37]

1. The claim is false.
2. The claim is partially true and partially false.
3. The claim contains insufficient information.
4. The claim may be true, but the proof is false.
5. The claim may be 'literally' or 'technically' true, but creates a false implication.[38]

To these descriptions may be added three criteria for determining 'unfairness in advertising', as outlined in the 'unfairness doctrine':

1. The unsubstantiated claim – made despite the lack of a reasonable basis for making the claim.
2. The special audience claim – which may motivate vulnerable groups to engage in conduct deleterious to themselves.
3. The puffing claim – which cannot be objectively disproved but offers promises unlikely to be fulfilled.[39]

In the Memorandum on the first draft Directive on Misleading and Unfair Advertising of the European Community, the general definition of misleading advertising given in Article Three set out the criterion of liability, namely the risk that the public would be misled. The concept of 'misleading advertising' was defined as follows in Article Four, which provided an elaboration of Article Three:

1. A claim is false; or
2. a claim that contains insufficient information; or
3. a claim that is partially true and partially false; or
4. a claim that is true but creates a false implication; or
5. a claim that is true but is falsely proved to be true; or
6. a claim that is not adequately substantiated; or
7. a claim that cannot be objectively disproved but that makes offers unlikely to be capable of fulfilment.[40]

In later drafts the specifications were changed, and in the final Directive of 10 September 1984 the points in Article Four were largely omitted. Article 3 on misleading advertising reads as follows in the final directive:[41]

ARTICLE 3

In determining whether advertising is misleading, account shall be taken of all its features, and in particular of any information it contains concerning:

(a) the characteristics of goods and services, such as their availability, nature, execution, composition, method and date of manufacture or provision, fitness for purpose, uses, quantity, specification, geographical or commercial origin or the results to be expected from their use, or the results and material features of tests or checks carried out on the goods and services;
(b) the price or the manner in which the price is calculated, and the conditions on which the goods are supplied or the services provided;
(c) the nature, attributes and rights of the advertiser, such as his identity and assets, his qualifications and ownership of industrial, commercial or intellectual property rights or his awards and distinctions.

Government regulation or self-regulation

In many parts of the world the question of which is most effective, government regulation or self-regulation, has been raised.

Oliver argues as follows:[42]

the government, in most cases, cannot regulate as well as the market place does. Businesses, far more painfully than politicians, pay the price for empty promises. Businesses, like individuals, have strong incentives to safeguard their reputations. In both the commercial and social world, your word is as good as your name.

This is not to say that there should be no role for government in the regulation of commercial speech, or that deceptive speech is something to be encouraged. But it is to say that government restraints on commercial speech must be carefully circumscribed and extremely limited in order to prevent the suppression of truthful information.

One may wonder if the tendency of governments to ban all advertising for certain products is an effective way of changing people's habits. Banning cigarette advertising will not make people stop smoking. It is a generally known fact that in countries where there is no cigarette advertising at all, or where cigarette advertising is banned from TV, people do not smoke any less than in countries where there are no limitations on cigarette advertising. It needs more than banning advertising to change people's behaviour.

▣ What should international advertisers do?

The extent and variety of rules and regulations worldwide is so large that international advertising specialists cannot know them all. Equally, they cannot all be described here.

Finding out about the many local laws and regulations is made easier by a score of international surveys conducted by the International Advertising Association, which deal with government regulations as well as with industry codes and guidelines that apply to advertising and sales promotion in many countries. The European Association of Advertising Agencies has published a book on laws and regulations concerning advertising in Europe, the so-called *Red Book on Laws and Regulations on Advertising in Europe*. This gives information on constraints relating to special product categories, advertising to children, sex role stereotyping, pornography, comparative advertising and sweepstakes. The IAA publishes a report on government regulation and industry self-regulation in fifty-three countries, *Barriers To Trade and Investment in Advertising*. Furthermore, several books have been written on the subject which give comprehensive overviews of the world situation concerning advertising laws and regulations, for example that by Barbara Sundberg Baudot,[43] and the European regulation of advertising, for example that by Rein Rijkens and Gordon Miracle.[44]

Boddewyn[45] suggests that international advertisers should take the following action:

1. Have in-house and external legal advisers check and double-check the true nature of advertising restrictions in relevant foreign markets.
2. Monitor and oppose the spread of regulations, taxes and other obstacles which hamper international advertising.
3. Initiate, support and assist the development of advertising self-regulation around the world.

▣ International regulatory bodies

The International Chamber of Commerce has been, and still is, the most important international regulatory body to influence worldwide advertising regulation. In 1984 the ICC was represented in 106 countries, with national committees in 57 countries.

International professional advertising organizations have always played an important role in the development of advertising regulation, and so have American and British advertising organizations. The main organizations are as follows:

The Advertising Association (AA)
American Association of Advertising Agencies (AAAA)
American Advertising Federation (AAF)
Association of National Advertisers (ANA)
European Association of Advertising Agencies (EAAA)
European Advertising Tripartite (EAT)
International Advertising Association (IAA)
Institute of Practitioners in Advertising (IPA)
World Federation of Advertisers (WFA).
Asian Federation of Advertising Associations (AFAA)

Of these organizations, the IAA has the most extensive worldwide network, with approximately 2,700 individual members in 74 countries in 1990. In Europe, the EAT has a very important function as the main lobbying body for the entire advertising industry.

Apart from the professional advertising organizations, the International Organization of Consumers' Unions (IOCU) plays an important role, with 135 member consumer organizations, an office in The Hague and a regional office for the Asia/Pacific region in Malaysia.

The World Health Organization (WHO) and the Food and Agricultural Organization (FAO), a UN organization, are concerned with the effects of multinational commercial activities on health. The United Nations Educational, Scientific and Cultural Organization (UNESCO) focuses on the cultural effects of global advertising. The United Nations Conference on Trade and Development (UNCTAD) has carried out studies on international advertising of specific manufactured products.[46]

■ Summary

The global advertising industry is under permanent pressure from consumers and governments who want to increase the constraints on it. On the other hand there is a worldwide tendency towards deregulation.

International advertising professionals must be aware that their profession may exert social and cultural influence which may be resisted by local governments or national and international organizations which aim to protect societies and consumers against the unwanted side-effects of commercial communications.

Many laws and regulations have already placed limitations on free commercial advertising. In many developed countries commercial advertising is already excluded from the right to freedom of speech. In less developed countries freedom of speech is in any case not necessarily a tradition. In future further restrictions may be expected from nationalistic factions which oppose multinational industries such as the fast food industry if they do not take into account national religious beliefs and customs.

Therefore, international advertising professionals must develop their own ethical standards and cultural sensitivity in order to avoid making cultural mistakes which may result in more legislation and regulation. This chapter has aimed to assist in this by describing cultural and technical constraints, the issues underlying regulation, and the development of laws and regulations.

The advertising industry must fight the growing number of restrictions on advertising. This last chapter concludes with the closing words of the IAA World President, Mr Roger Neill, at the 32nd World Advertising Congress of the International Advertising Association, held in Hamburg in 1990:

> Any product that is legally allowed to be produced, legally allowed to be sold, should be legally allowed to be advertised.

The International Advertising Association has made the fight for freedom of commercial speech one of its first priorities.

■ Notes and references

1. Barbara Sundberg Baudot, 1989: *'International Advertising Handbook: A User's Guide to Rules and Regulations'*, Lexington Books. Extracts from this book are reprinted by permission of the publisher (Lexington, Mass.: Lexington Books, D. C. Heath and Company, Copyright 1989, Lexington Books).
2. James P. King, 1988: 'Cross cultural reactions to advertising: the promise of non-verbal, continuous measurement'. *European Research*, February.
3. Ibid.
4. Ibid.
5. Ibid.
6. Francisco M. Nicosia, 1974: *Advertising, Management and Society: A business point of view*, McGraw Hill.
7. Ibid.
8. Ibid.
9. Daniel Oliver, 1988: 'Who should regulate advertising and why?', The Advertising Association President's Lecture 1987, *International Journal of Advertising*, 7, 1–9.

10. Vance Packard, 1957: *The Hidden Persuaders*, Longman, Green & Co.
11. Sundberg Baudot, 1989: op. cit.
12. Quoted in Nicosia, 1974: op. cit.
13. Sundberg Baudot, 1989: op. cit.
14. Ibid.
15. Ibid.
16. Daniel J.Boorstin, 1976: 'The rhetoric of democracy', *Advertising Age*, 19 April.
17. Stephen A. Greyser, 1972: 'Advertising: attacks and counters', *Harvard Business Review*, March/April.
18. J. T. Klapper, 1961: 'The effects of mass communication', Glencoe Free Press.
19. Erving Goffman, 1979: *Gender Advertisement*, Macmillan.
20. Sundberg Baudot, 1989: op. cit.
21. Rein Rijkens and Gordon E. Miracle, 1986: *European Regulation of Advertising*, North Holland.
22. Ibid.
23. Sundberg Baudot, 1989: op. cit.
24. Rijkens and Miracle, 1986: op. cit.
25. Ibid.
26. Ibid.
27. Sundberg Baudot, 1989: op. cit.
28. Ibid.
29. Ibid.
30. Rijkens and Miracle, 1986: op. cit.
31. Warren J. Keegan, 1989: *Global Marketing Management*, Prentice Hall.
32. Sundberg Baudot, 1989: op. cit.
33. Rijkens and Miracle, 1986: op. cit.
34. Ibid.
35. Sundberg Baudot, 1989: op. cit.
36. Rijkens and Miracle, 1986: op. cit.
37. Ibid.
38. D. Cohen, 1974: 'The concept of unfairness as it relates to advertising legislation', *Journal of Marketing*, July.
39. Ibid.
40. Rijkens and Miracle, 1986: op. cit.
41. Ibid.
42. Oliver, 1989: op. cit.
43. Sundberg Baudot 1989: op. cit.
44. Rijkens and Miracle, 1986: op. cit.
45. J. J. Boddewyn, 1988: 'The one and many worlds of advertising – regulatory obstacles and opportunities', *International Journal of Advertising* No. 7.
46. Sundberg Baudot, 1989: op. cit.

Appendix:
The IAA Diploma in International Advertising

■ **The International Advertising Association (IAA) and its Education Programme**

The IAA is the only global body dedicated to advancing the art, practice and interests of advertising throughout the world. The IAA, with headquarters in New York, binds together a global network of some 38 local IAA chapters in some 74 countries worldwide. In 1990 the IAA membership included close to 2,700 individuals. Working together with its local chapters, the IAA seeks to marshal local forces everywhere to protect business and the consumer in a wide range of areas. For example, the IAA defends free commercial speech, encourages responsibility in advertising, and explains the far-reaching economic and social values of advertising to the public and to governments.

EDUCATION PROGRAMME OF THE
INTERNATIONAL
ADVERTISING
ASSOCIATION

As just one facet of the many ways the IAA seeks to serve business and the public, it conducts an examination programme designed to establish world-class credentials by which competent practitioners can be identified: the examination for the IAA Diploma in International Advertising.

The examination is in two parts, both of which are required of all candidates. These are as follows:

Part I: Covers a broad range of knowledge about how to advertise on a worldwide basis.

Part II: Based on a communication case study which is supplied in advance of the examination.

The examination is held annually on the last Friday in May. Registration closes on 1 March of the same year. A candidate can sit for the examination in his or her own country provided that a local IAA chapter exists in that country.

Information is available from the IAA Education Secretariat at the following address:

Dellaertlaan 37
1171 HE Badhoevedorp
Netherlands

In order to give an impression of what the examination covers the questions and cases from the 1989 and 1990 examinations are reprinted on the following pages.

IAA Diploma in International Advertising, 26 May 1989

Paper 1

Candidates are allowed 3 hours to complete this paper plus $\frac{1}{2}$ hour if English is not their first language. Candidates must answer 5 questions. All questions carry equal marks.

1. 'The penetration of American films and TV shows is so extensive that most USA-derived TV ads can be used anywhere without amendment.' Discuss this view.

2. 'Global brand strategies imply a lessening of importance for indigenous marketing specialists.' Do you agree?

3. What would be the role and value of a globally published daily newspaper? What form might it take?

4. Is the concept of 'life-style' marketing relevant to advertising in Third World countries?

5. In what circumstances in planning advertising campaigns should the local objectives override HQ objectives?

6. 'There are no production benefits in making international ads. Indeed, it's a damned sight more expensive.' A harassed production manager's view. Is this always the case?

7. How would you correlate data from two research studies in different countries?

8. Is there any benefit in coordinating sales promotion between countries?

9. For an agency with business abroad but unable to find a working partner in a particular country, what alternative operating strategies are there?

10. Is 'the visit' the only reliable way of keeping abreast of market activity in a foreign market?

11. How can a public relations programme be introduced globally?

12. The various owners of satellite TV predict that it is the new dawn for advertisers. Do you agree?

IAA Diploma in International Advertising, 26 May 1989

Paper II

Candidates are allowed 3 hours to complete this paper plus $\frac{1}{2}$ hour if English is not their first language. Candidates must answer all questions.

1. You are Marketing Director for Tab, responsible for the launch of Trend. Write a briefing document for your agency, setting out objectives for a rolling launch commencing in January 1990. You should include a review of acceptable creative approaches and media strategies against the target groups you also define.

2. Outline the programme you would undertake to establish the global acceptability of the name Trend, and how you would find an acceptable alternative if it failed.

3. Prepare an international below-the-line plan for 1990 for Trend.

4. As Marketing Director, how would you deal with handling public relations internationally for the new cigarette?
   List your strategies.

Case for Paper II, May 1989

Trend, the smokeless cigarette

Tab, an international cigarette company, situated in Chicago, USA, has established a line of successful brands in the last fifteen years. They are all local brands, with different brand names in most of the countries in Europe, Asia and North America. In most countries these local brands are among the local top ten cigarette brands. Thus, Tab is one of the larger manufacturers of cigarettes. In each country the local brand of Tab has about the same market share as the rival well-known global brands such as Marlboro or Barclay.

For example, in Holland the market shares of filter cigarettes are as follows (%):

	1985	1986	1987	1988
Marlboro	9.0	9.6	11.2	12.4
Camel	6.1	6.5	7.3	7.8
Pall Mall	7.1	6.5	6.2	6.2
Local Tab	7.5	7.3	7.1	7.0

The production and marketing organization of Tab is decentralized: each country's subsidiary has responsibility for local production, marketing and advertising. A central marketing communications team sets the standards for product quality, distribution and quality of all marketing communication activities. All subsidiaries have to report twice a year to this team. R&D is also a centralized function. All subsidiaries work with local advertising agencies, most of them part of a global network of advertising agencies.

Tab produces three different products: plain, filter and light cigarettes. Together they have a world market share of 8.5 per cent. Tab is doing well financially. However, the developments in smoking behaviour have forced Tab to look for different products which can meet future challenges.

The product

Tab International has created a new product for which there are great expectations. It has been given the name 'Trend'.

The main principle of the new cigarette is that it produces nicotine for the smoker by heating instead of burning. Like all cigarettes, Trend consists of paper rolled tobacco. It looks like the usual filter cigarette. The difference is the carbon heat source at the end of the cigarette, followed by the tobacco segment and the tobacco filter. The cigarette has to be lighted in the usual way; the flavour is inhaled, but no ashes are formed, and there is no visual smoke, nor can it be smelled. As the 'smoke' (= blown out 'air') contains no smother and no tar, the cigarette produces no smoke in the traditional way, and by puffing out the inhaled (aromatic) air the smoker produces no smoke. After six minutes (normal smoking time), the cigarette will extinguish itself.

The shape of the cigarette does not change during smoking and the cigarette can be thrown away when it is extinguished. The advantages are that there will be almost no irritation for the environment and smoking Trend is much healthier because it contains no tar. It leaves no ashes or stubs. The whole cigarette remains and it does not leave stains. The taste of Trend is comparable to that of cigarettes from the full range of flavours.

The cigarette will be introduced in a hard box pack of twenty as is customary in the USA.

Price

The price of a hard box pack of twenty cigarettes is approximately 15 per cent higher than a hard box pack of twenty average international filter cigarettes.

Competitive situation

The product is unique, so there is as yet no competition for the product as such. However, as it will be seen as a substitute for traditional filter cigarettes, the whole cigarette market, and more specifically the filter cigarette market, will be the competition. For the first four years Tab expects no competitive market entries with a comparable product, because of its patent and the difficulties of product development.

As existing cigarette brands all have powerful identities, which have been promoted for ages, and appeal to specific life styles, it will be difficult to position Trend in the cigarette market.

Macro environmental situation

ATTITUDES
There is a substantial difference between attitudes towards smoking behaviour in the Western and Eastern part of the world. There are several reasons for these different attitudes:

Western world: more restrictions by law;
more anti-smoking attitudes and behaviour because of better knowledge about the effect of smoking on health.

Eastern world: almost no restrictions by law;
less anti-smoking attitudes as smoking is part of life-style and it confers status.

USERS
There is a worldwide tendency for women to smoke more than men, and more women smoke filter cigarettes. The reason for this is that women do not like plain cigarettes, because it leaves tobacco on the lips and teeth. Men, too, are beginning to smoke more filter cigarettes.

BRAND LOYALTY
Smokers are usually very loyal to their brand. They mostly stick to one brand and will not switch easily. Smokers have an 'evoked set' of only two or three brands, if their preferred brand is not available.

SEGMENTATION OF SOCIAL CLASSES
Fewer upper class people smoke than in the lower classes. The percentage of people who stop smoking is higher in the upper classes. The percentage of low-tar and low-nicotine cigarette smokers is higher in the upper classes.

DISTRIBUTION
The objective is to use the existing channels. The most important channels for cigarettes are (Europe): special tobacco shops (36 per cent), supermarkets (37 per cent), petrol stations (9 per cent), catering companies (8 per cent), and vending machines (8 per cent). Catering companies and petrol stations are growing distribution channels. Tab assumes there are several outlet possibilities for the new product, like supermarkets, special tobacco shops, petrol stations etc.

MARKET CHARACTERISTICS
Tab's objective is to get a 1 per cent market share of the filter cigarette market in the first year in the markets where it will operate. The objective is a market share of 3 per cent after three years.

Test markets
The primary objectives of test marketing are to yield a more reliable forecast of future sales.

Tab is considering three test markets in three different continents:

1. *North America.* One US state, Massachusetts, was selected. In Massachusetts a really big anti-smoking campaign was run with success. The consequences were that in all public buildings smoking was forbidden. After this smoking was more or less considered to be a sin. This will demand extra care for the communication around the introduction of Trend. Because of this heavy anti-smoking attitude there is some doubt about whether the regular distribution channels should be used. Massachusetts is a really wealthy state with less than 3 per cent unemployment. There are more women smokers than in other states and they smoke more filter cigarettes.
2. *Europe.* One country was selected, Holland. In Holland disapproval of smoking in public places is growing and the government has been active with anti-smoking

campaigns. The government also issues more restrictions on cigarette advertising each year. Smoking, however, is not yet seen as being as anti-social as in the United States. There is considerable propaganda about the unhealthy side-effects smoking has on the non-smoker, especially children. Women smoke more than men and they also smoke more filter cigarettes than men. Research findings show that the new product is seen as a speciality product, so distribution will focus on special tobacco shops and supermarkets with tobacco counters. There is no cigarette advertising on television or radio.

3. *Asia.* For Asia, Hong Kong was selected. Hong Kong has a mixed population of Chinese and expatriates, with a large upper class group. In Hong Kong smoking is very popular and the government has hitherto done little as to introducing laws restricting smoking. Almost 65 per cent of the people smoke. More men than women smoke, and they smoke more plain than filter cigarettes. Expenditure on advertising for cigarettes takes fourth place after leisure, retail and food. Currently advertisers are not permitted to aim cigarette advertising at young people. At the end of 1989 a partial ban on cigarette advertising on radio and TV will become fully effective.

Advertising

Advertising for the existing global cigarette brands is mostly life-style advertising. The cigarette industry has developed three types of life styles. Brands have been developed for the 'defiant, daring, adventurous smoker', the 'casual smoker' and the 'careful smoker'. Each cigarette brand has its own profile and image. Marlboro caters for the 'defiant smoker' and claims to be adventurous, sturdy and full of action with their cowboys. It also is typically American. Camel has also chosen 'adventure'. Barclay claims to be luxurious, charming and of high society with its James Bond figure. More important, it is a new low-tar cigarette with an unexpected taste.

Most advertising for cigarettes in the top ten brands is based on the claim 'adventure in combination with excitement and sensation'. The high society and quality-image cigarettes are situated between 11th and 20th place.

In most countries cigarette advertising on TV and radio is forbidden.

General restrictions on advertising in most countries are as follows:

1. Connections between the use of cigarettes and health are prohibited.
2. It is not permitted to stimulate smoking.
3. Suggestions that non-smoking is regarded less or implies lower status than smoking are prohibited.
4. Smoking should not be linked to sports.
5. Advertising is not allowed to influence people under 18 years old.

Communications objectives

The communications objectives are formulated in terms of brand awareness and claim recognition:

Target group: smokers of filter cigarettes, age 18+

Year one: 30% 'unaided' brand recognition
              50% 'aided' brand recognition

Year two: 30% 'unaided' brand recognition
              70% 'aided' brand recognition

Year three: 35% 'unaided' brand recognition
              80% 'aided' brand recognition

At least 50 per cent of the people who score on recognition must also be able to recall the proposition of Trend.

Consumer research

Before starting to invest, Tab did concept research to measure the interest in and appraisal of the cigarette Trend.

It was a test with concept boards, not the real Trend cigarette. The test was done in the neighbourhood of Tab headquarters.

The outcome of the research was as follows:

1. The appraisal of the new product is high: 60 per cent of the respondents to the questionnaire said it was a good idea to introduce a smokeless cigarette.
2. 77 per cent of the smokers said they would probably or certainly try Trend, provided the taste is excellent.
3. Of the non-smokers, about half would like to see people in their surroundings smoke Trend.

Later research among smokers concluded that smokers experienced the taste of Trend as reasonable to good. On an average, they marked it between 100 per cent and 65 per cent, while judging the norm for their own brand at 80 per cent. Most of the respondent-smokers were not feeling at ease, because they were inclined to tip off the ash and look at the smoke.

The positive reactions, however, won against the negative reactions.

Flavour segments

There are three main segments in the filter cigarette market:

full flavour segment: (c., 16 mg tar), which is growing
                        Marlboro, Camel
medium segment: stable
                        Peter Stuyvesant, Dunhill
light segment: declining
                        Philip Morris, Cartier

Of the 200 main brands, the ten biggest have 60 per cent of the market, the twenty biggest 77 per cent, and the forty biggest 90 per cent.

Conclusion

This case presents the introduction of a completely new product and brand, with no brand image at all. Tab International has decided to use the name 'Trend' for this revolutionary product in the United States. There has been no decision made yet on the brand name for other countries. The name will either be used worldwide (global brand) or just for the United States and possibly other countries in the Western world. This depends on the decisions taken by the local managers and the central marketing communications team, based on the feasibility of producing a global communications campaign for this type of product.

Tab has definitely decided to introduce the product in January 1990. Production will be possible in North America, Europe and East Asia (higher developed countries). There will be one standard pack (twenty cigarettes in a hard box), the decision on the price (approximately 15 per cent higher than the usual filter cigarette) is also definite.

Some important communication decisions have to be taken. You will be a consultant to the central marketing communications team which takes the decisions on the necessary marketing communication activities. Their specific questions will be put to you on 26 May 1989.

Be prepared!

Note:

This case is an adaptation of a case produced by Lintas Worldwide, International Division Headquarters, Amsterdam. Special thanks are due to Willy de Graaff of Lintas Amsterdam and Pieter Jan van Waesberghe. The data in this case are not taken from existing market research data, though attempts have been made to make them as realistic as possible.

IAA Diploma in International Advertising, 25 May 1990

Paper I

Candidates are allowed 3 hours to complete this paper plus $\frac{1}{2}$ hour if English is not their first language. Candidates must answer 5 questions. All questions carry equal marks.

1. The recent events in Eastern Europe will have a considerable impact on the European Community as a 'single market'. Discuss the effect that these events will have on advertising and marketing both within the Community and in the Eastern European countries.

2. What will be the role of international advertising specialists in Eastern Europe in the next five years?

3. 'Apart from movie channels, satellite TV has no role in international advertising.' Discuss.

4. Discuss, with examples, how far it is possible to produce multinational advertising that crosses language barriers.

5. Do you believe that large advertising agency groups are a good thing or a bad thing, taking into account the needs of media, advertiser, agencies and consumers?

6. Describe a 'perfect' agency/client reporting system for international advertising campaigns.

7. Describe what you consider to have been the best international sales promotion you noted in 1989, giving reasons as to why you feel that it was the best.

8. What steps would you take to carry out a PR launch of a new cosmetic simultaneously in two European countries?

9. Describe a creative and media strategy for a global campaign against atmospheric pollution.

10. A canned food factory in a small African state is eager to advertise and promote its products in Europe. How would you suggest they proceed?

11. Is there any truth in the statement that 'you can't buy media abroad without being swindled'?

12. Explain to an American manufacturer why his ads will have to be changed for Europe.

IAA Diploma in International Advertising, 25 May 1990

Paper II

Candidates are allowed 3 hours to complete this paper plus $\frac{1}{2}$ hour if English is not their first language.

The following assignment relates to the Mexx case study you have received before the examination:

You are an independent Marketing Consultant recently set up in business.

The owners of Mexx invite you to make proposals to them on how you might play a part in their organization, as a consultant.

They ask you for a document outlining your plan of work over a three-year period. They ask you to make initial recommendations about their organization for marketing and selling, and invite your thoughts on how they should tackle advertising.

They want recommendations on how they should plan, and control, their advertising.

They are interested in your views on what research they should carry out on a regular basis, and where.

They want your views on whether to use an outside company or set up a research department. They would like your advice on how to make sure Mexx is a 'global' brand.

Case for Paper II, May 1990

Mexx International*

Introduction

Mexx International is a well known and respected international brand.

For reasons of confidentiality certain information in the following case history has been changed or invented. Nevertheless, the case does represent a real situation.

Background

The fashion business in general is a very complex one. On the one hand there are many suppliers, on the other, brands emerge and vanish rapidly. The total market consists of regular brands, fake brands (labelled products), private labels and unlabelled products. The average fashion brand life-cycle is estimated at a maximum of seven years. Distribution tends to cover a very broad area: fashion is sold from shops (which can vary from a cheap, shabby looking outlet to a high-class fashion store or boutique) to chainstores, street markets, mail order and even selling from the back of a car.

Transactions between traders and retailers are still often made in cash. This, combined with the great diversity of brands and manufacturers, makes tracking studies on total fashion sales, like Nielsen's, hardly possible.

During the 1980s the total fashion business flourished, but a decline came in 1987. For years design and quality had remained at the same level while prices went up. The consumer just would not accept the high prices anymore. They simply waited for the 'Sales' period. For some companies this situation was disastrous, for retailers it was fatal. Many companies were forced to adapt themselves to the changing market and had to lower prices or improve quality. In 1988 the market slightly recovered.

Mexx International

In the early 1970s two Indian men started importing and selling cheap Indian fabrics in the Netherlands. These men, Rattan Chadna and P. K. Sen Sharma, built their business rapidly and were successful. At the end of the seventies they were also the official distributor in the Netherlands for Esprit, the successful Californian company.

---

* The Mexx case was prepared early 1990 by FHV/BBDO, and permission was given by Mexx to use their brand name. The background information was mainly derived from documentation found in interviews and other public sources and is based on the real history of Mexx. The market situation, as well as the objectives, were faked in order to adapt them to the needs of an examination case, which necessitated exaggerating the global situation.

As Mexx is a highly innovative company, their marketing and communication philosophies may have changed when the reader reads this case.

Based on their experiences, they decided to start a fashion company themselves. At the beginning of the 1980s they launched two brands: Emanuelle (for women) and Moustache (for men). After a few years the company wanted to internationalize these brands and, for practical reasons, had to find one brand name for the two collections. The 'M' of Moustache and the 'E' of Emanuelle were combined; two xxs, which stand for kisses, were added, and an international brand name was created: Mexx.

Mexx International's expansion

EUROPE

1984	1985	1986	1987	1988
Holland	Holland	Holland	Holland	Holland
Belgium	Belgium	Belgium	Belgium	Belgium
Germany	Germany	Germany	Germany	Germany
	Sweden	Sweden	Sweden	Sweden
	Finland	Finland	Finland	Finland
	Greece	Greece	Greece	Greece
	France	France	France	France
		Denmark	Denmark	Denmark
		UK	UK	UK
		Switzerland	Switzerland	Switzerland
		Norway	Norway	Norway
			Austria	Austria
				Spain
				Italy

NORTH AMERICA

1985	1986	1987	1988
USA	USA	USA	USA
	Canada	Canada	Canada

ASIA/PACIFIC

In the period 1990–1995 Mexx International is planning to introduce Mexx products in the following countries in the Asia/Pacific region:

1990	1991	1992	1993	1994	1995
Hong Kong	Hong Kong	Hong Kong	Hong Kong	Hong Kong	Hong Kong
	Singapore	Singapore	Singapore	Singapore	Singapore
	Thailand	Thailand	Thailand	Thailand	Thailand
	Malaysia	Malaysia	Malaysia	Malaysia	Malaysia
			Japan	Japan	Japan
			South Korea	South Korea	South Korea
					Australia
					New Zealand

SOUTH AMERICA

For the Latin American market Mexx has developed a special collection of casual wear for a try-out. In the period 1990–1992 Mexx will decide whether to continue with a specific collection for this geographical segment. Try-out markets are Chile, Argentina and Peru.

The company

Mexx International's headquarters are based in a small village near The Hague in the Netherlands. In 1988 total sales amounted to US $265,000,000.

The growth of the company, indexed, is as follows:

Year	Index
1983	100
1984	209
1985	309
1986	400
1987	432
1988	481

The organization

The Mexx organization is mostly centralized. Mexx International is responsible for all coordination and planning. The local offices translate the international guidelines and strategies into local strategies and tactics.

Basically tasks and responsibilities are as follows:

- Design and styling in Western Europe
- Production in Asia
- Sales in Western Europe and North America.

MEXX INTERNATIONAL HEADQUARTERS
Based in the Netherlands, responsible for:

- Holding company
- Design/styling
- Coordination of production
- Marketing services
- Advertising services
- Planning and organization
- Finance.

MEXX HONG KONG
Based in Hong Kong, responsible for:

- Production
- Quality control
- Global distribution
- Coordination of production in other countries like Sri Lanka, India, Thailand.

MEXX COUNTRY OFFICES
There are basically two different types of country offices:

- Mexx-owned offices. These are 100 per cent subsidiaries of Mexx International
- Private distributors. These are private agents or traders in fashion.

In general it depends on the size of the country or total sales whether the Mexx office is owned or private. Sometimes the situation has grown historically.
The responsibilities in each country are:

- Local sales and marketing
- Local distribution
- Local pricing
- Local coordination of advertising.

The marketing concept

Mexx offers fashion collections which are coordinated in design and timing, providing casual wear for men and women, 20–30 years old, 'followers'. Characteristics of this target group are: urban, outgoing, cosmopolitan.

The Mexx clients do not 'need' clothes, but are shopping for garments that fit their life-style, which is an attitude of fun, freedom and individuality. With Mexx fashion people buy a 'way of life'. This way of life is a reflection of Mexx's business vision: 'the need and want to be different'. This vision is not only relevant for the product but also for the style of working in the company. There is an emphasis on people's personalities with attitudes of freedom, personal responsibility and individuality.

The product itself, casual wear, can be best described as leisure wear for young, dynamic, colourful, daring and internationally oriented people.

As Mexx has not been advertising in the mass media for over a year and has only engaged in support for the retailers, brand awareness may have been weakened compared with others. Mexx may therefore have to consider re-launching their brand, or replacing it. A further consideration is the more widespread demand for higher quality in fashion goods. Mexx's rather low-quality image may put them at a disadvantage if this is the case.

The key to success for Mexx is the Mexx planning cycle. In the fashion industry it is common practice that retailers buy the next year's collections approximately six months in advance. Thus the manufacturer knows what has been sold and what has to be produced. The advantage is that there is no inventory problem. Everything which is produced has already been sold. The only problem is getting the goods delivered in time. One or two weeks' delay can be disastrous and, often, the goods may well be refused by the retailer if they are delayed. The Mexx planning cycle ensures that every aspect of the total process gets the time and attention it needs. This planning schedule is very tight and therefore delays are limited to a minimum. Everybody knows and sees immediately what will happen if things are delayed. Because of the efficiency of this planning cycle, Mexx has a delivery guarantee of 95 per cent while other brands in the market hardly reach 70 per cent.

The product

The product itself is mainly casual wear. Designs and styles change every few months and Mexx offers a broad range of products from basics (simple, down-to-earth trousers, shirts and sweaters) to more stylish and extrovert clothing – not really designer products, but commercial translations of top designers' work.

Although Mexx originally targeted their collections at 15–25 year olds, they have recently changed that strategy. They have split their collection into four separate parts:

- Mexx Woman collection
- Mexx Man collection
- Mexx Girls collection
- Mexx Boys collection

The first two are targeted at 20–30 year olds, and the third and fourth at 10–15 year olds.

The fashion business is based on seasons. Mexx operates with the following four seasons:

- Spring 1 + 2
- High Summer/Transition
- Fall 1 + 2
- Holiday, Early Spring

Each season is divided into two sections, these are the so-called delivery periods. Spring covers February–April, High Summer/Transition covers May–July, Fall covers August–January.

Spring and Fall are the major seasons and contribute approximately 75 per cent of total sales.

Distribution

International distribution is handled by the Hong Kong office. They ensure that everything is shipped out and delivered on time. The local offices, in turn, distribute the goods to local retailers. In general, Mexx casual wear is available in regular shops and large chain stores. Often these large chain stores have a 'shop-in-shop' formula. This means that a special counter or corner is reserved for a particular brand with a selection of its specific products, thus providing the opportunity to dress/merchandise the corner in the brand's style.

Additionally, countries which are large in terms of sales volume have one or two 'pilot' shops, which stock the entire Mexx collection. Besides this they offer the opportunity for both retailers and consumers to see, enjoy and experience the Mexx life style.

Pricing

In most countries the Mexx collections are moderately priced – not really expensive, not really cheap. Although there is a fixed price, the local distributor has some flexibility in adapting prices to the local situation.

Communication

Mexx International started with catalogues of the available collection, which were distributed among retailers. From 1984 Mexx started communicating with a regular advertising campaign. This campaign proved to be very successful. The essence of the concept was 'Streetlife'. It portrayed young people in the hectic atmosphere of big cities of the world; young people who are happy to meet each other and kiss. But the kissing does not denote a 'love' relationship – it is more of a friendly kiss. Their fashion is adventurous and extrovert.

MEXX INTERNATIONAL TOTAL ADVERTISING EXPENDITURES
Split by media (US $000):

	1984	1985	1986	1987	1988
TV	–	250	250	500	500
Magazines	–	1,050	1,950	2,050	2,450
Newspapers	–	–	1,000*	200	350
Cinema	–	–	200	300	500
Outdoor	–	100	100	150	200
Total	–	1,400	3,500	3,200	4,000

* Only in 1986 was a large newspaper campaign used for achieving higher brand awareness.

Competition

As always competition is fierce. Very many brands and manufacturers are competing in this market. Competitors for Mexx are listed below:

BENETTON

The well-established Italian wool and knitting brand. A large franchise chain, it operates centrally from Italy. Its advertising campaigns are well known ('United colours of the world') with, in general, two completely different young people next to each other, fully dressed in the Benetton style. Primary media: magazines and outdoor.

SISLEY

The secondary brand of the Benetton company, still very small but with a distinctive image and life style. Its use of media was striking, though expensive. Sisley used the last 5–6 pages in magazines and turned its advertisements upside down, thus giving the impression of Sisley having a magazine of its own. Media: only magazines.

ESPRIT

The well-known California-based brand. Their collection is mainly targeted at women in all age brackets. It is one of the largest companies in this segment. Their advertising campaigns always show beautiful, attractive people and radiate a kind of purity. Media: magazines and outdoor.

Note: The above mentioned brands have been very consistent in their advertising over the years.

INWEAR/MATINIQUE

InWear for women and Matinique for men are from a Scandinavian (Danish) company and mainly European-oriented. Products are middle of the road, not extrovert. Advertising campaigns have differed over the last few years. Media: magazines.

NEW MAN

A French company, primarily male oriented, and in essence comparable with Matinique. Campaign as well as media expenditures have been low-scale over the past years.

STEFFANEL

A rather new, Italian company, using a similar approach to Benetton, yet their products are somewhat more daring. Advertising is still low scale but includes television in Europe.

OTHER

Further competition consists mainly of local (and very many!) brands.

Next steps 1990–1995

Mexx is aiming for global scale operations. Following the theories of Theodore Levitt it has a preference for optimal standardization with respect to product design and production, brand image and advertising and other promotional efforts. Although its goals for the coming five years are quite ambitious, it has full confidence in the future.

This case was prepared by Marc Klamer at FHV/BBDO by courtesy of Mexx International for the examination for the IAA Diploma in International Advertising on 25 May 1990. Copyright 1990 IAA/BBDO.

Index

R